D0906703

SECULAR MOVEMENTS IN PRODUCTION AND PRICES

THEIR NATURE AND THEIR BEARING UPON CYCLICAL FLUCTUATIONS

SECULAR MOVEMENTS IN PRODUCTION AND PRICES

Their Nature and Their Bearing
Upon Cyclical Fluctuations

BY

SIMON S. KUZNETS, Ph.D.

Reprints of Economic Classics

Augustus M. Kelley · Publishers
new york · 1967

First Edition 1930

(Boston: Houghton Mifflin Co., *The Riverside Press*, 1930)

Reprinted 1967 by
AUGUSTUS M. KELLEY · PUBLISHERS

LIBRARY OF CONGRESS CATALOGUE CARD NUMBER
67 - 16341

PRINTED IN THE UNITED STATES OF AMERICA
by SENTRY PRESS, NEW YORK, N. Y. 10019

PREFACE

THIS series of books owes its existence to the generosity of Messrs. Hart, Schaffner & Marx, of Chicago, who have desired to encourage a wider interest in the study of economic and commercial subjects. For this purpose they have delegated to the undersigned committee the task of selecting or approving of topics, making announcements, and awarding prizes annually for those who wish to compete.

For the year 1928 there were offered:

In Class A, which included any American without restriction, a first prize of $1000, and a second prize of $500.

In Class B, which included any who were at the time undergraduates of an American college, a first prize of $300, and a second prize of $200.

Any essay submitted in Class B, if deemed of sufficient merit, could receive a prize in Class A.

The present volume, submitted in 1928 in Class A, was considered worthy of publication.

The Committee is not responsible for any opinions of an author.

J. LAURENCE LAUGHLIN, *Chairman*
University of Chicago
JOHN B. CLARK
Columbia University
EDWIN F. GAY
Harvard University
THEODORE E. BURTON
Washington, D.C.
WESLEY C. MITCHELL
Columbia University

AUTHOR'S PREFACE

THE present investigation attempts to inquire into the nature of the long-time movements in production and prices, as well as into their influence on cyclical fluctuations. It attempts to establish some uniformly observed characteristics of the so-called secular movements, and in the process to draw analytic distinctions between different groups of these movements. The latter are studied as they appear in the available statistical series of various countries. The aim is to formulate these movements in such a way as not only to reveal their common characteristics, but also to facilitate measurements of the relation between cyclical oscillations and the underlying secular changes.

A definite hypothesis concerning characteristics of industrial growth forms the basis of our statistical description of long-time movements. This hypothesis is derived from a preliminary observation of the wide field of statistical evidence and from material furnished by the chronicles of specific industries. The exact formulation of this tentative generalization and the historico-statistical material on which it rests are presented in Chapter I.

The conclusions of the first chapter furnish a definite approach to the methods of statistical analysis which can be applied to the body of available material. A consideration, however, of some of the general principles of statistical description of long-time movements makes clearer the exact type of analysis to pursue. This consideration forms the contents of Chapter II.

Chapter III presents the body of statistical data drawn from five countries; United States, Great Britain, Belgium, Germany, and France. Altogether about 60 series of industrial output and 35 series of prices are analyzed. The secular movements are segregated from the cyclical oscillations and are analyzed into two distinct groups of changes, the primary and the secondary. Each pair of production and price series is accompanied by brief comments drawn from the history of the particular industry whose output and prices are described quantitatively.

The measurable characteristics and the nature of the

secondary secular movements, whose existence is established in Chapter III, are discussed in Chapter IV. The discussion inquires into the causes of these secondary secular movements in production and prices, and deals with the question whether they can properly be called major cycles. The appendix to the chapter surveys the more important theories of major cycles set forth by various writers.

In Chapter V, the influence of secular movements on the cyclical oscillations is studied statistically. The aim is to discover the existence or absence of correlation between the rapidity of secular growth and the amplitude of cyclical oscillations.

The theoretical connection of these two measures of forces as revealed by contemporary business cycle theory is treated in Chapter VI.

The concluding chapter deals briefly with the theoretical significance of the results of the investigation and attempts to evaluate them in the light of economic theory, both past and present.

The investigation was begun in the summer of 1925, and was carried on uninterruptedly to the end of the calendar year 1926, during which time I enjoyed the opportunities of a research fellow of the Social Science Research Council. The study was not completed, however, before the summer of 1927, and has been materially revised since. Throughout these years I profited much by the help of many kind friends. Professor Wesley C. Mitchell was an inspiring and kind critic whose interest was of great assistance. To him especially I wish to express my deeply felt gratitude. Professor Henry Schultz and Dr. Hans Staehle read the manuscript and made a number of valuable suggestions. Dr. Dorothy S. Thomas's friendly interest was frequently most helpful. Professor Edwin F. Gay suggested a recasting of the manuscript which resulted in a considerable improvement. Mr. Irving Allen has gone through the arduous task of stylistic editing. And in the tedious labor of reading the proofs I was greatly relieved by the kind help of Miss Edith Handler. To all these friends I express my sincere thanks.

SIMON KUZNETS

NATIONAL BUREAU OF ECONOMIC RESEARCH, INC.
NEW YORK CITY

CONTENTS

Gompertz curves. The application of the logistic curve to cases showing a decline. The arbitrary element involved in our choice of curves. The methods of fitting.

Appendix: Some properties of the simple Gompertz curve. The simple equation for a curve of decline.

The procedure followed for each pair of production and price series. The concept of *primary* and *secondary* secular movements. The significance of secondary secular movements. The general nature of the comments accompanying each pair of series.

The data presented. United States: wheat, corn, potatoes, cotton, anthracite coal, bituminous coal, petroleum, pig iron, steel, Portland cement, copper, zinc, lead, salt, cotton consumption, silk imports, deflated bank clearings (six cities given separately), locomotives. United Kingdom: coal, pig iron, steel, cotton imports, ships cleared, tea consumption. Belgium: coal, pig iron, steel, zinc. Germany: coal, pig iron, steel, copper, zinc, wheat, cotton. France: wheat, coal, pig iron, steel, zinc, petroleum. Other countries. The cases of declining secular movements.

The tentative character of the comments given. General conclusions of the survey. Warning against over-interpretation.

The correlation between secondary movements in production and prices. The precedence of the price movements. The average duration of the swings.

The explanation of the movements in production, those in prices being taken for granted. The decline in the purchasing power of wage rates and the rise in profits — both during an upward secondary movement in prices. How can production of consumers' goods accelerate in these conditions? Tentative answer: larger employment, diminution in savings, larger stocks, etc.

The factors tending to carry forward a price increase. The lag of production movements behind price movements. The 'gestation' period. The disparity in movements between producers' and consumers' goods industries.

The retarding factors. The decline in the productivity of

labor. The diminishing output of monetary metals and of metals entering circulation.

Are the secondary secular movements 'major cycles'? Limitations of the discussion in the chapter.

Appendix A: Note on the studies of major cycles.

Appendix B: Comparative amplitude of secondary secular movements in industries producing producers' and consumers' goods.

The measures of the rate of growth and of the amplitude of deviations from the various trend lines. The four sets of relationships to be studied.

The comparisons of various industries within each of the countries. United States. United Kingdom. Belgium. Germany. France. Summary. The table of rank coefficients of correlation.

The comparisons of various national branches of the same industry. Coal. Pig Iron. Steel. Zinc. Copper. Wheat. Summary. The rank coefficients of correlation for these groups.

General summary of conclusions.

Change of the amplitude of deviations within the same series with the passage of time.

Appendix: Formulæ for computing the average percentage rate of increase. Logistic and Gompertz curves.

The influence of rate of growth upon the amplitude of secondary secular movements. The probable reasons for it. The influence of cycle-duration upon the amplitude of secondary secular movements — argument and test.

The influence of rate of growth upon cyclical fluctuations. The support in business cycle theories. The somewhat uncertain character of the latter.

Brief presentation of arguments. The theories that make the processes of industrial growth themselves the source of cyclical fluctuations. The factors determining uncertainty and the secular changes in them. The factor of emotional contagion. The disparity between savings and investments.

The disparity between volume of output and volume of purchasing power disbursed. Other factors.

Can there be cycles without upward secular movements?

The influence of secondary secular movements upon cyclical fluctuations.

The present status of the problem of long-time movements in economic theory.

Survey of the path traced in this study. Brief summary of the conclusions. The limitations of this study.

The theoretical significance of the investigation. Possibilities of future development in economic theory. Its present state. The probable future of its static and dynamic aspects.

TABLES

Chapter I

Appendix

Chapter IV

APPENDIX

CHAPTER V

APPENDIX TO CHAPTER III

CHARTS

Chapter III

In this chapter each chart, except the ones marked with *b* after their number, presents the original data and the line of primary trend. The charts marked *b* after their number present each the relative deviations from the primary trend lines.

CHAPTER IV

Secular Movements in Production and Prices

.·.

CHAPTER I

RETARDATION OF INDUSTRIAL GROWTH

Ceaseless change as the dominant characteristic of the modern economic system. Problem of the long-time movements of economic phenomena. Factors discussed by economic historians: growth of population, changes in demand, technical changes. Four reasons for the decline in the rate of an industry's growth: (I) the slowing down of technical progress. Examples from the cotton industry, woolens and worsteds, iron and steel, shoe manufacturing, paper, copper. The steam engine. The extractive industries. Summary of the dynamics of technical changes in industry. (II) Slower growing industries exercise a retarding influence upon the faster growing complementary branches. Similar influence of the rapidly growing industries upon the competitive branches. Statistical data for the United States on the ratio of value added by manufacture to the cost of materials: metals, machines, lumber and woodworking, textiles. (III) The funds available for expansion decrease in relative size as the industry grows; the automobile industry. (IV) Retardation of an industry by competition from the same industry in a younger country; Great Britain. Summary of factors that tend to cause a decreasing rate of growth of an industry within a nation. A word of caution regarding the validity of the hypothesis.

Appendix: Statistics of patents.

OUR modern economic system is characterized by ceaseless change. We may conceive this restless mobility as the feature that distinguishes the present economic organization from the system of the Middle Ages. Or we may see in it only a consequence, one of the manifestations of a more fundamental trait; perhaps the essential rationality of our economic behavior as contrasted with the traditionalism of past times. Whatever be our approach, the variety and frequency of changes strike our eye and challenge our understanding.

Certain groups of persistent fluctuations have been singled out by students and made the subject of prolonged discussions. Economists know a good deal about cyclical fluctuations and seasonal changes. They know little of the nature of random variations. On the subject of secular or long-time movements, what is said rests upon a small volume of vague knowledge combined with fervent beliefs.

It is true that long-time changes in prices are discussed by economists and statisticians in concrete terms, if not always dispassionately. But views of industrial progress or decay tend to be articles of belief, colored by recent experience. A country which has been prosperous for a generation or two, acquires faith in the unlimited possibilities of economic development, in the inexhaustible opportunities provided by technical progress and the energy of its people. In another nation, which has just suffered defeat in an exhausting war, the prevailing views stress the inevitability of decline, once a certain stage of development has been reached. We hear likewise a good deal of bright and dark futures in industry, of the eclipse of one locality and rise of another. In the discussion of long-term development these beliefs tend to color the whole argument and predetermine to a large extent the conclusions arrived at.

This diffusion of man's hopes and fears into vague generalizations is favored by the scarcity of exact knowledge. Aside from the seemingly prevalent growth of the physical quantity of goods produced, and of the long swings in the price level, little is definitely known of the course of long-time movements of economic phenomena. Indeed, questions of industrial development in their general aspects have become suspect to all conscientious economists and statisticians. We find hardly any discussion of the problem in the standard treatises which have appeared since the great days of the English Classical School. In reaction against the too facile generalizations of the latter, economic theory proper has restricted itself largely to static problems. While the Historical School in Germany promoted a number of specific investigations which enriched our concrete knowledge, it established no results of general validity. The problem of in-dustrial growth has been left to the more speculative minds.

Such a division of the field may have been expedient at the time when economic students had but few data for a thorough investigation of the course of economic develop-ment. But ignorance of long-time trends reduces the value of all the other work in economic science. Long-time move-ments must influence the briefer changes. And how can our study even of the instantaneous, static reactions of demand and supply be complete, if we know neither the general course of the changes about which these reactions take place, nor the influence which the former may have exercised upon the latter?

More cold light may be thrown upon the problem, if we can utilize the evidence accumulating in histories of indus-tries and in statistical records of growth. Postponing the problem of long-time movements in prices, we can discuss presently the growth in the volume of economic activity. But before concrete data can be examined, the current vague statement of the problem must be made definite. For, to paraphrase an old German proverb, in scientific problems 'Mastery lies in limitation.'

The picture of economic development suffers a curious change as we examine it first in a rather wide sphere, then in a narrower one. If we take the world from the end of the eighteenth century, there unrolls before us a process of uninterrupted and seemingly unslackened growth. We ob-serve a ceaseless expansion of production and trade, a con-stant growth in the volume of power used, in the extraction of raw materials, in the quality and quantity of finished products.

But if we single out the various nations or the separate branches of industry, the picture becomes less uniform. Some nations seem to have led the world at one time, others at another. Some industries were developing most rapidly at the beginning of the century, others at the end. Within single countries or within single branches of indus-tries (on a world scale) there has not been uniform, un-retarded growth. Great Britain has relinquished the lead in the economic world because its own growth, so vigorous through the period 1780–1850, has slackened. She has been overtaken by rapidly developing Germany and the United States. The textile industries which had so spectacular a rise toward the close of the eighteenth and the beginning of the nineteenth century ceded first place to pig iron, then to steel, while in turn the electrical industries assumed the leadership in the '80s and '90s.

The view becomes further variegated if we distinguish the different industries in their national units. The rapid development of the English textiles came much earlier than that of the American. The Belgian coal output had reached nearly stable levels in the beginning of the twentieth century when American and German coal production was still showing substantial growth. Industries within the limits of one country frequently show a retardation of development as compared either with the national industry as a whole or with the same industry on a world-wide scale.

We might go further and distinguish various localities within one national system, or different stages within one industry, making the view still more kaleidoscopic. The whole procedure is not unlike that of observing a distant object with field glasses of varying power. The naked eye will see but a uniform blur of color, the glasses will reveal parts of different hues, and the latter will dissolve still further if the magnifying power is increased. The stage at which one stops in concentrating and deepening the field of vision depends upon the purpose in mind.

Here the decisive criterion is the expectation of significant results from study in terms of one unit as contrasted with larger or smaller units. Both our historical records and our statistical data show mostly events and changes within a national branch of an industry. It seems advisable to resolve the general problem of economic growth into the narrower question as to the long-time changes which can be observed in various national branches of production and trade.

The prevailing impression of this procedure, as represented by everyday knowledge, may be summarized as follows: As we observe the various industries within a given national system, we see that the lead in development shifts from one branch to another. The main reason for this shift seems to be that a rapidly developing industry does not continue its vigorous growth indefinitely, but slackens its pace after a time, and is overtaken by industries whose period of rapid development comes later. Within any country we observe a succession of different branches of activity leading the process of development, and in each mature industry we notice a conspicuous slackening in the rate of increase. For example, the vigorous development of copper mining during the years 1880–1900 in the United States did not continue unabated, nor did that of steel after 1870–1900, nor railroad construction after 1830–1880.

This observation is not likely to be disputed. But contrasted with our belief in the fairly continuous march of economic progress, it raises a frequently overlooked question. Why is there an abatement in the growth of old industries? Why is not progress uniform in all branches of production, with the inventive and organizing capacity of the nation flowing in an even stream into the various channels of economic activity? What concentrates the forces of growth and development in one or two branches of production at a given time, and what shifts the concentration from one field to another as time passes?

These questions can best be answered by an inspection of the historical records of industrial growth, focussed upon the processes that underlie economic development. The plausible and vague generalization concerning the slackening of expansion observed within separate industries of a national system will guide us through the maze of concrete data we must utilize. Used as a centering rod for our findings, it will help us to answer the first and most simple queries in this vast and complicated problem.

Of the numerous factors discussed by economic historians in connection with the history of an industry, three groups stand out as the dynamic, the pushing forces. They are: (1) growth of population; (2) changes in demand; (3) technical changes, including both mechanical or engineering progress, and improvement in business organization.

These groups of factors are, of course, not independent of one another. The growth of population is conditioned to a large extent by the standard of living (demand) and the supply of means of subsistence, the latter in its turn depends upon the state of technical arts. Changes in demand usually follow changes in technique, while the volume of demand is in close and definite connection with the size of the population. And technical progress comes to be realized in response to some felt needs, which may be brought about by the pressure of population or by changes in demand. No sooner do we start with one of the factors than it leads us immediately to the other two in a kind of chain relationship. A more detailed consideration of this interdependence will clear a path into the problem.

The growth of population appears to us human beings as a self-generating process, itself independent, yet influencing nearly all social phenomena. But in the industrial system of a country, population is just another productive factor, and its size from year to year is of the same significance as, for example, that of the annual output of pig iron. Like the volume of iron production, it predetermines in a broad way what and how much will be produced in the next time unit. To treat the growth of population as an independent dynamic factor implies an anthropocentric delusion as to the specific function of man in his productive and procreative capacities.

This thesis will appear somewhat less shocking when we look at the factors which controlled population growth during the last century and a half: the birth-rate, death-rate, and immigration. While the birth-rate tended to decline in European nations through the nineteenth century with growing wealth, the extraordinary increase in population is to be accounted for by the great decline in the death-rate. This decline was due to the progress of medicine, both preventive and curative, and to the developments which made possible such improvements as sanitary water supply, sewerage, and hygienic clothing and buildings. To quote the latest work on the subject, 'Whatever may have been the proximate causes of the subjection of pestilence in Western Europe, this subjection was undoubtedly associated with advancing civilization. It was the result of the same practical, yet adventurous spirit, that gave us the steam engine, the railway, and modern agriculture, and of which we have a further manifestation in modern medicine.' [1] It is also a matter of common knowledge that immigration is conditioned by the same forces that make for economic growth.

But while the increase of population is not independent of industrial and technical development, it influences the latter. A larger population in the industrial system, while made possible only by the preceding expansion of the industries, may in its turn account for the further growth in the volume of productive activity. In this connection it is interesting to observe that according to the latest investigations, there was a definite decline in the rate of increase of population in most of the European countries during the nineteenth century. [2] No matter what specific curves are fitted to the graph of population growth, the abatement in the percentage increase is to be observed in nearly all the countries.

Were changes in population the only factor in industrial development, this tendency towards a smaller rate of increase would both confirm and explain completely our hypothesis concerning a similar tendency in the growth of industries. The explanation would then run somewhat as follows.

Start with an initial population of a given size. It produces all the commodities and also the next generation. Since we assume that all the other factors in their relation to the population factor are constant, the next generation will have the same per capita output as the initial one. If population shows a decreasing rate of growth, the volume of industrial output will show the same.

Such an explanation is, of course, just a schematic description which shifts the burden of discussion to the problem of population growth. But even if we take the

[1] See M. C. Buer: *Health, Wealth and Population in the Early Days of the Industrial Revolution.* London, 1926.

[2] See R. Pearl: *Studies in Human Biology*, Baltimore, 1924, and other numerous studies by the same author.

latter for granted, the description is too simple to be true. If it were exact, we should have a stable per capita output and a uniform growth in all the various branches of production. But per capita output has been rising rapidly in most countries and in most industries throughout the last century, while the various branches of production within the national systems show a bewildering variety of rates of increase and rates of retardation. The actual picture is not one of even growth nor of a harmonious slackening in the various industries.

The factor of population is thus only one of the forces of development. While its behavior supports strongly the initial working hypothesis, it seems to have no direct bearing upon the more conspicuous aspects of the problem. Why does the per capita output grow at different rates at different times? Is there no expansion of the productive system that would allow an unretarded growth of population? Or, if there is the latter, why do the forces that make for an increase of per capita output distribute their influences so unevenly as to allow a slowing up of the older industries and the appearance of entirely new branches of production? To answer these questions we must turn to the two other groups of factors — changes in demand and changes in technique.

In the discussion of demand it is best to distinguish the demand of ultimate consumers from that of producers. The needs of manufacturers and of traders often provide a direct stimulus to technical progress. Such connection is to be observed in the invention of the steam engine, of the spinning jenny, of the puddling process, to name some notable cases. But while necessity is truly the mother of invention, the demand of producers exercises its influence on industrial growth only through the medium of the technical changes it calls forth.

A different relation exists between consumers' demand and industrial progress. Changes in the latter are called forth by technical innovations that bring a new or a greatly improved commodity within reach. Demand for tea, cotton cloth, radios, electric light, automobiles appeared only after the progress of technique had made all these commodities available. It is true that we may observe self-generating vagaries in consumers' tastes, but these passing changes are confined to a restricted number of commodities and affect even these but slightly.

Being a passive influence, consumers' demand cannot be treated as an independent dynamic factor in industrial growth. It is often considered, however, a retarding force. There are definite and often narrow limits to the amount of a commodity a man may consume, and we can visualize a situation in which an industry's growth is retarded by the saturation of the total volume of consumers' demand. The production of consumers' goods having slowed down, a corresponding abatement in expansion would manifest itself in the output of producers' goods.

But demand in many cases is elastic and depends to a large extent upon the costs of the product as compared to the available purchasing power. Both factors are a reflection of the state of the productive arts. A lowering of costs by technical progress may proceed far, and the same result may be brought about by an increase of purchasing power through expansion of production in other fields. Within the last century, a prolonged retardation of industrial growth was called forth, not by the satiation of the maximum possible demand, but by a lack of effective demand arising from lack of purchasing power in the face of high costs. Both were obviously the reverse of an abatement in technical progress. Only when demand is definitely inelastic does it serve as an immediate retarding force; but inelasticity is itself frequently an effect of the cheapening of commodities resulting from technical development.

We are thus brought to the factor of technical changes as the most important group of processes in an industry's development. While all three forces are interdependent, the charges in technique most clearly condition the movements in both population and demand, while the dependence of technical progress upon population and demand is less clear and immediate. In the chain interconnection of the three, this link seems to be the most prominent. While not denying the significance of the other two, we shall discuss in detail only the changes in technique as the factor most promising of significant findings.

In many industries there comes a time when the basic technical conditions are revolutionized. When such a fundamental change takes place, a new era begins. In the manufacturing industries it is frequently the period when the machine process first supplants hand labor to a substantial extent. In the extractive industries, it is either the moment when the sources and use of a commodity are discovered (petroleum) or when a new and wide application is found for a commodity hitherto but little used. As concrete examples of such periods, one may mention the decade 1780–90 for the cotton industry and pig iron production in Great Britain, the decade 1860–70 for steel, the decade of the '80s for the copper industry, the decade of the '30s for anthracite, and of the '40s for bituminous coal in the United States, the first and second decades of the nineteenth century for zinc smelting (Belgium-Saxony), the '60s for petroleum (United States), and the decade of the '70s for lead (United States). In all these cases we observe a revolutionary invention or discovery applied to the industrial process which becomes the chief method of production. Our generation has been the eye-witness of such changes in the automobile and radio industries.

When such a change occurs, the industry grows very rapidly. The innovation is rarely perfect at the start, and further improvements take place continually after the main invention or discovery. The use of the continually improving and cheapening commodity spreads to larger areas, overcoming obstacles which may have limited demand in the past. Population grows and helps to swell the total volume of output. But with all this, after a time the vigorous expansion slackens and further development is not so rapid. What are the processes which underlie this change?

In an attempt to answer this question we have grouped together trends observed in the life histories of a number of industries. The findings may be summarized as follows:

I. Technical progress slackens.

II. The slower growing industries exercise a retarding influence upon the faster growing complementary branches. The rapidly growing industries exercise a similar influence upon competitive branches.

III. The funds available for the expansion of an industry decrease in *relative* size as the industry grows.

IV. An industry in one country may be retarded by the competition of the same industry in a younger country.

These tentative generalizations call for support and amplification.

I. Technical Progress Slackens

The slowing down of technico-economic progress was noted twenty years ago by the prominent German economist Julius Wolf. One of his four 'laws of retardation of progress' reads: 'Every technical improvement, by lowering costs and by perfecting the utilization of raw materials and of power, bars the way to further progress. There is less left to improve, and this narrowing of possibilities results in a slackening or complete cessation of technical development in a number of fields.'[1] Wolf illustrates the thesis by a number of examples, but undertakes no study to show that such retardation of technical progress has actually taken place.

Such a study must begin with a distinction between the manufacturing and extractive industries. In the former a spectacular technical development took place during the last century and a half, a process that must be observed rather closely to reveal the tendency towards retardation. In the extractive industries, technical progress was less conspicuous, and its failure to overcome the limiting influence of exhaustion can be demonstrated more simply.

To illustrate the technical changes within the manufacturing industries, brief accounts relating to a few separate branches were compiled. These chronicle the most important inventions within the fields and show the diminution in the number or importance of inventions as an industry grows older.

A thoroughgoing study of technical changes in the manu-

[1] See *Die Volkswirtschaft der Gegenwart u. Zukunft*, Leipzig, 1912, pp. 236–37.

facturing industries is a Herculean task, not to be attempted in the present study. Even for a single industry the field is a vast one, so we can do no more than to give an impressionistic summary of a few industries as illustrative, and the lack of reliable, up-to-date materials prevents us from considering these results as final.

The textile industries offer the best illustrations of an apparent decline in the rate of technical progress. The cotton, wool, and the worsted manufactures are among the branches of production in which the Industrial Revolution began long ago. Here there has been time for the tendency to manifest itself in a more or less perceptible fashion.

Cotton. Most of the revolutionary inventions in the cotton manufacturing industry came close together in the last thirty years of the eighteenth century. The spinning jenny was invented by Hargreaves in 1767, patented in 1770, and introduced immediately. Arkwright's first patent for the water-frame was taken out in 1769; his mill built at Crompton in 1771. In 1779 Crompton invented the mule. In 1785 Arkwright's patents were thrown open to the public, but they had been widely and unscrupulously utilized before that date. Meanwhile a pressing need for raw cotton had developed. In response Whitney's saw gin was invented in 1793 and improved in 1795. Three years prior Crompton's mule was greatly improved by Kelly. In 1785 Cartwright invented the first power loom, but it was not efficient, and its use did not spread until essential improvements were introduced much later. A number of subsidiary machines were also invented during the last quarter of the eighteenth century. The carding machine (cylinder) was introduced in Lancashire in 1760 and greatly improved in 1772 by John Less. The scutching machine was invented in 1797.

By 1800, however, serious defects in some of the most important machines and a number of gaps in the mechanical equipment of the industry still remained, but most of these were remedied during the first half of the nineteenth century. Thus the mule was made self-acting by Roberts in 1825, and about the same time the throstle was introduced into the water-frame. The final improvement which made the power loom practicable was carried through by Kenworthy and Bullough in 1841. Important improvements in the carding machine were made in 1823, 1834, and 1850.

It is interesting to observe that few important inventions were made after 1860. In the careful study of the technical development of American cotton manufactures made by M. T. Copeland,[1] of the five groups of manufacturing processes distinguished, only one seems to have benefited from new inventions. Of course, there was marked improvement in the machines already in use by 1860, but most of the industry's machines were available by that time. To cite a few illustrations: 'In the machinery used for the initial processes the chief changes have been in the direction of perfecting machines already employed in 1860' (p. 56). The openers and pickers were available by 1860. The stationary flat cards had been known for a long time, although they were materially improved by Wellman in the '50s. The revolving flat card was taken up in the '60s in England. The cotton combing machine was invented in 1845. In the drawing frame there were no great changes after 1860, except improved construction and the introduction of better stop motion (electric). The fly frames had already superseded the speeders in most cases by 1860. The type was modern, but many improvements were made.

In spinning no important new mechanisms were introduced after the '60s. In spooling, however, two new devices appeared, Wade's wire bobbin holder (invented in the '70s) and the Barber Knotter (1900). In warping and sizing the same machines were used after 1860.

The single revolutionary invention after the '60s was the Northrop Automatic Loom (put on the market in 1894). It combined a number of important features and cut the labor cost of weaving one half, 'a fact which is particularly significant since the labor cost of weaving previously constituted one half of the entire labor cost of manufacturing cotton cloth.'[2] The automatic loom was improved later on and adapted to the weaving of cloth from different colored thread. (Crompton and Knowles.)

[1] *The Cotton Manufacturing Industry of the United States*, Harvard University Press, 1917, chapter 4.

[2] *Ibid.*, p. 86.

In converting and finishing, most of the processes remained essentially unchanged. 'The methods of bleaching have undergone few changes during the last fifty years, or even during the last century.... As in bleaching, so in printing no new types of machines have been introduced during the last half century.'[1] The only recent development of importance was in the mercerization process. In the drying and finishing machinery there was considerable improvement but no new inventions.

The general impression from this survey is that the bulk of the machine equipment was introduced into the industry before 1860, and after that the number of important inventions was much smaller. While the eighty years preceding this date witnessed a number of inventions of a revolutionary character, there were only one or two of similar rank after 1860.

The economic effects of technical improvement are reflected in the cost of capital and labor per pound of cotton yarn. The data are supplied by Th. Ellison.[2]

	Yarn 40 hanks to the lb.			Yarn 100 hanks to the lb.	
	shillings	pence		shillings	pence
1779	14	0	1786	34	0
1784	8	11	1796	15	6
1799	4	2	1806	4	2
1812	1	0	1812	2	10
1830	0	6.8	1830	2	2.8
1860	0	6.3	1860	1	5
1882	0	3.4	1882	1	0.4

It is to be seen that as measured in absolute savings the effect of the technical progress seems to grow smaller and smaller. But even the rate of decline in the cost of capital and labor was diminishing although not continuously. Thus in the first 51 years this cost (in yarn 40 hanks to the lb.) declined from 14 shillings to 6.75 pence, or 96 per cent; in the next 52 years it declined from 6.75 to 3.375 pence, or only 50 per cent. The decline is still more obvious in the case of yarn, 100 hanks to the lb. It is interesting to notice that the cost of raw cotton does not exhibit the same decline.

[1] *Op. cit.*, p. 94.

[2] Th. Ellison: *The Cotton Trade of Great Britain*, 1886, p. 61.

The cotton in yarn, 40 hanks per lb., cost 2 shillings in 1779, 7.75 pence in 1830, and 7.125 pence in 1882 (6.875 *d.* in 1860). Thus the cost of cotton constituted in 1779, 12.7 per cent of the selling price, in 1834, 54 per cent, in 1882, 68 per cent.

Woolen and Worsted. The woolen and worsted industries received most of their machinery from the cotton industry, with two important exceptions: Kay's fly-shuttle and the wool combing machine. The mechanization of operations in the industry was thus completed quite early, and after the 1860s no great inventions seem to have been introduced into either the woolen or the worsted branch of production.

To cite a few details: In the preparation of the stuff for spinning, the machines and processes in use were introduced before the '60s. The Burr Picker was introduced in 1833–34, the Burr Cylinder was attached to the carding machine about 1846. The carbonization process of cleaning was introduced in Germany in the '50s. In washing and scouring, the modern processes were also established fairly early. The slashing machine (invented in 1835) was brought to its modern form by 1860.

The carding machines were essentially in their modern form by the '30s. Spinning likewise did not benefit from any important inventions after the '30s. Only in weaving did the woolen and worsted industries profit from that revolutionary invention first made for the cotton industry, the automatic loom. But the importance of this device is appreciably less in the woolen and worsted manufactures than in cotton.

In finishing machinery there was no progress in the size and efficiency of the apparatus. Gig mills and mechanical shearing were pretty well established by the beginning of the nineteenth century. The latest important inventions were in the specifically worsted operations of combing. The first machine technically suitable for wool was achieved by the introduction of the 'nip' process by Heilman (about 1840), and brought to its final efficient shape by Donisthorpe and Lister (1851). Other important changes were made by Isaac Holden (square motion in 1854) and Noble (1853).

The decline in the rate of technical progress in wool and

worsted is attested by a careful investigator.[1] After sketching the vigorous technical advance in the American industry the author says in his general summary in the preface, 'But this early woolen advance has not persisted. Indeed, with it the degree and rapidity of technical progress during more recent decades in this branch of the industry, and the technical situation that has confronted the worsted cloth manufacture throughout its whole career in the United States, present rather sharp contrasts. As for the former, advances have been progressively less significant as the years have gone by, until recently improvement has chiefly taken the form of refinements upon existing mechanisms, coming either from within the domestic industry or from abroad. In the worsted manufacture, a manufacture which on a factory basis goes back in this country only about 75 years — a complete equipment of well-developed, quasi-automatic machinery was originally borrowed from abroad, and, since its introduction here, it has undergone scarcely any improvement in type. To be sure, certain apparatus for use in processes auxiliary to the main manufacturing operations have been introduced, and as in the woolen branch much progress has been made in the perfection of preëxisting machinery. Moreover, with regard to both woolen and worsted machinery, one should note the recent advent of the automatic loom — a significant exception to the statements just made. Though this mechanism does in fact promise less for the wool manufacturing industry than a similar machine has already accomplished for the allied cotton-cloth manufacture, and indeed has made little progress in the woolen branch of the former industry, still it must be viewed as a notable improvement. On the whole, however, marked changes and conspicuous advances have been rare during recent decades in the mechanical equipment of either the woolen or the worsted manufacture. In short, there appears to be a tendency toward stability in technological form — observable, I believe, in other industries as well. Progress undoubtedly will come in the future, but seemingly at a generally slower rate. The Industrial Revolution has here about spent its force.'

[1] A. N. Cole: *The American Wool Manufacture*, Harvard University Press, 1926, pp. ix–x.

Iron and Steel. For these most important branches no recent general surveys of technical and economic development are available. The summaries given below are necessarily meager, and the impression is uncertain. One branch of production, cast iron and moulding processes, is entirely omitted.

England was again the leader in introducing the modern technical processes in iron smelting. According to Scrivenor, attempts to substitute pit coal for charcoal were first made early in the seventeenth century by Dudley (1618), later by Copley (1656). According to T. S. Ashton,[1] coke smelting was first successfully introduced by the elder Darby in 1709. But in 1734 ironmasters were still experimenting unsuccessfully in the same direction. The reason was that the inventors were reticent about their processes, the production of sound coke iron was not generally successful, and the coke iron did not possess the tensility and ductility necessary to make good malleable iron. For a long time therefore the coke smelting process was restricted to castings.

The coal smelting process spread extensively in the 1760s. Ovens began to be used instead of open piles, and in 1763 Smeaton had invented the double-acting blowing cylinder to produce a stronger air blast. By the introduction of the steam engine the operation of these cylinders was greatly facilitated. Only then was the victory of coal over charcoal complete.

Developments in smelting practice after that were concerned mostly with improving the shape of the furnace and the blast. Both were, on the whole, gradual, and represented modifications of the essential revolutionary change, that from charcoal to coal. The big single inventions were the introduction of the hot blast instead of the cold (by Neilson in 1828), which was applied to the manufacture of pig iron with anthracite coal in 1837 by Crane. After that there was little development up to the twentieth century. In the first decade of the latter century a fuel saving dry blast was introduced by Gayley. But as in similar cases, while the saving was considerable, the blast furnace had achieved such a degree of efficiency that the saving in the

[1] *Iron and Steel in the Industrial Revolution*, Manchester, 1925.

smelting cost had little effect on the selling price of pig iron. Still, the history of the smelting phase of the iron industry does not leave a clear impression of decline in the rate of technical progress, for we find an important invention rather late in the industry.

In wrought iron the situation is clearer. Wrought iron was long produced by fusion of cast iron on charcoal forges, but this was expensive and moreover required a highly scarce commodity. The problem was solved by Cort. The whole history of wrought iron is well summarized by J. P. Roe.[1]

As a natural sequence of the successful use of coke in the blast furnace, the metallurgists of those days sought means by which to use either coke or raw coal for the conversion of cast iron into wrought iron. To use coal successfully it was essential to avoid contact between the iron and the fuel. This led to the introduction of the reverberatory furnace. . . . [The Granage in 1776 and the Onions in 1783 seem to have been unsuccessful.]

In 1784 Henry Cort patented the process . . . to him belongs the credit for first using coal for refining iron, and for introducing what was later known as the puddling process. . . . When first introduced, the iron loss was excessive, taking two tons of pig iron to make one ton of bars; and for some years after the process was well known, the loss was from 50 to 70 per cent. Such an iron loss would have been intolerable, exceeding as it did that in any of the older methods, had it not been for the fact that this process made available a cheap and abundant fuel. . . . [For this reason the process spread without delay.]

The original process was improved by the use of air cooled, cast iron bottoms. . . . The process was subsequently known as *dry puddling* after the method of *pig boiling* appeared. . . .

The pig boiling process was invented by J. Hall about 1830, and from the time of its introduction to the present it has been the chief producer of wrought iron, and to-day is known under the broad term of puddling. The only changes made in the reverberatory furnace for puddling have been those of increasing the size and working from both sides. . . . [2]

---

[1] 'The Manufacture of Wrought Iron,' in *The A B C of Iron and Steel*, edited by A. O. Backert, Cleveland, 1915, pp. 96–97.

[2] *Op. cit.*, pp. 96–97.

While Cort's puddling process replaced the old methods of fusion, and was finally changed in the first half of the nineteenth century, his other invention, the rolling process (1782), replaced the labor wasting procedures of stamping and hammering previously used in the production of the iron bar. There seems to be no record of any marked changes in this process after Cort introduced it, except, of course, improvement in size, force, particular shape, etc.

Steel presents a good example of the course of inventions within an industry. It was produced after 1740 by the Huntsman process, but modern steel production was not possible until after the introduction of the Bessemer pneumatic procedure. While its principle was known as early as 1855, the Bessemer process failed in 1855 and 1856 to produce successful results. Only when R. Mushet added *spiegeleisen*, in 1856, was it possible to produce good steel from pig iron in the Bessemer converter. But the pig iron had to be of low phosphoric content which limited the use of the process, especially in those countries where the phosphoric content of the ore was high.

Almost immediately after the introduction of the Bessemer process improvements and inventions of efficient methods followed, and these account to-day for the imposing output. If we divide into two periods the sixty years since the decade when the modern steel industry really began, we find that most of these improvements and inventions fall within the first half. There was first the open-hearth process which is the most widely used to-day. It was originally applied by Siemens and the Martins (separately) in the early part of the '60s (the Siemens furnace was patented in 1856), and introduced into the United States in 1869. The main advantage of this method is that the phosphoric content of the pig iron and scrap does not matter so much as in the Bessemer process. Also the open-hearth process allows greater control during the process of smelting. Another big improvement was the Gilchrist-Thomas de-phosphorizing process, first patented in the United States in 1877, applicable both to the Bessemer and the open-hearth methods, which permits the use of pig iron of any phosphoric content. This invention made available the ore deposits of Germany and the United States. Even the electric steel processes, which so far account for only a small part of the steel output, were initiated by the Siemens electric furnace in 1880, although great changes were made in the '90s and constant improvements are still occurring.

This concentration of inventions in the period 1855–90 does not mean that no improvements occurred later. After 1890 there were changes in the different alloys used in the furnace to produce a final product. The product became greatly diversified, and even to-day we read of new kinds of steel being produced. There were of course improvements in the converter and the hearth, the handling of materials, etc. But what seems on the whole certain is that the essential processes of manufacture, those which made possible its production and use on a grand scale, were all introduced in the early history of the industry. What followed was the gradual process of technical refinement. The rate of technical progress as reflected by single inventions recorded was undoubtedly higher in the first thirty years after the Bessemer process than in the succeeding thirty years.

A recent general source such as the Encyclopædia Britannica (13th edition) corroborates the statements concerning each of these important changes. 'Developments during 1910–26 in iron and steel were improvements in process and equipment rather than new methods....' The most important recent changes according to this account were the exploitation of gas (in the blast furnace processes), the splitting of the steel refining process into two phases, and the rapid growth of electric furnaces for producing high quality steel.[1]

The general conclusion concerning iron and steel manufacturing is the same as that for textiles. If not iron smelting, wrought iron and steel show in the dynamics of their productive process the same phenomenon of a decrease in the number of important inventions after the industry started on a modern basis.

Shoe Manufacturing.[2] Here we have an entirely different

[1] Vol. II, pp. 537–41.

[2] See F. Behr: *Die Wirkung d. Fortschreitender Technik auf die Shuhindustrie,* Leipzig, 1909; also the article by Rehe, *Beiträge zur Geschichte d. Technik u. Industrie,* 1911, Enc. Brit., 11th ed., vol. 24, p. 933.

branch of production, one in which all operations were at one time of a manual type, and no reliance was placed as in iron and steel upon chemical processes.

The working actions involved in shoe manufacturing may be divided into three groups: (1) cutting of the parts; (2) joining of the parts; (3) polishing of the finished product. Of these, the second group involves more time and labor than the others.

The saving of manual labor in the first group was comparatively easy by applying cutting forms and driving them sharply through the material with a great wooden hammer. But the large stance machines soon replaced this process, especially early for soles and heels. These machines were first driven by hand presses, but in the '80s power began to be supplied by motors. Stance machines were not widely applied in the manufacture of uppers because changes in fashion were too likely to render them uneconomical.

In the second group of operations the elimination of manual labor began very early, in the first decade of the nineteenth century, when pegging was introduced instead of sewing (attributed to various people — Randolph, Walker). In 1810 M. J. Brunnel patented a range of machinery for fastening soles to uppers by means of metallic pins or nails, and the use of screws and staples was patented by R. Woodman in the same year. The simplification in the manual operations introduced by pegging paved the way for the application of the machines. The final shape of these machines, the champion pegging machine, which is still in use, was introduced in 1851.

Meanwhile the sewing machine was invented by Howe (1845) and imitated by Singer. It was quickly taken over for the sewing operations on the uppers (Chevalier's machine in the '50s) and a decade later adopted for the fastening of the sole (Mackay machine — 1867). A modification of the latter was the Keats machine ('the iron shoemaker') in 1878 and the Goodyear of 1874–75. These sole sewing machines are the most important in shoe manufacturing.

The third group of operations was mechanized in the '80s, but this seems to have been of little significance in the history of the industry. By the end of the '80s the only important operation not yet taken over by machines was the nailing of the uppers to the inner sole, an operation requiring a careful nipping motion. A machine for this purpose was first invented in the '70s by J. Matzeliger, an American negro (hence the name 'niggerhead'), but it did not prove very practical. In the '90s, however, it reached its final form, the consolidated lasting machine, and was widely adopted. After this no improvement of any importance occurred.

In the shoe industry, on the whole, the process of technical improvement seems to have been particularly intense in the thirty years from 1850 to 1880. During this time most of the important machines were invented and introduced: the pegging, the stance, and the sewing machine. In the '80s the comparative unimportant polishing machines, and in the early '90s the lasting machines appeared. By that time the process of mechanization had been completed, and consequently the rate of technical change as reflected by the number of new important machines introduced had considerably diminished. Thus the course of progress seems to have been more rapid in the earlier period of this industry, beginning with its industrial revolution, than later.

Paper. In this, one of the oldest of industries, the technical revolution seems to have taken place fairly early. The operations involved fall into two classes: (1) preparing the pulp; (2) transforming the pulp into paper. Problems in the first class are connected mainly with the question of raw material.

Until the middle of the nineteenth century rags furnished the only source of raw material, but by that time the growth and technical development of the industry had created a shortage in rags, and an intense search for a substitute ensued. This proved to be esparto discovered about 1860 and was first adopted in England. The process for treating it was patented by Routledge in 1861.

A much more important raw material was found in wood-pulp produced either by mechanical or chemical means, the latter being the more widely used since it gave a more durable paper. Mechanical wood-pulp (ground wood) was introduced into the United States in 1866, having originated in

Germany in 1840. The current processes of preparing chemical wood-pulp may be distinguished as the sulphite and the sulphate, the former used for book and fine paper and partly for newsprint, and the latter for Kraft and wrapping paper. The sulphite process was discovered by Tilghman in 1867, but it was not used extensively until seventeen years later, by which time essential improvements had been made in it. The sulphate process was invented in 1884, and was introduced into the United States in 1907. It has developed mostly during the recent decades, and has largely supplanted the older soda process.

The search for new raw materials continues unabated and with rags still used for very fine paper the variety of raw materials is considerable. Waste paper has been used for a long time, and the latest reports concern the possibilities of cornstalk. So the technical processes in the transformation of the raw material into pulp keep on changing, and it would be difficult to determine just when the technical progress slackened unless we were to study separately each specific method of treatment. We shall, therefore, pass on directly to the processes of manufacturing paper proper.

The processes for transforming pulp into paper are beating the half-stuff in the beating engine, where the remaining traces of chlorine are removed and where loading materials, color, and sizing are added. It then passes through the paper machine, which delivers the wet paper sheets, dries, cuts, and polishes them. Frequently the beaten pulp, however, is put through a refining machine before entering the paper machine.

Beating machines were introduced early. The Hollander, developed in the Netherlands about 1750, is the underlying type for all modern beating machines. 'The elementary Hollanders . . . contain in essence the features of the modern beating machine. At first worked by hand, they were afterwards propelled by steam or other motive power.' [1]

The beating machines have remained unchanged in principle. They have been improved only in efficient operation, and later years have brought about a complete omission of the beating process in the manufacture of newsprint. Since

[1] A. Dykes Spicer: *The Paper Trade*, London, 1907, pp. 7–8.

1921 a number of newsprint mills are mixing the screened mechanical pulp with the necessary amount of sulphite and passing the mixture directly to the paper machine. This practice prevails as yet only in newsprint mills.

The paper machine (Fourdrinier) was invented by Louis Robert in 1797–98. One of this type, built by Donkin, was installed at Frogmore, England, in 1803. Improvements followed in rapid succession. In 1808 Dickinson invented a machine for making paper on a cylinder covered with wire cloth (patented in 1809). T. B. Crompton patented a process for drying paper by means of steam cylinders in 1821 and a device for splitting paper by circular knives in 1828. In 1830 appeared the Dandy Roll invented by Marshall. In the same year strainer plates for removing dirt from pulp were introduced by Ibbotson. The latter, in coöperation with Barratt, also discovered an improved plan for water-marking paper and a method for producing rolls with a greater degree of accuracy (1830). After that there were no revolutionary changes, although the modern type of machine was not well established until the end of the '80s.

Of course, improvements continue. Recently an improved arrangement of the screens has been set up, and some modern machines permit the production of fine paper on a wide, high speed type instead of on the narrow, slow running form. But by and large one may subscribe to the statement of Spicer's. After he has described the inventions up to 1830, he says: 'We have watched the development of paper-making machinery detail by detail till we have, at length, reached a period when the whole art, as we now understand it, may be said to have been conceived in its broad outlines. Since then there have been many alterations and improvements, but they have been for the most part continuations of the same idea. For seventy years the development has progressed, by slow degrees and at irregular intervals, along the path already marked out in 1830.' [1]

The method of loading (adding of mineral to the pulp to give weight) and sizing (the process by which the surface is prepared to receive ink without absorption) were well known early in the industry's history: The latest change, noted in

[1] *Op. cit.*, p. 66.

Spicer's book, is the replacing of crystal alum by sulphate of alumina (used to fix the gelatine sizing to the paper). However, these processes are not very important in the industry and we shall not dwell upon them.

The broad conclusion of this rather brief survey is that as far as the manufacture of paper proper is concerned (as distinct from the production of pulp), technical progress has considerably abated during the later periods of the industry's history. Technical improvements are still made, and there is much room for mechanical development in handling of materials. But the mechanization of the industry is largely completed, and there is little prospect for important technical innovations, except in the field of raw materials.

Copper. In the copper industry we find an exception to the decline in the rate of technical change. The history of the industry on a modern basis goes back to 1880. It is true that the roasting and smelting processes have been greatly changed and improved during the 1880–1900 decades, for this period witnessed the development of the Bessemer process in copper smelting, the development of the pyritic smelting principle, the adoption of electrolytic refining and of the mechanically rabbled roaster furnaces. But on the other hand, after 1900 the basic lining was introduced into the converters, the manufacture of sulphuric acid from blast furnace (reverberatory furnace) gases gained in importance, coal-dust firing was introduced into the reverberatory furnaces, and the 'leaching' process of direct metal extraction appeared. Not to mention the processes of preparing the ore for refining, which have been revolutionized since 1900, we find in refining proper no slackening in the rate of progress.

Several reasons may be adduced for this. One is that the period since the industry entered the modern era is comparatively brief. But of more importance seems to be the growing scarcity of raw materials. The exhaustion of rich copper ore deposits proceeded at a threateningly rapid rate, and provided an ever-pressing stimulus for changes in technique. These changes while directed mainly to the process of ore concentration also affected refining. Thus the process of 'leaching' is an outcome of the scarcity of rich ore, which directed attention to the porphyry ore deposits in which the copper occurs as oxide or chloride, making mechanical concentration impossible.[1]

Thus far we have been dealing with manufacturing industries. Let us now take the case of a great invention, namely the steam engine, and trace its development and influences through different industries. Its familiar history calls for only a brief summary.

The steam engine was originally built with the definite intention of satisfying a demand for cheap power arising from: (1) the coal, tin, and copper mines for pumping water; the demand for coal growing out of the use of pit coal for smelting of iron; (2) the iron furnaces which needed power to supply a strong blast; and (3) waterworks in large cities to pump water. The invention was financed successively by Roebuck, Boulton, an English bank, and a Dutch firm.

'The story of the early progress of steam power (this includes the Newcomen engine) in industry is easily epitomized. At first it was used as a matter of sheer necessity by the mines; then later it enabled new methods to be employed in smelting iron and working textile machinery of a new and powerful description; then lastly it replaced other types of power in the rest of the industrial field, wherever coals became cheap.[2]

'The interdependence of the various movements of the mechanical revolution is very obvious. The steam engine provided power to drain the coal mines, which supplied coal for the new methods of smelting iron; which in turn provided the additional supplies of metal for the construction of engines and machinery. By 1800, industry had reached its modern stage mechanically; there is no radical difference between the methods of 1800 and those of 1900.'[3]

This gives a clear picture of the early development of the engine. Its history after Watt is discussed in great detail by

[1] The writer is indebted to Mr. F. E. Richter, lately with the American Telephone and Telegraph Company, for the information relating to the copper industry.

[2] John Lord: *Capital and Steam Power*, 1923, p. 180.

[3] *Ibid.*, pp. 221-22.

C. Matschoss.[1] He divides the nineteenth century into two parts, and the story of the development and spread of the engine illustrates well the difference between the early and the late stages in the history of a fundamental technical change. The improvements and extension during the period 1800–50 may be summarized as follows:

I. Improvements in the stationary engine.
  1. Simplification of construction — better regulation of work done.
  2. The raising of the steam pressure and the application of the principle of expansion. The high pressure engines did not spread quickly so long as the materials used in the construction of the boilers and parts were unable to stand the strain of high pressure. Moreover, high pressure engines required a more precise adjustment. Hence they were little used in the '40s and became practical only in the '50s.
  3. The use of the same steam in two and three cylinders. Effected profitably by Woolf (1804–06).
II. The stationary engine in industrial use.
  Here the engine expanded to fields much beyond its original application in mines, blast furnaces, and cotton and wool factories. The single important invention was Nasmyth's steam hammer in 1838.
III. The applications in transport.
  This was the most important line of development. In 1807 appeared the first successful steamship. In 1838 a steamship crossed the Atlantic in 15 days, thereby cutting the time of passage in half. In 1843 the first transatlantic iron screw ship was launched. The application of the steam engine to railway transport is well known. In the '30s we already find in England the railroad promotion boom and crisis.

As compared to these changes in the first half of the century, what were the developments in the second half and later? Of course, improvements in the engine itself continued. With the better quality of materials it was possible to increase the steam pressure. Overheated or mixed steam began to be used with the spread of mineral oil lubrication. Construction was improved. But the great single advance was the introduction of the Corliss regulator, with its precise delivery of power according to the work to be done. This

[1] *Entwicklung der Dampfmaschine*, Berlin, 1908.

was first introduced in 1849 and was soon adopted in all the engines.

In industry the chief innovations arose out of the growing use of electricity. The dynamo called for motive power which was supplied by the steam engine, and an entirely different type was developed — the steam turbine. The modern type dates from 1884 (compound by Parsons), and was improved in 1891. It was first employed only in electric works, but later applied to marine propulsion (first in 1897) and then adopted by large and fast ships. The steam turbine is practicable only where great power and speed are required, and hence did not spread to industry. The steam engine, however, found industrial application in the form of the traction engine in agriculture, and the modern steam pump-pulvometer in waterworks (1871 by Henry Hall).

In transport, other than the introduction of the steam turbine on fast ships, there were no particular developments after this, except the improvements and economies achieved by raising pressure, overheating steam, etc.

This in brief is the development of the steam engine. The following observations may be made:

1. In the early period, i.e., until 1850, the use of the steam engine spread rapidly in mines, blast furnaces, and waterworks, where the demand for it gave rise to the invention of the mechanism in its modern form. Almost simultaneously it spread to industries, where the introduction of machinery called for power supply, particularly in the textile and paper-making industries. Later it was applied in the field of transportation, and here the task of the inventor was to provide modifications which would render the 'moving' engine practicable.

Having spread in its early history to these various fields, the steam engine then occupied a position of dominance as the chief source of power supply for industries. Its expansion in the second half of the century was less significant, and was contingent upon the appearance of inventions and mechanism which had no direct connection with the steam engine itself, the latter being reduced to a subsidiary mechanism. The traction engine had no place in agriculture before the invention of heavy farm machinery, and the application to the dynamo obviously had to wait upon the appearance of the dynamo. The significance of these extensions is small in comparison to those of the locomotive and the steamship in the earlier half of the century. The steam turbine was and remained of comparatively limited application.

2. It must be remarked that the steam turbine is technically an entirely different type of engine, since it uses steam directly and not through a system of cranks and shafts. The basic pattern of the steam engine remained throughout the century and continues even to-day to be of the type constructed by Watt. The last important improvement in it was the Corliss regulator of 1849, and with that the engine seems to have reached comparative perfection.

The steam engine presents the only case of a power engine having a long history, but the two major characteristics of its history, viz., the great rapidity and importance of expansion in its early period, and the achievement of comparative perfection after a certain stage of development are paralleled by power motors such as the electromotor, internal combustion and gas engines. Thus the electric power supply spread most rapidly and immediately after 1880 to those spheres in which steam power was unsuitable (such as electric lighting). In the later period it began to penetrate fields formerly served by the steam engine in which cheap electric power was more convenient and economical (interurban lines). In this period, when the new motive power was being extended to fields formerly supplied by a different although not greatly inferior power supply, the rate of expansion was probably slower than in the first period.[1]

[1] It is interesting to contrast the introduction of electric and other motors with the introduction of steam. Steam power was the first mechanically produced supply of power independent of weather conditions and changes of stream, which were such handicaps in water-power. It reduced enormously the cost of energy in its productive applications. The saving afforded by electricity was not very significant compared with that effected by the first mechanical power supply. The only exact calculations illustrating this statement we found in *Die socialpolitische Bedeutung d. Kleinkraftmaschinen*, by Karl Bauer, Berlin, 1907. The cost of human power for one horse-power hour is estimated at 630

In closing this brief account of a few cases of technical changes in industry, we should make clear that they are presented merely as illustrative and in no sense as proof. It would be impossible to assert the existence of the tendency discussed above throughout all industry without a thorough investigation, quite beyond the scope of the present study. The general impression, however, is that in manufacturing industries in which the so-called industrial revolution occurred long ago, the rate of industrial progress has diminished with the passage of time, and the industrial arts in their technical aspects are gradually approaching stable forms.

Thus our illustrations show that the number of important inventions within an industry with an unretarded supply of raw material tends to diminish as time goes on. A considerable amount of arbitrariness is involved in deciding which is an important invention and which is not. The selection by economic and technical historians in their presentation is not the ideal test, although the best available. Another assumption justified only by forced ignorance is the conception that the inventions cited are of equal significance. But the evidence points with emphasis to a diminution in the number of important innovations.

The main reasons for such a trend come easily to mind. The introduction of the initial invention is a stimulus which soon creates a corresponding change and improvement in the other processes within the industry. The number of

pfennigs. One horse-power hour delivered by a steam engine of 6 h.p. capacity and working five hours per day is 11.8 pfennigs, and the same by an electric motor 11.7, the difference between steam and electricity being insignificant. It is more apparent for a smaller engine. For a steam engine of 1 h.p. capacity the cost is 31.5 pfennigs, for an electromotor of the same capacity, 13.9. Of course, the introduction of the steam engine did not mean a drop in the cost of energy from 630 pfennigs to 11.8 or to 31.5, because the service of the modern steam engine is much more effective and cheaper than those in use at the beginning of the last century, and on the other hand, human labor was much cheaper. Still, it seems reasonable to suppose that the saving involved in the change from human power to the steam engine was much greater than that in the transition from steam to electricity as far as mere volume of energy is considered.

these other processes is limited, and as the industry thus advances technically, the economic stimulus to further innovations becomes weaker.

Technically a branch of production is a series of a small number of separate operations that lead in an invariable sequence from the raw material to the finished product. Once an important process in this chain is revolutionized by an invention, pressure is exercised upon the other links in the chain to become more efficient, otherwise the disparity in performance at the different stages prevents a full exploitation of the innovation. Many important inventions came in response to such pressure from a preceding technological change. Whitney's cotton gin, a classic example, was aimed to satisfy the great demand for raw cotton caused by the mechanical inventions of the preceding decade. The application of the drilling process to petroleum and the resulting enormous production called for better transportation facilities, and pipe lines appeared. The use of coal in iron smelting necessitated a strong blast, and the Smeaton blowing cylinder was invented.

The stimulus for technical changes in other processes of the industry is thus present from the moment the first major invention is introduced. It may take long, in response to this stimulus, before the necessary technical improvements are made. But the initial invention itself paves the way, for it usually standardizes the product at that stage when ready for further working over. This standardization facilitates a more mechanical and precise future treatment, thus provoking technical progress at the later stages within the industry.

While the stimulus for further inventions appears early, the number of operations to be improved is limited and gradually becomes exhausted. In a purely manufacturing industry technical progress consists mainly in replacing manual labor by machines. When all the important operations are performed by machines which have reached a stage of comparative perfection, not much room is left for further innovations. If in addition to that, the chemical processes are perfected to a point allowed by modern machinery, no great new improvements may be expected. As inventions take over one process after another, a very limited field is left to the later periods of an industry's history, and the rate of progress in terms of separate inventions declines.

This gradual spending of the protracted 'industrial revolution' is accompanied and furthered by the weakening of the economic stimulus. After the cost of a commodity has been reduced from luxury levels, its low price renders the demand for it largely inelastic, and further possible reductions are too small to have any appreciable effect. In addition to that, as Julius Wolf pointed out, there is resistance to radical innovations in the existing capital investment, which is larger, the older the industry.

We have thus a considerable argumentative basis for the tentative generalization concerning the decline in the number of noted inventions. The succession of these does not exhaust, however, the possibilities of technical progress within an industry. For the improvements in the inventions themselves and changes in the labor element are to be considered. Both processes are gradual, and no definite factual material is to be gathered from the historical accounts. But the following general observations can be made.

An invention already has a long history by the time it appears in its first practical form. Every important change in technology has a long list of predecessors; witness the steam engine, the water frame, coal smelting, etc. If it replaces an operation performed by hand, it follows a series of unsuccessful types starting with a plain imitation of the motions performed by hand and ending up with a successful modification of these motions and practicable mechanical performance. If the invention comes to perform a function impossible before, it is usually a result of a drawn-out process of the application of a scientific principle first stated as a theoretical proposition long prior to its successful introduction. Only when a close similarity of functions in two industries permits a carrying over of an innovation from one to the other (smelting of various metal ores) has the invention no history so far as its application within this specific industry is concerned.

Our listing of inventions describes them at this point of

their first successful application, at the period when their first practicable form is reached. After that numerous improvements take place. Their cumulative effect is often much larger than that of the first application itself. But the essential contents of the invention usually remain unchanged; the improvements occurring only in the details. The modern steam engine employs exactly the same principle of steam expansion used by Watt. The modern combined mule and frame embody the same mechanical ideas, and in essentially the same forms first introduced by Crompton and Arkwright. In the histories of industries and of technological procedure one finds time and again assertions that the principles of the invention remain the same although the efficiency of its practical form may be considerably improved.

But these improvements, which come with an ever-extending practical use, are minor in character, and the field for them is limited, since there comes a time when the machine or the process is practically perfect. The same rule of exhaustion operates here as within the larger field of the industry itself. Improvements tend to come at a faster rate during the early periods of use, immediately after the faults are indicated by the practical operation of the innovation. They tend to diminish because there is less to improve. It is true that some of the improvements may be delayed because they have to wait upon development in other industries. Thus pressure in steam engines could not be raised until boilers were constructed of more durable materials cut with greater precision. But this need, if intense enough, provides a stimulus for improvements in the related branch and hastens its development.

The statement that improvements tend to diminish with time as the invention nears perfection can be partly substantiated by patent statistics. The relative number of patents indicates the amount of attention paid by the inventive capacities of a nation to the mechanism of the process in question. The general results of the data on patents (for detailed treatment see Appendix) indicate that for specific inventions or even whole fields of them, the attention paid declines very early. The cumulative effect of an invention thus may be presumed to change at a diminishing rate and gradually approach a stable level, the level of perfection.

Of the third constituent element in technical progress, the changes in the labor factor, we know least. In the history of an industry, one of the first important changes is the development of efficient labor. One is liable to underestimate the importance of this change, but the reports concerning the troubles of the pioneer manufacturers reveal its significance. Their main task was to teach the former manual workers in the field greater alertness, care with the expensive machines, concentrated attention to the work. Not until the younger generation was old enough to enter the factories did the pioneer steam engine builders, spinning manufacturers, and others have at their disposal a reliable working group. The same difficulties are encountered in any new process. Experienced workers are not to be found, and they either have to be imported or to be trained at home. But usually this problem was solved rather early in the industry's history.

Now with the growth of an industry there develops a lessening dependence upon the labor supply. The introduction of automatic machines enabled the performance of operations by relatively unskilled workers, while calling for an increased number of skilled machinists to keep the 'automatics' in order. But even where the far reaching division of the process into a number of small operations has not yet resulted in the introduction of automatic machines, the growing specialization makes the industry less dependent upon the supply of skilled labor. This suggests the possibility that even after the technical equipment and processes of the industry have reached stable levels, there may be continued improvement from a better analysis and a more scientific management of the manual operations still to be performed.

These two streams of improvement in the labor element, one coming immediately after the technical innovations, the other after the industry has reached comparative stabilization, seem to draw out, to attenuate the decline in the rate of technical change that would otherwise have resulted.

But the consideration of the labor factor gives no basis for denying the tentative conclusions as to the existence of such a decline inferred from specific evidence and general reasoning concerning the changes in industrial techniques proper.

In our discussion of the technical development in manufacturing industries, we examined the succession of inventions within specific branches, considered the tendencies to improvements in these important innovations, and briefly pointed out the changes within the labor element — all to indicate the ground for the tentative generalizations regarding the decline in the rate of technical progress. In the extractive industries, however, the declining effects of technical developments in the face of exhaustion are clearly reflected in the pertinent statistical indexes. We shall review the few available statistical series to show that with rare exception these data indicate a diminution in rate of growth, a definite approach to stability or even decline.

The indexes to be used in the analysis of growth of agricultural production are, of course, acreage and yield per acre, the total crop being the product of the two. The course of technical progress is reflected in both measures: in the yield per acre for quite obvious reasons, in the acreage in so far as the work of expansion or of reclamation of non-cultivated territory may be considered essentially an extension of technical development. In both of these aspects technical progress has definite limits. As the data cited below will show, in most cases the growth in these two components reveals conspicuously an approach to stable levels, the curve being roughly a convex second degree parabola on an arithmetic scale. In a few cases one of the components exhibits an increasing absolute increment, but then the other component is stable or declining. The specific data, put into the form of decennial and quinquennial averages, follow (see tables, page 36).

In all four cases for the United States the growth of acreage is described by a convex parabola, even for cotton where the increase in the area cultivated has been rather rapid. The lines of the yield per acre present a less regular picture.

1. Acreage and Yield per Acre, Four Crops, United States, 1866–1925

(Decennial averages; acreage — thousands of acres; yield in bushels)

	Wheat		Corn		Potatoes		Cotton	
	Acreage	Yield	Acreage	Yield	Acreage	Yield	Acreage	Yield
1866–75	20,470	12.0	37,216	26.1	1,261	93.0	8,810	176.2
1876–85	34,433	12.4	61,671	25.4	1,998	81.2	15,209	170.7
1886–95	37,500	12.7	74,274	23.8	2,653	73.8	19,421	176.9
1896–05	49,591	13.4	92,067	25.8	3,008	85.3	26,115	189.0
1906–15	48,838	15.1	101,499	26.8	3,595	97.7	33,248	186.2
1916–25	58,366	13.8	103,898	27.4	3,797	101.6	36,236	153.7

(See *Yearbook of Agriculture*, 1922, pp. 583, 571, 668, 711; 1925, pp. 743, 788, 913, 952.)

In the case of wheat the line, a concave parabola, indicates a continuous rise to 1916, with a drop in the decade 1916–25. In all the other cases, however, the increase in the yield per acre has been neither continuous, nor certain. They all show a decline during the first two decades (cotton during the first only) and a rise thereafter (cotton to 1916), but with the absolute increment diminishing. Thus, except for the yield for wheat, the American data indicate a growth in acreage and yield approaching a limit, showing a decline in the absolute increment.[1]

The data for other countries support this generalization. Thus in the German series for three crops:

2. Area and Yield per Hectar, Three Crops, Germany, 1878–1912

(Quinquennial averages; area — thousands of hectars; yield in doppelzentners)

	Wheat		Rye		Potatoes	
	Area	Yield	Area	Yield	Area	Yield
1878–82......	1822	13.0	5941	9.9	2766	76.5
1883–87......	1921	13.3	5839	10.0	2916	87.4
1888–92......	1942	13.6	5719	9.9	2919	81.1
1893–97......	1961	16.8	5980	13.9	3047	117.0
1898–02......	1905	18.5	5948	14.8	3198	129.8
1903–07......	1867	19.8	6080	16.1	3288	131.3
1908–12......	1912	20.7	6168	17.8	3315	133.4

(Data for 1878–92, *Statistisches Handbuch für das Deutsche Reich*, Berlin, 1907, pp. 448–49; the remaining — *Statistisches Jahrbuch*, 1908, pp. 30, 32; 1914, pp. 43–44.)

[1] The curves on an arithmetic scale are similar to those expressing the Mitscherlich law of diminishing returns.

The line of area in all cases that show a rise is convex. So is the line of yield per hectar, with the possible exception of that for rye, although even there, if the first two stable averages are disregarded, the rise is larger (absolute size) from 1888 to 1898 than in the decade following. Thus the German data indicate also a retarded movement in the line of growth of area and of yield per hectar.

The French series covering a much longer period of time indicate a similar tendency.

3. Area and Yield per Hectar, Two Crops, France,
1815–1910

(Averages, area — thousands of hectars; yield in hectolitres)

	Wheat		Potatoes	
	Area	Yield	Area	Yield
1815–18.............	4600	10.0		
1820–29.............	4860	11.8		
1830–39.............	5270	12.4	775	93.8
1840–49.............	5761	13.7	983	99.2
1850–59.............	6349	14.0	933	87.1
1860...............	6993	14.4	1103	101.1
1871–80.............	6851	14.2	1212	99.0
1881–90.............	6968	15.6	1417	99.3
1891–1900..........	6804	16.2	1533	105.9
1901–10.............	6568	17.6	1508	111.6

(Data from *Annuaire Statistique de France*, 1914–16, pp. 43–44.)

The picture of area expansion is blurred by the change resulting from the war of 1870. Taken continuously the line of area in both crops is convex. The same is true for the line of yield. It must be noticed, however, that the wheat area in France started to decline only after 1870, and until that time it was rising with an increasing absolute increment.

In young countries, area may grow along a concave line, i.e., with an increasing size of the absolute increment. But in such cases the yield does not usually exhibit any conspicuous rise. The latter appears only when territorial expansion stops and production is increased without extending the area cultivated. An example of an accelerated rise of the acreage is presented by Australia.

4. ACREAGE AND YIELD PER ACRE, WHEAT, AUSTRALIA, 1860–1921

	Acreage (thousands of acres)	Yield (bushels)
1860–61	644	15.9
1865–66	818	11.8
1870–71	1124	10.8
1875–76	1423	13.2
1880–81	3054	7.6
1885–86	3277	8.4
1890–91	3229	8.4
1895–96	3774	4.8
1900–01	5667	8.5
1905–06	6123	11.2
1910–11	7372	12.9
1915–16	12485	14.3
1920–21	9072	16.1

(Data from *Official Yearbook of the Commonwealth of Australia*, no. 9, 1916, pp. 314–15; no. 15, 1922, pp. 244–45.)

While the area cultivated was increasing along a concave line, the average yield declined considerably through the first 35 years and began to recover only in the second half of the period. Thus, for the entire 60 years, it was only the acreage that contributed to the growth of the total crop.

This statistical survey, brief as it is, indicates adequately the movement of technical improvement within the agricultural branches of production. The two measures of acreage and yield both show a declining size of absolute increment, thus illustrating the progressive influence of a limiting condition on expansion and on technical progress. In a few cases one index (usually acreage) may show an increase in the absolute increment, but this is offset by the absence of increase in the other factor.

In the second group of extractive industries, the mining group, the output per worker is a good indication of the long-time trend in the technical changes in the industry, or rather in the effect of these changes as over against the adverse influence of the gradual exhaustion of resources. If the rate of technical progress showed a constant tendency to increase, such that it overcame the deterioration in the natural conditions of production, the output per worker would show a constant increase. If the output showed a retarded growth which soon turned into a decline, one would be justified in supposing that the course of technical improvement was not strong enough to overcome the exhaustion of the resources.

While the statistical data below cannot be considered as proof, for other factors except the approach to the limit may be responsible for the decline, they offer strong evidence in support of the hypothesis. The data are fully available only for Germany. Let us consider the annual output per worker in four important minerals.

5. ANNUAL OUTPUT PER WORKER OF FOUR MINERAL ORES, GERMANY, 1860–1909

(Quinquennial averages, metric tons; total work force (Mittl. Belegschaft) as the denominator)

	Bit. Coal	Iron Ore	Copper Ore	Zinc Ore
1860–64................	174.2	92.6	22.0	35.1
1865–69................	202.7	124.6	30.0	35.1
1870–74................	201.9	149.4	37.2	40.9
1875–79................	223.8	186.7	44.0	48.7
1880–84................	265.2	214.5	42.6	50.0
1885–89................	276.3	277.8	36.8	53.3
1890–94................	256.9	319.8	40.3	51.2
1895–99................	268.0	406.4	48.7	49.1
1900–04................	247.(¹	463.1	47.8	45.1
1905–09................	253.8	551.3	44.4	43.4

(Data to 1905, from the *Statistisches Handbuch*, pp. 252–55. For 1905–09 from the *Statistisches Jahrbuch*, corresponding years.)

Three of these series, bituminous coal, zinc, and copper show a rise along a convex curve up to a certain point and a determined decline thereafter. Thus the conclusion from the evidence of these three minerals is that the technical development means an increased output up to a certain point only, and from then on the approach to the limit becomes apparent. Even while output is on the increase, the size of the absolute increment is already declining. This shows that the net effect of technical progress, as expressed by these indexes, is gradually diminishing, and hence is greater in the earlier periods of the industry's history than later.

This is not true in the case of iron ore, where the abundance of resources placed no limiting pressure on the increase of output.

The data for other countries refer only to coal output.

The figures for Belgium reveal the same type of movement as in Germany.

6. ANNUAL OUTPUT PER WORKER OF COAL, BELGIUM, 1831–1924

(Quinquennial averages, metric tons per worker)

1831–35	85.2	1861–65	132.4	1891–95	168.4
1836–40	97.0	1866–70	143.0	1896–1900	178.0
1841–45	110.2	1871–75	143.8	1901–05	166.4
1846–50	114.2	1876–80	148.4	1906–10	165.8
1851–55	127.0	1881–85	169.4	1911–15	143.6
1856–60	118.2	1886–90	178.8	1916–20	133.2
				1921–24	132.8

(Data from *Bulletin de la Societé de l'Industrie Minérale* and the *Annuaire Statistique de la Belgique*, courtesy of Mr. H. G. Villard, National Bureau of Economic Research, Inc.)

Here, too, we have an increase through the first part of the period, along a convex line on an arithmetic scale. A definite decline began in the '90s.

A similar long-time trend line may be observed in the output per worker of coal in Great Britain and France.

7. ANNUAL OUTPUT PER WORKER OF COAL, GREAT BRITAIN AND FRANCE, 1887–88—1911–12

Great Britain (av. per underground worker, tons, annual)		France (av. per total force, metric tons, daily)	
1888–92	360.9	1887–91	0.728
1893–97	335.3	1892–96	0.708
1898–02	354.9	1897–1901	0.728
1903–07	345.7	1902–06	0.695
1908–12	314.7	1907–11	0.678

(Data for Great Britain from J. W. F. Rowe: *Wages in the Coal Industry*, London, P. S. King & Son, 1923, p. 13. Data for France from M. Saitzew: *Steinkohlenpreise u. Dampfkraftkosten, Schriften d. Verein f. Sozialpol,* vol. 143.2, p. 141.)
Note: In this book of Saitzew, the author undertakes a thorough analysis of the technical development of coal mining from the point of view of the past and the future costs of production. His definite forecast is that output per worker will decline, and that this tendency cannot be overcome by any continued rise in wages, for it is due to an ever-progressing deterioration in the natural conditions of production (pp. 168–69). Having analyzed the influence of machinery, the author says, '.... the introduction of machinery in several parts of the productive process has resulted in considerable saving. In other parts a rise in the capacity of the engines with the accompanying intensification of production could also bring about considerable decrease of costs. But ... it is clear that the savings become gradually smaller and smaller, and that the time of considerable decreases in costs is in the past rather than in the future.' The law of exhaustion is thus showing itself more and more in this branch of industry.

These two series for annual output per worker of coal covering the latest period only indicate a decline in the per capita output from the start.

Unfortunately we do not possess any other series on output per worker in the extractive industries. The United States figures from the Census of Manufactures are too far apart and too much subject to accidental influences to be reliable. The few series we have examined indicate a generally prevailing decrease in per worker output of coal, and of copper and zinc in Germany. In the case of the mining branches, the statistical proof might be considered in the nature of supererogation. For here we have the ideal example of an industry where limited deposits are being gradually exhausted, and where the difficulty of production increases the nearer we approach to the limit.

The lengthy discussion of the dynamics of technical change in industry may now be summarized. In most branches of productive activity the rate of technical progress slackens, provided we measure it from the beginning of the modern era. In the manufacturing industries, which have profited more than any others by the development of technology during the last century and a half, the 'industrial revolution' turns out to be a protracted process of a gradually retarded character. This is illustrated by the important inventions with their tendency to concentrate in the early phases of an industry's history. A similar tendency of slackening improvement and retarded spread is revealed by the history of such an important single invention as the steam-engine. The technical progress of some industries is continually stimulated through the impoverishment of the raw materials, with the consequence that we do not witness a slowing down of progress. For the extractive industries the diminishing net effect of technical improvements due to an increasing exhaustion of resources is illustrated by the few statistical data available.

II. The Slower Growing Industries Exercise a Retarding Influence upon the Faster Growing Complementary Branches — The Rapidly Growing Industries Exercise a Similar Influence upon their Competitive Branches

The slower growth of the extractive as compared with the manufacturing industries is another retarding force operating within specific branches of production. In the economic development of a nation industries are interconnected and a slow growth of one eventually exercises a check upon the development of the others.

Let us take the not altogether probable case of an industry whose processes are being technically improved, while the state of the industrial arts in the other branches of productive activity is at a standstill. Let us also suppose that we are dealing with an isolated industrial system. What will be the development of the technically progressive industry, A, first in regard to its total output of product, and second as to the cost composition of the final price of the product?

The increase in the total volume of the particular product of A will obviously meet a check in the stability of technical conditions in the other industries. For the product of A, the developing industry consumes as raw materials commodities B, C, D, etc. With the growth in the volume of production by A, there will be a larger demand for B, C, D (although not in direct proportion to A's increase). This demand can be satisfied only by diverting a larger and larger supply of labor and capital to those industries producing B, C, D, and thus making available less capital and labor for the A industry. The savings realized by the technical progress in the latter, do not all flow back to be reinvested in the industry, but are drawn upon to subsidize the increase in the industries supplying A. The larger A grows, the greater is the diversion of labor and capital to the technically stable industries, for we are assuming an isolated system with limited productive opportunities. Evidently there comes a time when the technical improvement in A no longer liberates funds to provide for its own future growth.

This last statement will be clear when we examine the changes in the cost composition of A's product. The economic result of the continuous technical improvement in this industry will be that the 'value added by manufacture' will grow smaller and smaller, while the 'cost of raw materials' will either remain stable or grow larger and larger. In the final price of the product, the element of value added is thus going to comprise a smaller and smaller percentage.

And while the technical progress may go on at an unabated rate (which we have seen above to be improbable), the economic effects of this technical development will become progressively smaller. The time will come, when the value added forms such an insignificant percentage of the total price of the product, that no further change in the productive process, be it ever so important technically, will be of any economic effect in expanding demand and permitting a larger output. Without technical changes in the related branches of industry, a given branch A cannot go on expanding indefinitely, no matter how great its own technical progress may be. At a certain point any further technical improvement would just balance in its saving the extra effort needed to supply the additional quantities of raw material necessary.

We took the extreme case of an industry developing within an otherwise stable industrial system. But the same reasoning applies to a less extreme situation in which we find technically rapidly changing branches of production and those slowly changing. In such a case the difference between the rates of change within the two groups will serve to provide the same kind of check in both its aspects, the technical and economic.

This applies directly to the contrast between the extractive and the manufacturing groups. Undoubtedly the manufacturing group enjoyed a greater technical progress than the other, or at least the effects of such progress were not counterbalanced so much by the paucity of resources. But in the long run the slow development of one group tends to become a check on the development of the other. The effects of a rapid technical progress in a group of industries assume less and less importance, when measured from the point of view of the industrial system as a whole.

We may make use of some statistical data to illustrate the statements outlined above. The United States Census of Manufactures provides us with data on 'value added in process of manufacture' and 'cost of raw materials' within the separate industries, some series going back to 1840. Of course the figures (given decennially, quinquennially, and lately biannually) are subject to variations in the price level (both being in dollars), but by taking the ratio between 'value added' and the 'cost of raw materials' we eliminate a large part of these variations. If the statement hypothetically illustrated above is true, the ratio of value added to value of raw materials ought to be declining in those industries that have developed technically faster than the others. Let us now survey the data, beginning with the metals group (the data are all from the abstract of the Census for 1921 checked by that of 1923).

8. Ratio of Value Added to Cost of Materials — Metals and Metal Products

(Cost of materials taken as 100)

	Blast Furnaces	Steel Mills and Rolling Works	Cutlery and Edge Tools	Safes and Vaults	Hardware
1849.........	79.0	....	165.0	.....	130.7
1859.........	69.8	....	170.5	152.0	147.6
1869.........	53.1	52.8	175.0	181.8	142.0
1879.........	52.4	56.2	149.1	134.2	124.3
1889.........	32.3	53.4	220.7	152.1	162.4
1899.........	57.2	52.8	190.4	132.6	145.4
1904.........	29.6	52.8	208.8	144.8	175.2
1909.........	22.1	49.9	216.5	146.6	154.4
1914.........	20.1	55.5	212.0	174.3	152.2
1919.........	27.9	68.3	242.1	131.4	164.0
1921.........	16.3	47.4	229.5	165.1	193.6
1923.........	21.8	54.3	322.4	169.6	167.9

Of these five branches of metal production only one, the blast furnaces, stands in immediate connection with the underlying extractive branch, i.e., with iron ore. The steel mills used until recently pig iron as their principal raw material, the three other branches mostly steel. It is thus interesting to observe the difference in the movement of the ratio in these five cases. The most definite and precipitous decline is in that for blast furnaces. The decrease in cost of production in the steel mills just kept pace with the cheapening of pig iron, and the ratio was on the whole stable. The other three groups were also technically improving, but the pace of technical changes there was much slower than in steel and iron, and their ratios consequently show a definite upward trend. This example thus supports the statement made above: the value added by the manufacturing industries as over against the cost of the materials supplied by the extractive groups declined rather steadily. True, as we ascend the industrial ladder, we may find that the rate of improvement in the production of the semi-raw product is higher than in the later processes of its manufacture. But this evidently only acts as a check upon the continued technical progress within the most rapidly developing stage of production.

Another interesting case is presented by that group of more or less complicated mechanisms such as washing machines, sewing machines, typewriters, and motor cars.

9. RATIO OF VALUE ADDED TO COST OF MATERIALS — MACHINES
(Cost of materials taken as 100)

	Sewing Machines and Parts	Washing Machines and Wringers	Typewriters	Motor Vehicles
1859............	556.8	252.0	.....	.....
1869............	335.1	203.3	.....	.....
1879............	162.5	101.2	.....	.....
1889............	235.6	83.7	473.5	.....
1899............	123.3	71.7	394.4	163.2
1904............	144.3	73.5	469.0	128.6
1909............	146.7	105.3	383.7	79.9
1914............	167.0	83.2	345.4	72.0
1919............	137.4	74.3	226.7	51.3
1921............	138.3	81.7	288.0	51.0
1923............	158.8	95.7	275.6	47.3

Here we observe a precipitous decline of the ratio in the production of all four kinds of machines. It is noteworthy that the two longer series indicate a retardation of the decline. The same tendency may be seen in the case of blast furnaces. This may be ascribed either to cheaper raw material in the second half of the period as compared to the first, or to the slowing down of the effects of technical progress as expressed in the absolute cost of production. Of the two explanations the latter seems the more probable.

An interesting case is the movement of ratios in the lumber and woodworking group:

10. Ratio of Value Added to Cost of Materials — Lumber
and Woodworking

	Lumber Products	Lumber Planing Mills	Boxes, Wood, Packing	Furniture
1849............	113.3	164.8	113.6	190.0
1859............	117.5	74.4	107.0	213.3
1869............	103.3	71.0	95.3	167.0
1879............	59.7	62.2	65.3	117.1
1889............	115.1	75.1	79.1	146.3
1899............	128.8	68.5	40.3	128.1
1904............	215.6	72.9	70.4	131.5
1909............	183.7	67.0	62.1	120.7
1914............	153.7	67.0	63.8	118.7
1919............	194.6	67.2	72.7	118.5
1921............	138.8	70.0	67.3	116.5
1923............	160.8	72.7	73.1	126.9

The first series of this group, that of lumber products, belongs to the extractive industries, since lumber products embrace all the raw materials of the forest before they have been worked over by the planing mills. For this reason the ratio is declining only until the '80s and shows an unmistakable rise thereafter. The other three groups are, however, manufacturing industries, and their ratios all decline as would be expected.

The group of textiles does not present the same clear-cut picture:

11. Ratio of Value Added to Cost of Materials — Textiles

	Woolen Goods	Silk Goods	Linen Goods	Knit Goods
1849.........	67.8	65.4	.....	147.7
1859.........	69.2	69.4	116.5	127.4
1869.........	61.2	56.2	94.4	87.2
1879.........	59.3	82.6	59.2	91.7
1889.........	62.4	71.2	80.6	87.6
1899.........	66.8	71.9	71.2	87.2
1904.........	62.2	75.7	56.5	78.5
1909.........	63.2	82.7	61.0	81.6
1914.........	63.0	75.9	62.3	76.5
1919.........	67.4	77.2	67.0	67.0
1921.........	92.0	72.8	83.9	75.9
1923.........	80.7	58.9	87.5	75.2

Of the four indexes cited only two show a declining tendency, the one for linen goods and most clearly the one for knit goods. In the woolen goods industry the ratio is, on the whole, stable. In silk goods it shows an upward tendency, evidently because the raw material declined in price and because of greater economy in its use in the production of the commodities.

On the whole the data show that in the case of manufacturing industries technical progress results in a lessened importance of the rôle played by the manufacturing processes in the price of the product. This is the economic expression of the fact that the slower developing industries supplying the raw materials act as a check on the growth of the industries favored by the advantages of technical development. The slower growth of mining and agriculture is bound to retard the manufacturing industries, which have' to rely on the former for their supply of raw materials.

This check is the stronger the more isolated the industrial system in question and the more limited its natural resources. What actually happens, of course, is that the given industrial system in its technical development has to depend more and more upon the supply of raw materials provided by the extractive industries of other countries. This removes to a large extent the pressure of limited natural opportunities. But there are definite territorial and political obstacles to the unretarded spread of an economic system.

The cases discussed so far concerned those goods whose production is related in a complementary way, as e.g., a manufactured commodity and its raw materials. In these cases the slower growth of the raw material will retard and a rapid growth will facilitate the development of the manufacturing industries affected. But where competition between industries exists, rapid growth in the production of one commodity will act as a brake upon the growth of the other.

The obvious examples need only to be mentioned. The development of the carriage industry has been retarded or the industry largely displaced by the rapid rise of the automobile. The technical development of the electrical industry has checked the extension of steam engines. Ice manufacture may very well be limited by the use of domestic refrigeration. In these examples we have obviously competitive industries where the rapid growth of one retards or even displaces the other.

This competition may likewise affect branches of industry where no such obvious relation as that of their products satisfying one and the same set of wants exists. The recent observations regarding the deterrent effect on the purchase of clothing by the spread of the automobile indicate that within the economic system there is constant competition between various goods; a competitive process whose ramifications are the more significant and far reaching the wider the margin of purchasing power directed to comparatively dispensable wants. Whether in consumers' or producers' goods, there are always alternatives of choice not only among various goods satisfying the same want but also among various goods satisfying different wants. When the satisfaction of one set of desires is given up in order to satisfy others, the rapid growth of a certain commodity may adversely affect the development of another industry not directly complementary. The most immediate retarding effect of a rapid technical progress and spread of a new commodity will be upon the production of the older product for which the new one is a substitute. Its next most decided adverse influence will be upon the production of the commodity most easily dispensed with, and which at the same time stands in no complementary relation to the new industry. And obversely, this rapid growth of a new commodity will exercise a stimulating effect upon the development of industries that stand in a complementary relation to it.

Thus we see that because of the ties connecting different branches of industry, whether of a complementary or competitive sort, a considerable discrepancy in the rates of growth between a given industry and all those related to it will tend to be reduced with the passage of time. A rapidly growing industry will feel the retarding effect of the slower growth of those industries supplying it with raw materials or with complementary goods. On the other hand, an older industry may be retarded still further by the rapid growth of a new, directly competitive industry, or by the generally faster growth of the new industries which may divert the supply of capital and purchasing power from this older industry, even though no direct relation exists either in demand satisfied or in raw materials used.[1]

III. The Funds Available for the Expansion of an Industry Decrease in 'Relative' Size as the Industry Grows

Before the fundamental invention or discovery is introduced, and for some time thereafter, the industry affected may have been insignificant as compared to other branches of production. Thus the cotton cloth industry of Great Britain prior to 1780 was one of the smallest, most insignificant branches of industry. So was pig iron production in England before the introduction of coal smelting, for the timber available for smelting was approaching exhaustion; likewise steel production was practically insignificant before the introduction of the Bessemer process. This remark applies with least qualification to commodities that are products of a new process or discovery, such as petroleum, Portland cement, electrical apparatus.

But the rise of a new industry or the revolutionary expansion of an old one implies a considerable new investment. Capital must be provided either from the returns of the industry concerned, or from the returns (or possibly capital) of the other industries. Considering for the present only subsidies from the outside, it seems clear that the funds available relative to the size of the subsidized industry are greater in the early periods of growth than later on.

Good illustrations are provided by the steam engine and railroad. The invention and production of the first steam engines were financed in succession by Roebuck, who made his money in iron, by Boulton, a successful hardware manufacturer, and by both British and Dutch Banks. The extensive production of engines which started after 1800, when

---

[1] This brief discussion suggests significant leads as to the study of comparative rates of growth. We cannot go further into the question either here or in the subsequent statistical discussion owing to the limitations on the size of the manuscript, but we plan to take it up at some future time.

the Watt patents expired, was financed by funds not derived from the Boulton firm. In the early days to produce a steam engine cost much more than at present. One of the earliest made by Watt cost £2000. But the ratio of the available funds to the then current volume of production was higher than when the production of steam engines had become a substantial percentage of the country's total output.

The case of the railroads is still clearer. About the middle of the '30s, when the annual addition to the net may have amounted to a hundred miles, the surplus funds available for expansion were more ample than, say, in the '80s, when the annual addition was about 10,000 miles. By the time an industry becomes so large that it produces a considerable percentage of the whole country's total output, when its capital ties up a large part of the total capital of the country, the funds coming from outside cannot be so large proportionately to the current output as in the days of its beginnings.

A somewhat different group of cases is presented by those industries where inventions supplant an old branch of production, for example, in automobile and carriage making. In these instances the new industry may derive much of its equipment and funds from the old one. This source is evidently richer in the early stages, for later on the old industry is almost completely displaced.

It must be observed, however, that in a number of industries the capital withdrawn from other branches of activity is of comparatively small significance in the early periods of expansion, due mainly to the lack of stability in the industry and the lack of assurance on the part of would-be creditors that it is a good risk. To cite the most notable case, the American automobile industry obtained its original capital from two sources: the savings and capital of entrepreneurs (coming from other industries) and the credit extended by the part-makers. But the bulk of the present capital came from re-invested profits, which were consistently high in the successful concerns. Aside from bank loans, the capital market did not come to the assistance of the industry until much later, when its important place in the industrial system was assured and it had achieved comparative technical stability.[1]

Thus the relative diminution of available capital fund exists only *cæteris paribus*, i.e., under unchanging conditions of capital attraction. But obviously these conditions do not stay unchanged. They comprise mainly two sets of factors: the amount of profits achieved, and the degree of assurance connected with their receipt, both determining the magnitude of profit expectation. Therefore it is only by assuming a constancy in the expectation of profits that we can give a definite meaning to the statement of the larger proportional size of funds in the early periods of growth. This raises the question as to the changes in this expectation of profits, to the movement of the net returns in the developing industry, to the sources of financing the growth from within.

The information scattered in the histories of industries seems to indicate that the ratio of net returns to capital invested is larger in the early periods of growth. When a branch of production is just beginning to develop successfully (and we treat only those which later become the more important industries of a country), the returns to the pioneers are, in proportion to the size of the actual investment, much larger than later on, when the industry achieves bulk and stability. The chief reasons for these large returns during early growth seem to lie in the rapid rate of technical change, rapid improvement of the product, and lowering of costs. The stability that comes eventually is a reflection of the retarded rate of technical changes and of their economic effects. This slackening of technical progress, the dynamics of change in industry was examined at considerable length above.

[1] Ralph C. Epstein: *The Automobile Industry*, 1928, chapter IX. Also L. N. Seltzer: *Financial History of the American Automobile Industry*, Boston, 1928.

IV. An Industry in One Country may be Retarded by
    the Competition from the Same Industry in a
    Younger Country

The best illustration is provided by the industrial history
of Great Britain. The main inventions in the stream which
started in the second half of the eighteenth century were
introduced in England. Being less affected by the French
Revolution and the Napoleonic Wars than the continent of
Europe, it was the first country to enjoy the bloom of industrial capitalism, and in the early periods of its modern era
supplied goods not only to herself and dominions, but also
to practically all of the European countries. The insufficiency of her extractive industries was made up by extensive imports from other countries. It is true that this
became something of a burden, when iron ore had to be
imported in large quantities, and when the copper and tin
mines approached exhaustion. Nevertheless, throughout the
first half of the nineteenth century, Great Britain enjoyed
an undisputed leadership in industry and trade. In the
second half the situation changed, because of the rapid
economic development of other countries, notably the
United States and Germany. With the superior natural
opportunities which these countries enjoyed, their rapid
progress was undoubtedly one of the main causes for the
retardation in the growth of the British industrial system
after the '60s.

It is to be seen that this factor applies to an industry only
within national bounds, while the other factors discussed
above may well exercise their influence on a wide scale.
Their influence is, however, not of a very obvious nature,
and does not bear so directly upon the question of national
supremacy and power. For this reason in the many discussions concerning the industrial development of nations, the
factor of national competition is credited with undue importance.

Let us now briefly recapitulate the factors which tend to
bring about a decreasing rate of growth of an industry
within a nation. As an industry starts from small beginnings and develops rapidly to a substantial output, it is

enabled to do so mainly by progress in the technical conditions of production. But as it grows to considerable size, the volume of surplus funds available for further expansion becomes comparatively smaller, because up to a certain point this industry develops faster than all the others, and thus the funds coming from the outside do not grow in proportion to the output. The funds which come from within the growing industry itself decrease too, because the effects of technical progress show an unmistakable tendency to slacken. This slowing down is due either to retardation in technical progress itself or to the pressure of the exhaustion of resources. Added to that is the check exercised by the groups of productive activity, whose industrial arts do not improve so rapidly nor with the significance of the industry in question. And finally, if it happens that one country is the first to benefit from the introduction of major inventions, the development of other countries may create a serious obstacle to the unabated rate of growth in the first.

The hypotheses developed above must be taken with a great deal of caution. The list of factors as they influence the processes of growth of an industry is not complete, nor are the generalizations formulated proved beyond doubt. We have directed our attention chiefly to the technical conditions and to the economic in their technical aspects. But we did not examine the changes in the personal element from the productive and cost sides, nor the changes in the organization of the industry, nor a number of other forces whose influences go to form the stream of events termed the history of an industry. We have singled out a factor whose importance seemed to us paramount in the growth of industries, and we have studied the dynamics of its changes only. Some of the data used indicate, it is true, the effect of this factor within the complicated conditions of the totality of events. But the other proofs concern the particular element only *cæteris paribus*, and the hypothesis presented must be considered far from complete.[1]

[1] As far as we can see at first glance, consideration of some of the other factors, such as the change from free and fierce individual competition to trusts and syndicates, the rise in the workers' budget and

Nor may the proof of the hypothesis advanced be considered final in any sense. In one most important generalization, we adopted the crude method of listing and dating the important inventions. The possibilities of omission and wrong emphasis in such a procedure are rather numerous. In the other cases the data cited were not exhaustive. The most that can be claimed for the suggestions set forth is that they strengthen our impression of the general course of the development of an industry; offer plausible grounds for expecting a retardation in the growth of every national branch of production from the time its modern technical conditions are first established.

This retardation in the rate of growth is now to be investigated at some length. The statistical records of long-time movements at our disposal can be used to ascertain whether industries do reveal a declining rate of growth. The observations concerning such a decline will then assume the form of a more thoroughly tested inductive generalization, and will rest upon the accompanying analysis for its argumentative basis. The statistical description of the long-time movements will convey a more exact knowledge of their nature, and the analysis involved will then permit us to study the bearing of these long-time changes upon cyclical fluctuations.

APPENDIX. THE STATISTICS OF PATENTS

The statement that improvements tend to diminish as time goes on and as an invention nears perfection can be substantiated in part by the statistics of patents. Of course, only a very small percentage of the patents issued represents changes that have been or will be actually introduced. What the number of patents really indicates is the amount of attention that the inventive capacities of the nation pay to problems connected with a specific mechanism or process. Such an index is valuable in itself. But it may be used to measure technical progress under two assumptions: (1) that an equal per-

---

the intelligent factory laborer, the increased emphasis on conservation, saving, and more efficient management rather than on further technical improvements — all these only seem to support our proposition regarding the declining rate of growth as largely a reflection of the declining rate of technical progress.

centage of the improvements covered by patents is being actually introduced every year; (2) that the improvements are equivalent units. There is a good deal of arbitrariness involved in these assumptions, therefore the data below have only a limited relevance to the statements developed in the chapter.

The figures on the number of patents for different mechanisms and in different groups were obtained by straight counting from the Annual Reports of the Commissioner of Patents (Alphabetical List of Inventions). We give them in quinquennial averages.

12. NUMBER OF PATENTS ISSUED FOR TYPEWRITERS IN UNITED STATES, 1872–1923

Years	Number of Patents, Average per Year	Cumulative Number	Average Ratio of the Annual to the Total Number Issued in Last Year of the Period (1:10,000)
1872–76........	5.8	29	4.34
1877–81........	11.2	85	8.62
1882–86........	29.6	233	13.82
1887–91........	115.8	812	51.12
1892–96........	123.0	1427	56.46
1897–01........	121.2	2033	52.26
1902–06........	194.4	3005	67.06
1907–11........	320.2	4606	92.28
1912–16........	299.2	6102	76.78
1917–21........	227.5	7240	59.08
1919–23........	198.4	7678	52.44

The cumulative number is computed to the end of each fifth year. The ratio is over the total number of patents issued for that year.

The data in this case indicate that the absolute number of patents issued rises up to a certain time and then falls off. If the total number (cumulative) is in any way representative of the long-time course of technical progress, then the latter follows a curve of a diminishing rate of increase. In this particular case, the ratio, which purports to express the relative share of attention which the inventive capacity of the nation devotes to the problem of the typewriter, follows closely the absolute numbers. In other cases, however, it is not so. Take for example the sewing machine. (See Table 13.)

The movement of the absolute number is in this case similar to that of typewriters: a rise in the early period, then a decline (here very gradual). But the ratio is at its highest around the '60s, at exactly the time when the sewing machine was being introduced into practical use. The ratio should be ascribed greater significance than the absolute number of patents. For by indicating the comparative share of attention devoted to the improvement of a par-

13. Number of Patents Issued under the Title 'Sewing Machine,' United States, 1849–1923

Years	Absolute Number, Average per Year	Cumu-lative Number	Ratio 1:1000	Years	Absolute Number, Average per Year	Cumu-lative Number	Ratio 1:1000
1849–53	5.2	27		1889–93	183.0	6004	7.84
1854–58	50.2	278	19.88	1894–98	165.8	6833	7.82
1859–63	59.4	575	15.98	1899–03	165.6	7661	6.30
1864–68	91.4	1032	11.24	1904–08	163.8	8480	5.10
1869–73	230.2	2183	19.12	1909–13	184.4	9302	4.70
1874–78	148.0	2923	11.46	1914–18	257.4	10559	6.06
1879–83	230.6	4074	13.96	1919–23	158.4	11351	4.20
1884–88	203.0	5089	9.70				

ticular invention, it tends to indicate also the comparative progress in this invention — comparative to the average rate of improvement prevailing in the industrial system.

A peculiar feature is revealed if we compare the movement of the number of patents issued for a complete engine or tool with those for its parts — thus comparing a wider and a narrower field of improvement. Below are the data for the plow and the plow sulky.

14. Number of Patents Issued, Plow and Plow Sulky, United States, 1850–1923

Years	Plow. Number issued, Av. per Year	Plow Sulky. Number issued, Av. per Year	Plow. Ratio to total 1:100	Plow Sulky. Cumulative Number
1850–54.....	60			
1855–59.....	204		13.24	
1860–64.....	277		14.58	
1865–69.....	827	35	15.00	35
1870–74.....	750	29	12.52	64
1875–79.....	837	131	12.96	195
1880–84.....	819	164	9.66	359
1885–89.....	755	80	6.94	439
1890–94.....	575	44	5.06	483
1895–99.....	501	16	4.60	499
1900–04.....	552	16	4.04	515
1905–09.....	658	15	3.98	530
1910–14.....	791	11	4.44	541
1915–19.....	754	5	3.68	546
1920–23.....	377	3	2.50	549

It is interesting to note that while the absolute number of patents issued for plows declined very slowly beginning with the '80s, the number for plow sulkies rose and fell very rapidly, its cumulative frequency forming a curve rapidly approaching a stable limit.

Evidently because of a narrower field of application, the absolute
number of suggested improvements declined much more for the
sulky than for the plow. The ratio for plows shows, however, a
very considerable decline from the '70s.

The same difference is revealed for the patented improvements in
the field of electricity. Let us take first the number of patents issued
under the general name of electrical cables, wires, machines and all
the various appliances. We then have the following picture:

15. NUMBER OF PATENTS ISSUED IN THE ELECTRICAL FIELD
TOTAL, UNITED STATES, 1866–1924

Years	Absolute Number, Annual Average	Ratio to Total 1:10,000	Years	Absolute Number, Annual Average	Ratio to Total, 1:10,000
1866–70...	7.8	6.34	1896–1900.	422.0	187.04
1871–75...	20.4	16.44	1901–05...	583.6	203.70
1876–80...	49.8	38.88	1906–10...	586.2	170.10
1881–85...	328.4	166.18	1911–15...	726.0	194.68
1886–90...	447.4	200.92	1916–20...	747.8	191.32
1891–95...	464.8	214.24	1921–24...	687.3	179.50

The absolute number of patents is on the whole increasing throughout the period although there is a retardation toward the end. The
ratio to the total number of patents definitely increases only to the
first half of the '90s, and a slow but undoubted decline starts after
that.

Let us compare with this movement the changes in the number of
patents issued for specific electrical appliances, such as motors,
meters, wires, cables, etc.

16. NUMBER OF PATENTS ISSUED FOR VARIOUS ELECTRIC
APPLIANCES (I), UNITED STATES, 1872–1921

Years	Electric Light, etc. Absolute Number, Annual Average	Electric Cables Absolute Number, Annual Average
1872–76................	1.0	
1877–81................	17.2	
1882–86................	34.6	16.4
1887–91................	27.2	8.0
1892–96................	30.2	7.8
1897–01................	17.4	8.4
1902–06................	18.0	4.4
1907–11................	26.6	7.4
1912–16................	33.2	4.8
1917–21................	32.0	3.8

In the field of electric light, arc light and light systems, the total number of patents issued per annum shows no marked decline, but when taken as a percentage of the total number of patents issued in the field of electricity, it does. The patents for electric cables and for electric wires and wire systems show a decline in their absolute number from the start. The same is true of electric motors and electric meters:

17. Number of Patents Issued for Electrical Appliances (II)
United States, 1879–1923

(Absolute number, annual average)

	Motors	Meters		Motors	Meters
1879–83	5.4		1904–08	40.6	19.2
1884–88	32.6	7.6	1909–13	12.8	10.4
1889–93	55.8	20.2	1914–18	11.8	9.2
1894–98	45.8	18.8	1919–23	14.6	3.6
1899–03	57.8	33.2			

In both cases we have an appearance of a frequency curve: the number of patents increases through the first half of the period and declines just as decidedly in the second half.

The data surveyed indicate that patents for a limited field show an appearance either of a frequency curve or of a curve declining outright. The ratio to the total shows generally a very early decline. If the number of patents represents technical improvement, the data show that a retardation eventually sets in, the earlier periods showing a rise in technical improvement and the later ones a decline. If the ratio be considered a more reliable measure of actual technical progress, the retarded character of the process becomes still more conspicuous, especially in the more limited fields.

CHAPTER II

THE STATISTICAL DESCRIPTION OF LONG–TIME MOVEMENTS

The definition of secular movements. The dependence of the concept upon our definition of cyclical fluctuations. Two groups of purposes pursued in the analysis of time series. The influence of the choice of purpose upon the period taken, the method of description, and the method of fitting the line of secular trend.

The choice of methods in our specific case. The need of a curve embodying some assumptions. Our assumptions stated and made more specific. The choice of the logistic and the Gompertz curves. The application of the logistic curve to cases showing a decline. The arbitrary element involved in our choice of curves. The methods of fitting.

Appendix: Some properties of the simple Gompertz curve. The simple equation for a curve of decline.

THE analysis of time series into their constituent parts is of recent development. Attempts to represent long-time movements by a curve go back to the '6os, and seasonal variations were studied by the elder Jevons. But with the accumulation of long-range statistical data, the development of the method of correlation, better knowledge of cyclical fluctuations, and the interest in forecasting business and industrial conditions, since the beginning of the present century, a more refined analysis of time series has become insistent.

The term 'secular movements' was first introduced into economic discussion by A. Cournot. His definition still holds true: '... articles such as wheat... are subject to violent disturbances; but, if a sufficient period is considered, these disturbances balance each other, and the average value approaches fixed conditions.... This will not make it impossible for the value so determined to vary, nor prevent it from experiencing absolute variations on a still greater scale of time. Here, as in astronomy, it is necessary to recognize *secular* variations, which are independent of periodic variations.' [1] If by periodic variations we under-

[1] *Researches into the Mathematical Principles of the Theory of Wealth,* English translation, 1897, p. 25.

stand cyclical fluctuations, the definition is precise enough for our purposes.

Secular movements are continuous, irreversible changes which underlie the cyclical fluctuations of a time series. Obviously the criteria of continuity and irreversibility are relative to some scale of time, the scale being determined by the duration of the cyclical swings, and changes in these cyclical swings considerably affect the results of the procedure adopted in determining secular movements. The precision of our knowledge of these movements depends to a large extent upon the definiteness of our conception of cyclical variations. Nor is this dependence dissolved by any refined mathematical methods of curve fitting or smoothing. Before these can be applied, the period of smoothing and the general character of the curve must be determined. In this determination our knowledge of cyclical fluctuations plays an important part.

The purposes for which the analysis of time series is undertaken may be divided into two groups. In the first, the interest is in measuring the cyclical fluctuations themselves, and the secular movement is determined only to be eliminated and forgotten. In the second, the long-time changes are described in order to be studied at greater length and made further use of. To the first group belong all investigations of correlation or of some characteristics of 'pure' cyclical swings; to the second, studies in long-range forecasting, comparisons of past changes, and the attempts to generalize as to the course of long-time movements.

The purpose of analysis should influence the methods used in determining secular changes. In the first group of purposes we are not interested in any particular form or shape of the secular trend line, and the elimination is guided by the concept of cyclical fluctuations undisturbed by long-time factors. Here the methods employed should be fairly flexible. In the second group, because of our primary interest in the secular movements themselves, the methods are more rigidly circumscribed. The desire to forecast, to make comparisons, or to verify an hypothesis determines the particular description, that which best satisfies the purpose in mind.

This difference in purpose affects the choice of the period of the secular movement as well as its method of determination. If our purpose is simply to get rid of the long-time changes in order to measure the cyclical fluctuations, any period of time will do, provided it is longer than a cycle and contains a number of complete cyclical swings. But for the purposes of the second group, the period must be carefully chosen. If forecasting is the aim, choice must permit the inclusion of all those influences, and only those, which are most likely to persist in the future. If comparisons are to be made, the period is, of course, fixed beforehand. And if some tentative generalization as to the course of secular changes is to be tested, the period must be so chosen that the forces presumably operating can have exercised their influence undistorted by any other factors.

Again, the purpose of analysis is of consequence for the method of description. Where we wish to eliminate only the long-time movements, the most flexible types of description are proper. A simple or weighted moving average is probably best; for without making any limiting assumptions as to the nature of secular changes, its smoothing operations are based upon given characteristics of the cyclical fluctuations themselves. The defects of this method arise from the fact that cyclical swings present in specific time series do not always exhibit the characteristics assumed. But varying the period and smoothing overcome a share of the difficulties; while the flexibility of the method assures a completeness of elimination of long-time changes seldom achieved by a mathematical curve. Such complete elimination is supremely important in correlation studies.

The moving average, by virtue of its flexibility, may be used in the second group of investigations, but as a first step only, for the final description of secular movements must in all such cases be simpler and reveal uniformities more conspicuously than can the moving average. In forecasting we need a curve that permits extrapolation of most probable values. Comparisons call for a line that embodies most prominently the unit of comparison. And if a hypothesis is to be verified, the secular movements should be described by a curve that incorporates the assumptions to be tested.

In all these cases, therefore, a moving average is but a first step toward the final description of long-time changes by a mathematically expressed curve.

Our purpose, however, does not greatly affect the methods of fitting the mathematically expressed curve (once the general equation and the number of constants are determined). But we must bear in mind the essential uncertainty of the whole process of separation, or we shall be unduly influenced by mechanical methods of fitting. The method of least squares may save the investigator the trouble of decision in fitting to selected points, and may appear more objective in the sense that identical results will be reached by different investigators. But mechanical arbitrariness is no whit better for being mechanical, and the method of least squares does not assure satisfaction of the two most obvious criteria of goodness of fit; namely, the balance and the minimizing of relative deviations from trend within each cycle.[1] In a series which shows a great change in the absolute size of items from one end to the other, the investigator would be better advised to use more flexible methods of fitting.

These brief remarks suggest the methods of statistical description best adapted to our investigation. Starting with an hypothesis to verify, we must select for the expression of long-time changes that curve which most fully embodies this hypothesis. This curve we shall attempt to fit by appropriate methods to series covering periods sufficiently long to reveal the influences affecting the growth and decline of industries discussed in Chapter I.

The thesis to be tested asserts that industries reveal a retarded growth or, in mathematical terms, a declining rate of percentage increase. Growth is not so much an increase in the absolute size per unit of time as the rate which this increase bears to the level previously achieved.[2] The selected

[1] Neither has the connection of the least squares procedure with the theory of probability any significance in the analysis of time series. See the admirable early discussion by W. Lexis, *Zur Theorie der Massenerscheinungen in der Menschlichen Gesellschaft*, Freiburg, i. B., 1877, pp. 31–33.

[2] See the interesting discussion by W. S. Jevons, *The Coal Question*, chapter IX, 'On the Natural Law of Social Growth.'

curve should thus exhibit a declining rate of percentage increase.

This still leaves a wide field of curves from which to choose. A declining rate of percentage increase is not incompatible with an ever-present absolute increase in the absence of finite limits. Together with parabolas and other complex curves approaching a limit, the simple straight line exhibits a declining percentage increase. Hence, a closer scrutiny of the change in the rate of absolute increase is necessary in order to narrow the field of choice.

The question whether the increasing output of a growing industry has an absolute final limit can be answered positively. The volume of output of a single branch of productive activity in a country cannot grow indefinitely, no matter how far from the final limit it may be at any given time. Thus, the curve chosen must describe an output (or any other index of activity) growing from zero to a finite level of maximum size.

In this movement from zero to the limit, how does the rate of absolute increase change? Observation reveals that it rises throughout the greater part of the life of an industry. While the rate of percentage increase may be steadily declining, the average amount by which the output of a given year exceeds that of the preceding grows in size. The diminution in the rate of absolute increase appears much later, when the limiting conditions begin to exert their pressure.

These limiting influences were discussed above. But what is it that augments the absolute increment? To what measurable factor in the industry are we able to relate it in simple terms in order to gain a more definite knowledge of the equation and curve to be fitted to the statistical data?

That measurable factor is the level of output attained by the industry in the preceding time unit. A branch of production with a large volume of output in one year may fairly easily achieve a considerable increase in this volume during the next. For example, an industry producing ten million tons of pig iron annually may readily expand this volume by 100,000 tons in the subsequent year, but for a branch whose total output is only 1000 tons any such increase would be an extraordinary feat. We may say that the current volume of activity in an industry indicates the size of the existing plant and indicates whether the output may be easily expanded. It thus furnishes a sort of measure of the source of reinvestible funds and of the possibility of an industry's growth.

The size of the absolute increase is therefore largely determined by the volume of output already achieved, and the process of growth becomes to that extent self-stimulating, or, as the chemists express it, autocatalytic. On the other hand, where there is a decline in the percentage rate of growth, the retarding influence makes finally for a diminution in size of the absolute increase as the limit is approached. We now have a more definite notion as to our choice of a curve. It should have a finite limit, exhibit a declining rate of percentage increase, and show the changes in absolute increase as dependent upon the stimulating influence of size of output and the retarding influence of the approach to the limit.

The simplest curve embodying these assumptions, and one which is found to fit a large number of cases, is the symmetrical logistic curve applied by Pearl and Reed to the study of population growth. Its equation is $y = \dfrac{L}{1 + e^{a-bx}}$ where L is the final limit, and b is positive. Thus, when x is increasing, i.e., as time passes, the denominator grows smaller and y larger. When x is infinitely large, the denominator becomes 1, and y is equal to L. The absolute rate of increase in y is a function of the product: size of y by the distance still left to the limit (i.e., by $L - y$). The rate of percentage increase is declining throughout the range of the curve which rises from O to L.[1]

The symmetrical logistic is the simplest curve of all those which satisfy the conditions, because it puts the rate of

[1] For the best discussion of the assumptions underlying the curve see A. Lotka, *Elements of Physical Biology*, pp. 64–66. A clear exposition also appears in R. Pearl, *Studies in Human Biology*, chap. 24, pp. 558–83.

Some interesting implications are discussed in T. B. Robertson, *The Chemical Basis of Senescence and Growth*. See also an interesting recent book in Russian, *The Cycles of Capitalism and the Economic Reconstruction of the U.S.S.R.*, by V. Bazarov, Moscow, 1927 (especially chap. v).

absolute increase in a simple arithmetic relation to the size of y and to the limit. But this is merely one of many possible ways of expressing this dependence, and the simple logistic is thus only one of many possible curves. The same logistic could have more than three constants and hence imply a more complex relationship between absolute increases and the two groups of influences. The other curve used in this study, however, is not the higher degree logistic, but a three constants Gompertz curve of the equation $y = ae^{b^x}$.[1] It satisfies the same criteria, with the difference that the absolute rate of increase is here a function of the product *log* of the current y by the ratio of the y to the limit.[2]

Both curves are curves of growth, hence applicable only to industries which show an increasing output. But even in such a vigorously growing nation as the United States, a number of branches of production reveal a decreasing volume of output. In order to describe these declining secular movements in a manner analogous to those of growth, we must select the important factors whose influence can be expressed in a tentative, mathematically formulable generalization.

As for these factors, an industry may be declining because of competition from other industries. Thus canal traffic has diminished by reason of railroad competition; the tonnage of sailing vessels because of the steamship. In many cases of extractive industries there is an apparent diminution of natural resources. But in most of these it is comparative diminution with regard to the same industries in other countries rather than absolute. That is, competition from the more favorably situated industry in another country makes for the decline ascribed to the impoverishment of resources.

In a third group decline occurs through exhaustion of the area of exploitation; a noticeable example is found in the annual addition to railroad miles. To this group belong generally all those accumulated durable goods, further pro-

[1] The particular form we use is $y = Ce^{A(1-R^z)}$, where R is always less than 1.

[2] For a mathematical description of this implication see Appendix to chapter.

duction of which is for the most part unnecessary. Were 'railroad miles' like cotton consumed in a year, obviously there would be no decline in their annual production. For this third group also, decline can be ascribed to growth elsewhere within the economic system.

That every protracted decline in an industry must be offset by growth elsewhere is a direct consequence of the fact that, within the period of time we are considering, no civilized economic system has shown a prolonged contraction in absolute terms. If within such a stable or growing productive system an industry's output is declining, it must be the result of competitive pressure from another industry, or from the same industry in a foreign country, or it may arise from the accumulation of products within the declining industry itself.

But since decay is the opposite of growth, and having surmised something of the nature of the latter, we can now make a reasonable supposition as to the general course of decline. We have seen that the logistic and Gompertz curves satisfy certain assumptions concerning the course of growth of developing industries. The competitive pressure of these industries on those declining can be assumed to reveal the same general mathematical form, and not knowing exactly to what extent developing industries influence those on the down grade, we may make the simplest assumption, namely, that this influence is directly proportional to the growth of the rising industries throughout the secular movement.

This enables us to formulate the general course of decline in the following terms. After an industry has reached its maximum, decline sets in and generally assumes the shape of a logistic (or a Gompertz) curve. The equation for such a declining movement is then $y = L - \dfrac{L_1}{1 + e^{a-bx}}$ where L is the maximum output attained by the industry. And the whole expression prefaced by the minus sign is a logistic curve expressing the negative influence exercised on the given industry by the growing competitive factors.[1]

---

[1] The equation actually used was simpler. For the transformations see Appendix to chapter.

This formula was applied to the few series which exhibited a decline over a considerable period. It was found to fit some of them in its above simple form. In others, however, a constant had to be added, because the industry usually did not decline to the full limit expressed by the curve. After reaching a low level industries show a considerable retardation in their downward movement. At these low levels output is so diminished that the competitive pressure cannot be expected to exert its full force. The addition of the constant to the curve thus makes the lower limit not zero, but that low point at which the decaying industry continues to stagnate.

This brief discussion of the three types of curves chosen and of their implications indicates both their simplicity and formal character. They are applicable to many processes in various fields of the universe, and are thus similar to the general methods of quantitative determination in which the breadth of assumptions permits application to different disciplines of human knowledge. Nothing in the implications discussed would seem to be in disagreement with our knowledge of economic phenomena. On the contrary, they reflect the plausible expectations of the investigator.

It must not be thought, however, that no arbitrary elements are involved in our choice of the three types of curves. Granted all the assumptions as to the movements of rates of absolute and relative increase and the existence of finite limits, it is arbitrary to choose only the simplest equations which satisfy the conditions. One might plausibly argue that the rate of percentage increase need not be decreasing from the start; that the relationship between the rate of absolute growth and other factors need not be so simple as presented by either the logistic or Gompertz curves. And thus one might choose to fit parabolas on a *log* scale, or logistic and Gompertz curves on a *log* scale instead of an arithmetic.

In selecting the simplest equations we made an arbitrary choice. But a further narrowing of assumptions did not seem feasible, and the curves discussed present a clear and concise expression of the hypothesis. This justifies the choice of the logistic and Gompertz curves. They are not the *only* mathematical expressions possible, but tentative equations to be used in attempting a uniform, analytic description of secular movements.

The questions of period and method of fitting can be treated briefly. The hypothesis applies to an industry in broadly homogeneous conditions of development, from the time its essential technical processes are first established. But to ascertain such homogeneity and the exact starting point is somewhat difficult. The procedure actually followed was to take the series for the entire period available. Exceptions were made in cases where fundamental changes in conditions were too obvious to be denied. Obviously, we should not study the imports of cotton into England before and after the industrial revolution, as taking place under continuously similar conditions. In few cases did the series not extend over a time long enough to include periods essentially different. On the other hand, in order that the general process of development should not be obscured by temporary and particular influences, the span had to be the longest possible. So in most cases the period for which the data were available was taken.

The method of fitting was that of selected points, the points being chosen usually from original data averaged for each nine-year period. The method of least squares can be applied to the logistic and the method of moments to the Gompertz curve.[1] But both are laborious, and when applied to absolute data give results not appreciably better than the method of selected points. It was considered more important to use the less time-wasting procedure and thus cover a wide field of observation, than to indulge in refinement of the constants by laborious correction. The justification of this choice becomes more apparent in the review of the series analyzed.

[1] For the former, see T. B. Robertson, *Chemical Basis of Senescence and Growth*, Appendix, pp. 323–34; for the latter, L. E. Peabody, 'Growth Curves and Railroad Traffic,' *Journal of the American Statistical Association*, December, 1924, p. 479.

APPENDIX

Properties of the Gompertz Curve

$$Y = Ce^{A(1-R^x)}; \quad \log Y = \log c + A - (1 - R^x); \quad (I)$$

$$\frac{1}{y}\frac{dy}{dx} = -AR^x \log R; \quad \frac{dy}{dx} = -y \log R \cdot AR^x;$$

But from (1) $\quad AR^x = -\log y + A + \log C$

Consequently $\quad \dfrac{dy}{dx} = (-\log R) \, y(\log C + A - \log y) \quad (II)$

$$\underset{\underset{K}{\text{positive constant}}}{\downarrow}$$

The limit of the curve is Ce^A, the *log* of the limit is: $\log C + A$

Thus the equation II reads:

$$\frac{dy}{dx} = Ky \, (\textit{log of limit} - \log y)$$

The relative rate of increase in the curve is a straight line but in terms of *log y* and not of *y* (as in the logistic). Thus:

$$\frac{1}{y}\frac{dy}{dx} = -AR^x \log R = (\log y - A - \log C) \log R$$

$$= \boxed{- \log R \, (A + \log C)} + \boxed{\log R} - \log y$$

$$\qquad\quad \underset{a}{\downarrow} \qquad\qquad\qquad \underset{b}{\downarrow}$$

$a-$ is always positive because *log R* is negative and C always larger than 1

$b-$ is always negative because *log R* is negative, R being less than 1

The Equation of a Declining Trend

The equation given in the test was: $\quad Y = L - \dfrac{L_1}{1 + e^{a-bx}}$

But we can declare: $L_1 = L$

Then: $\quad Y = L - \dfrac{L}{1 + e^{a-bx}} = \dfrac{L + Le^{a-bx} - L}{1 + e^{a-bx}} = \dfrac{Le^{a-bx}}{1 + e^{a-bx}}$

$$= \frac{L}{e^{-a+bx}(1 + e^{a-bx})} = \frac{L}{e^{-a+bx} + 1}$$

Thus the formula is the same logistic only with its direction reversed

CHAPTER III

THE STATISTICAL MATERIAL PRESENTED

The procedure followed for each pair of production and price series. The concept of *primary* and *secondary* secular movements. The significance of secondary secular movements. The general nature of the comments accompanying each pair of series.

The data presented. United States: wheat, corn, potatoes, cotton, anthracite coal, bituminous coal, petroleum, pig iron, steel, Portland cement, copper, zinc, lead, salt, cotton consumption, silk imports, deflated bank clearings (six cities given separately), locomotives. United Kingdom: coal, pig iron, steel, cotton imports, ships cleared, tea consumption. Belgium: coal, pig iron, steel, zinc. Germany: coal, pig iron, steel, copper, zinc, wheat, cotton. France: wheat, coal, pig iron, steel, zinc, petroleum. Other countries. The cases of declining secular movements.

The tentative character of the comments given. General conclusions of the survey. Warning against over-interpretation.

THE analysis of the series presented below has a twofold purpose. First, to show whether a curve of one and the same logical type, having an equation embodying certain general presuppositions, fits the data satisfactorily. If it does, our assumptions are verified. The second step is to discover whether the general formula describes *all* the long-time movements in the series. If a scrutiny of the deviations from this 'logical' trend line discloses residual long-time movements, the analysis must be extended to describe these as well, in order to account fully for the phenomena subsumed under the aggregative name of secular variations.

The procedure followed may be illustrated with the first series; namely, wheat crops in the United States. Table 1 (see Appendix, pages 332, 333) and Chart 1 present the annual crops as estimated by the Department of Agriculture for 59 years from 1866 to 1924. The smooth curve on Chart 1 is the Pearl-Reed logistic fitted by the method of selected points. On inspection, the curve gives a good description of the long-time movement on the scale of the period as a whole. Its shape indicates the more rapid growth from

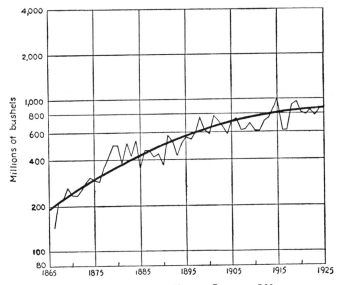

CHART I. WHEAT CROPS, UNITED STATES, 1866–1924
Original Data and Primary Trend Line

1865 to the end of the century, and the much slower relative increase during the decades 1900 to 1920. The fit is good. In short, the logistic curve can be said to form an adequate description of the long-time movements in the volume of wheat crop in the United States.

But does the curve take account of all the long-time changes, understanding by these all the continuous movements which underlie the cyclical fluctuations? To answer this question one must inspect Chart 1b, where the broken solid line represents the relative deviations of the original series from the fitted trend line. It is easily seen that the cyclical oscillations still have long-time movements underlying them, e.g., the rise from 1866 to about 1879; the decline from that year to about 1890, etc. These long periods of rise and fall can hardly be said to constitute cycles; or if one prefers to term them cycles, care must be taken to distinguish them from the shorter and more frequently recurring oscillations called 'business cycles.'

We shall term these movements the *secondary* secular variations. This distinguishes them from the *primary* variations described by the general formula first fitted to the original data. Formally speaking, the determination of these secondary variations is a second step in the process of describing secular movements by a series of successive approximations. Technically, they are traced by smoothing a moving average (arithmetic) passed through the relative deviations from the line of primary trend. The smoothed line does not deviate greatly from the broken line of the average itself, and wherever possible, is passed through the center of the brief cycles.

A question immediately arises as to the significance of this analysis, namely, what is the exact meaning of the secondary secular variations? The function, purpose, and meaning of a line of trend, taken as a single line or single formula describing the total volume of long-time movements, is a familiar notion. But these first and second approximations — are they merely a technical method for simplifying the descriptions of movement difficult to describe in one step; or a method of analysis that reveals groups of phenomena known to be essentially different by other means than a statistical splitting of the series? Is the description of the secondary variations merely a technical supplement refining a rough description given by the logical formula for the primary trend, or does it describe the influence of a distinct group of factors known to us in other ways?

Before answering, it should be pointed out that there is nothing in the statistical procedure adopted that creates artificial secondary movements through a wrong application of the tools of statistical analysis. This might happen were the original data misrepresented by a poorly fitting line of primary trend. For example, to take an extreme case, if the original series plotted ran like a convex parabola, and the trend fitted was a concave parabola or straight line, deviations from these trends would reveal conspicuous secondary movements of an artificial character, provided no direct and preponderant evidence existed to prove that the lines fitted expressed a definite group of influences.

The cases under consideration, however, are different.

All the primary trend lines fit fairly well, and the secondary movements result not from misrepresentation or from a direct disagreement with the course of the data, but from a comparative inadequacy of description in the line of primary trend. In other words, secondary variations appear because of a change in the scale of 'long' in the definition of long-time movements, and not because the line of primary trend diverges from the data within the same period.

In the case of wheat crops in the United States, secondary movements have been observed by students who did not use elaborate statistical analysis. For example, 'The increase in wheat production in the last 55 years has been due largely to increase in the area harvested. The increase has not been continuous and regular. Periods of expansion have been followed by a few years of little change or by a slight decline in acreage. Since 1866 there have been three periods of marked expansion, from 1873 to 1880, from 1890 to 1899, and from 1913 to 1919,'[1] Chart 1b shows the secondary movements closely following these periods of 'marked' expansion.

Thus, while the closeness of fit characterizing the line of primary trend assures the genuineness of the revealed secondary variations, their nature and the factors whose influence they describe must be explained. The explanations are to be found in the chronicles of industries whose growth we are examining statistically. For example, in the article just quoted it is said that from 1870 to 1879 'both acreage and production nearly doubled.... This was due in part to the policy of homestead settlement of public lands which followed the close of the Civil War, and partly to the development of machinery which made extensive production possible. The self-binder... and the large separators driven by tractor engines played important parts in this expansion of wheat growing.'[2] The marked increase during the last decade of the century may be attributed to the opening of the Far West and the introduction of giant threshers which

[1] C. R. Ball and others: 'Wheat Production and Marketing,' *Yearbook of Agriculture*, 1921, pp. 77–160.

[2] *Ibid.*, p. 93.

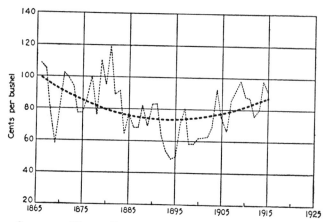

CHART Ia. WHEAT, DECEMBER FARM PRICES, UNITED STATES,
1866–1915
Original Data and Primary Trend Line

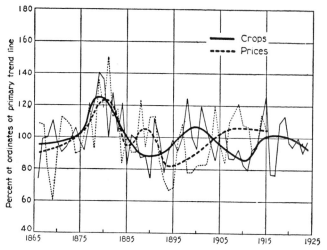

CHART Ib. WHEAT, CROPS AND PRICES, UNITED STATES,
Relative Deviations from Primary Trend Lines

made extensive dry farming possible. As for the last expansion, 'the rapid rise in acreage and production beginning in 1915 was due, of course, to the demand for wheat caused by the outbreak of the World War.' [1]

These constitute specific explanations of particular secondary movements; but there is one powerful factor which always seems to exert an influence. This is the movement of the price of the commodity itself. The secondary secular variations of the indexes of production synchronize somewhat with the periods of rise and fall in the price level. Hence arises the purely statistical problem of examining the long-time movements in prices to discover a possible general explanation of the secondary movements in production and trade.

The analysis of price series is closely analogous to that of the production series. The line of primary trend, a curve of the same order as in production, is fitted. There are, however, no *a priori* assumptions concerning the long-time movements of prices; therefore a second degree parabola, i.e., a curve with the same number of constants as the curve used in production series, is fitted by the method of least squares. Moving averages are made of relative deviations from this parabola, and then smoothed into the line of secondary secular variations. The period of smoothing is usually the same as for the corresponding production series, and the line, wherever possible, is made to pass through the short cycles.

On Chart 1a the actual data and the primary trend for prices are given. On Chart 1b the light dash line presents the deviations and the heavy dash line describes the secondary secular movements.

The correspondence of the two heavy lines on the chart is obvious. Thus, the movement is upward both in price and production to the end of the '70s and downward after that. The rise in the price movement subsequently lags, however, behind the rise in production. Owing to the arbitrariness involved in the determination of the lines of secondary movements, fine comparisons are unwarranted. On the other hand, arbitrariness is inevitable, for the phe-

[1] *Op. cit.*, p. 85.

nomena dealt with possess no marked regularity which permits application of a rigid formula either for smoothing or for interpolating.

With the line of secondary trend determined, the cyclical fluctuations as relative deviations from this trend can be ascertained. This permits us to examine the connection of these fluctuations with the underlying secular movements, with each of their two distinct parts, or with the total — an inquiry we make in Chapters V and VI.

To recapitulate the statistical procedure: To the series for production or trade (nearly all commodity volumes), a line of primary trend of the logistic or Gompertz type is fitted by the method of selected points. To the relative deviations from this primary trend line, a second line obtained by smoothing a moving average of these deviations is fitted. This second line purports to describe the secondary secular movements, and its elimination is part of the process of obtaining the cyclical fluctuations. The price series, usually for the same period as production, is analyzed in an analogous manner. A second degree parabola is fitted by the method of least squares. A moving average of the relative deviations from this parabola is computed and smoothed into the line of secondary secular variations. These secondary movements in both prices and production are then compared to find whether there is a close concurrence between them.

Note: In distinction from a number of other students of the long-time movements in production we preferred to deal with the indexes of the total volume of output rather than with the per capita figures. The reasons for this choice may be briefly stated:

1. We expected to study the cyclical oscillations in the series, and wanted to have as unconfused a record of movements in output as possible. The elimination (by division) of the changes in population, without our knowing the exact nature of these changes, would introduce an ambiguity in the resulting series which is absent in the uncorrected series of the volume of output. For if there are oscillations in population movement, it is quite probable they are interconnected with the changes in output in more than a direct multiplicative way, and it is better to leave the factor in.

2. While there may be some sense to the per capita output of consumers' goods, per capita output of producers' goods is of significance only for comparisons from country to country (at the same point of time) but of hardly any meaning for the study of the long-time changes.

3. And even for the consumers' goods, the per capita figures have ambiguous meaning. With the retardation in the rate of growth of population, with the changes in the birth-rate and in the death-rate, the age composition of the population changes appreciably, and the mere number of living souls does not mean the same number of consuming units.

Since most of the series dealt with covered the output of producers' goods, such as coal, pig iron, steel and the like, it was considered advisable to deal with the indexes for total output.

In the following presentation of the various series only short textual comments will be made. The important events in the history of an industry, which may throw light on the particular causes of the secondary movements and the agreement or disagreement of these changes in production and prices, will be cited. Of course no exhaustive treatment is possible. At present we are interested in presenting the data and noting the similarities, differences, etc. The task of inference must be kept in mind, however, and will later be taken up in detail.

2. *Corn, United States.* In the case of wheat crops we found a rough correspondence of secondary movements in production to those of prices, the latter lagging considerably in one instance. In the series of corn crops the correlation is much more clearly marked.

Chart 2 shows the line of primary trend, which is again a logistic curve. The fit is fairly good, and the secondary movements (Chart 2b) are approximately the same as those for wheat. A rise occurs from 1866 to the end of the '70s, especially conspicuous in the second half of the latter decade. An historical explanation is at hand:[1] 'The Civil War retarded development during the sixties and less corn was reported by the census of 1869 than in 1859. Rapid expansion took place in the following years.... Returning soldiers of the Civil War gave further impetus to the settlement of the prairies and improved machinery came into use. The acreage in corn increased from 44 million to 66 million acres in the 5 years from 1875 to 1880, and the average corn product per farm doubled in the decade 1869–1879.' The great increase in the second half of the '70s was due to

[1] C. E. Leighty and others: 'The Corn Crops,' *Yearbook of Agriculture,* 1921, pp. 161–226.

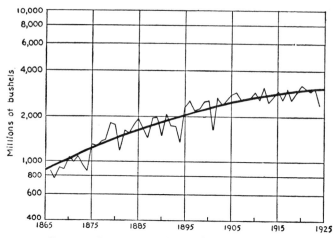

CHART 2. CORN CROPS, UNITED STATES, 1866–1924
Original Data and Primary Trend Line

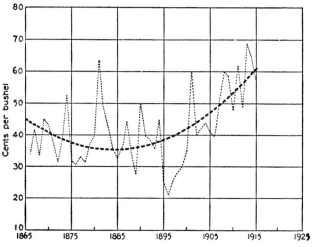

CHART 2a. CORN, DECEMBER FARM PRICES, UNITED STATES,
1866–1915
Original Data and Primary Trend Line

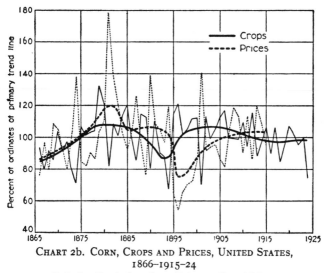

CHART 2b. CORN, CROPS AND PRICES, UNITED STATES,
1866–1915–24

Relative Deviations from Primary Trend Lines

increased exports and lower freight rates. 'Beginning with
1876 there was a very great increase in the exports of both
corn and meat products. The decline in freight rates about
this time favored the transportation of farm products from
the Corn Belt. The methods of culture in the West improved
as the machinery improved, and as land values rose more
intensive cultivation was encouraged....'

The decline from this point to the middle of the '90s was
no doubt owing to a slackening of the impetus given by the
above factors. The upward movement which began again
in the second half of the '90s and continued through the
first half of the first decade in the new century is noted by
the writers quoted and is connected with the expansion in
the Far West, the main increase occurring in Oklahoma.
The decline developing immediately afterwards is similar
to that of the wheat crop. But while the latter rose considerably during the World War period, the corn crop
secondary movements continued to decline or remained on
an unchanging level as a result of wheat competition. 'The

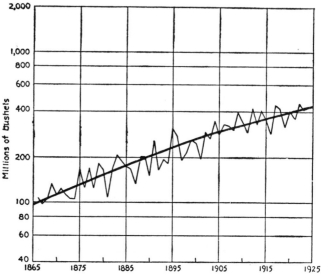

CHART 3. POTATO CROPS, UNITED STATES, 1866–1924
Original Data and Primary Trend Line

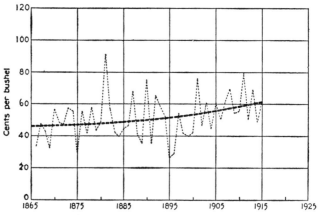

CHART 3a. POTATO, DECEMBER FARM PRICES, UNITED STATES,
1866–1915
Original Data and Primary Trend Line

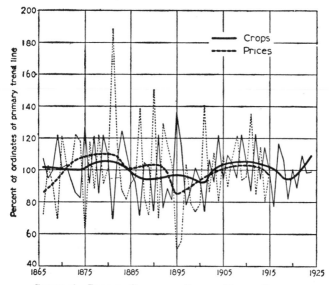

CHART 3b. POTATO, CROPS AND PRICES, UNITED STATES,
1866–1915–24
Relative Deviations from Primary Trend Lines

demand and guaranteed price for wheat during and immediately following the World War and the scarcity of labor resulted in marked increases in the wheat acreage and decreases of corn acreage in many other states. The full effect of this tendency was felt in 1919.'[1]

The secondary secular movements in corn prices are fairly synchronous with those of crops (Chart 2b). As with wheat, prices began to recover late in the '90s.

The cyclical fluctuations show a varying regularity. The correlation between prices and crops is distinct and negative, large crops resulting in low December prices and vice versa.

3. *Potatoes, United States.* The logistic curve fitted to potato crops for the same 59–year period presents a good description of the long-time movements. The secondary secular variations are rather small (Chart 3b), but similar in kind to those of wheat and corn. A rise to the end of the

[1] *Op. cit.*, pp. 174–75.

'70s, a decline to the '90s, and a rise in the second half of that decade continuing to the first decade of the new century may be observed. These movements were due chiefly to changes in output per acre. The following explanations have been advanced:

'Another interesting feature of the data is that of the decline in yield per acre from the first to that of the fourth cycles (i.e., from 1875–79 to 1890–99) and the subsequent upward trend in yield from that point on. Several factors are thought to be responsible for this yield-depression period, of which the following are considered the most important: (1) the ravages occasioned by the Colorado potato beetle during the early period of its invasion, when adequate control measures had not as yet been evolved; (2) the decline of agriculture due to financial depression; and (3) a gradual depletion of the natural fertility of soil.

'Similarly the upward trend in per acre yields may be explained on the basis of certain influences, as for example that of the agriculture experiment stations, agricultural colleges, the U.S. Department of Agriculture through its extension workers and investigators....'[1] The retardation during the war was again due to a low yield per acre. 'This low average acre production is in a large measure attributable to a rapid expansion of acreage during the war period resulting in the planting of land unsuited to the crop, or in sections where the climatic conditions were unfavorable. Poor seed was also a factor in low yields.'

The secondary secular variations in prices show a close correspondence to those of crops with the same number of up and down swings well timed with the crop movements. It is interesting to note the precedence of the secondary movements in prices in the '90s and thereafter.

The cyclical fluctuations in potato prices and crops are fairly regular and brief. The correlation between crops and prices is conspicuous and decidedly negative.

4. *Cotton, United States.* The series for cotton crops is used only from 1866 because of the Civil War and its effects on cotton growing. The logistic curve fitted presents a good description of the movements for the 59-year period.

[1] L. C. Corbett and others: 'Fruit and Vegetable Production,' *Year-book of Agriculture*, 1925, pp. 347–48.

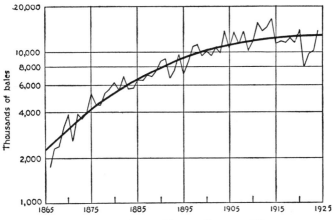

CHART 4. COTTON CROPS, UNITED STATES, 1866–1924
Original Data and Primary Trend Line

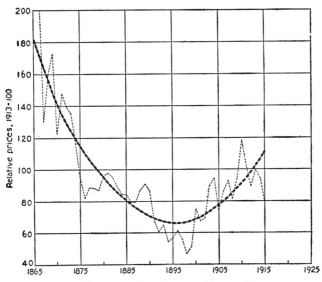

CHART 4a. PRICES OF RAW COTTON, UPLAND MIDDLING,
NEW YORK, 1866–1915
Original Data and Primary Trend Line

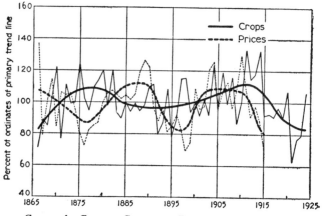

CHART 4b. COTTON, CROPS AND PRICES, UNITED STATES,
1866–1915–24
Relative Deviations from the Primary Trend Lines

In studying the secondary secular movements the influences of the Civil War must be borne in mind. The movements in production are similar to other crops. To quote
an historical account: 'The blockade during the Civil War
temporarily ruined the cotton industry of the South. During
the war some cotton was produced, but for the most part
agricultural activities were diverted to the production of
food. In 1865 the South was again free to return to a high
degree of specialization in cotton. The recovery of production was necessarily slow. The crop of 1866 was less than
two million bales, which was less than half that of 1859
and a little greater than the crop of 1839. High prices stimulated production by the farmers along the Northern border
of the Cotton Belt and in Arkansas and Texas... by 1879
conditions in the South were fairly stable again, and the
crop of that year was the largest that had ever been produced....' [1] There was a slight retardation in development
during the decade 1880–90. In the second half of the '90s
the secondary movement again turns upward. 'The de-

[1] A. M. Agelasto and others: 'The Cotton Situation,' *Yearbook of
Agriculture*, 1921, pp. 323–406.

velopment of Oklahoma and Western Texas added a large acreage to the cotton production area between 1899 and 1909. The total acreage increased 52 per cent in the decade and continued to increase up to 1914.... Since 1914 production of cotton has been reduced considerably by the ravages of the boll-weevil. The crop of 1919 was only a little larger than the crop of 1909, which was a short crop for that period.'[1]

Until the '90s the secondary movements in cotton prices show considerable divergence from the movements in crops. From 1866 to the second half of the '70s there was a decline from the high price levels created by the war shortage. The rise in the '80s no doubt reflects the high price level of commodities, except that other prices were declining in the second half of the decade as compared with the first. Subsequently the secondary movements of cotton prices show a fairly good correspondence to those of crops.

The prices analyzed here are not December farm prices, which were taken for the other crops, but October spot quotations on the New York market. The cyclical fluctuations show a clear positive correlation with a conspicuous one year lag of crops behind prices.

5. *Anthracite Coal, United States.* The series for anthracite coal output in the United States covers a hundred-year period. Of the two lines of primary trend fitted, the Gompertz curve gives the better description. The fit is fairly close.

The secondary secular variations in output result from both changes in technical conditions during the century (mainly transportation) and the underlying price movements. The first period up to 1834 is characterized as the period of canals,[2] though the influence of canals could hardly have been important before 1825.

Eliot Jones says: 'The main features of the early development of the anthracite industry may be briefly summarized as follows: The Wyoming field was first developed on any

[1] A. M. Agelasto and others: 'The Cotton Situation,' *Yearbook of Agriculture,* 1921, pp. 323–406.

[2] Eliot Jones: *The Anthracite Coal Combination in the United States,* Howard Press, 1914.

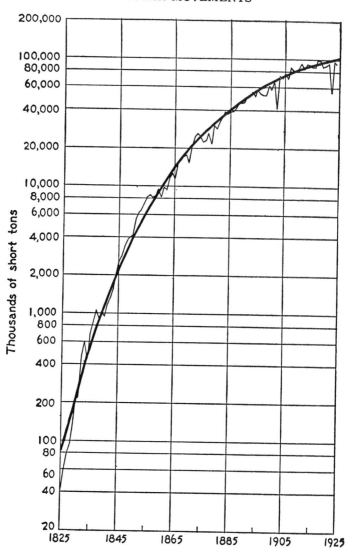

CHART 5. ANTHRACITE COAL OUTPUT, UNITED STATES, 1825–1924
Original Data and Primary Trend Line

considerable scale by the Delaware & Hudson Canal Company... [The canal and connecting gravity railroad were completed in 1829].... The Lehigh Region was developed by the Lehigh Coal and Navigation Company. [After carrying coal on a highway, it built a gravity railroad in 1827. The Lehigh Canal was completed in 1829.] In the Schuylkill region, the Schuylkill Canal [completed in 1825] soon became primarily a coal-carrying canal.' [1]

None of the canals and connecting railroads was completed before 1825, which is therefore the proper date to begin the period. Eliot Jones closes it at 1834; but the next period, that of railways, did not really start until the '40s. 'As the result of the rapid extension of transportation facilities between 1834 and 1873, of the opening of many new mines, and of the increased demand for anthracite consequent upon the growth of population and a more general recognition of the value of hard coal as fuel, the anthracite coal trade experienced a considerable growth during this period. From 1834 to 1842 the growth was gradual. Inasmuch as navigation was closed during that part of the year when demand for anthracite for domestic purposes was greatest, a very rapid growth could not be expected. In 1842, however, the Reading Railroad entered the Southern coal field, and removed the difficulties incident to intermittent navigation, so far as that field was concerned. About 1840, also, anthracite began to be used to a greater extent in manufactures, especially in the manufacture of iron, and was successfully used also on steamboats. These factors taken in connection with the speedy growth of population after 1840, and the decrease of forests presented conditions favorable for a more rapid growth of the trade. The shipments which had been about a million tons in 1842, had doubled by 1845, and had trebled by 1848. There was an uninterrupted increase until 1856....' [2]

On Chart 5b may be observed the secondary movements in output describing the two swings which correspond to the opening of the canal and railroad periods respectively. The declining movement begun in the second half of the '50s was arrested by the outbreak of the Civil War, which stimulated

[1] *Op. cit.*, pp. 7–22.   [2] *Op. cit.*, p. 38.

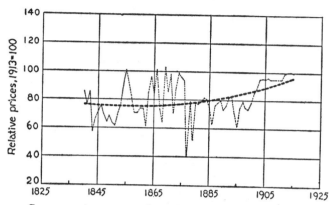

CHART 5a. ANTHRACITE COAL, STOVE, WHOLESALE PRICES,
UNITED STATES, 1840–1915
Original Data and Primary Trend Line

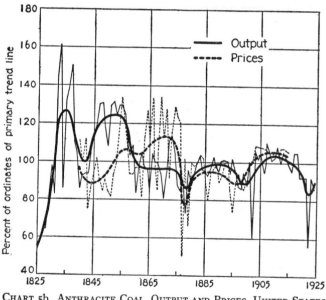

CHART 5b. ANTHRACITE COAL, OUTPUT AND PRICES, UNITED STATES,
1825–1924
Relative Deviations from Primary Trend Lines

the demand for coal. After that the variations correspond to the general type of variations pointed out in the movements of crops: a rise to the '80s, a decline through the second half of that decade and the early '90s, and a rise thereafter. In the second decade of the present century the secondary movement is again downward.

The secondary movements of anthracite prices show a good correspondence to output, with the possible exception of the Civil War period. There the price movement describes a large cycle similar to that in production, but prices are on a relatively higher deviation level than in the preceding decade, while production is on a lower. Except for that, correspondence between the two is very good, with the secondary movements of prices tending to precede the movements in output.

The cyclical fluctuations reveal a decided decrease in amplitude with the passage of time. The cycles in output seem to be more frequent than those in price, especially during the first decade of the twentieth century when monopolistic price fixing and stabilization appeared. The correlation is positive.

6. *Bituminous Coal, United States.* Previous to the early '40s, when the first railroad was opened, bituminous coal output was comparatively insignificant. This series, therefore, is taken from 1840. The first important field was the Georges Creek (Appalachian Region). 'With the advent of the B & O Railroad into the field in 1842 a great impetus was given to the mining industry. In the meantime the Chesapeake & Ohio Canal, which was started at the same time as the railroad — in 1828 — was completed between Cumberland and Georgetown in 1850.... We thus find the field enjoying rather unusual transportation facilities....' [1]

The secondary movements in output were rather small until after the Civil War. The subsequent accelerated growth reflects the general growth of the nation's industries and the increased use of coke in pig-iron production. After that the movements closely correspond to other branches of activity.

[1] A. T. Shurick: *The Coal Industry,* Boston, Little, Brown and Company, 1924, p. 12.

In prices, the secondary movements are fairly similar to output, frequently preceding the latter. It might be inferred that movements in output are a reflection of prices. The single exception is the continued upward price movements after 1910, but the instance is uncertain owing to the war influence.

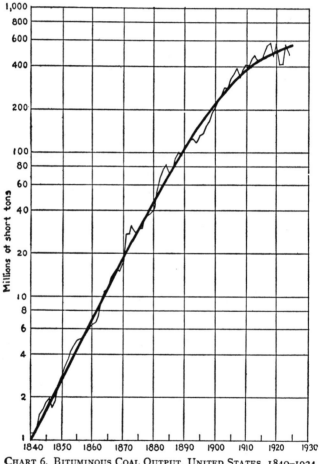

CHART 6. BITUMINOUS COAL OUTPUT, UNITED STATES, 1840–1924
Original Data and Primary Trend Line

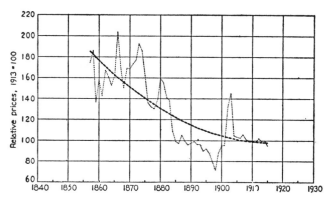

CHART 6a. BITUMINOUS COAL, WHOLESALE PRICES, UNITED STATES, 1857–1915
Original Data and Primary Trend Line

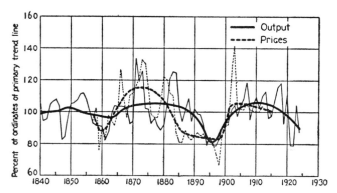

CHART 6b. BITUMINOUS COAL, OUTPUT AND PRICES, UNITED STATES,
OUTPUT, 1840–1924 — PRICES, 1857–1915
Relative Deviations from Primary Trend Lines

The cyclical fluctuations in production show both a decrease in amplitude and a briefer duration with the passage of time. The cycles in production and prices appear to be fairly well correlated in a positive relation.

7. *Petroleum, United States.* The logistic curve fitted to

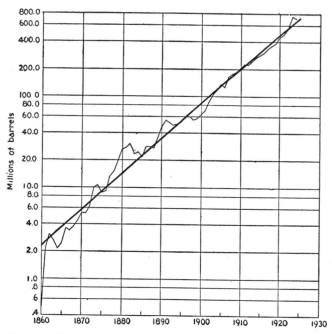

CHART 7. CRUDE PETROLEUM OUTPUT, UNITED STATES, 1860–1924
Original Data and Primary Trend Line

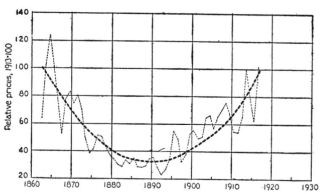

CHART 7a. PRICES OF CRUDE PETROLEUM, UNITED STATES,
1862–1916
Original Data and Primary Trend Line

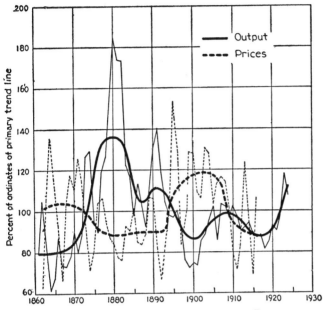

CHART 7b. CRUDE PETROLEUM, OUTPUT AND PRICES,
UNITED STATES, 1860–1924
Relative Deviations from Primary Trend Lines

this series as the primary trend resembles a straight line, since the oil industry for the 64 years taken shows but slightly retarded growth. The beginnings of the industry date back to 1859, the year Drake drilled the first well in Pennsylvania. A feverish expansion followed almost immediately, then a reaction. Once begun the industry developed rapidly, reflecting in its secondary movements the same periods of acceleration and retardation observed in other industries. The increase is rapid until 1881, is retarded to the end of the '90s, then rapid again. After 1910 the secondary trend moves downward for a time, prolonged by the outbreak of the war. After the war vigorous development again begins.

Secondary movements in price of petroleum are quite different from those of other prices. We have here a typical

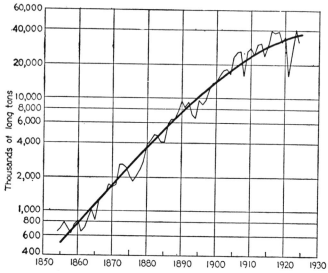

CHART 8. OUTPUT OF PIG IRON, UNITED STATES, 1854–1924
Original Data and Primary Trend Line

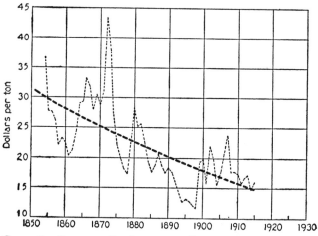

CHART 8a. PRICES OF PIG IRON, NO. 1, FOUNDRY, UNITED STATES,
1854–1915
Original Data and Primary Trend Line

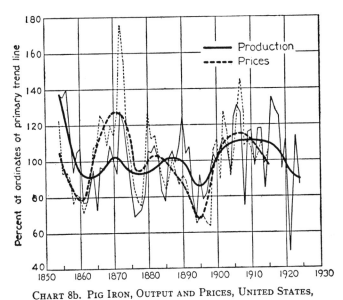

CHART 8b. PIG IRON, OUTPUT AND PRICES, UNITED STATES,
1854–1924
Relative Deviations from Primary Trend Lines

case of the price movement of a new commodity with its
fall from the high levels of a luxury to the low levels of a
necessity. This is the obvious explanation of the price
decline accompanied by a greatly accelerated growth of
output from the '60s to the '80s. The direction turns in the
'80s, but recovery is slow until the '90s, after which the
secondary price movements follow those of the general price
level. Comparing variations in production and price, we
thus find correspondence only in the series' second half.
In the first, there is divergence, the result of a great discovery. This is a typical case, illustrations of which we
shall find in a number of other series.

In the cyclical fluctuations an appreciable diminution in
amplitude and duration occurs with the passage of time.

8. *Pig iron, United States.* The series used starts in 1854,
when the Iron and Steel Institute began publication of continuous reports of output. Data for earlier periods are

merely estimates of varying authority. Moreover, in the '50s the widespread use of mineral fuel in iron smelting initiated a new era in the industry.

The logistic curve as the line of primary trend yields a good description of the original series. The secondary secular variations in price and production correspond admirably. Those in output are, on the whole, similar to movements in other branches; a retarded growth in the '50s continuing through the Civil War; then acceleration. But the upward movement breaks in the '70s, a break which may be explained by the extreme severity of a purely cyclical depression. The change, however, is not very appreciable, and production movements are on approximately the same level to the end of the '80s. After that the secondary variations follow the usual course hitherto observed.

The price series, usually preceding production, repeats the same up and down swings. The only apparent difference is that it rises to a much higher deviation level in 1870 and exhibits a more conspicuous decline from that date to the '90s. With that exception the correspondence is very close, and supports the notion that the secondary secular variations in production are a reflection of those in prices.

The cyclical fluctuations in the two series are also very closely correlated. The correlation is positive and simultaneous.

9. *Steel, United States.* Large-scale production of steel in the United States as elsewhere began only with the introduction of the Bessemer process. The first steel rail was rolled in this country in 1865, but it was not until certain patent litigations were settled in 1866 that large-scale production was possible.[1] Lacking the proper kind of pig iron and skilled workers, the industry labored under severe handicaps.

The Gompertz curve as the line of primary trend gives a satisfactory description of the series. The secondary movements are very similar to those of petroleum; in production they are intensified replicas of those common to many other branches, but in prices quite divergent. In

[1] J. M. Swank: *History of the Manufacture of Iron in All Ages,* 1890, pp. 409–13.

production there is a rise to the '80s, a decline thereafter, accelerated growth beginning in the second half of the '90s, and retardation in the first half of the decade 1910–20. The prices present a case in which an epoch-making invention cuts the quotations drastically. Thus the price of steel rails per ton was about $120 in 1867 and about $43 in 1877.

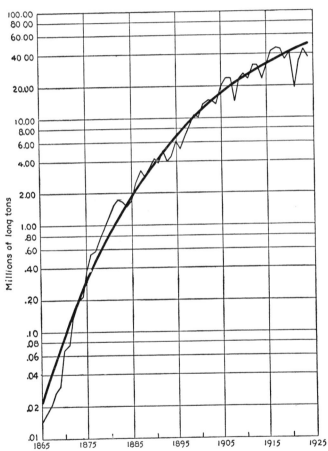

CHART 9. CRUDE STEEL PRODUCTION, UNITED STATES, 1865–1924
Original Data and Primary Trend Line

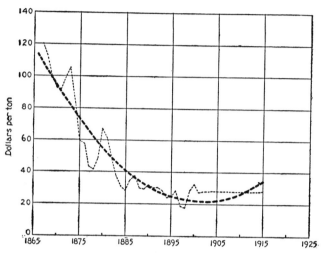

CHART 9a. PRICE OF STEEL RAILS, UNITED STATES, 1867–1915
Original Data and Primary Trend Line

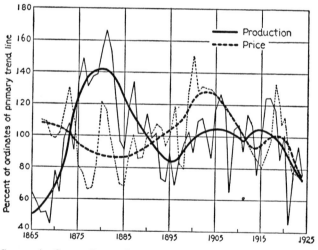

CHART 9b. CRUDE STEEL, PRODUCTION AND PRICES, UNITED STATES,
1865–1924
Relative Deviations from Primary Trend Lines

Of course, this rate of decline did not continue. We observe the secondary secular variation in the price of steel moving downward from the '60s to the '80s and not upward as with other prices. The upward movement starts about 1885, and after the '90s the variations resemble those observed before. A change in the character of deviations is introduced by quasi-monopolistic price fixing which started in 1901. The secondary secular movement is, however, similar to that of production. As in the case of petroleum, we find here divergence in movements between price and production in the first half of the series and good positive correspondence in the second half.

The cyclical fluctuations in prices and production reveal a good positive correlation, except, of course, for the decade of price fixing.

10. *Portland Cement, United States.* Large scale production of Portland cement took place still later than that of either steel or oil. 'The cement industry had made great strides in England and Germany, but no real attempt was made to advance its manufacture in the United States until about 1872, when a plant was built at Kalamazoo, Michigan. This project... was a complete failure. In 1875, however, a true Portland cement was being made at a small plant located in Western Pennsylvania.'[1] In the meantime a small quantity of Portland cement was produced in the Lehigh Valley district as a by-product of the natural cement industry. Large-scale production became economically possible only when the old stationary kilns and millstones were replaced by the rotary kiln and modern grinding machinery, which allowed a cheap transformation of the hard, dry raw materials of the Lehigh district. The rotary kiln was first used in 1889. 'The next step in development of manufacturing methods began about 1895, when powdered coal was substituted for petroleum as fuel.'[2]

The series analyzed describes the production of Portland cement beginning with 1880 and indicates an amazingly rapid growth. The logistic curve fitted reveals fairly well

[1] H. P. Willis and J. T. B. Byers: *Portland Cement Prices*, Appendix I, pp. 81–82.

[2] *Op. cit.*, p. 83.

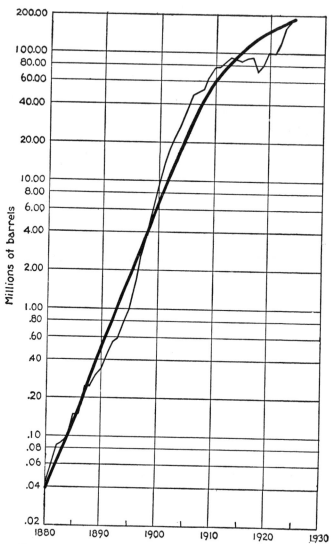

CHART 10. PORTLAND CEMENT PRODUCTION, UNITED STATES,
1880–1924
Original Data and Primary Trend Line

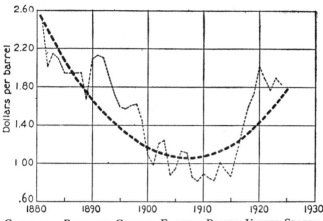

CHART 10a. PORTLAND CEMENT, FACTORY PRICES, UNITED STATES,
1881–1924
Original Data and Primary Trend Line

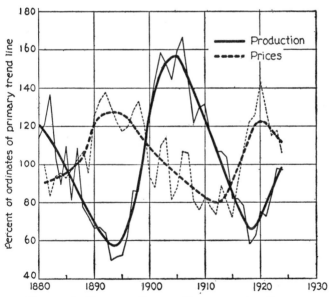

CHART 10b. PORTLAND CEMENT, PRODUCTION AND PRICES,
UNITED STATES, 1880–1924
Relative Deviations from Primary Trend Lines

the general trend, allowing for considerable relative variations around it. The conspicuous secondary movements in production follow the usual course: a decline from the '80s to 1895, a rise after that to 1903–07, again a decline protracted by the curtailment of building activity during the war, and a recovery afterward to supply the needs of postwar building.

While production displays the same movements as in most of the other industries, the secondary variations in prices run an entirely different course, a course opposite in part to that of the general price level. Thus, the secondary price variation is rising from the '80s to 1895, and falling from then to 1912. Only during the war did cement prices display the same inflationist rise as other commodities. Whether this peculiar movement was due to business control aimed at a constant volume of trade, or whether the price decline after the '90s was due to the influence of technical improvements, one cannot say. The latter hypothesis seems unlikely, since in other industries technical improvements were introduced in the '90s and still the secondary variations in prices followed the usual upward course into the twentieth century. As may be seen from the charts, the secondary movements in production and prices of cement are in opposite directions most of the time. This tendency is easily explained for the war years, but for the whole period up to the outbreak of the war is not accounted for.

The cyclical fluctuations in both production and prices are fairly regular and closely correlated. The correlation is positive with price cycles tending to lag behind production.

11. *Copper, United States.* Although the copper industry is one of the oldest of industries, it was not until the late nineteenth century that it assumed modern dimensions. With the development in the '80s of the ammunition industry, the rise of the electrical industry, and the opening of the Montana and Arizona deposits, its rapid growth begins. Output increased from 16 million pounds in 1860 to 28 in 1870 and to 60 in 1880, but for the decade from 1880 to 1890 the output rose to 260 millions, i.e., more than quadrupled. While the data for crude copper output extend back to 1845, and while a trend line could be fitted to the entire series, it is

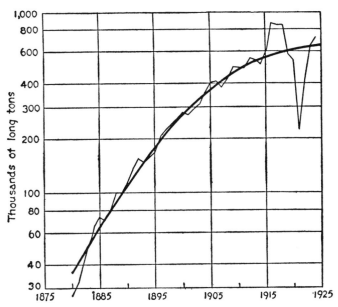

CHART 11. COPPER PRODUCTION, SMELTER, DOMESTIC ORE,
UNITED STATES, 1880–1924
Original Data and Primary Trend Line

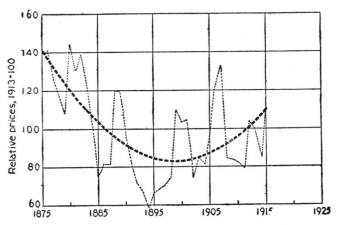

CHART 11a. PRICES OF COPPER, UNITED STATES, 1876–1915
Original Data and Primary Trend Line

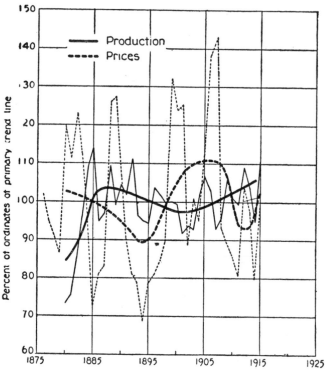

CHART 11b. COPPER, PRODUCTION AND PRICES, UNITED STATES, 1880–1915
Relative Deviations from Primary Trend Lines

both advisable and justifiable to include only the modern period and begin the series in 1880.

The logistic curve fitted describes the data fairly well. The secondary movements in output and prices reflect the influence of mine discoveries and the activities of various copper syndicates. Thus while all other industries show a declining secondary variation after 1880, copper output moves upward. In the early years of the decade this was evidently due to exploitation of the newly opened Montana-Arizona mines; in the later years it was the influence of the Secretan Syndicate. The latter, organized in 1887 with the aim of cornering the total copper output of the world, permitted the contract mines to produce within 20 per cent above their 1887 output. With prices high, the mines made the most of their opportunity. The policy of the syndicate also stimulated output by the outside mines, with the result that production was on high levels up to and through 1892.

Consequently, while the declining secondary movement in copper production is delayed more than in other industries, it continues for a longer period, up to 1902. This was partly a result of the overstocked condition, partly a matter of conscious policy of the newly formed American Copper Trust (1899). The subsequent recovery is similar to the rising movement in other branches of industry, except that it moves directly into the war period without retardation after 1907–08.

The secondary secular variations in copper prices likewise reflect the activity of the syndicates. The declining movement is delayed until the end of the '80s, because of the price rise initiated by the Secretan combination. The rising movement after 1895 is accentuated by the American Trust policy. Hence, the correlation between the secondary movements of production and prices is not very obvious, for during the 1900–10 decade output was directed with conscious conservatism to attain stability, while prices were affected by the movement of the general price level.

In the cyclical fluctuations we observe small and frequently recurring cycles in production, while those in prices are longer and much more conspicuous. The correlation is positive with a lag of varying direction and duration.

12. *Lead, United States.* Antimonial lead was produced in this country as early as 1720. But the extensive application of the method of producing argentiferous lead by desilverizing the ore did not take place until about 1870. At this time the Montana-Nevada mines began to supply the country with the product, which was transported over the Union Pacific Railroad (completed 1869). The first reports of output began in 1873, and in that year the output of argentiferous lead was only slightly less than the total of antimonious lead for 1872. At present argentiferous lead

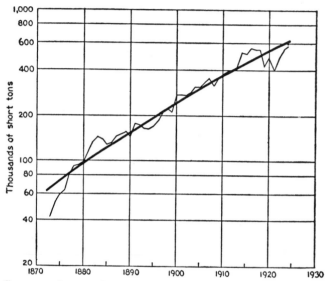

CHART 12. REFINED LEAD OUTPUT, DOMESTIC ORE, UNITED STATES,
1872–1924
Original Data and Primary Trend Line

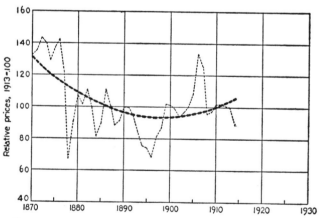

CHART 12a. PRICES OF PIG LEAD, UNITED STATES, 1870–1914
Original Data and Primary Trend Line

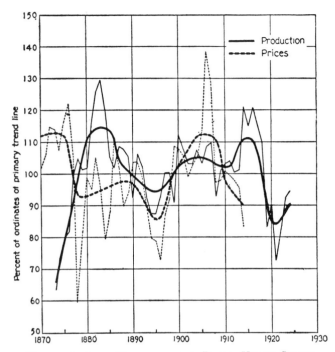

CHART 12b. LEAD, PRODUCTION AND PRICES, UNITED STATES,
1872–1924
Relative Deviations from Primary Trend Lines

comprises over 70 per cent of the total lead output in the
United States.

The production series is therefore taken from 1873, and
the fitted logistic curve offers a good description of the data.
The secondary movements in output again reveal a close
correspondence to the other series. The only noticeable
difference is the more rapid rise in the '70s for lead production. The probable explanation is found in the feverish
exploitation at that time of the newly opened mines by the
modern and cheap methods of metallurgical transformation.

Consequently, we observe here a situation somewhat
similar to that of oil and steel. The decline in the secondary
movements of prices begins immediately after the opening

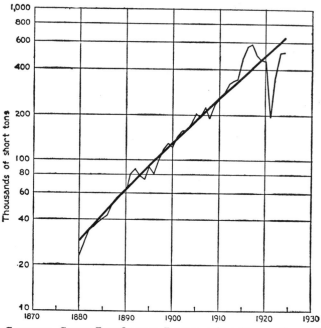

CHART 13. CRUDE ZINC OUTPUT, DOMESTIC ORE, UNITED STATES,
1880–1924
Original Data and Primary Trend Line

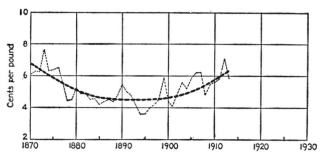

CHART 13a. PRICES OF SPELTER ZINC, UNITED STATES, 1870–1914
Original Data and Primary Trend Line

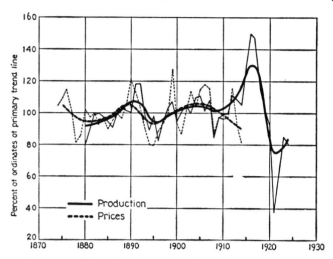

CHART 13b. ZINC, PRODUCTION AND PRICES, UNITED STATES,
1875–1924
Relative Deviations from Primary Trend Lines

of the new deposits and continues to the middle of the '90s, with the exception of a slow rise from 1880 to 1887. After 1895 the agreement of the secondary movements in production and prices is close. Previous to this date we may notice a rough correspondence of the swings, except in the '70s the general movements are opposed.

The cyclical fluctuations are fairly regular, with close correlation. The price cycles, particularly in the first half of the series, precede production cycles by one year.

13. *Zinc, United States.* Large scale production of zinc began in the United States in the 1870s. Data are available, however, only since 1880–82. The Gompertz curve chosen as the line of primary trend yields a good fit.

In the secondary movements we find a markedly close correspondence between prices and production. Production movements follow the usual course, but because of the absence of data fail to show high levels in the '70s. The rise, however, may be surmised from the price line. There is the familiar decline in the '90s with its following upward move-

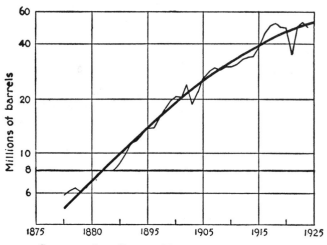

CHART 14. SALT OUTPUT, UNITED STATES, 1880–1924
Original Data and Primary Trend Line

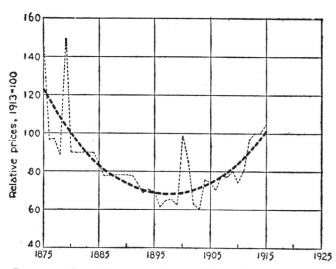

CHART 14a. SALT, WHOLESALE PRICES, UNITED STATES, 1875–1915
Original Data and Primary Trend Line

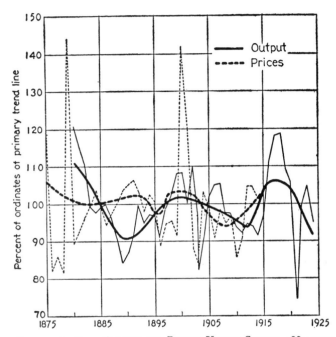

CHART 14b. SALT, OUTPUT AND PRICES, UNITED STATES, 1880–1924
Relative Deviations from Primary Trend Lines

ment. In prices, the secondary movements are similar, with a slight tendency to precede.

The cyclical fluctuations appear to be well correlated, the price cycles tending to precede those in production. As in a number of other cases, the price cycles are less broken, i.e., of longer duration and larger amplitude than the production cycles.

14. *Salt, United States.* The data for salt output are available only from 1880. Chart 14 shows the industry's vigorous growth, and the logistic curve fitted offers a good description of the long-time movements.

The secondary secular variations both in production and prices are affected although but slightly by the activity of the Salt Trust. The production movements show the usual retardation from 1880 to the '90s and an early recovery thereafter. The peak of the subsequent rise, however, appears in 1900 and not in 1905–10 as in the other industries. This is attributable to the overproduction induced in 1899–1902 by the expansion policy of the National Salt Company (organized early in 1899).[1] With the breakdown of the company early in 1902 output declined abruptly, and the secondary secular movement turns downward. In the last two decades the variations follow the usual course.

The secondary movements in prices also show the influence of the trust; the variation is sharply upward to 1900 and declines thereafter. With that exception they follow the ordinary course.

The correspondence between the secondary variations is thus fairly good, except that prices do not exhibit the same determined decline after 1880 as observed in output.

The cyclical fluctuations are fairly small with the correlations between production and prices clear and positive. The price cycles tend to precede production cycles in the early part of the series.

15. *Cotton Goods, United States.* The amount of raw cotton consumed is the best single index of cotton goods production in this country. The available data begin in 1870, and the logistic curve employed as the line of primary trend yields a good fit.

The secondary secular movements in production follow the course hitherto observed so often. There is the upward movement to 1880, a decline from that date to 1895, a subsequent rise continuing through the World War, with a retardation after 1905–07.

Prices reflect the influence of the Civil War and post Civil War conditions, and thus repeat, in a somewhat attenuated form, the secondary movements in the price of raw cotton. (See Chart 4b.) They drop abruptly immediately after the war, and except for a slight rise in the late '80s, continue to decline to 1895. After 1895 the secondary movements in price pursue the familiar course. Apart from the difference in the '70s, the correlation between production and price movements appears to be good.

[1] A. S. Dewing: *Corporate Promotions and Reorganizations*, Cambridge, 1914, chap. VIII, pp. 203–26.

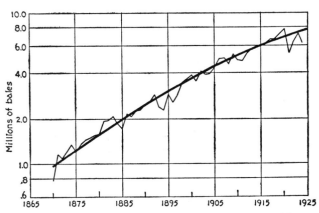

CHART 15. CONSUMPTION OF COTTON BY TEXTILE MILLS, UNITED
STATES, 1870–1924
Original Data and Primary Trend Line

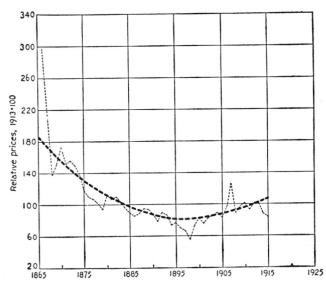

CHART 15a. COTTON TEXTILES, WHOLESALE PRICES, UNITED STATES,
1866–1915
Original Data and Primary Trend Line

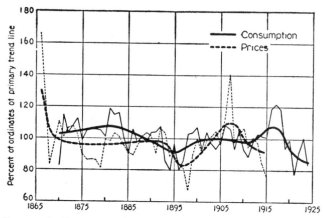

CHART 15b. COTTON TEXTILES, PRODUCTION AND PRICES, 1866–1924
Relative Deviations from Primary Trend Lines

The cyclical fluctuations are clear-cut and closely correlated, with the price cycles lagging behind those of production.

16. *Silk, United States.* Raw-silk imports constitute the best single index of silk manufacturing in the United States. The data extend back to 1864. The line of primary trend fitted is a Gompertz curve, more suitable than the logistic because of the exceptionally rapid and undiminished growth in volume through the sixty years. The description given by the curve is fairly adequate.

The secondary secular movements in imports do not follow closely those previously observed in other fields. Thus after a high level in the '60s a retardation appears, continuing to the middle of the '70s. This may be due to adulteration of the raw material practiced by Chinese merchants, which raised a pressing problem in 1870.[1] As a result a great decline in silk imports occurred, and for the time being no other source of supply was available. The recovery which followed resulted from the extensive Japanese culture

[1] F. R. Mason: 'The Silk Industry in the United States and the Tariff,' *American Economic Association Quarterly*, vol. XI, no. 4, 1910, pp. 15–18 and ff.

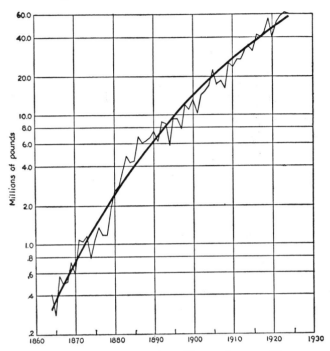

CHART 16. IMPORTS OF RAW SILK, UNITED STATES, 1864–1924
Original Data and Primary Trend Line

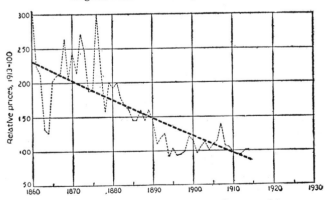

CHART 16a. PRICES OF RAW SILK, UNITED STATES, 1860–1914
Original Data and Primary Trend Line

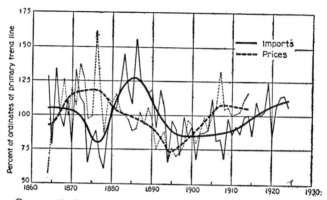

CHART 16b. RAW SILK, IMPORTS AND PRICES, UNITED STATES,
1864–1924
Relative Deviations from Primary Trend Lines

just beginning, which yielded a much more reliable raw
material and an improved quality of Chinese raw silk, an
effect of Japanese competition. The secondary movements
after that follow the usual path. There is no marked rise,
however, to 1907, probably because of the Russo-Japanese
War. Beginning with 1910, the movement is strongly upward.

In the price series (Italian raw silk prices until 1890,
Japanese raw silk after 1890) the secondary movements
follow the usual course, except that the peak of the upward
movement comes somewhat before 1880. This may have
been due to the failure of the Chinese to supply reliable raw
material, a failure which sent all silk prices upward, including those for the fine Italian grade. Subsequent movements
are similar to those observed in numerous other cases.

The cycles are clear-cut both in prices and imports. The
correlation is fairly close and positive, price cycles lagging
behind those in imports.

17–21. *Bank Clearings, United States.* The data for bank
clearings may be taken as a fairly good index of a city's
total volume of trade for the period given. Such data are
available over a long time for a number of cities, and we
can discover whether or not the total volume of trade

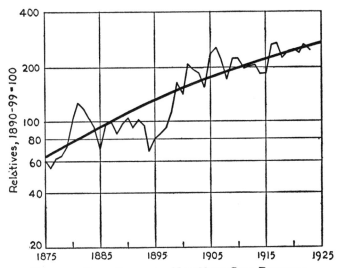

CHART 17. BANK CLEARINGS, NEW YORK CITY, DEFLATED,
1875–1923
Original Data and Primary Trend Line

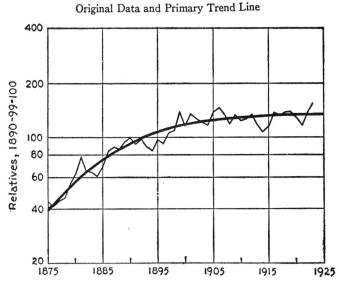

CHART 18. BANK CLEARINGS, BOSTON, DEFLATED, 1875–1923
Original Data and Primary Trend Line

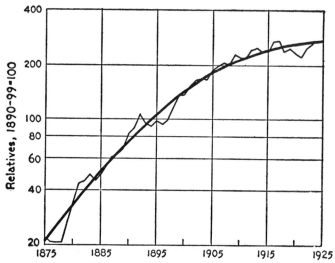

CHART 19. BANK CLEARINGS, CHICAGO, DEFLATED, 1875–1923
Original Data and Primary Trend Line

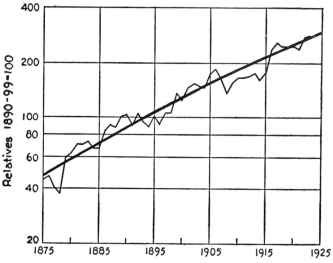

CHART 20. BANK CLEARINGS, PHILADELPHIA, DEFLATED, 1875–1923
Original Data and Primary Trend Line

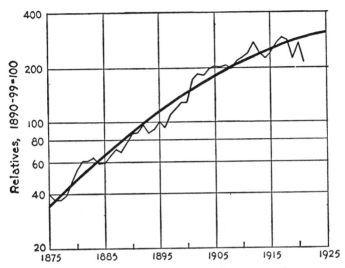

CHART 21. BANK CLEARINGS, ST. LOUIS, DEFLATED, 1875–1921
Original Data and Primary Trend Line

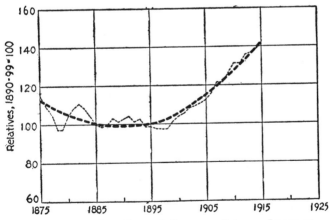

CHART 17–21a. CARL SNYDER'S INDEX OF GENERAL LEVEL OF
PRICES, UNITED STATES, 1875–1914
Original Data and Primary Trend Line

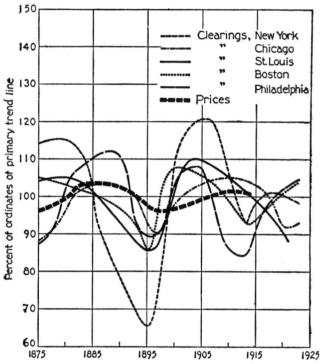

CHART 17–21b. BANK CLEARINGS AND GENERAL PRICE LEVEL,
5 CITIES, UNITED STATES, 1875–1923
Relative Deviations from Primary Trend Lines

follows the same type of curve found to fit the long-time changes in so many branches of industry.

The series 17–21 present bank clearings, beginning with 1875, for five of the largest cities: New York, Chicago, Philadelphia, Boston, and St. Louis. All these series have been deflated by Carl Snyder's index of the general price level, specially devised for the purpose of deflating bank clearings.[1] To each of the series a logistic curve was fitted as the line of primary trend. The descriptions are all satis-

[1] See his article, 'A New Index of the General Price Level from 1875,' *Journal of the American Statistical Association*, June, 1924, p. 195.

factory and in two cases, Chicago and Boston, extremely good.

On Chart 17–21b all of the secondary movements are plotted together. The heavy line represents the secondary variations in the general index of prices, that is, the Snyder index employed for deflation. One may easily note that the secondary movements in clearings for the different cities pursue a fairly similar course. They all reveal the retardation around 1895, although this begins at different points in the various series. Again the secondary movements show a recovery to the first half of the 1900–10 decade (in Chicago continuing to 1910), and most of them register a decline to the war, with subsequent recovery. To this movement Chicago and St. Louis form exceptions.

The secondary movements in the price index follow the same course, but with a marked retardation as compared to clearings. Whether this retardation is due to the composition of the index, which includes more slowly moving items than those which constitute clearings, it is impossible to say with any degree of assurance.

The cyclical fluctuations show a good correspondence between the clearings' movements for the various cities and those in prices. Price cycles are rather attenuated and lag fairly regularly behind the clearings' cycles.

22. *Baldwin Locomotive Works, United States.* In series 22 we have an interesting case of output by one enterprise only. This enterprise is, however, of large proportions, having recently produced over 2000 locomotives annually. The data extend back to 1835, and the fitted logistic curve describes the long-time movements rather well.

The interesting aspect of the statistical analysis of this series is the line of secondary movements. These present accentuated reproductions of those in other branches of industry. For comparison, the secondary variations in the price of pig iron are plotted (Chart 22b), and the correspondence between locomotive output by a single establishment and the price of the main raw material is surprisingly close.[1] That we are here dealing with a single establishment

---

[1] The relationship is, however, roundabout. For the movements in pig-iron production are well correlated with the movements in railroad expansion, and the railroads are the only consumers of locomotives.

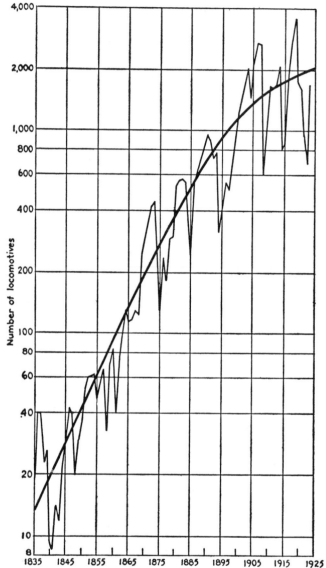

CHART 22. NUMBER OF LOCOMOTIVES PRODUCED, BALDWIN WORKS,
1835–1923
Original Data and Primary Trend Line

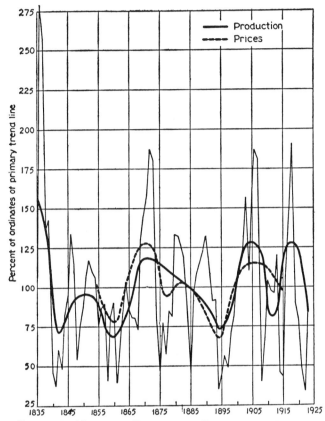

CHART 22b. NUMBER OF LOCOMOTIVES PRODUCED AND PIG-IRON
PRICES, 1835–1923
Relative Deviations from Primary Trend Line

accounts for the extreme violence of the movements. On a
national scale the relative deviations from the line of primary
trend would presumably be much milder.

The cyclical fluctuations in locomotive production, while
much more violent than those in the production of pig iron,
are very similar to the latter.

23. *Coal, United Kingdom.* We have confined ourselves
thus far to series for the United States, and it might be

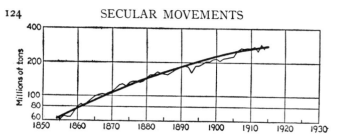

CHART 23. COAL OUTPUT, UNITED KINGDOM, 1854–1914
Original Data and Primary Trend Line

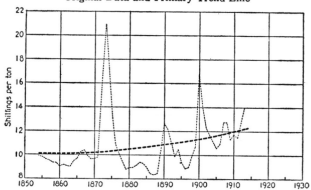

CHART 23a. EXPORT PRICES OF COAL, UNITED KINGDOM, 1854–1913
Original Data and Primary Trend Line

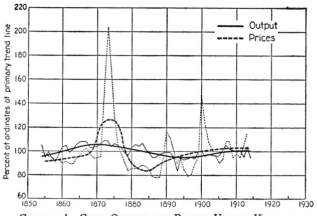

CHART 23b. COAL, OUTPUT AND PRICES, UNITED KINGDOM,
1854–1914
Relative Deviations from Primary Trend Lines

thought that the fit of the curves used is just an accident of economic development in one country, even though shared by many industries and observed in many branches of economic activity. But we shall presently see that the curves apply to many series in other countries as well.

Thus the logistic curve applies to coal output in the United Kingdom. The industry began in the eighteenth century but data are available only from 1854. For the 61 years which the series covers, the logistic curve presents a very good description. The series, like all others for the European countries, was brought up only to 1914.

The secondary secular variations are comparatively small, but run a course similar to the American series. There is a rise to 1870, a gradual retardation from that point to 1895, and again an acceleration of growth after 1895. Were the series taken for the war years, the line would no doubt have reflected the usual rise and reaction.

The secondary secular movements in prices are much more conspicuous than those in production, especially in periods of war, as e.g., in 1870 and 1900, but they do show a rough correspondence to the more attenuated movements in production. The synchronization is not very complete, for in prices the decline starts later in the '70s than in production, and the rise begins in the late '80s, not in the '90s. But the number of swings is the same, and a casual observation of Chart 23b reveals a fair correspondence.

In the output series cyclical fluctuations are very mild; in the price series they are longer and much more conspicuous.

24. *Pig iron, United Kingdom.* Here we have a series of data on production which extends back to 1788, and a series of prices which starts in 1785. To the production series a logistic curve was fitted. Inspection reveals a good description of the long-time movements over the 125 years embraced by the original data (see Chart 24).

The secondary secular variations in production could not be ascertained exactly for the first half of the period, because annual data are lacking. But it may be seen (Chart 24b) that these variations correspond to price movements. Both prices and production rise to 1800–05. After that a down-

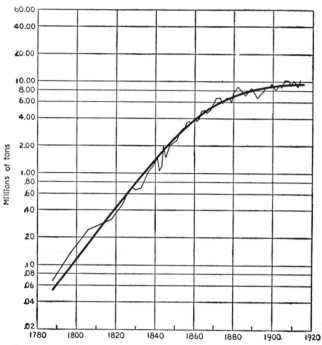

CHART 24. PIG IRON PRODUCTION, UNITED KINGDOM, 1788–1913
Original Data and Primary Trend Line

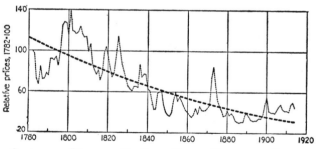

CHART 24a. PRICES OF PIG IRON, UNITED KINGDOM, 1782–1913
Original Data and Primary Trend Line

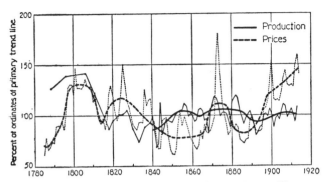

CHART 24b. PIG IRON, PRODUCTION AND PRICES, UNITED KINGDOM,
1788–1913

Relative Deviations from Primary Trend Lines

ward movement begins and continues, on the whole, through the first half of the nineteenth century, with an interruption by the 20-year swing from 1815 to 1835. In the recovery, i.e., the beginning of another upward secondary movement, output precedes prices considerably, the former starting in the early '40s, the latter in 1851. After that there is again a fairly good correspondence, somewhat distorted by the high prices in the '70s. In the decline to the '90s, price movements reach the low point earlier than production movements, in 1885 and not in 1895. In the accelerated growth after 1895, prices tend upward more sharply than production.

Thus while we have a fairly close correlation of the secondary variations in production and prices, a scanning of the historical records of the industry reveals important specific occurrences associated with each particular up and down swing. For example, the upward movement of output after 1785 may be traced to the introduction of the important inventions of Sir Henry Cort, which enormously cheapened the production of bar iron (puddling and rolling instead of stamping and hammering). As a result production rose to high deviation levels never again reached.

In November, 1806, came the declaration of the Continental Blockade, which considerably curtailed Great

Britain's exports, and was one of the contributing causes to the downward secondary movement after 1805. The recovery, which began in 1815, is linked with the cessation of the war and the reopening of the European markets, with Great Britain able to deliver a superior product at lower prices than continental producers.

The turn after 1825 may have been a simple reaction, or due to the drastic reduction of import duties on pig iron in 1826; a reduction brought about by the pressure of consumers of pig iron who were suffering from the high prices. The drop in prices started a decline in production, reflected in the secondary movements of both series.

By 1833 the railroads' demand for iron began to grow and from the early '40s to the '70s, the demand constantly expanded as new uses for iron developed. Thus in the early '40s came its extensive application in steamship construction and building. Moreover, exports increased vigorously as other nations built up their railroad structures and made other capital investments without being able themselves to supply cheaply the essential materials. The decline of prices, which continued until the '50s, stimulated the demand for iron. These facts explain the rising movement, which lasted to the '70s. Subsequent movements do not seem to be associated with any specific happenings; but the general downward trend after 1870 no doubt reflects the change in Great Britain's world position as compared with her rôle in the first half of the century.[1]

The cyclical fluctuations in production and prices are regular. Correlation between the price and production cycles is quite close and positive, price cycles lagging behind production. Here again, as in a number of other cases, the cyclical fluctuations in prices are more violent than those in production.

25. *Steel, United Kingdom*. The Bessemer process, which made possible the modern steel industry, was patented in 1856, but large-scale production did not begin until the '70s. To the series, which extends back to 1875, a Gompertz curve was fitted. It yields a fairly good description of the long-

[1] The facts noted were gathered from Scrivenor's *History of the Iron Trade*, and Beck's *Geschichte des Eisens*.

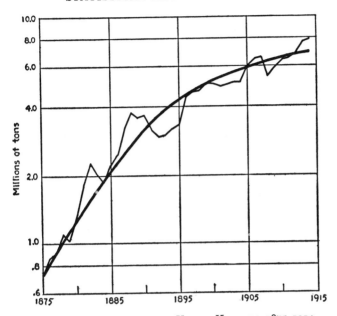

CHART 25. STEEL PRODUCTION, UNITED KINGDOM, 1875–1914
Original Data and Primary Trend Line

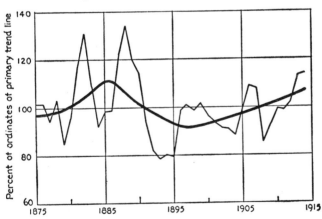

CHART 25b. STEEL PRODUCTION, UNITED KINGDOM, 1875–1914
Relative Deviations from Primary Trend Line

time movements, and was found to be a much better fit than the logistic curve.

The secondary movements in output are roughly similar to those for pig-iron production, although the peak of the upward movement occurs much later than in the latter. No series of steel prices in the United Kingdom could be found, so no comparison with the secondary movements of prices was possible.

The cyclical fluctuations are clear-cut and seem to diminish in amplitude with the passage of time. They show a good correlation with the cycles in pig-iron production, plotted on the same chart for comparison.

26. *Tonnage of Ships Cleared, United Kingdom.* The tonnage of ships cleared from the ports of the United Kingdom is the best available index of the volume of foreign trade (i.e., of the indexes that cover a long period of time). The data extend far back, but they are discontinuous up to 1815. Moreover, it was in 1815 that steamships became known to the world and a new era in shipping began, although extensive transatlantic steamship traffic arose only in the late '30s.

The logistic curve, taken as the line of primary trend, yields a good description of the long-time changes for the hundred years covered by the data. In the secondary secular movements we observe a correspondence between the shipping series and the index of the general level of prices (the Jevons-Saurerbeck index, beginning in 1781). We may also notice a considerable similarity between the secondary variations in shipping and those in pig-iron output. The movements decline from 1815 to about 1835. Whether the decline was a prolonged reaction from the high levels of the early Industrial Revolution (1780–1800), or a reflection of the declining movement in prices, or both, cannot be said with any degree of assurance. While prices continue to decline until 1850, secondary variations in shipping turn upward after 1836. That date marks the beginning of a period of extremely vigorous export trade, to which we referred when commenting on the series of pig-iron output in the United Kingdom. The brief retardation after 1857 and to 1865 may have some connection with the

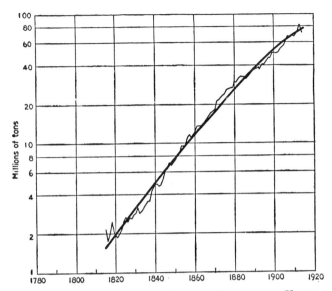

CHART 26. TONNAGE OF SHIPS CLEARED, PORTS OF THE UNITED
KINGDOM, 1815–1913
Original Data and Primary Trend Line

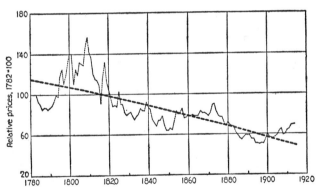

CHART 26a. INDEX OF THE GENERAL LEVEL OF PRICES, UNITED
KINGDOM, 1782–1914
Original Data and Primary Trend Line

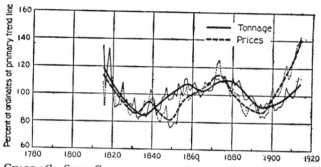

CHART 26b. SHIPS CLEARED AND THE GENERAL LEVEL OF PRICES,
UNITED KINGDOM, 1815–1914
Relative Deviations from Primary Trend Lines

Crimean War, but probably more with the United States
Civil War, which removed from the market one of the most
important customers of English industries. After that developments are typical: a vigorous rise up to the end of the
'70s, a decline toward 1895, and again a rise after that date.

The secondary movements in prices decline until 1850,
then rise to 1873, and in the decade 1855–65 exhibit the
retardation found in production movements. Developments
thereafter follow the ordinary course and show, as they do
practically throughout the entire period, a close correlation
with the movements in the shipping series.

The cyclical fluctuations are fairly regular, with the cycles
in prices and shipping closely correlated.

27. *Cotton imports, United Kingdom.* The data on imports
of raw cotton form a good index of changes in the volume
of cotton manufacturing in the United Kingdom. It is the
only series available over a long period, and the reëxports
being fairly small, the imports indicate with a certain precedence or lag the consumption of cotton by the manufacturers of the country. The series was taken from 1781, since
the epoch-making inventions were introduced and the modern era of cotton manufacturing launched in the 1780s.

The logistic curve fitted as the primary trend describes
quite well the long-time changes throughout the 133 years
covered by the data. The secondary movements describe

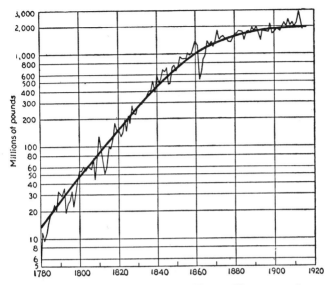

CHART 27. IMPORTS OF RAW COTTON, UNITED KINGDOM, 1781–1914
Original Data and Primary Trend Line

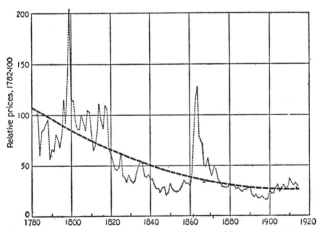

CHART 27a. PRICES OF RAW COTTON, UNITED KINGDOM, 1782–1913
Original Data and Primary Trend Line

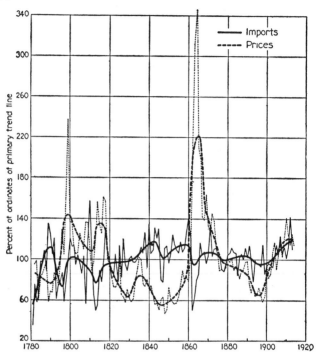

CHART 27b. RAW COTTON, IMPORTS AND PRICES, UNITED KINGDOM, 1781–1913
Relative Deviations from Primary Trend Line

a number of swings which may be easily explained, by the numerous historical accounts of the industry, and by correlation with the corresponding secondary movements in cotton prices.

The rapid rise beginning in 1781 is evidently due to the introduction of the revolutionary inventions of Arkwright and Compton (the spinning jenny first patented in 1778; the mule in 1779). The Arkwright patents were thrown open to the public in 1785, but were used extensively by outsiders before that. The reaction and decline after 1790–91 is apparently due to the lack of raw materials and the great rise in the price of raw cotton. Thus Ellison records that in 1788 the East India Company was pressed to increase cotton growth in India. The price reached a great height in 1799.

In 1793 the cotton gin was invented, and its rapid spread enabled the United States to become an important source of supply for the raw material. This together with an augmented Indian crop lowered prices and stimulated cotton manufactures again. The secondary movement in imports thus turns sharply upward in 1796. The Continental Blockade served to retard growth slightly, although the price disparity between the English and Continental markets finally served to break down the restrictions, and in 1809–10 a phenomenal upswing of the trade ensued. In 1812 war between England and the United States caused a break in the imports and a high level in prices. The trade, however, recovered very quickly.

After 1812 we observe a steadily rising secondary movement in imports up to about 1860. The acceleration is highest during 1830–45, and is coincident with a corresponding swing in prices. This period marks a great expansion of English trade in general, although in the particular case of cotton imports the acceleration may have been connected with the introduction of the Roberts self-acting water-frame (1825) and of the throstle, about the same time; just as the power loom, whose successful introduction dates about 1844, may have been partly responsible for the recovery. There is likewise a recovery in the secondary movements of prices. The outbreak of the Civil War in 1861 accounts for the great decline in imports and rise in prices. After that the movements follow the usual course. They decline to 1895 and rise thereafter.

The secondary movements in the price of cotton from 1795 show the same number of swings as the imports and at about the same time. But the wars of 1812 and 1861 sent prices to very high deviation levels, hence the particular swings have as their basis a continuously declining movement from these war peaks, with the declining price movements diverging from those of imports. Prices reveal a declining movement, on the whole, from 1812 to 1841, while the secondary trend in imports is rising through this period.

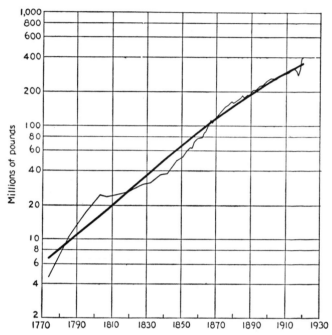

CHART 28. CONSUMPTION OF TEA, UNITED KINGDOM, 1780–1920
Original Data and Primary Trend Line

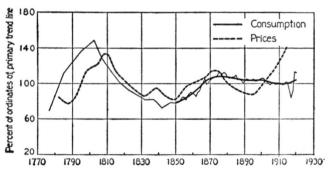

CHART 28b. CONSUMPTION OF TEA AND GENERAL PRICE LEVEL,
UNITED KINGDOM, 1780–1920
Relative Deviations from Primary Trend Lines

Again imports show nothing like the rise to 1861 exhibited by the secondary price movements, which decline after that point. Another disagreement occurs in 1780–95, when cotton prices were declining because of more extensive cultivation, and cotton imports were rising. While the separate swings are similar and simultaneous for prices and imports, there is a considerable divergence between them as a result mainly of wars and their extreme effects on prices.

28. *Tea Consumption, United Kingdom.* This might be considered a typical case of consumption series, such as whisky, coffee, tobacco, etc., available for the United Kingdom. The series was not used previous to the 1780 decade, since that may be said to mark the beginning of the modern economic era. The logistic curve fitted yields a fairly good description of the long-time changes.

The secondary variations are plotted together with the secondary movements in the general level of prices (Chart 28b). They show a rather good correspondence. Both have a great upward movement toward the first decade of the nineteenth century; from then to the '40s there occurs a continuous decline in tea consumption, while price movements decline up to the '50s. This discrepancy coincides with that noted in several other English series, e.g., pig iron and shipping. The movements from then are upward to the '70s and decline after 1875–80. No appreciable recovery, however, in the tea consumption series after 1895 is observable. What may be the reason, we are at a loss to say.

Cyclical fluctuations in tea consumption are quite attenuated, as is to be expected. They reveal a good, positive correlation with the cycles in the general level of prices.

29. *Coal, Belgium.* Most of the production series for Belgium, which we are now to treat, date back to 1831, about the time the independent kingdom was established. From then until the late war, there were no outstanding external disturbances which greatly affected the country's productive activity. Currency and prices were, however, disturbed by the wars of France.

The logistic curve fitted to coal output offers an excellent description of the changes in volume through the 83 years

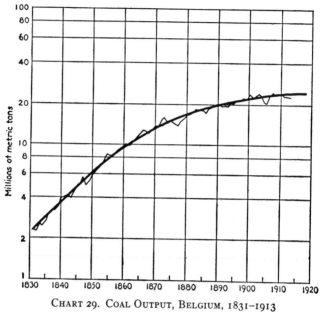

CHART 29. COAL OUTPUT, BELGIUM, 1831–1913
Original Data and Primary Trend Line

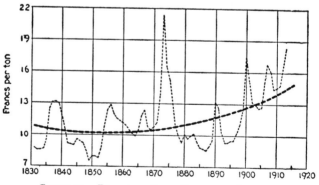

CHART 29a, PRICES OF COAL, BELGIUM, 1831–1913
Original Data and Primary Trend Line

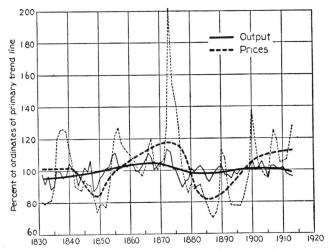

CHART 29b. COAL, OUTPUT AND PRICES, BELGIUM, 1831–1913
Relative Deviations from Primary Trend Lines

covered. So excellent in fact, that the secondary movements prove to be very attenuated, and do not reflect fully the variations in the price series. When traced, however, these movements in production follow the course observed for the same period in other countries. An upward movement definitely begins in the late '30s. It continues until the early '70s and then turns downward. A recovery appears about 1885, with a slow rise to 1905 and a retardation thereafter. In this pattern Belgian coal output repeats, on the whole, the series for the United States, save that its swings somewhat precede the latter.

With one divergence in the early part of the series, the secondary movements in prices follow a similar course, but reveal throughout much more striking deviations from the primary trend than the movements in output. Prices show a decline toward 1850, especially abrupt after 1839. This may reflect the price movement in other European countries at the time, or the prolonged depression into which Belgium was plunged after the Treaty of 1839, when the country was burdened with a share of Holland's national debt. Sub-

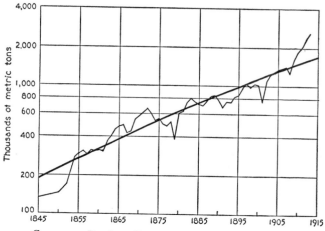

CHART 30. PIG-IRON PRODUCTION, BELGIUM, 1845–1913
Original Data and Primary Trend Line

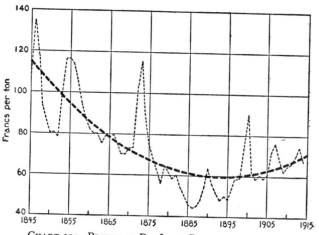

CHART 30a. PRICES OF PIG IRON, BELGIUM, 1845–1914
Original Data and Primary Trend Line

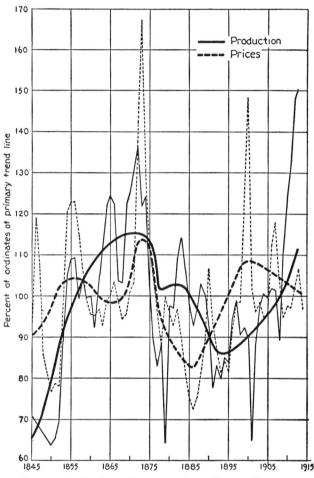

CHART 30b. PIG IRON, PRODUCTION AND PRICES, BELGIUM,
1845–1913
Relative Deviations from Primary Trend Lines

sequent movements repeat those for output; a rise to the
first half of the '70s, a decline to the end of the '80s, and a
rise thereafter gradually retarded at the end. Correlation
between the two groups of movements is fairly good.

The charts reveal rather mild cycles in output, with those for prices markedly conspicuous. The correlation is close and positive; price cycles showing a tendency to lag behind those of production.

30. *Pig iron, Belgium*. In this case we have data for annual output from 1850. The logistic curve yields a fairly satisfactory description of the changes over the 70 years, although it leaves room for rather violent secondary movements.

The latter trace the usual course: a rise to 1873, thence a decline to the first half of the '90s, and a rise again to 1913. The somewhat exceptional movement is the extreme rise after 1909. This is found in a number of other series for both Belgium and France.

The secondary variations in prices show a greater number of swings, with a temporary retardation occurring during the decade, 1857–65. Whether this retardation is related to the new technical processes then introduced or to the great English exports, one is at a loss to say. But a similar retardation is present in English pig-iron prices, so it may be connected with the withdrawal of the United States from the market for the time being, both as a purchaser of goods and source of the monetary metal. After this retardation, the secondary movements in prices run the familiar course, except that the recovery starts somewhat early, i.e., after 1886. This is undoubtedly to be linked to the formation of the Belgian Iron Syndicate in 1886. On the whole, there is a rough correspondence between the secondary movements in production and prices, the former lagging in the recovery during the '90s.

The cyclical fluctuations are clear-cut for both, and show a remarkably close positive correlation. The price cycles appear to lag behind those in production.

31. *Steel, Belgium*. This series describes the output of steel by the modern processes only (Bessemer-Martin), but nearly all of the country's output is produced by these processes. The series goes back to 1875. A Gompertz curve fitted as the primary trend line yields a good description of the longtime movements.

Determination of the secondary movements is difficult

because of the brevity of the period studied and the violence of the cyclical fluctuations. There seems to be, as in other series, a decline from 1875 to the early part of the '90s, but a recovery takes place immediately in the second half

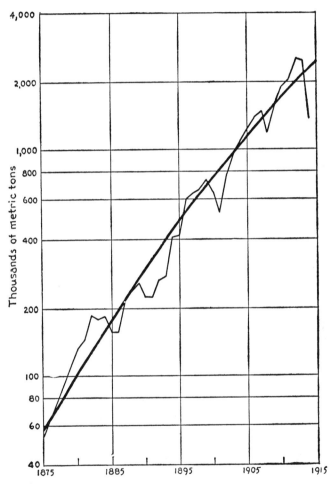

CHART 31. STEEL PRODUCTION, BELGIUM, 1875–1913
Original Data and Primary Trend Line

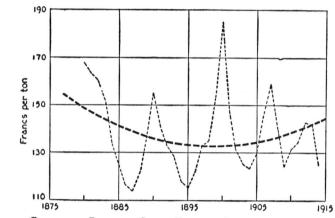

CHART 31a. PRICES OF STEEL, FINISHED PRODUCTS, BELGIUM,
1880–1914
Original Data and Primary Trend Line

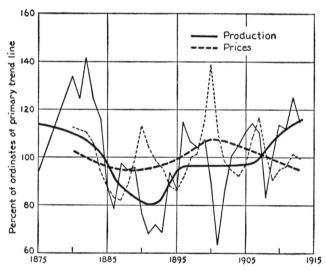

CHART 31b. STEEL, PRODUCTION AND PRICES, BELGIUM, 1875–1913
Relative Deviations from Primary Trend Lines

of that decade. Then follows an even rise up to about 1905, and an acceleration afterward, although here we may be observing merely the first phase of an incomplete cycle.

The secondary variations in prices show a rough correspondence to those in production. There is a decline to the end of the '80s, and a rise to 1900, the latter corresponding to the rise in production at the end of the '90s. After 1900, the movement in prices continually declines without reflecting anything like the rising movement in production after 1908. This discrepancy is similar to that observed in pig iron.

The cyclical fluctuations both in production and prices are fairly prominent. The correlation is close, with the price cycles lagging definitely behind production.

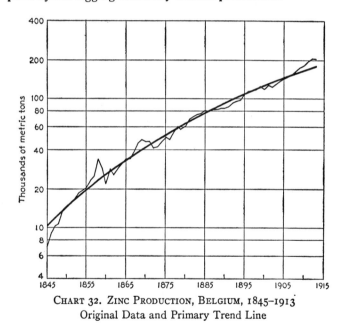

CHART 32. ZINC PRODUCTION, BELGIUM, 1845–1913
Original Data and Primary Trend Line

32. *Zinc, Belgium.* Belgium was one of the two pioneer countries in the production of zinc. In 1805 the Belgian method of zinc ore roasting had already been discovered by

Dony, but need for perfecting the process and creating a market for the new metal still remained. It was only after 1837 that substantial development began.

The series used extends back to 1845. The Gompertz curve offers a fairly good description of the long-time changes over the 69 years covered.

In the secondary secular variations we observe a number

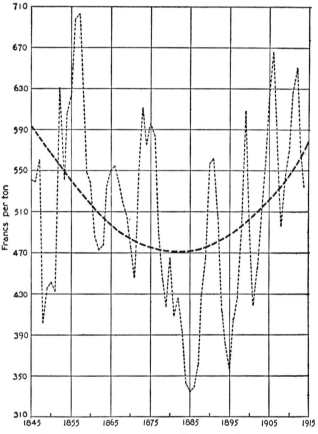

CHART 32a. PRICES OF ZINC, BELGIUM, 1845–1914
Original Data and Primary Trend Line

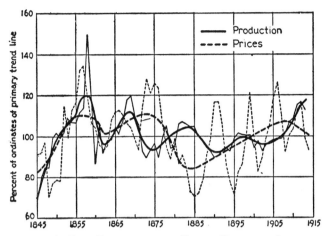

CHART 32b. ZINC, PRODUCTION AND PRICES, BELGIUM, 1845–1913
Relative Deviations from Primary Trend Lines

of swings but they are easily explained by the historical
facts and the relation of the movements in production to
those in prices. There is in both sets of movements a rather
vigorous rise toward the second half of the '50s, similar to
other series both in Belgium and Great Britain. The retardation about 1857–64 is the same as was observed and commented upon in pig-iron prices. It seems to have been as in
other cases a reaction from the expansion in the two preceding decades (marked by railroad and shipbuilding consequent upon inventions), and partly due to the withdrawal
of the United States from the world market because of the
Civil War. With the disappearance of these retarding factors, recovery sets in and up to the middle of the '60s
movements in production and prices run closely together.

The divergence immediately after 1870 was occasioned by
the Franco-Prussian War. The Belgian zinc industry was
supplying the French market, and Belgium's monetary
system was bound up with that of France. With the outbreak of the war came high prices, lower exports, and lower
levels of production. With the resumption of normal conditions, an upward production movement and a downward

price movement set in. In 1885 the declining movement in prices was arrested by the formation of a syndicate, and the upward movement thus begins earlier than in other commodity prices. The syndicate also limited production and was partly responsible for the continued declining movement in output until 1891, when it decided to allow an increase in volume.[1] After that the long-time movements in production seem to be correlated with the very long price cycles, a result, perhaps, of the syndicate's conscious policy. The secondary movements in prices, however, follow the usual course.

The cyclical fluctuations are comparatively mild for production and rather violent for prices, the contrast being especially marked in the second half of the series. This with their difference in duration gives an apparent lack of correlation though some can be traced. In the first half of the series the price cycles appear to precede those in production.

33. *Wheat, Germany.* This series describes a branch of economic activity in its last stages of growth, and approaching stability in absolute volume of output. The series dates back only to 1878. The logistic curve fitted describes admirably the long-time changes for the 36 years.

In the secondary movements for production the influence of the variations in the price level is complicated by the changes in Germany's tariff policy. Under the pressure of international competition and reflecting the declining movement in prices, the secondary variations in crops is downward from 1878 to 1890. But in 1885 the Reichstag raised the duties on wheat and other grains, and pressed by the agricultural interests increased them again in 1887 and 1890.[2] This increase in duties was directed mainly against the Russian imports. The resulting rise in prices stimulated production, and the secondary movement in crops turns upward, 1890–95. The causes for the rise, and hence the acceleration itself were short-lived, for after 1890 Germany

[1] See H. Denis: *La Dépression Économique et Sociale et l'Histoire de Prix*, Ixelles-Bruxelles, 1892–95, pp. 302–03.

[2] Waltershausen, Sartorius von: *Deutsche Wirtschaftsgeschichte, 1815–1914*, Jena, 1920, pp. 308–09.

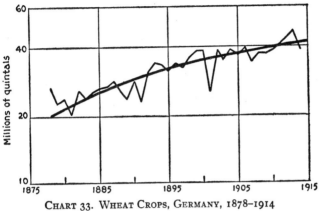

CHART 33. WHEAT CROPS, GERMANY, 1878–1914
Original Data and Primary Trend Line

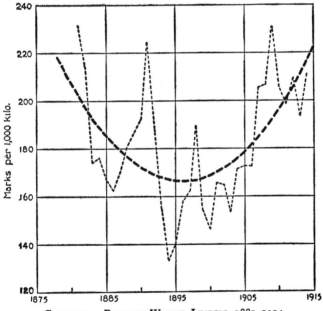

CHART 33a. PRICE OF WHEAT, LEIPZIG, 1881–1914
Original Data and Primary Trend Line

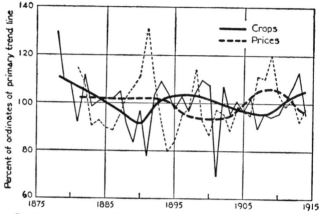

CHART 33b. WHEAT, CROPS AND PRICES, GERMANY, 1878–1914
Relative Deviations from Primary Trend Lines

emerged from her tariff isolation. In 1891 a treaty of preferential treatment was concluded with Austria-Hungary which admitted Hungarian grain. In 1894 a similar treaty was concluded with Russia. The German grain prices declined, and a declining secondary movement in crops set in.[1] Thereafter the developments in prices follow the course observed for other countries. In crops the movement continues downward until 1909, when evidently as a reflection of the high prices of 1908–09, it turns upward. On the whole, there is a fair correlation between the secondary movements in production and prices, the former lagging considerably behind the latter, and both deviating from the usual course because of changes in tariff policy.

In the cyclical fluctuations, we find rather violent swings in prices, with those for crops more broken. Nevertheless, there is a fair degree of correlation.

34. *Coal, Germany.* The series used gives the output of brown and bituminous coal and exhibits a vigorous growth of these industries. The data go back to 1860, when the unified German state was emerging. The logistic curve

[1] Waltershausen, Sartorius von: *Deutsche Wirtschaftsgeschichte, 1815–1914*, Jena, 1920, pp. 383–88.

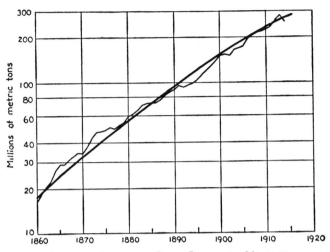

CHART 34. OUTPUT OF COAL, GERMANY, 1860–1914
Original Data and Primary Trend Line

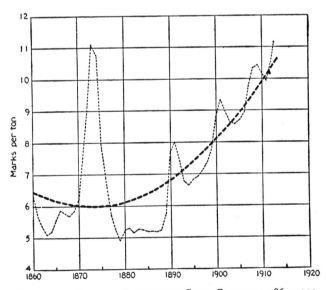

CHART 34a. PRICE OF BITUMINOUS COAL, GERMANY, 1860–1913
Original Data and Primary Trend Line

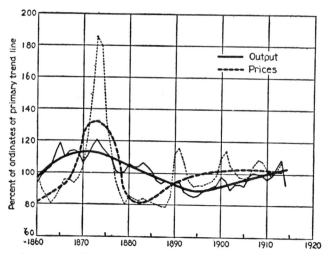

CHART 34b. COAL, OUTPUT AND PRICES, GERMANY, 1860–1914
Relative Deviations from Primary Trend Lines

fitted yields a good description of the changes throughout
the 50 years (Chart 34)

The secondary movements in output follow the frequently
observed course in other branches of production for other
countries. There is the rise to the first half of the '70s,
thence a decline to the first half of the '90s, and a subsequent
rise These movements portray a fairly good correspondence
to the secondary variations in prices. The latter similarly
rise to the first of the '70s, then start to decline. The price
movement recovers earlier than output, however, i.e., at the
end of the '80s and not in the '90s. Whether this earlier
recovery in the upward movement of prices is attributable
to the Coke Syndicate, the first successful forerunner of the
Rheinisch Westphalian Coal Syndicate,[1] or whether to the
earlier effect of factors that induce an upward secondary
movement, we cannot say with any certainty. After 1890,
the variations in prices pursue the familiar course. On the
whole, correspondence between the secondary movements of
production and prices is rather good. Even though after

[1] A. Stockder: *German Trade Associations*, New York, 1924.

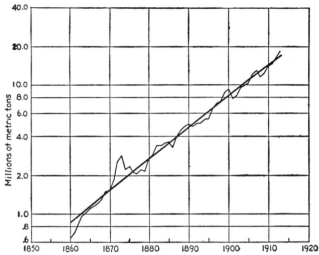

CHART 35. CONSUMPTION OF PIG IRON, GERMANY, 1860–1913
Original Deviations and Primary Trend Line

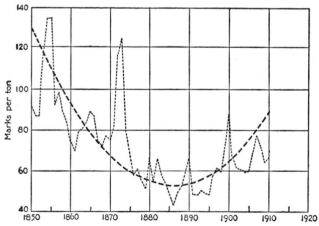

CHART 35a. PRICES OF PIG IRON, GERMANY, 1850–1910
Original Data and Primary Trend Line

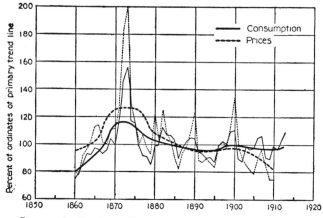

CHART 35b. PIG IRON, CONSUMPTION AND PRICES, GERMANY,
1860–1913
Relative Deviations from Primary Trend Lines

1893 the industry was practically controlled by the two
Rheinisch Westphalian Syndicates in succession, this correspondence is undisturbed.

Comparing the cyclical fluctuations in production and
prices, we find an unusually close positive correlation. But
the price cycles are much more violent and tend to lag
behind those of output, especially in the series' latter half.

35. *Pig Iron, Germany.* Here we have a case of extraordinary, vigorous growth with no appreciable abatement during
the 55 years covered by the data. Hence, the logistic curve
fitted looks almost like a straight line on a log scale. The
fit is fairly good.

In the secondary secular variations we have another instance of almost perfect correlation between prices and
production, in spite of the fact that the industry was subject
to a number of effective cartels. The movements follow the
usual course — a rise to 1873, and subsequent decline to the
first half of the '90s.

It is interesting to note here the difference which a number
of German and other continental series show in their development after 1895 compared to series for the United

States. In the United States we observed a recovery late in the '90s, with an upward movement to the second half of the 1900–10 decade. In Germany, the recovery sets in in the first half of the '90s, and is no doubt related to the extraordinary growth of cartels and to the absence of currency difficulties then present in the United States. The

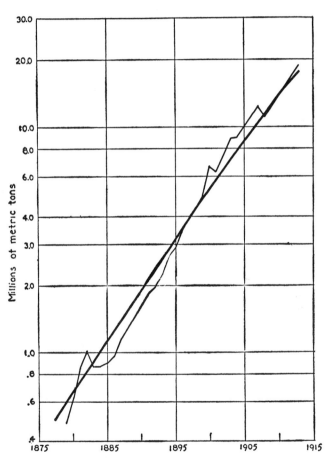

CHART 36. CRUDE STEEL OUTPUT, GERMANY, 1879–1913
Original Data and Primary Trend Line

period immediately following, 1895–1900, was for Germany one of most vigorous activity in a number of branches of production.

The correlation of the movements in prices and production is almost perfect. The conspicuous retardation in prices

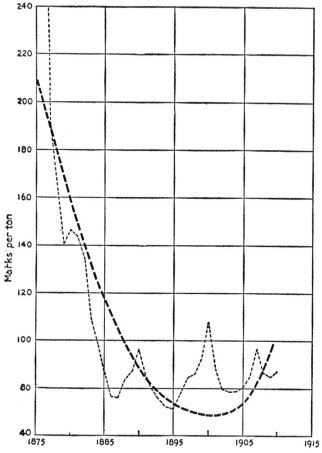

CHART 36a. Prices of Ingots and Steel Billets, Germany, 1877–1910
Original Data and Primary Trend Line

after 1900 as compared with production marks the only noticeable flaw.

Chart 35b reveals clear-cut cyclical fluctuations. The correlation is simultaneous, with prices tending to lag slightly.

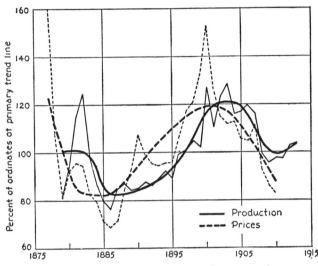

CHART 36b. STEEL, OUTPUT AND PRICES, GERMANY, 1879–1913
Relative Deviations from Primary Trend Lines

36. *Steel, Germany.* The data on steel production for Germany are available only since 1879. It is appropriate, nevertheless, to begin observations from that year, for while the Bessemer process was introduced into the country much earlier, Germany's modern steel industry arose with the important Thomas and Martin processes about that time. Because of the high phosphoric contents of the ore, the original Bessemer process was unsuitable. The Gompertz curve fitted to the data offers a good first approximation.

In the secondary secular variations we again see a close correlation between prices and production, but both sets of movements differ somewhat from the usual course. There is a rapid decline in prices after 1877, coincident with similar movements in prices of other commodities. The recovery, however, starts early, toward the end of the '80s. Production movements portray the same pattern to that point. Then both sets swing upward considerably, prices to 1900, production to 1903. The declining movement from this period was shared by many branches of German industry, while their rise from 1895–1900 was extraordinarily great. It is interesting to note that the operations of the powerful Stahlverband (organized in 1904) only smooth the price decline, and in no way prevent it.

In the cyclical fluctuations, production seems to fluctuate more frequently than prices, but in a much milder fashion. Correlation between the two is thus partly concealed.

37. *Copper output, Germany.* The data in this case refer to the output of crude copper by the Mansfield works, but this establishment produces practically all of the country's output. While the series goes back to 1860, annual data begin only in 1870. The logistic curve fits the data admirably.

The secondary secular variations in production can be interpreted only from 1880. The high levels about that

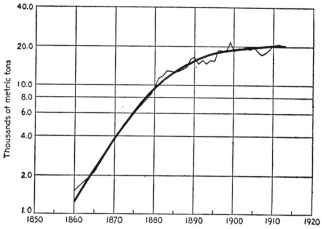

CHART 37. COPPER PRODUCTION, MANSFIELD WORKS, GERMANY, 1860–1913
Original Data and Primary Trend Line

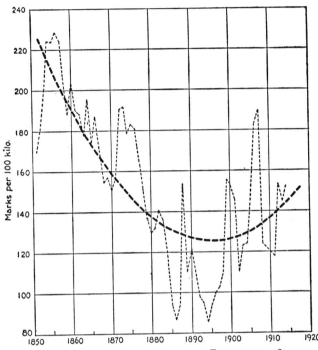

CHART 37a. PRICE OF COPPER, HAMBURG, FRANKFURT, 1851–1914
Original Data and Primary Trend Line

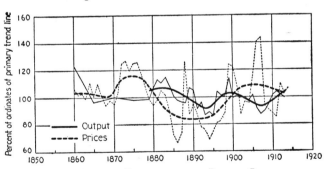

CHART 37b. COPPER, PRODUCTION AND PRICES, GERMANY,
1860–1913
Relative Deviations from Primary Trend Lines

year (whether marking a decline or a rise from 1870 cannot be said) are probably accounted for by the activities of the Secretan Syndicate. There is the usual decline up to the first half of the '90s. After the '90s the movements of copper production trace those of steel, pig iron and wheat, i.e., rise to 1900 and decline thereafter.

The secondary movements in prices follow a somewhat different course, being closely correlated with the movements of prices in other countries. They likewise decline to the '90s, but rise after that to 1905–07, thus moving on high levels while output is declining.

Chart 37b reveals violent cyclical fluctuations in prices but much milder for production. The correlation is, however, fairly close, with the price cycles tending to lag behind production.

38. *Zinc, Germany.* Zinc smelting is one of the oldest industries in Germany. It began in Silesia in 1780, and the Silesian furnace was introduced in 1809. The data are available from 1845, and to this series, as to all others for zinc production, a Gompertz curve was fitted. The description obtained is quite satisfactory.

The secondary secular movements in production are a reflection of the movements in prices, complicated by war and the output policy of syndicates. The rise from 1845 to the end of the '50s reflects the corresponding upward variation in prices, and is similar to movements in that period of other branches of industry for the various countries. After 1857 a retardation in the movement of prices develops, with a marked decline in the movement of production. Prices turn upward again immediately after 1870, and rise to peak levels in 1873–75. But the movement in production continues to decline throughout the Franco-Prussian War, recovering, however, immediately after, and continues to rise until 1885. This recovery might be, in a measure, a result of the preceding high prices and restrictions imposed by the war, and in part a consequence of the spreading use of blende as raw material. In 1885 the syndicates appeared, and there begins an upward movement in prices accompanying a curtailment in production. The price movement rises from 1885, while production turns upward only at the end

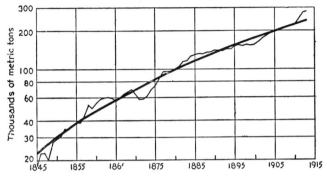

CHART 38. CRUDE ZINC PRODUCTION, GERMANY, 1845–1913
Original Data and Primary Trend Line

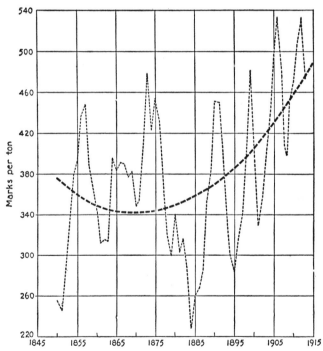

CHART 38a. PRICES OF ZINC, BRESLAU, 1850–1913
Original Data and Primary Trend Line

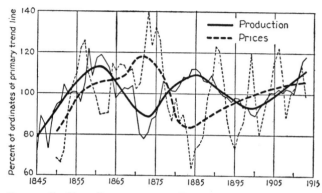

CHART 38b. ZINC, PRODUCTION AND PRICES, GERMANY, 1845–1913
Relative Deviations from Primary Trend Lines

of the '90s. Owing to the disturbing influences of war and
syndicate policies, close correlation between the secondary
variations in prices and production is absent.

In the cyclical fluctuations we observe much more conspicuous cycles in prices than in production. The latter
cycles are mild, especially in the second half of the series.
Correlation between the two is apparent only in the first
half of the period, with the fluctuations of production lagging
behind those of prices.

39. *Consumption of Cotton, Germany.* While these data
are found only in quinquennial averages, the series is used
because it is one of the longest available for Germany. The
logistic curve fitted gives an excellent description of the
long-time movements.

The deviations from this line of primary trend clearly
picture the course followed by the secondary variations.
For the purpose of comparison we plotted on the same
chart (39b) the Otto Schmitz index of wholesale prices in
Germany, computed in the same averages as the cotton
consumption series, and taken relatively to 1851–1913 as
100. The chart shows a very good correspondence between
the movements of the two series, both picturing the course
of secondary variations of other series heretofore surveyed.
Thus we have another instance to add to the numerous

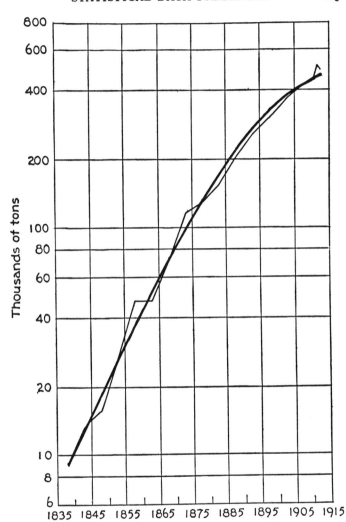

CHART 39. CONSUMPTION OF RAW COTTON, GERMANY, 1836–1913
Original Data and Primary Trend Line

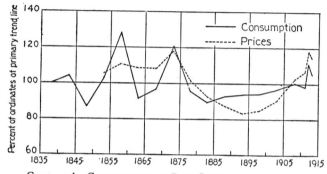

CHART 39b. CONSUMPTION OF RAW COTTON AND INDEX OF
WHOLESALE PRICES, GERMANY, 1836–1913
Relative Deviations from Primary Trend Lines

examples already cited of a close correspondence between secondary movements in production and prices.

40. *Wheat, France.* The series of wheat crops for France extends back to 1815. Since after 1870 considerable change in territory and acreage occurred, it was deemed advisable to divide the series into two parts, one up to 1870, the other beginning in that year. A logistic curve fitted to each of the two parts yields a fair description of the long-time changes, which are obscured by the violent year-to-year fluctuations in the original data.

The secondary movements in wheat crops are comparatively insignificant. There is a slight rise after 1815, which marks a recovery upon the cessation of war, and then, as a reflection of the downward movement in prices, a slight decline to the middle of the '40s. The upward swing, which sets in after that and continues to about 1857, is evidently again a reflection of a similar movement in prices. After 1857 the latter begins to decline, only to rise once more with the outbreak of the Franco-German War, and production movements pursue a similar path. Developments after the war portray the familiar pattern: a decline to the '90s, with an upward movement thereafter, terminating in the first half of the 1900–10 decade, as with a number of other series.

The secondary variations in prices are, as indicated above, similar to those in crops. There is a sharp drop after 1815, obviously a post-war deflation, thence a slow decline to the beginning of the '30s, with a succeeding rising movement. This reaches its highest point about 1857, but continues on to 1870–73. From that time the usual decline to the '90s appears, with the subsequent rise. It should be noticed that this later and considerable upward movement in prices after the '90s is accompanied by a slow decline in the growth of the volume of crops.

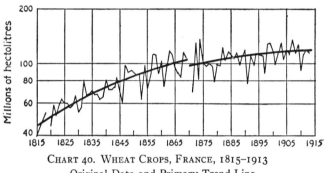

CHART 40. WHEAT CROPS, FRANCE, 1815–1913
Original Data and Primary Trend Line

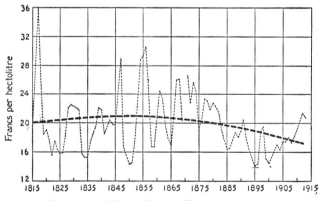

CHART 40a. WHEAT PRICES, FRANCE, 1815–1913
Original Data and Primary Trend Line

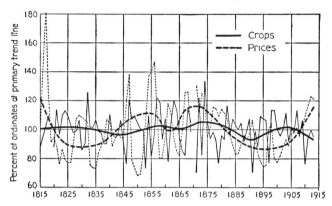

CHART 40b. WHEAT, CROPS AND PRICES, FRANCE, 1815–1913
Relative Deviations from Primary Trend Lines

The cyclical fluctuations both in crops and prices are conspicuous. The cycles in prices are less broken than those in crops, and appear to precede the latter in a number of instances. Otherwise the correlation is positive, although not very close, owing to the difference in duration.

41. *Coal, France.* This series dates back to 1811, giving us one of the longest descriptions available. It was found possible to treat the data as continuous throughout, because with the slow spread of mining technique in France the loss of the provinces after 1870 was a loss of potential coal wealth rather than of coal actually produced. The logistic curve fitted offers a rather good description of the long-time changes as they developed over the 103 years.

In the secondary secular variations we observe a good correspondence between production and prices. In prices, the movement declines from 1811 to the second half of the '40s. The same tendency may be observed in output, but in that instance the marked decline ceases after 1820, when, no doubt, with the restoration of normal conditions and the raising of tariff barriers (mainly against England) the pressure of English competition was not so severe as immediately after the Napoleonic Wars.[1] The next marked decline in

[1] I. H. Clapham: *Economic Development of France and Germany, 1815–1914*, Cambridge University Press, 1923, p. 233.

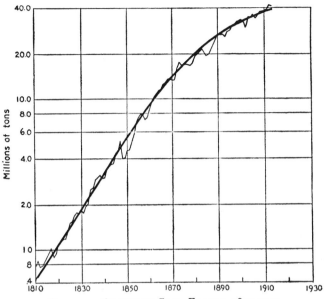

CHART 41. OUTPUT OF COAL, FRANCE, 1810–1913
Original Data and Primary Trend Line

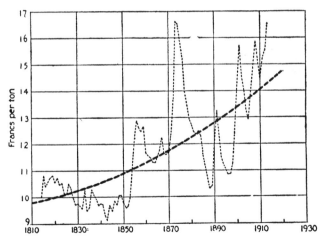

CHART 41a. AVERAGE PRICE OF COAL, FRANCE, 1814–1913
Original Data and Primary Trend Line

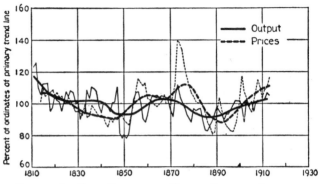

CHART 41b. COAL, OUTPUT AND PRICES, FRANCE, 1810–1913
Relative Deviations from Primary Trend Lines

production appears in 1848–52 and is associated with the
political disorders of the time. The price movement turns
upward at the end of the '40s. Output recovered with the
cessation of political troubles, and proceeds upward until
the middle of the '60s. These 20 to 25 years during the
building of the railway system (completed about 1855–60)
mark a period of accelerated growth in French industry.

While the price movement starts downward in the late
'50s, output turns downward in the '60s, and continues its
course through the Franco-Prussian War years down to the
second half of the '80s. The price movement, of course,
turns upward in the '70s, because of the war, and resumes
its decline only in the second half of that decade. Its downward movement therefore comes later than that of output
and terminates later; namely, in the first half of the '90s.
After the '90s, correspondence between the secondary trend
lines in production and prices is rather close. On the whole,
there is fair correlation between these movements throughout the length of the series, with the divergences accounted
for largely by wars and to some extent by tariffs.

The cyclical fluctuations in output are regular. In prices
there is the curious phenomenon of intensified fluctuations
after 1850, the cycles up to that date being very mild. Correlation between the cycles is close, those in prices lagging
behind output.

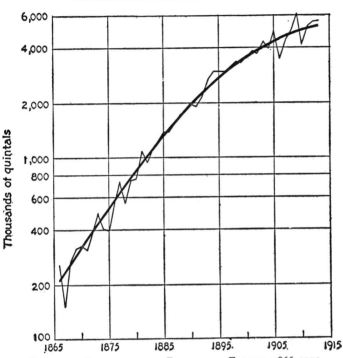

CHART 42. CONSUMPTION OF PETROLEUM, FRANCE, 1866–1913
Original Data and Primary Trend Line

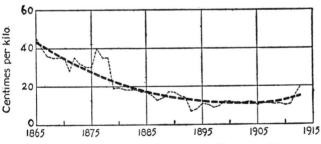

CHART 42a. PRICES OF CRUDE PETROLEUM, FRANCE, 1865–1913
Original Data and Primary Trend Line

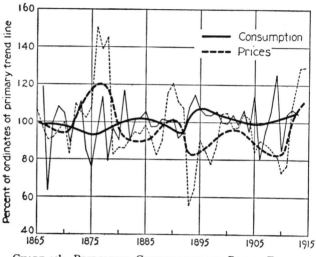

CHART 42b. PETROLEUM, CONSUMPTION AND PRICES, FRANCE,
1866–1913
Relative Deviations from Primary Trend Lines

42. *Petroleum, France.* The data used in this case refer
to the consumption of petroleum (both crude and products)
and were obtained by subtracting the exports from the
imports. The series goes back to 1866, when petroleum was
first used. The logistic curve fitted describes admirably the
long-time changes over the 48 years covered.

The secondary secular variations in consumption are
comparatively insignificant. It is interesting to note that
they do not in any way reflect the movements in petroleum
prices (except possibly inversely), but rather the general
changes in growth of the nation's economic life. After a
slight decline in the '60s, the movement tends gradually
upward to the first half of the '80s, a period of accelerated
growth of industry in France. After that, again as a reflection of the general movements, there is a decline to the '90s.
The exact reason for the appreciable rise immediately
following cannot be pointed to with assurance, but the
pronounced tariff reduction of 1893 may be cited. Thence
follows a decline to about 1903 accompanied by an upward

movement in prices. The succeeding rise to 1911 is partly explained by the large imports of 1909, occasioned by the fear that the general tariff schedules would be applied to the American imports.[1]

In studying the secondary movements in prices one notices their close correlation (after the '70s) with the movements in the American prices, and their inverse relationship with the secondary variations in French consumption. After a slight decline in the '60s, the movement turns abruptly upward in the '70s, a result of general monetary inflation in the country. The succeeding sharp drop to the '80s patterns the secondary movement in price for the same series in the United States, and is connected with the overproduction at that time of the American wells. The following recovery to the beginning of the '90s is also similar to that in the United States, just as are the rise to 1901 and the movements which follow. With nearly every movement in prices, the variation in consumption tended in the opposite direction. Whether this relationship is fortuitous or whether it marks a case of elastic demand it is impossible to say.

The cyclical fluctuations are quite regular both in consumption and prices. Here we observe rather good positive correlation, on the whole, synchronous.

43. *Pig Iron, France.* This is another long series which describes the output of a most important branch of industry. It may be taken continuously throughout the entire period, for in the regions lost to France after 1870 the pig-iron industry was not appreciably developed. The logistic curve fits the data fairly well, although leaving room for considerable secondary secular movements.

In the production series these secondary secular movements resemble those for coal output, except that the swings are still more accentuated. There is a decline to the '30s, with a considerable rise following to the second half of the '40s. The break in 1848–52 is again due to political disorders. The subsequent acceleration, the result of the resumption of railroad construction, follows a rising movement in prices. The peak of this upward movement in production

[1] A. Levy: *La Commerce et l'Industrie de Petrole en France*, Paris, 1923, p. 34.

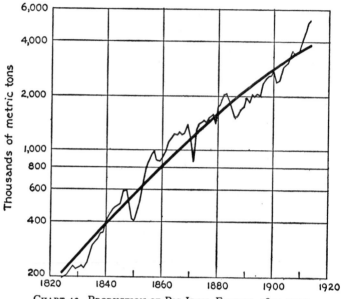

CHART 43. PRODUCTION OF PIG IRON, FRANCE, 1824–1913
Original Data and Primary Trend Line

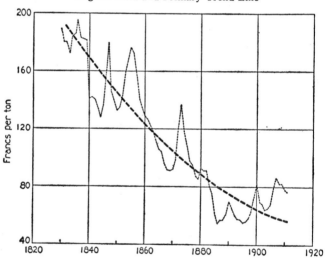

CHART 43a. AVERAGE PRICE OF PIG IRON, FRANCE, 1830–1915
Original Data and Primary Trend Line

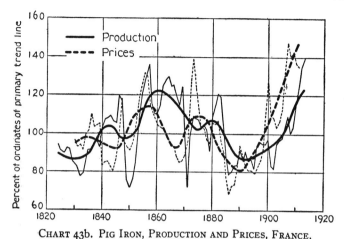

CHART 43b. PIG IRON, PRODUCTION AND PRICES, FRANCE,
1824–1913
Relative Deviations from Primary Trend Lines

occurs about 1860; in prices a year or two earlier. From
then on, the secondary variation in production is declining
to the first half of the '90s, with a temporary recovery in
the decade 1873–83, portraying with a certain lag the movements in prices. After 1890 the movement in production
proceeds steadily upward.

The secondary movements in prices, as pointed out above,
are similar to those in production, occurring either syn-
chronously with the latter or preceding them. The movement is downward to the first half of the '40s and upward to
the second half of the '50s. The rather conspicuous decline,
which then sets in, is interrupted by an abrupt rise after
1870, which is, however, very brief. The course thence is
downward to 1890, and sharply upward after that date. On
the whole, the correlation of secondary variations in prices
and production is very good.

In the cyclical fluctuations we also observe a close correlation between prices and production. It is positive and, on
the whole, simultaneous.

44. *Steel, France.* In this case the data go back to 1870,
and give the output of steel products (rails, plates, bars,

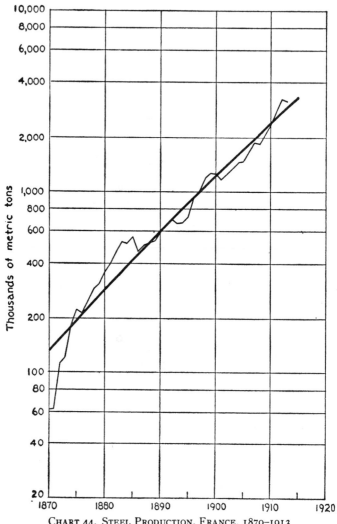

CHART 44. STEEL PRODUCTION, FRANCE, 1870–1913
Original Data and Primary Trend Line

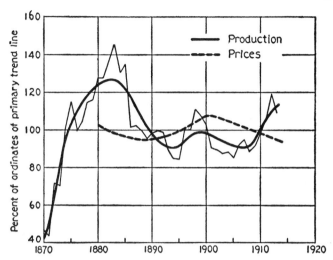

CHART 44b. STEEL PRODUCTION, FRANCE, AND STEEL PRICES,
BELGIUM, 1870–1913
Relative Deviations from Primary Trend Lines

etc.). The Gompertz curve presents a fairly good description of the long-time changes.

As Clapham records, the output of Bessemer steel in France had reached over 100,000 tons by 1869, and in output of steel and wrought iron combined France was then second only to the United Kingdom. But the Franco-Prussian War and its consequences greatly altered this situation. Thus the secondary movement in production starts at a very low point, and rises rapidly to the first half of the '80s. In this and in the decline toward the middle of the '90s, the steel industry patterns the movements observed in other branches of production. In the succeeding period, however, it shows a development different from other industries, but similar to that of steel production in Belgium and Germany. There is a rapid rise toward 1900, thence a decline to about 1908, and an apparent rise subsequently.

For the purpose of comparison we charted the secondary movements in steel prices for Belgium. (French prices are available only from 1900.) Chart 44b reveals a fairly good

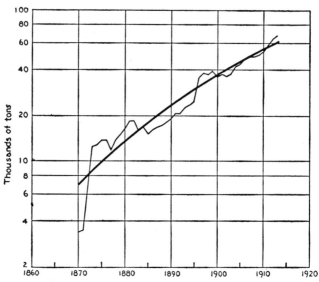

CHART 45. CRUDE ZINC PRODUCTION, FRANCE, 1870–1913
Original Data and Primary Trend Line

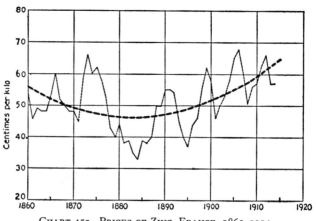

CHART 45a. PRICES OF ZINC, FRANCE, 1860–1914
Original Data and Primary Trend Line

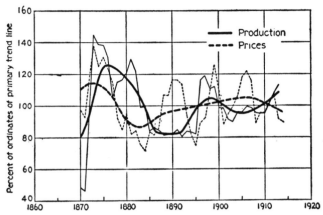

CHART 45b. ZINC, PRODUCTION AND PRICES, FRANCE, 1870–1913
Relative Deviations from Primary Trend Lines

correspondence of the movements in prices and production, except for the discrepancy after 1907–09 which was observed in an analogous comparison for the steel industries of Belgium and Germany.

The cyclical fluctuations in steel production are clear-cut. They reveal a very good correlation with the cycles in Belgian steel prices, with the latter tending to lag.

45. *Zinc, France.* The zinc smelting industry may be said to have begun in France in 1870, when the separation from Belgium stimulated the development of domestic manufacture. To the series, which extends back to 1870, a Gompertz curve was fitted (as to all the series for zinc production). It offers a fairly good description of the long-time changes for the 45 years taken.

In its secondary movements zinc production follows a course similar to steel output. A considerable rise to the first half of the '70s appears, with an immediately following decline, evidently a result of the resumption of foreign competition and a reflection of an analogous movement in prices. The decline continues until about 1890, after which the movement repeats the variations for steel: a vigorous upward movement in the second half of the '90s, a decline to about 1905–07, and a rise thereafter.

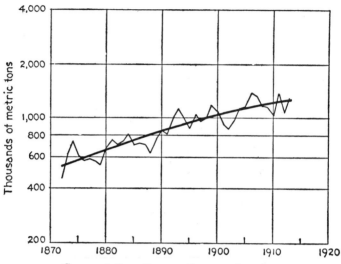

CHART 46. SALT OUTPUT, FRANCE, 1872–1913
Original Data and Primary Trend Line

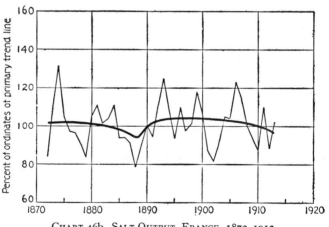

CHART 46b. SALT OUTPUT, FRANCE, 1872–1913
Relative Deviations from Primary Trend Line

The movements in prices were, on the whole, similar: they rise in the '70s and subsequently decline. But this downward movement terminates about 1885, i.e., about five years earlier than in production, and thence a slow upward variation toward 1905–07 occurs, interrupted by considerable cyclical fluctuations. Prices were controlled mainly by the Continental zinc syndicates, established about 1885. The only considerable divergence between the movements of prices and production is after 1905–07, when production accelerates while prices show a declining secondary variation.

There is a fairly good correspondence of the cycles in production and prices, the latter tending to lag, especially in the first half of the series.

46. *Salt output, France.* This series presents the output of marine and mineral salt from 1872. The logistic curve yields an excellent description of the long-time movements.

The secondary variations are comparatively mild. No specific explanations for their peculiar character can be given, nor are corresponding prices available. The course of movements is somewhat similar to the usual one, but precedes the latter by a five to seven year period. The series is one of those in which we are unable to account for the secondary secular variations because of the lack of other data.

The five series commented on below are included in our study in order to make more thorough comparisons between long-time changes in the same industry for different countries. In addition to the series for the five countries heretofore surveyed, these series cover branches of production in other countries for which data are available over a long period.

47. *Wheat crops, Australia.* The data for the volume of wheat crops in Australia go back to 1860 and are given annually from 1875. A logistic curve was fitted to the series. It yields a satisfactory description of the changes through the 60 years, although it leaves room for rather considerable secondary movements.

In order to explain the latter, we plotted on the same chart the secondary variations in wheat prices in the United

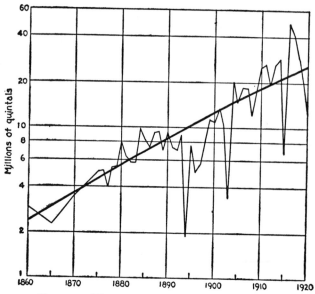

CHART 47. WHEAT CROPS, AUSTRALIA, 1860–1920
Original Data and Primary Trend Line

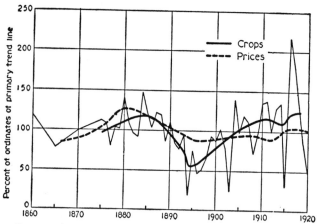

CHART 47b. WHEAT CROPS, AUSTRALIA, AND WHEAT PRICES,
UNITED STATES, 1860–1920
Relative Deviations from Primary Trend Lines

States, on the supposition that these variations in the American prices are quite similar to those in the English, Australian, or whatever prices at which Australian wheat was being sold. The chart shows a remarkably close correlation between these movements in crops and prices, the latter tending to precede somewhat the former. There is in both an upward movement to the '80s, in prices toward 1880, in crops to about 1884. After that there is a decline to 1895, and thence a rise in the movements of crops to 1910, in prices to about 1907. After a temporary retardation in both, they picture the war rise and decline. The correspondence, on the whole, is nearly perfect.

We did not extend the comparison to cyclical fluctuations, for in this case we can hardly expect a close correlation of American prices with those at which the Australian crop was sold.

48. *Wheat crops, Argentine.* Argentine is another important source of the international wheat supply. The data, however, are available only from 1881. A logistic curve was fitted to the series, yielding a fairly good description of the long-time changes for the 40 years covered.

The secondary secular movements are considerable, and show, on the whole, a rough similarity to those observed in Australia and the United States. There is the decline from the '80s, only it terminates somewhat earlier than in the other countries, i.e., in 1890 and not about 1895. From 1890 a vigorous upward movement toward 1910 ensues, repeating the variations in production and prices for other countries. The subsequent decline continues through the war, for while the war occasioned higher international prices for wheat, it cut off the supply of labor and capital from Argentine and retarded the vigorous peace-time growth.[1] Recovery sets in at the end of the war. On the whole, then, there is considerable correlation between these secondary movements in wheat crops and prices in Argentine and those for other countries.

49. *Wheat crops, Japan.* In this series the Japanese wheat crop is given beginning with 1877. This branch of produc-

---

[1] O. A. Krause: *Argentiniens Wirtschaft während d. Weltkrieges,* Berlin, 1919, pp. 93–94.

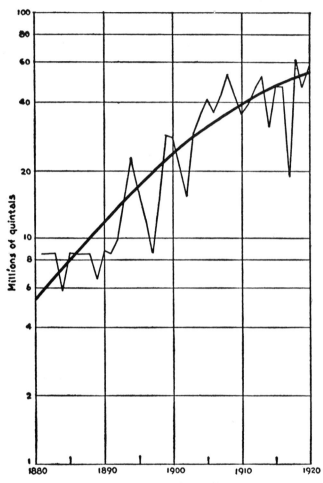

CHART 48. WHEAT CROPS, ARGENTINE, 1881–1920
Original Data and Primary Trend Line

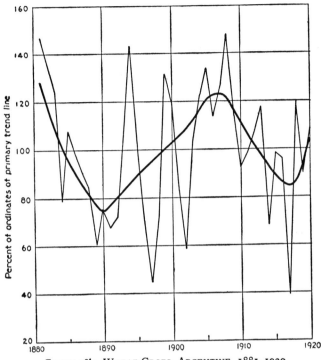

CHART 48b. WHEAT CROPS, ARGENTINE, 1881–1920
Relative Deviations from Primary Trend Line

tion appears to be slowing up considerably in its rate of growth, and the logistic curve fitted yields a close description of the long-time changes.

In the secondary movements we find peculiarities to which we can only point without offering explanation, because we lack pertinent information. The series fails to show the appreciable drop in the '90s present in most of the others, but it displays a considerable decline in the decade 1900–10. Whether this decline was due to the Russo-Japanese War, we cannot tell. The marked acceleration during 1915–20 may, however, be safely ascribed to the World War.

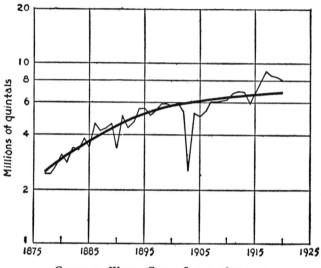

CHART 49. WHEAT CROPS, JAPAN, 1877–1920
Original Data and Primary Trend Line

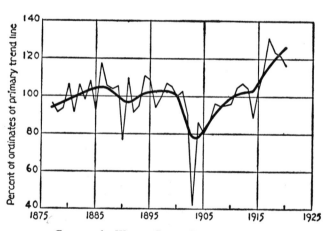

CHART 49b. WHEAT CROPS, JAPAN, 1877–1920
Relative Deviations from Primary Trend Line

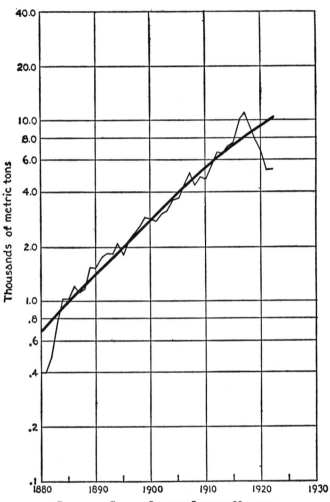

CHART 50. COPPER OUTPUT, JAPAN, 1881–1922
Original Data and Primary Trend Line

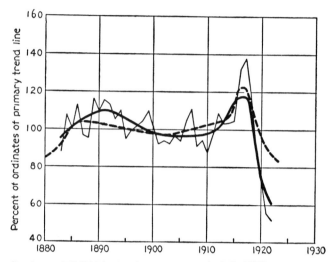

CHART 50b. COPPER OUTPUT, JAPAN (——), AND COPPER OUTPUT, UNITED STATES (————), 1879–1922
Relative Deviations from Primary Trend Lines

50. *Copper output, Japan.* This series extends back to 1879. The logistic curve describes the long-time movements rather well.

The secondary variations are similar to those for the United States, but lag behind the latter by three to four years. We find here the same rise to the '90s, the slow decline to the 1900–10 decade, thence a slow recovery accelerated tremendously during the period of the late war. This marked similarity of the secondary movements with those for the United States suggests a close connection between these two national branches of the copper industry.

51. *Copper output, Canada.* This series begins with the intensive modern development of the copper industry and the logistic curve describes rather well its rapid growth in Canada.

The secondary secular movements in production seem to be a magnified replica of those for the United States. There is the same strong upward swing to the beginning of the '90s and a decline to the latter part of that decade. The

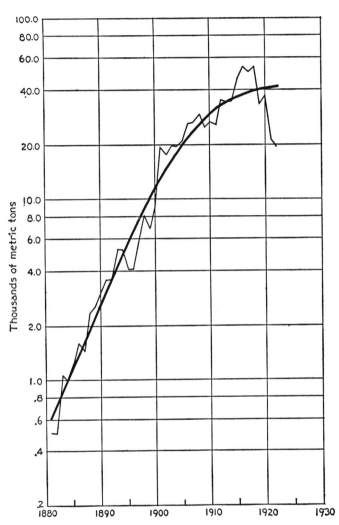

CHART 51. COPPER OUTPUT, CANADA, 1881–1922
Original Data and Primary Trend Line

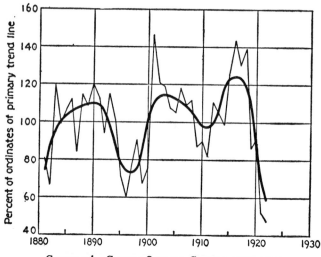

CHART 51b. COPPER OUTPUT, CANADA, 1881–1922
Relative Deviations from Primary Trend Line

industry shows, however, a pronounced swing during 1900–
10. The variations thereafter reflect the effects of the war
demand, observed in all other national branches of the copper industry.

Cases in which the secular movements show a decline in
absolute terms differ essentially from those we have been
studying. We have seen above that in order to formulate
a curve of a logical character that would describe such cases,
we must make additional assumptions, and that the resulting curves are somewhat more complicated than those for
the rising trend lines. This loss of simplicity, both in a
logical and technical sense, prevents us from exploiting the
results of the statistical analysis as fully as we exploit the
much more numerous series of a growing character.

For this reason the statistical procedure applied to declining series covers only the first two steps, i.e., it is limited to
fitting the primary secular trend line and to ascertaining the
first deviations. The line of secondary movements is not
determined exactly, but its course is obvious from a cursory

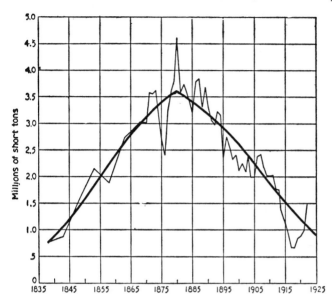

CHART 52. TONNAGE OF FREIGHT MOVED ON THE ERIE CANAL,
1837–1922

Original Data and Primary Trend Line

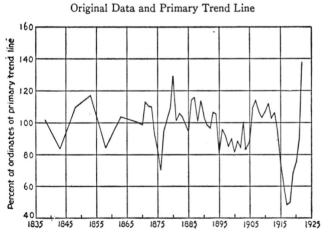

CHART 52b. TONNAGE OF FREIGHT MOVED ON THE ERIE CANAL,
1837–1922

Relative Deviations from Primary Trend Lines

inspection of the broken line of first deviations. It must be added that the number of declining series investigated is rather small, for we can utilize only data which exhibit a decline for a considerable number of years, and not many such series are available. The number taken is, however, ample to indicate the pertinence and possibility of applying a logical assumption curve to the long-time process of economic decay.

The brief comments which accompany the charts (there are two charts for each series) relate to the goodness of fit obtained and to the character of the secondary secular movements.

52. *Tonnage of traffic, Erie Canal, 1836–1925*. Here we have a characteristic case of rise and decline, the latter caused by railroad competition. The peak of development was reached about 1880. The curve fitted to the data is the simple logistic in the positive part, and the inverted logistic to the decline. The fit as may be seen is admirable. The presentation of the series on a log scale would only accentuate the closeness of fit.

The secondary movements, easily discerned on Chart 52a, seem to follow the general course for industries in the United States, with the exception of the World War period. There is a rise in the '50s, and a decline in connection with the Civil War. Thence occurs the commonly observed upward movement to the '80s and a decline to the second half of the '90s. Succeeding developments pursue the familiar course, except for the decline in 1915–18.

53. *Increase in railroad net, United States, 1831–1922.* This series was included mainly because Professor Wesley C. Mitchell considered it a typical example of a declining industry. The difficulty with it as taken is that it contains negative items in 1918–19, when the mileage instead of increasing was diminishing. The positive part is a typical logistic curve case; the trend on a log scale is at first a straight line, and then slopes up to a level limit. To the declining phase we fitted an inverted logistic curve with an additional constant. It may be seen to fit the data rather closely. The secondary variations were not plotted separately, but from Chart 53 it may be observed that they would follow the usual course,

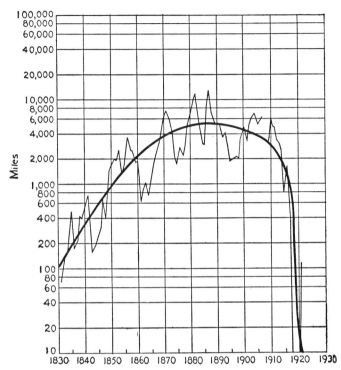

CHART 53. NUMBER OF RAILROAD MILES ADDED ANNUALLY,
UNITED STATES, 1831–1922
Original Data and Primary Trend Line

i.e., decline from the '80s to the second half of the '90s and
then rise to about 1910, declining again during the war
period. This case shows that the inverted logistic curve
with the added constant is very elastic, and that it can
describe a decline of any degree of abruptness.

54. *Copper output, United Kingdom.* This is another case
of an extreme decline, but here it prevails over a much
longer period than in the series for the railroad net, thus
presenting a more severe test of the curve. The one fitted
is an inverted logistic with an added constant. In this case,
as in all others, the limit is chosen by inspection, and the

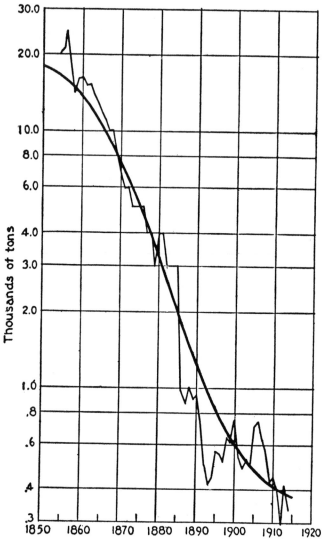

CHART 54. COPPER OUTPUT, UNITED KINGDOM, 1854–1914
Original Data and Primary Trend Line

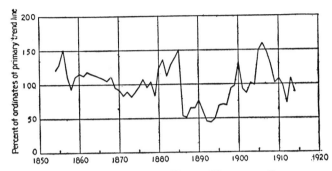

CHART 54b. COPPER OUTPUT, UNITED KINGDOM, 1854–1914
Relative Deviations from Primary Trend Line

other constants fitted by the method of selected points. The fit is good.

In the secondary movements we recognize the course familiar to us from the other series. After a decline to the beginning of the '70s, there is a rise to the '80s protracted by peculiar developments in the world copper market. Thence occurs a decline to the '90s, with a rise to the end of the first decade of the twentieth century, followed by a downward movement similar to that in many other industries.

55. *Lead output, United Kingdom, 1854–1915.* This is another instance of a decline extending over 63 years. The

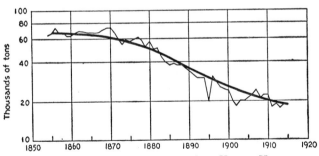

CHART 55. LEAD OUTPUT, DOMESTIC ORE, UNITED KINGDOM,
1854–1914
Original Data and Primary Trend Line

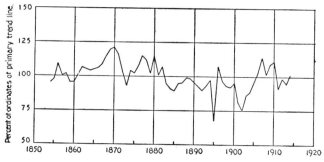

CHART 55b. LEAD OUTPUT, UNITED KINGDOM, 1854–1914
Relative Deviations from Primary Trend Line

curve fitted, a logistic with an additional constant, yields an admirable fit.

The secondary variations (Chart 55b) follow approximately the course of copper output, but precede it in the upward movement during the decades 1860 to 1880 and in the decline to the '90s which follows. After the '90s there is again the rise to the end of the 1900–10 decade, with a downward turn thereafter.

56. *Tonnage of sailing vessels, entered and cleared, France, 1845–1915.* In this series we find both a phase of development and of decline. The peak of growth appears about 1870, after which a slow decay sets in. The curve fitted to

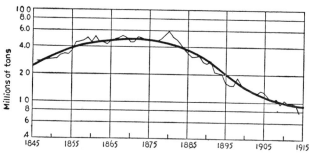

CHART 56. TONNAGE OF SAILING SHIPS, ENTERED AND CLEARED, PORTS OF FRANCE, 1847–1914
Original Data and Primary Trend Line

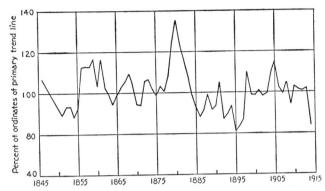

CHART 56b. TONNAGE OF SAILING VESSELS, ENTERED AND CLEARED,
PORTS OF FRANCE, 1847–1914

Relative Deviations from Primary Trend Line

the rising phase is the ordinary logistic. The curve for the decline is a logistic having the same maximum limit, inverted, and with an additional constant. The fit is quite close.

The secondary variations appear to follow the usual course, except for the decline to the '70s followed by a belated rise to the '80s, a movement probably associated with the Franco-Prussian War. Thence the movements repeat the familiar decline to the '90s, the rise to the second half of the 1900–10 decade, and the downward trend thereafter.

57. *Zinc ore output, Belgium, 1840–1913.* During these 74 years the industry was growing only for about 16 years. For the other 60 years or so, it exhibits a steady and considerable decline. The curves fitted are the positive logistic and the inverted logistic, the latter without an added constant. The fit obtained may be seen to be fairly good.

The path of the secondary variations is somewhat peculiar. True, there is the usual decline at the end of the '50s and the rise to the '70s, but the subsequent recovery appears very early, namely, in the beginning of the '80s. And all the succeeding movements precede the usual course by at least a decade.

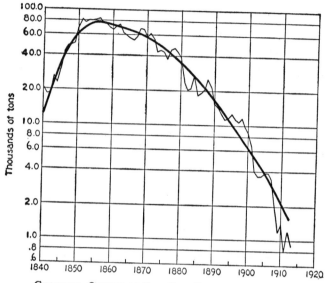

CHART 57. OUTPUT OF ZINC ORE, BELGIUM, 1840–1913
Original Data and Primary Trend Line

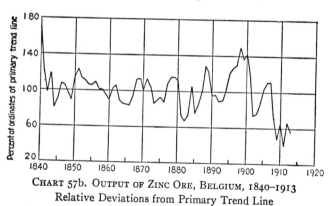

CHART 57b. OUTPUT OF ZINC ORE, BELGIUM, 1840–1913
Relative Deviations from Primary Trend Line

We have now completed our survey of the data and are ready to draw our first tentative conclusions. Before we do so, however, let us note certain peculiarities of the work.

It must first be remarked that the 57 series presented are

practically all of the significant series reviewed for analysis. Of the few important series omitted only one or two showed long-time movements that grew with an undiminished rate of growth, and thus could not be described by either the logistic or the Gompertz curves. It was felt, however, that even in these cases, were a longer period of time taken, the picture would agree with the observations recorded in so many branches of economic activity. The survey presented is therefore comprehensive, in the sense that there was no biased choosing of series merely because they could be well described by the curves with whose assumptions the investigation started.

On the other hand, reservations must be made concerning the attempted explanations of the secondary variations. It is obvious that in order to explain these fully and thoroughly, one would have to go deeply into the history of each specific industry and take into account the numerous influences which shaped the movements in each particular decade. But such an intensive investigation was not feasible within the limits of the present study, and the comments made present but the more obvious factors, which might account for the specific character of the secondary secular movements. No claim for exhaustive treatment is made, and in a few cases no explanation could be advanced for lack of relevant information. This leaves us in a mood of hesitancy concerning the complete validity of the secondary variations, i.e., as to the thoroughness of the agreement of the results of the statistic analysis with the findings of our historical knowledge.

With this reservation in mind we may set forth the rather clear conclusions of our statistical survey. We have found that:

1. The simple logistic and Gompertz curves, mostly the former, describe well the long-time movements of growing industries, and, with certain modifications, those of declining industries.

2. The secondary secular variations in production are in most cases similar to those in prices, the latter following a rather general course in agreement with the well-known historical periods of the rise and fall in the general price

level. The specific movements in production are usually confirmed by the history of the industry.

3. The elimination of the primary and secondary secular movements leaves clear-cut cyclical fluctuations, which do not reveal (as a rule) any movement longer than that of the prevailing cycle.

The significance of the first conclusion should be made clear to prevent overvaluation. The good description of the series yielded by the logistic and Gompertz curves should not lead one to infer that they are the only ones that yield such description, that they embody the law of growth and are for that or for some other reason the superior forecasting curves. In forming a good description of the long-time movements, these curves only corroborate the general assumption concerning the decline in the percentage rate of industrial growth (within specific industries) and lend some weight to the hypothesis which makes this decline a function of the level attained and of a finite limit. The conclusion of the statistical analysis supports therefore only a limited historical generalization. But the specific constants arrived at in the process of fitting have in themselves scarcely any forecasting value, nor are the forms of the equations to be treated as expressions of 'a law of growth.'

While the description of primary secular changes by a mathematical curve has significance only as a generalization covering a limited past, the separation itself of the total secular movement into primary and secondary appears to be of the utmost significance. It distinguishes movements and groups of forces, which must be distinguished, if an understanding of the nature and bearing of long-time movements is to be attained. It may be that the curves chosen to describe the primary movements are too simple. It is quite possible that future investigators will find the methods of determining secondary variations used here as too rough. But some separation of the total long-time movements into their constituent parts similar to the primary and secondary, as defined above, is clearly necessary if the investigator is interested in the secular movements themselves.

This completes our discussion of the primary secular movements, although the materials presented invite further study. We could compare the lines of percentage increase derived from the primary secular trend lines for various branches of industry in different countries, and probably learn a great deal more about the processes of industrial development. But it was found advisable for technical reasons to confine the discussion only to the general traits of the phenomena studied, and thus to defer the more detailed treatment to some future time.

We are now ready to take up the nature and mechanism of the secondary secular movements.[1]

[1] The tables of series on which are based the charts and the discussion in chapter III will be found at the end of the book. These tables give the original data, the primary and secondary trend ordinates, and the deviations. Each table is accompanied by the equation of the primary trend line and by an indication of the sources from which the original data were taken.

CHAPTER IV

THE NATURE OF
SECONDARY SECULAR MOVEMENTS

The correlation between secondary movements in production and prices. The precedence of the price movements. The average duration of the swings.

The explanation of the movements in production, those in prices being taken for granted. The decline in the purchasing power of wage rates; the rise in profits — both during an upward secondary movement in prices. How can production of consumers' goods accelerate under these conditions? Tentative answer: larger employment, diminution in savings, larger stocks, etc.

The factors tending to carry forward a price increase. The lag of production movements behind price movements. The 'gestation' period. The disparity in movements between producers' and consumers' goods industries.

The retarding factors. The decline in the productivity of labor. The diminishing output of monetary metals and of metals entering circulation.

Are the secondary secular movements 'major cycles'? Limitations of the discussion in the chapter.

Appendix A: Note on the Studies of Major Cycles.

Appendix B: Comparative Amplitude of Secondary Secular Movements in Industries Producing Producers' and Consumers' Goods.

BEFORE we discuss the nature of the secondary secular movements and the mechanism by which they are brought about, we must consider more carefully and at greater length than we have thus far, the results of the statistical analysis of the series. We saw in Chapter III that the lines of secondary variations in production and prices for a commodity reveal a fairly good correlation in most cases. It was also pointed out that certain factors such as wars, trust policies, and radical inventions interrupted and disturbed this concomitance of the secondary movements and frequently accounted for the changes peculiar to production or to prices alone.

In the table below we attempt to summarize the results of the statistical analysis which bears upon correlation between the secondary movements in production and prices. The characterization of the correlation is in terms of 'good,' 'fair,' and 'poor,' and the classification of every particular pair of series is based upon inspection of the charts. Of course, such characterization can be only approximate, and the whole method is one of arbitrary rule of thumb. But it must be remembered that in the determination of the lines of secondary movements there was a considerable element of arbitrariness. Consequently, it would be incongruous to apply exact methods for computing a coefficient of correlation. We must satisfy ourselves with rough characterizations, our check always being the chart itself. The critical reader may turn back to the chart and see for himself whether the characterization of the correlation in the table is suitable. Our method is to be preferred to the laborious and exact methods for ascertaining the coefficient of correlation in the cases we are dealing with.

The results of the characterization are as follows:

1. Tabular Summary of the Correlation of Secondary Movements in Production and Prices

Number of Series	Character of Correlation	Secondary Movement which Precedes
1	fair	production
2	fair (except during the war)	production
3	good	prices
4	poor until the first half of the '90s	undetermined
5	good	prices
6	good	prices
7	poor until the first half of the '90s, fair thereafter	undetermined
8	good	prices
9	poor until the first half of the '90s, good thereafter	undetermined
10	poor	
11	fair	undetermined
12	good	production
13	good	prices
14	fair	prices
15	poor until the first half of the '90s, fair thereafter	production
16	fair to poor	prices
17	good	clearings
22	good	simultaneous
23	fair to good	undetermined

Number of Series	Character of Correlation	Secondary Movement which Precedes
24	fair	prices
26	good	prices
27	fair	prices
28	fair	simultaneous
29	fair to good	production
30	fair	undetermined
31	poor to fair	
32	fair	undetermined
33	poor	
34	fair	prices
35	good	simultaneous
36	good	prices
37	fair to good	prices
38	poor	
39	good	undetermined
40	fair	prices
41	good	prices
42	poor	
43	good	prices
45	fair	undetermined
47	good	prices

It may be seen from this table that of the 40 series for which comparison of the secondary movements in production and prices is possible, 15 show good correlation, 4 (United States series) show lack of it during the first half of the period, 15 show fair correlation, and only 6 no positive correlation at all. Such a bare summary as presented in the table, however, underestimates the degree of significant connection. We have found time and again that there is a definite explanation for the lack of correlation. Nevertheless, such instances are recorded in the table as unconnected. On the other hand, in this rough estimate of the character of correlation, a single discrepancy will be hidden by the majority of concurrent swings. As it stands, the table reveals significant correlation, and accepting this fact, let us further examine it, in order to determine the nature and mechanism of these major swings in prices and production.

There arises first the question regarding lag and precedence. Do prices precede production in these secondary movements, or do they lag as in most of the cyclical fluctuations? The third column of the above table gives a first approximate answer. Of 34 series which reveal sufficient correlation for the observer to judge regarding the time sequence of the movements, 17 series or exactly one half show prices preceding. Eight series are marked as indeterminate, which means that the time sequence shifts without indicating a preponderance of lag for either prices or production. In three cases the correlation is simultaneous, and only in six does production definitely precede prices in the secondary movements. Of these six cases one is that for bank clearings.

This characterization of the time sequence is, however, too rough. One more exact may be arrived at, if we date the peaks and the troughs of the secondary movements and compare the contiguous point of time for production and prices. Of course, even in this procedure, there is an arbitrary element in the choice of swings, which are recognized as correlated and thus compared as to their timing.

We have dated altogether 89 pairs of turning points in production and prices. Their distribution into pertinent groups is shown in the following table.

2. DISTRIBUTION OF TURNING POINTS (PAIRS — PRODUCTION-PRICES) IN THE SECONDARY MOVEMENTS

	Revivals			Recessions			Both		
	Production Precedes	Prices Precede	Simultaneous	Production Precedes	Prices Precede	Simultaneous	Production Precedes	Prices Precede	Simultaneous
Absolute numbers.......	10	26	8	16	23	6	26	49	14
Per cent of total.......	23	59	18	36	51	13	29	55	16
Average discrepancy in years. ...	3.3	4.7		2.4	3.5		2.7	4.1	

It should be noticed that in the recession group there are a number of cases in which the production movement precedes prices in the down-turn from the high levels caused by the World War. This reduces the significance of the 16 cases in this group. But even as they stand the figures show a definite tendency on the part of the secondary movements in prices to precede those in production, this tendency being especially conspicuous in revivals.

Granted that there exists significant correlation between the secondary movements in production and prices, and that prices tend to precede production in these variations, what is the period of time occupied by such swings?

In measuring the duration of the swings, we have dealt with upward and downward movements and not with a complete swing. An upward or downward movement was counted as separate, if it was longer than the average cycle in the series (or in the neighborhood of that swing, if the duration of the cycles changed appreciably with time). The upward movement was counted from a point after the trough to the last highest point inclusive; the downward, from its highest point to its lowest inclusive. Incomplete movements (at the ends of the series) were counted separately, but were not taken if shorter in length than the average cycle for the series.

The frequency distribution of these upward and downward movements by their duration is given in the two following tables.

3. FREQUENCY DISTRIBUTION OF PERIODS OF RISE AND FALL IN THE SECONDARY SECULAR MOVEMENTS

Years	Production Series					
	United States		Other Countries		Total	
	Not including incomplete	Including all	Not including incomplete	Including all	Not including incomplete	Including all
3– 5......	7	13	5	7	12	20
6– 8......	20	28	20	24	40	52
9–11......	24	32	9	16	33	48
12–14......	13	21	13	18	26	39
15–17......	6	9	10	16	16	25
18–20......	2	3	3	7	5	10
21–23......	1	1	5	7	6	8
24–26......	0	1	1	3	1	4
27–29......	0	0	2	2	2	2
30–32......	0	0	0	1	0	1
33–35......	0	0	0	1	0	1
Total.....	73	108	68	102	141	210
Average..	10.9	10.1	12.2	13.0	11.1	11.6

The distribution for the price series yields approximately the same results.

4. FREQUENCY DISTRIBUTION OF PERIODS OF RISE AND DECLINE IN THE SECONDARY SECULAR MOVEMENTS

Years	Price Series					
	United States		Other Countries		Total	
	Not in-cluding in-complete	Including all	Not in-cluding in-complete	Including all	Not in-cluding in-complete	Including all
3– 5....	12	16	3	7	15	23
6– 8....	15	23	13	19	28	42
9–11....	10	16	16	21	26	37
12–14....	14	17	11	15	25	32
15–17....	3	6	7	9	10	15
18–20....	2	2	3	6	5	8
21–23....	1	1	5	8	6	9
24–26....	1	1	6	7	7	8
27–29....	0	0	1	3	1	3
30–32....	0	0	1	2	1	2
Total...	58	82	66	97	124	179
Average	9.7	9.5	13.3	13.6	11.6	11.7

The distributions (see Charts 1 and 2) show a fairly regular shape in the total groups both for production and prices. In the price series, however, the distribution seems to be less

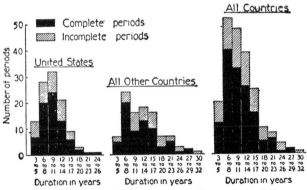

CHART 1. FREQUENCY DISTRIBUTION OF PERIODS OF RISE AND FALL IN THE SECONDARY SECULAR MOVEMENTS
Production Series

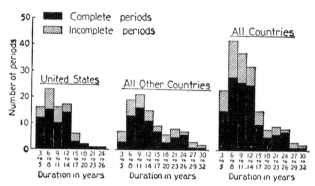

CHART 2. FREQUENCY DISTRIBUTION OF PERIODS OF RISE AND
FALL IN THE SECONDARY SECULAR MOVEMENTS

Price Series

homogeneous than in the production series. The averages
are, on the whole, fairly representative.

We thus obtain about 22 years as the duration of a complete swing for production and 23 years for prices. In the
United States the duration seems to have been smaller than
in European countries, but this difference is due mainly to
the fact that different periods of time were represented by
the two groups. In the European countries there are more
series that go back of 1860 than in the United States.

Thus we find these secondary variations in production and
prices substantially similar, of an average length of slightly
more than 20 years for a complete swing, and with a tendency for the price movements to precede those of production.
What are the factors that cause these variations, and what is
the nature of the mechanism underlying them?

In order to simplify the problem, let us assume the secondary movements in prices as given, and conceive them as the
moving cause. We have seen that in most cases the secondary variations in prices precede those in production. While
this is, of course, no proof that the movements in prices cause
the movements in production, we may make such an assumption as a temporary working hypothesis. The question then
may be formulated as follows: Why is it that with a con-

tinuous rise and fall in prices there is a continuous acceleration or retardation in the rate of growth of industrial output?

The question seems simple, but it is only superficially so.
The easiest answer is that when prices rise, the prospect of
profitable sales becomes brighter and increased production
results. But the rise of prices, which we are discussing, is not
the simple and immediate change from three to four dollars
for a unit of product. It is a drawn-out movement underlying and concealed by cyclical fluctuations and other disturbing changes. It is revealed only by long-range statistical
analysis, where the concept of the normal or the base from
which we measure is given a long-time significance. But to
the business man in his immediate experience price changes
are relative to prices current at a given moment of time, and
only such changes may be conceived as direct stimuli to an
increase of production. Prolonged price changes do not bear
upon the immediate activity of the business community and
cannot in themselves be taken as active causes to explain
the changes with which we are concerned.

In order to ascertain these causes and to be able to point
out the factors which immediately influence business activity
and in the longer run result in an acceleration or retardation
of an industry's growth, we must inquire more closely into
the effects of a secondary movement in prices on the distribution of the national product among the different economic
groups, as well as among the different groups of industries.
In considering the effects of a secondary movement in prices
on the distribution of the national product, we shall find
what happens to the relative shares of the national income,
and in the inquiry we shall see how the interaction of the
different groups within the economic system contributes to
the appearance of a prolonged rise or decline in the rate of
business activity.

It is a fairly well-established generalization in economic
theory that during a period of a long rise of prices, money
wages[1] lag behind the prices of commodities, both retail and
wholesale, so that real wages during such periods show a tend-

---

[1] In the present discussion we use money wages estimates corrected or
uncorrected for employment. It does not affect the argument concerning
the expected movement of profits.

ency to decline. On the other hand, in periods of falling prices, money wages do not decline so rapidly or so far as commodity prices and consequently real wages move upward. This refers, of course, to secondary movements in prices and wages, the underlying primary trend being left out of consideration.

Here we shall refer only briefly to the statistical evidence in support of this statement. The latest comprehensive calculation of an index of real wages in the United States is that of A. Hansen.[1] He surveys the period from 1820 to 1923 and arrives at the following conclusions:

With the exception of the decade of the seventies, real wages move inversely with the general price level. . . .

This relationship between real wages and price fluctuations holds true of both the major and minor movements. Five major price and wage movements are apparent. The tendency of real wages was upward from 1820 to 1849 while the trend of prices was downward. From 1849 to 1865 the general trend of prices was upward, and in this period real wages tended downward. From 1865 to 1897 the price trend was heavily downward while the real-wage movement was strongly upward. From 1897 to 1919 the general trend of prices was upward but real wages at first fell and then remained stationary. With the heavy fall in prices beginning with 1920, real wages rose sharply.[2]

Mr. Hansen also gives a brief sketch of how this happens:

If prices rise, the benefit accrues immediately to the entrepreneurial class. In time, however, competition among entrepreneurs compels them to bid up the prices paid for labor, land and capital until the surplus profits are absorbed. In the mean time, however, a fresh rise in prices has created a new margin of profits above costs. Entrepreneurs, naturally, do not pass on these gains to the other factors until compelled to do so by the pressure of competition. It is therefore inevitable that in rising-price periods wages and other costs should lag behind prices. . . .

Evidence for the same relationship between prices and real wages is available for the United Kingdom and France. A general index (that of G. H. Wood) of money wages, re-

[1] 'Factors Affecting the Trend of Real Wages,' *American Economic Review*, 1925, pp. 27–42.
[2] *Op. cit.*, p. 39.

tail prices, and real wages brought up to 1910 may be found in W. T. Layton's *An Introduction to the Study of Prices* (Macmillan, 1920), p. 184. The accompanying chart clearly shows that the rise in real wages was fastest during the three decades from 1870 to 1900, that is, when prices were on the whole declining. During the decades from 1850 to 1870 real wages in the United Kingdom were rising only very slowly, and in the first decade of the present century they were falling. But during this latter period the price movement was distinctly upward.

The same inverse relationship existed up to the '50s, as may be seen from the summary of Mr. Bowley.[1] In this table the following description is given:

Periods	Prices (Wholesale)	Real Wages
1790–1810	rising very fast	falling slowly
1810–1830	falling fast	rising slowly
1830–1852	falling slowly	rising slowly

It must be remarked, however, that the same table records positive correlation for a few of the periods.

For France there is available a general index of money wages by decades and later quinquennially, from 1806. We also have a cost of living index (food, rent, light and fuel) by decades since 1810. We are able therefore to compute an index of real wages. The data are taken from *Salaires et Coût d'Existence à diverses époques jusqu'en 1910*, Ministère de Travail et de la Prévoyance sociale (Paris, 1911), pp. 20 and 105.

5. MOVEMENT OF WAGES AND THE COST OF LIVING, FRANCE, 1810–1900

1900 = 100

Year	Money Wages	Cost of Living	Real Wages
1810	41	74	55
1820	43	80	54
1830	45	80	54
1840	48	83.5	54
1850	51	85.5	60
1860	60	95.5	63
1870	71	103	69
1880	82	110	75
1890	92	103	89
1900	100	100	100

[1] Layton, p. 185.

The underlying primary trend in real wages is very conspicuous and somewhat obscures the secondary movements. It is to be observed that real wages declined from 1810 to 1830, while prices, as indicated by the cost of living, were rising. From 1830 to 1840 prices appear to have been stable, but real wages rose. From 1840 to 1880 prices rose, and real wages rose, too, but in the latter we must distinguish the underlying primary trend from the shorter secondary variations. Thus while the greatest rise of prices was from 1850 to 1860, the rise in real wages during that time was only one half of the rise for the previous decade. From 1880 to 1900 prices were falling, while real wages increased and at a faster rate than formerly.

These data support the truth of the generalization that money wages do not rise so fast as the cost of living during periods of increasing prices, and consequently real wages are falling, while the reverse is true in periods of declining prices. Now the cost of living, determined as it is by retail prices, is generally rising and declining less than the index for wholesale prices. It follows from this that money wages do not rise so much as the value of output rises, nor do they fall so far as the latter, when this value is falling and rising in connection with corresponding changes in prices.

The latter statement calls for but little statistical confirmation. We need but refer to the material in H. L. Moore's study on the *Law of Wages*, where the average daily wage is compared with the value of the daily product, with the long-time primary trends eliminated (p. 52, Chart 6). One readily sees that during the big swings the average daily wage moves much more steadily than the value of the daily product.

But other production costs besides wages must be considered. Charges rigidly contractual in character such as interest on long-term investments, rent for ground and buildings, amortization charges, are all fixed over a considerable period of time. Therefore they do not rise with an increase in prices even though the latter is continuous over a fairly long period, simply because they are settled at the time the obligations are incurred, and are not continually readjusted to a change in prices.

Of production costs it is only the cost of materials that keeps pace with a rise in prices. While large as this item may be for some branches of industry, the lag of wages and supplementary costs is sufficient to keep the total costs of production below the rise in the value of output. Hence over a prolonged period of price increase, there is a rise in profits. For similar reasons, in periods of price decline there is a falling-off in net earnings, whether measured in money or commodity terms.

This concurrence in the movement of profits with those of prices is well established, even though the data for profits covering long periods of time are scarce. But the few available all point unmistakably to the truth of the above generalization.

In H. Denis, *La Dépression Economique et Sociale et l'Histoire des Prix* (Ixelles-Bruselles, 1895, p. 61), we find data on net earnings (*benefices net*) for all the Belgian joint stock companies. Reducing them to index form and dividing by the index of wholesale prices, we obtain:

6. NET EARNINGS OF BELGIAN CORPORATIONS, 1870–90, DEFLATED
Average of 1872–82 = 100

1870........ 82.2	1877........ 69.9	1884........ 130.5
1871........ 149.4	1878........ 75.9	1885........ 117.3
1872........ 107.7	1879........ 81.9	1886........ 159.2
1873........ 136.0	1880........ 92.0	1887........ 130.3
1874........ 123.4	1881........ 106.7	1888........ 141.5
1875........ 91.4	1882........ 136.6	1889........ 156.6
1876........ 81.8	1883........ 135.1	1890........ 190.0

It is to be seen that net earnings decline to the end of the '70s and rise thereafter. Disregarding cyclical fluctuations, the trough in 1877 is much lower than in 1885, and would be even lower were we to make allowance for a primary secular trend line.

This being the case it is interesting to observe that corporate profits began to recover considerably earlier than prices. True, the recovery was inappreciable until about 1881, but the prices of pig iron and coal (to which branches most of the *sociétiés Anonymes* belonged) began to recover only in 1885.

For Germany we have data for net earnings of stock companies by separate industries, expressed as a percentage of capital. These are given below (Table 7) for three important branches: coal, iron, and the machine building industry.

7. NET EARNINGS OF GERMAN CORPORATIONS, PER CENT OF THEIR NOMINAL CAPITAL [1]

	Coal	Iron	Machines		Coal	Iron	Machines
1870....	9.24	5.19	15.59	1886....	3.45	1.84	7.80
1871....	12.20	12.66	?	1887....	3.98	6.34	8.18
1872....	20.52	13.61	?	1888....	5.39	6.34	8.58
1873....	21.06	6.29	2.46	1889....	6.43	7.79	10.39
1874....	16.37	3.50	?	1890....	17.85	9.10	12.40
1875....	4.90	2.47	?	1891....	16.38	7.74	12.06
1876....	2.97	3.47	?	1892....	8.55	5.06	10.04
1877....	?	?	?	1893....	5.66	4.84	7.95
1878....	.64	?	?	1894....	4.09	3.57	8.91
1879....	1.95	3.96	2.93	1895....	7.00	4.90	10.97
1880....	4.26	4.00	0.78	1896....	9.07	7.45	12.75
1881....	3.52	3.51	3.66	1897....	11.28	11.24	14.73
1882....	4.52	5.35	3.93	1898....	11.66	12.17	13.94
1883....	5.60	4.73	8.46	1899....	12.40	15.14	15.42
1884....	4.45	4.25	9.70	1900....	17.64	13.62	12.91
1885....	2.97	3.94	9.34				

[1] See Ed. Wagon, *Die Finanzielle Entwicklung Deutscher Actiengesellschaften von 1870 bis 1900*, etc., Fischer, Jena, 1903, pp. 175–76, 182.

Here we see again the rise and fall of profits concomitantly with the prolonged periods of rise and decline in prices. And here again net earnings recover much earlier than prices. The secondary variations in the price of German coal turn upward about 1882–83, those of pig iron about 1892. But the net earnings recovered in 1880 and 1887 respectively, thus showing a precedence of a few years (see Charts 3, 4, and 5).

It is this movement of profits during periods of continuous changes in the price level that accounts for the appearance of analogous changes in the commodity volume of output. For profit is the immediate incentive, which, under the conditions of the money economy, stimulates independent economic activity, that is, entrepreneurial activity, and results in increased output and a higher rate of industrial growth. This group of economic agents is motivated mainly by prospective net earnings. A continuous rise in prices furnishes a condition for a continuous rise in profits, and provides the incentive for an accelerated tempo of business activity.

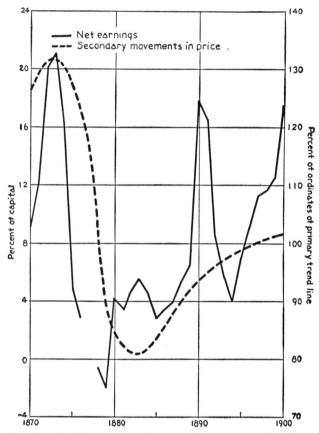

CHART 3. NET EARNINGS OF GERMAN CORPORATIONS, PER CENT
OF NOMINAL CAPITAL, 1870–1900
Coal Industry

From the point of view of the secondary variations, the
lines of primary trend describe the movements of the equilibrium situation. From the point of view of the primary
trend movements, the secondary variations are disturbances
from that equilibrium to be accounted for by specific causes.
We see now that, if we accept a continuous change in prices
as given, the different ways in which the various cost factors in

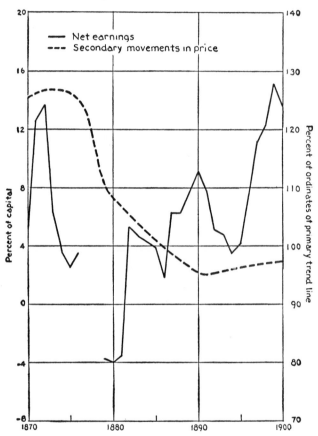

CHART 4. NET EARNINGS OF GERMAN CORPORATIONS, PER CENT
OF NOMINAL CAPITAL, 1870–1900
Iron Industry

production respond to such change results in a modification
of the profit flow, and thus accounts for a simllar movement
in output; a relative acceleration or retardation of the rate of
growth, not described by the lines of primary trend.

Another significant result of a continuous change in prices,
largely a corollary to that just described, is the difference in
the response of various industries to the change in the level of

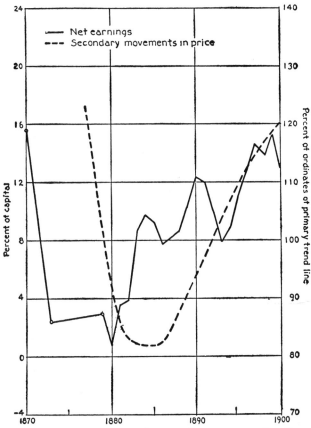

CHART 5. NET EARNINGS OF GERMAN CORPORATIONS, PER CENT
OF NOMINAL CAPITAL, 1870–1900
Machine Industry

prices. As will be seen below, the secondary variations in
industries producing consumers' goods are not so considerable as those in branches making producers' goods. But the
remarkable thing is that both groups show a positive correlation with the secondary variations in prices which occur
for both in approximately the same periods of time. This
raises the intriguing question as to the possibility of an ac-

celeration of output when real wages are falling. Does it not mean that the purchasing power distributed to wage-earners and to persons with fixed incomes is getting relatively smaller? And if so, how is it possible for industries producing consumers' goods to accelerate their output? We shall attempt to answer this question at once.

It must first be remarked that the data used to prove the decline of real wages are not fully corrected for changes in employment. The series used by Mr. Hansen are based upon full time rates. Mr. Wood's series is corrected for full unemployment, but not for partial. The general references to falling real wages seem to be based mostly on the decline of the buying power of rates of pay, rather than on a decline in the actual amount paid in wages. Whether this amount declines one cannot determine with any precision. At any rate, it may be safely assumed that the decline, if any, in the total volume of real wages paid, is less than the decline in such volume, when computed at full time.

The second qualifying suggestion is that wage-earners and receivers of salaries and fixed incomes from investments are not the only consumers in society, although they may be said to form the bulk of the urban consumers. The business men enjoy greater profits, as do all classes which benefit immediately from a rise in prices. To this group belong also the numerous agricultural producers, who in an upward movement of prices obtain correspondingly larger sums of money for their products, and whose demand for consumers' goods may be rising as compared to periods when their money incomes are not so large or steady. While the influence of this prosperity of the entrepreneurial classes may not be great on commodities of inelastic demand, it may be of significant character in the markets for such goods as textiles, furniture, etc.

But even these classes, which presumably suffer a decrease in the flow of purchasing power disbursed to them, do not necessarily contract their demand for consumers' goods. With the flow of larger money incomes there is an appearance of prosperity and an incentive to spend. And it is quite possible, although no exact proof is forthcoming, that during periods of continuously rising prices, a change takes place in the attitude of consumers towards goods and money, a change which is outstanding in periods of rapid money inflation. Money becomes depreciated in the eyes of consumers, goods seem more desirable than formerly, the stimulus for saving money is weakened, and this desire to acquire goods receives an economic justification in view of their continual appreciation and the decline in the value of money. It is therefore highly probable that during these periods of rising prices the classes which receive slowly adjustable incomes spend a much larger part of them and save less than in periods of declining prices. This would help them to maintain the old level of consumption and even to raise it, and the justification would lie in the changes that take place in the relative conditions of money and commodity supply.

Statistical proof for the support of these statements is possible only in part. Let us first present the data and then discuss their bearings on the point.

We have data on the amount of money paid out and received year by year since 1867 for the post-office and trustee savings banks in the United Kingdom. These data refer only to accounts current at the beginning of each year. Subtracting the amounts paid out from those received, we obtain the following series. (See Table 8, page 418.)

The question we are attempting to answer is what is the share of money wages spent and the share saved over various periods of price changes and its bearing upon the possibility of acceleration of output when real wages are falling. If it is assumed that the statistics on savings refer to savings by wage-earning and salaried classes only, then we are able to compare the changes in savings with those in money wages for these groups. If during periods of rising prices (and hence of money wages) savings remain stable or decline, it follows that a smaller relative share of incomes is being saved. If savings rise, but less so than money wages and salaries, the same conclusion holds. But if savings rise proportionately with incomes, then we may conclude that the relative importance of saving has not diminished.

In the case under consideration, the data for the United Kingdom indicate that in periods of falling prices, such as

8. Net Amounts Received by the Post-Office and Trustee Savings Banks, United Kingdom, 1867–1914 [1]

(Triannual averages, thousands of £)

1867........		1885........		1900........	
1868........	883	1886........	2308	1901........	−650
1869........		1887........		1902........	
1870........		1888........		1903........	
1871........	1754	1889........	2797	1904........	−2237
1872........		1890........		1905........	
1873........		1891........		1906........	
1874........	1741	1892........	2181	1907........	−2517
1875........		1893........		1908........	
1876........		1894........		1909........	
1877........	1161	1895........	7328	1910........	452
1878........		1896........		1911........	
1879........		1897........		1912........	
1880........	663	1898........	4863	1913........	1170
1881........		1899........		1914........	
1882........					
1883........	2252				
1884........					

[1] National Monetary Commission, *Statistics for Great Britain, France, and Germany,* p. 22. Also *Statistical Abstract for the United Kingdom, 1903–17,* no. 65, pp. 344–47.

from the '70s to the second half of the '90s, the net receipts of the savings banks were rising (see Chart 6), while during the periods of rising prices such as began at the end of the '90s, these net receipts were decidedly falling. Knowing that money wages were rising and falling on the whole together with prices we cannot but conclude that in times of an upward price movement (of the type of a secondary variation) the share of incomes saved was declining. While this is true, it does not necessarily mean that the funds thus diverted were used to purchase consumers' goods. One might argue they would be invested, the opportunities being attractive during upward price movement periods and comparatively poor in times of falling prices. That this factor may be of some importance cannot be denied. However, the average size of a deposit account was below thirty pounds in the decade 1910–20 (the highest), and one would hardly suspect the investment motive to be of considerable influence.

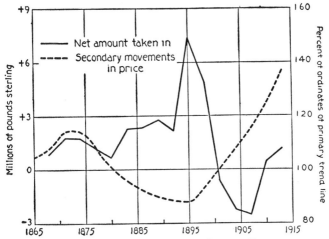

CHART 6. NET AMOUNTS RECEIVED BY SAVINGS BANKS OF THE
UNITED KINGDOM, 1867–1914

While the English data are thus favorable to the hypothetical generalization suggested above, analogous figures
for France leave us in doubt. The net receipts (deposits
minus withdrawals) are as follows:

9. NET RECEIPTS (MILLIONS OF FRANCS), CAISSE D'EPARGNES ORDI-
NAIRES, FRANCE, 1870–1908 [1]

1870...... −76		1885...... 113		1897..... −54	
1871......−115	−78	1886...... 22	34	1898.....−126	−91
1872...... −42		1887...... −34		1899..... −92	

1873...... 0		1888...... 43		1900.....−242	
1874...... 18	28	1889...... 96	88	1901..... −12	−139
1875...... 65		1890...... 126		1902.....−164	

1876...... 74		1891...... 41		1903.....−210	
1877...... 65	86	1892...... 69	−25	1904..... −35	−71
1878...... 120		1893......−185		1905..... 33	

1879...... 100		1894...... 45		1906..... −42	
1880...... 83	88	1895...... 3	−21	1907..... 9	0
1881...... 80		1896......−112		1908..... 32	

1882...... 187	
1883...... −3	107
1884...... 137	

[1] National Monetary Commission, *Statistics for Great Britain, France, and Germany,*
p. 338.

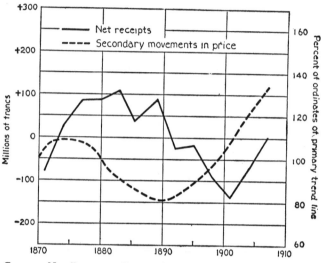

CHART 7. NET RECEIPTS, CAISSE D'EPARGNES ORDINAIRES, FRANCE, 1870–1908

In this case (see Chart 7) the line of net receipts would follow, although with a lag, the secondary variations in prices and money wages. The average deposit rises in size from below 300 fr. to about 475, thus is not very large. Whether the rise and decline in savings was greater or less than that in money earnings it is impossible to ascertain in the absence of exact data on money earnings. This case, if not showing definitely that the income saved increases or remains stable during the periods of rising prices, does leave us in doubt whether it definitely and decidedly diminishes.

For the United States, instead of taking the absolute data, it is better to use the year to year change in the savings deposits, since the latter indicates the balance of withdrawals and payments (interest accrued being disregarded). This we can compare with the year to year change in money wages as given by Hansen (*loc. cit.*, p. 32). Both series have been first turned into relatives on the base of 1913 as 100 (or rather 1912 as 98, since the deposit series does not extend to 1913). The table then runs as follows:

10. Year to Year Change in the Average Size of Deposits in Savings Banks, and in the Rate of Money Wages, United States, 1854–1912

(Underlying Data = Relatives, 1913 = 100)

Deposit	Wages	Deposit	Wages	Deposit	Wages
1854*... +1	+2	1874.... +2	−3	1893.... +3	0
1855.... +1	+1	1875.... +3	−5	1894.... 0	−3
1856.... +1	0	1876.... +1	−3	1895.... +1	+1
1857.... +1	+1	1877.... −8	−6	1896.... +1	+1
1858.... 0	+1	1878.... +2	−1	1897.... 0	0
1859.... +1	0	1879.... −3	−1	1898.... −1	0
1860.... +2	+1	1880.... −1	0	1899.... +1	+1
1861.... −1	0	1881.... +0	+2	1900.... +2	+2
1862.... +1	+1	1882.... +1	+2	1901.... +1	+1
1863.... +4	+7	1883.... 0	+1	1902.... 0	+3
1864.... +2	+9	1884.... 0	0	1903.... +1	+2
1865.... +1	+8	1885.... 0	−1	1904.... 0	0
1866.... +4	+4	1886.... +1	0	1905.... 0	+2
1867.... +4	+2	1887.... 0	+2	1906.... +2	+3
1868.... +4	+1	1888.... −1	+1	1907.... −1	+4
1869.... +2	+4	1889.... +1	0	1908.... −1	−1
				1909.... +5	+1
1870.... +6	+1	1890.... +1	+1		
1871.... +1	+2	1891.... 0	0	1910.... +5	+2
1872.... +6	−1	1892.... −1	+1	1911.... −3	+1
1873.... 0	0			1912.... +2	+3

* Changes from preceding year to year given in the table.

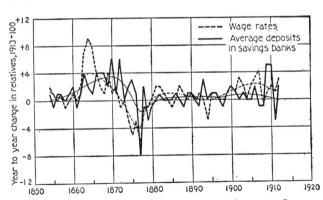

Chart 8. Year to Year Change in the Average Size of Deposits in Savings Banks and the Money Wage Rates, United States, 1854–1912

On Chart 8, both series are plotted, and a free-hand line of moving averages is drawn in. Two observations can be readily made: 1. There is a positive concurrence of movements in savings deposit and wage changes, the former, however, lagging considerably behind the latter; 2. the savings do not rise or fall so much on the average as the wage-rates. Both series underestimate probably the fluctuations in earnings and savings, since one refers only to wage-rates and the other does not cover the change in the number of depositors. But as they stand, the evidence is that with increased earnings a smaller share of the incomes goes to savings, hence the latter do not increase in the same proportion as earnings. We may infer, although none too confidently, that in periods of rising prices these groups spend a larger part of their current income than in times of falling prices, and this provides a partial explanation why industries producing consumers' goods find it possible to accelerate the rate of their growth, in spite of the fact that full time wages distributed may indicate a decline in purchasing power.

Another explanation for the accelerated growth for those industries producing consumers' goods may be that during periods of rising prices the relative size of stocks may be increasing. Unfortunately, we do not possess any long-time data on the size of stocks of commodities, hence we cannot answer definitely the question whether the secondary variations in prices are accompanied also by analogous secondary variations in the absolute or relative size of the stocks. It is, however, evident that in such periods, when with increasing prices the enterprisers obtain larger profits and when such increasing profits permit larger use of bank funds, there is an incentive to carry larger stocks than at other times. A continuous rise in prices while stimulating increased production makes possible more funds to carry an absolutely larger stock and such a policy is profitable, for the supply at the next instance of time at higher prices will be met from stocks obtained at lower costs. The longer the time a commodity takes to reach the buyer from the moment it is finished the larger the gain thereon to the producer. While this may not be apparent within the immediate experience of the business man, for the price changes we are dealing with are in the nature of drawn-out secondary variations, there may be a slow, gradual change in the stock policies as an unwitting adaptation to the changed economic conditions.

To sum up the four suggestions that may be brought in to explain the accelerated rate of growth in production of consumers' goods during periods of rising prices:

I. The volume of employment is increasing, and this counteracts the loss of purchasing power in the wage rates.[1]

II. Groups of consumers other than wage-earners and salaried classes enjoy an increased flow of real incomes.

III. The wage-earning and salaried classes spend in periods of rising prices a larger part of their current incomes and save less than in periods of falling prices.

IV. Stocks carried by the enterprises are probably larger during those periods of rising prices than at other times.

While the production of consumers' goods thus expands in periods of upward price movements, it cannot expand relatively as much as the production of producers' goods. For changes in the distribution of the national product which take place during these periods, favor the entrepreneurs and leave in their hands larger funds for expansion. This expansion results of course in accelerating the rate of growth of producers' goods beyond what it would be when stimulated by a rise of prices alone. On the other hand, the consumers' goods branches cannot expand so rapidly, since they do not profit greatly from the funds in the hands of entrepreneurs and are slowed down because of the decreased or stable, or only slightly increased flow of purchasing power into the hands of the bulk of the consuming body. For this reason, branches producing consumers' goods show secondary variations considerably milder than those for producers' goods.[2]

---

[1] This does not weaken the argument developed above that the decrease in real wages and salaries implies an increase in profits. For provided the productivity of workers does not decline, a decrease in real payment per unit of time implies a larger margin left to the entrepreneurs.

[2] See Appendix (B) for statistical test of this proposition.

In our discussion so far we assumed a continuous rise or decline in prices. We took the secondary variations in prices as given, considered them as an independent cause, and saw how the different responses to them by the various elements of entrepreneurs' costs result in a larger volume of profits, thus stimulating increased production, and we saw how this factor of increased profits accounts for the different amplitude of the secondary variations in the two groups of industries. But such a presentation shifts the whole burden of the problem to the question of secondary variations in prices. What is the cause of these? And have we the right to treat these secondary secular movements of prices as entirely independent of the analogous variations in output? Is the relationship only unidirectional, so that variations in prices are continuously the cause and those in production always the effect?

In the large but not very illuminating literature on the causes of the great decline or rise of the price level, which has appeared in an attempt to explain the continuous changes in prices, which we have termed the secondary variations, price movements are treated as an effect and are looked upon either as a result of continuous changes in the output of monetary metals, or ascribed to a change in the supply of commodities. But the changes in output of commodities are not analyzed, and the supply of goods is treated as an independent factor. In few of these writings is there a suggestion of an interaction of the commodity and price elements. Rather, they treat prices, the output of monetary metals, and production of other commodities as separate elements in a rigid cause and effect relationship, instead of revealing them as influencing one another in a highly complex relationship similar to that found within the cyclical fluctuation proper.

Now our account of the processes which take place in connection with the secondary variations in prices gives to the whole phenomenon a resemblance to cyclical fluctuations. There is the same maladjustment between production of consumers' and producers' goods. There are the changes in the purchasing power of wage rates and salaries. It thus appears probable that the secondary variations must be in part, at least, due to peculiarities of our exchange and production system in the money economy similar to those which play such an important rôle in the explanation of cyclical fluctuations.

It seems to be an unnecessary simplification of the problem and offers merely a one-sided explanation to assume continuous variations in prices as given and then to explain movements in production as a parallel effect. It is more realistic to start with a given increase of prices and see how, in response to the latter, the present-day economic system creates conditions that tend to perpetuate and continue the price increase, even after the immediate stimuli for such an increase have disappeared. We must keep in mind, however, that we are discussing secondary variations, those protracted swings of 22–23 years' duration, and not the shorter cyclical fluctuations.

Let us now suppose that for some reason or other a considerable rise of prices extending over four or five years has taken place, i.e., an increase not entirely due to cyclical fluctuations. The usual results will follow. Profits will increase, reserves will grow, the production of producers' goods will forge to a higher deviation level than the output of consumers' goods and there will be an accelerated growth of output all around. The real wage rates will decline, but this will be offset by larger employment, less savings, etc. Suppose further that the cause of this continuous upward movement of prices has disappeared, and from this point on the conditions of money supply keep pace with production, resulting in stable prices, stable on the level attained. What will be the immediate and more remote consequences of this cessation of the rise in prices?

The immediate conclusion is that prices are not going to remain on this level, but turn downward instead. For in the processes of adjustment which follow this price stabilization, expenses which lagged behind during the preceding period of a continuous price increase are going to mount and reduce profits from their comparatively high levels. Indeed the pressure of the wage-earners for a readjustment of wages, of salaried men, of creditors, all will serve to raise the cost of production even after the rise in prices has ceased. This will presumably cut into the prospective profits, provided, of course, prices cannot be further increased. This decline in prospective profits will reduce production, increase unemployment, and start prices on the downward path. It would seem, then, that with the cessation of the cause which made for the initial rise of prices, the secondary variation will turn downward and will not be prolonged in the absence of an outside stimulus.

A closer attention to the problem shows, however, that we have overlooked the probable influence of two groups of factors. One group comprises those factors that account for the lag of secondary movements in production behind those in prices. The second is the discrepancy between the production of consumers' and producers' goods in their response to an increase in prices. The probable effects of both of these groups of factors is to prolong the price rise beyond the initial period.

It was remarked above that the secondary movements in production lagged in the majority of cases behind those in prices on an average of about four years, although this lag is much smaller if the cases of simultaneity are included. The reasons for this lag are not easily discovered. There is, of course, the fact that while profits rise when (or before) prices begin to rise, this recovery may take some time to result in an increase of production. For, while profits may begin to recover, they may still be below normal and the enterprise may be inclined to await the accumulation of reserves before expanding production. There is also, of course, the question of the period of 'gestation.' For while expansion on the scale of cyclical fluctuations is possible without increasing greatly the current equipment of the enterprise, changes of the character of secondary variations cannot be accomplished without a preceding change in equipment. While secondary variations may be as considerable (or less) than the cyclical, they are more continuous, and an enterprise cannot continue increased production for a long time without an increase in equipment. Therefore, besides the reluctance of the body of business enterprises to prepare for an increasing output until the accumulation of better profits paves the way, there is probably also the period of waiting before equipment is supplied to make such expansion economically and technically possible.

It must be noticed that in at least one particular case this period of gestation is considerable. The changes being brought about by secondary variations may accelerate the need for such a major type of adjustment as the building of a long trunk line railroad. Now, such an enterprise takes about five or six years, although parts of the line may be opened for operation as soon as completed. We can cite a few illustrative instances. To build the Central Pacific line of 883 miles took from January, 1863 (ground broken at Sacramento), until May, 1869 (completed at San Francisco), i.e., slightly more than six years.[1] The California Pacific, incorporated in 1865, made no material progress for two years and the road was not finished until 1869 (total length 163 miles). With the Canadian Pacific, the contract for construction was signed in October, 1880, and the road completed in November, 1885.[2] Ground was broken for the Union Pacific in October, 1863, and the last rails laid in May, 1869. These examples show that it takes five or six years to build a long trunk line of 800–900 miles. But it is exactly this kind of production of producers' goods that is frequently called for by secondary variations, when accelerated growth requires changes and readjustments between the different parts of the economic system. And while in the early stages the rise of prices and production calls for these changes, the time it takes to bring them about may account for a continued rise of prices in the later stages beyond the initial point.[3]

But to whatever reasons the lag of secondary movements in production behind those in prices may be ascribed, let us accept this lag as a given fact, and investigate its implications.

[1] See J. Dagett, *History of the Southern Pacific*, New York, 1922, p. 83.

[2] See H. A. Innis, *A History of the Canadian Pacific Railway*, London, 1923, pp. 98–128.

[3] From this point of view it is interesting to notice that the dates quoted above fall in the decade of the '60s and bring us up to the decade of the '70s. It is probable that the building of railroads and the period of waiting involved is at least one of the reasons for the prolongation of the secondary movements to the '70s and in some industries beyond that. On the other hand, railroad construction had pretty much ceased by the beginning of the twentieth century so that it could have been of but little importance in the later secondary variations.

The first is that the consequences of a given rise of prices, i.e., the increased profits, reserves, etc., result in a changed supply of goods only after a certain time elapses. This may be explained in two ways: either increased profits and reserves themselves appear with a certain belatedness, or there is a delay after their appearance before change in supply results. In either case, we shall have after a period of increase of prices a volume of current or prospective purchasing power at the disposal of the business enterprises without a current possibility of satisfying the demand.

Let us suppose that a continuous price increase takes place for four or five years. At the expiration of the fifth year, we find either accumulated funds in the hands of the business enterprises, a result of good profits realized during the last four or five years, or we have the prospect of profits to be realized when the goods just produced are sold. The actual situation is a combination of the reserves accumulated and prospective profits. Production, however, begins to rise only in the last year or two of the upward price movement. At the end of the fifth year of the movement we thus have reserves accumulated for five years, or five years minus the period for which the output is not yet sold, and the supply increased so far to a much smaller degree. The effect of this will be that in the next year, even if the cause making for the initial rise of prices has ceased to operate, we shall still have an increase of purchasing power in the hands of the entrepreneurs and a rise of production that is not sufficient to satisfy the increased demand. Under such conditions it is not likely that a price decline will set in. It is rather more probable that an adaptation to the conditions will be made by entrepreneurs, and that in response to the pressure on the part of the wage-earners for an increase in wages and a rise in the other items of production costs they will attempt to raise prices. Because of the lag of production in adjusting itself to the changed price and commercial demand conditions, a price movement can be continued beyond its initial stage, and this continuation, as may be readily seen, prepares the ground for a further advance.

It must be emphatically pointed out again that we are speaking of secondary secular movements and not of cyclical fluctuations. The significance of this difference is that we have no place in this discussion for the factor of 'competitive illusion' which is of such importance in the shorter cyclical fluctations. Its rôle there is to drive prices vigorously upward and to call forth an exaggerated response on the part of the productive system, which when realized puts an abrupt end to the upward movement of prices and production. In the secondary movements we have very few of these elements of exaggeration and overstimulation, those irrational factors in business activity. Here we find rather a slow and unconscious adaptation. But here also we have a projection of an initial disturbance because of the lag in adjustment by the productive system. The lag, however, is much more considerable than in the cyclical changes; the disturbance is more a gradual process of change, and there is no possibility of the disturbance becoming greatly exaggerated, which also means there is small possibility of its stopping abruptly.

In the lag of production movements behind those in prices we have a mechanism which implies a possibility of a slow, perpetual motion. When the initial impetus toward price increase has spent itself, prices will still increase for a time because production has not adjusted itself to the increased demand on the part of the business enterprises. This further increase of prices again results in the shift in the distribution of national income that accompanied the preceding rise of prices and plants the seeds for a further increase, and so on *ad infinitum.*

Of course the rise of prices which takes place after the initial rise will be presumably weaker than the latter. This is likely because during the period of the initial rise, we have for a time at least (in its later part) a combined effect of the outside cause and the self-induced rise, which combined effect prolongs the price rise beyond the initial point. While this continued increase beyond the initial point takes place, nevertheless the rise will slacken and as a result the maladjustment between prices and production will diminish. What we find then is a continuously diminishing rise of prices rather than an unretarded upward movement.

Another factor may prolong an upward movement of

prices once begun, although it comes much later than the first. This factor is the difference between the production of consumers' and producers' goods. It was noticed above that in response to a continuous price increase growth in the consumers' goods group does not expand relatively so much as in the producers' goods branches. This is mainly owing to the fact that consumers are not favored by the changes which take place in the relative distribution of the national income as a result of upward price movements. This unequal acceleration of growth of output in the two groups also implies that they do not increase their equipment relatively equally. For the industries producing consumers' goods do not have to enlarge their productive possibilities as much as the producers' goods branches.

What happens then when the price increase ceases? And let us suppose for a moment that this increase ceases in spite of the carrying-forward power of the lag. If the prices become fixed on a level basis, then as pointed out above, profits begin to decline and production follows a similar course. In other words, we witness the beginning of a recession.

But it is obvious the recession will tend to be checked by the increasing flow of purchasing power to consumers. For the demand for consumers' goods would not slump so much (if at all) as the demand for the producers' goods, and with lowered prices a revival of the upward movement may be effected by the demand of the consumers' goods industries for equipment in order to expand their production.

If the beginning price increase is of long enough duration to result in an upward movement of production, the underequipment of the consumers' goods industries as compared with the producers' goods industries will be comparatively large, and the reserve and profit funds accumulated during the preceding price-rise considerable. As a result, the advancing period of depression may be stopped by the continued demand for consumers' goods, easy funds, and the desire of the consumers' goods industries to equip themselves as well as the producers' group, since a large part of equipment is common to most branches of industry.

The initial rise of prices has thus two results: a larger than usual discrepancy between the two groups of industries in their productive equipment and a larger than usual fund of accumulated profits. With these consequences granted, it is seen how a following period of depression may be abruptly ended by the comparatively undiminished demand for consumers' goods and the incentive for this branch of industry to start expanding again. And the next upward movement of the cycle is thus likely to set in after only a brief period of recession and before the decline has proceeded very far.

Now this has two implications. One is that the first cycle with its period of prosperity long and relatively high and with its recession checked before it has developed very far will have an upward secondary movement underlying it. The second implication is that the next cycle starts with a larger fund of profits and reserves unimpaired by the depression. It will start also, by our suppositions, under conditions of money supply that will keep pace with the current production, i.e., with the long-time movements in the latter. In other words, even with the assumption of this money supply maintaining prices at the once established higher level, the next cycle would be on a higher level than the preceding one, but the underlying secondary movement would no longer be rising but remain on an unchanged level. The fact, however, that we start the cycle with larger accumulated funds and a short period of depression preceding it, might prolong the upward movement again and continue the discrepancy in expansion between the two groups of industries, although possibly not so great as before. This will in turn check the following period of depression, and we see the same picture of long periods of prosperity, short periods of depression and a continuous, if gradually slackening upward secondary movement.

It must be pointed out here that in the above reasoning we have made two assumptions. One is that after the initial price rise the conditions of money supply continue to keep pace with production, and prices remain stable on the level reached. The significance of this assumption will be discussed later. The second is that the initial rise is supposed to be longer than the 'average' period of prosperity, for only in this case is there an accumulation of funds and a discrepancy between the two groups of industries larger than 'usual,' and only this permits us to make deductions concerning the probable course of the following period of depression. It is this second assumption which must be briefly discussed in its present connection.

The two factors presented above, viz., the lag of production movements behind prices and the difference between the production of producers' and consumers' goods, as sustaining a continuation of an upward movement in prices and production after the initial upturn, are the more powerful the longer the initial rise assumed. That this is so we have seen just now for the second factor, that of the difference between the two groups of industries. But, evidently the lag of production movements behind prices, if it is to be of any influence at all, must be preceded by a rather long rise in prices and a considerable rise in production itself, for only in this case does the expansion of productive facilities become imperious and only in this case is there a necessity for the readjustments whose gestation occupies a considerable period of time. Within a comparatively brief initial period of price increase neither of these forces becomes effective, and the price rise probably will not be carried forward beyond the initial point.

In respect to this phenomenon of an initial disturbance the problem of secondary variations is quite different from that of cyclical fluctuations. In explaining the latter we also have to assume an initial disturbance. But the duration and size of this disturbance, in so far as they are required by the hypothesis, need not be very pronounced, hence the disturbance rarely presents a problem in itself. It is the relative weight of the mechanism creating the exaggeration and prolongation of this disturbance that is the more important, and which forms the real kernel of the problem. In secondary variations, however, the initial disturbance from the equilibrium (the latter being represented by the lines of the primary trend) must be considerable in order to set into motion the factors which prolong it. Such disturbances must be explained on their own account, and their appearance can hardly be presented as an inevitable occurrence out of a stream of similar disturbances. The initial movements that set up the secondary variations are rather specific, historically important happenings. It is for this reason that we shall hardly be able to conceive the secondary variations as large cycles, for they arise neither from purely random changes nor from initial disturbances cyclical in character.

We must therefore be cautious in accepting the significance of the two factors discussed above, lag in production behind prices and the maladjustment between producers' and consumers' branches. They require a fairly prolonged period of increase in the price movement and the assumption of an undiminished money supply in order to exercise any influence in prolonging the price and production upward movement beyond the initial point. For an upward secondary movement of average duration from eleven to thirteen years, there must be at least five to six years of an initial increase, in order that we may be able to ascribe significance to the factors of lag and to the difference between the two groups of industries.

Granted the fairly long period of initial increase we obtain a picture of a rather indefinite, endless prolongation of a price and production increase. For while, as described above, the upward movement would be gradually slackening, apparently no actual decline would set in. But what are some of the factors which act as brakes on such an endless upward movement of prices and production, bring about a cessation of the rise, and eventually set in motion a decline?

In considering these retarding factors, it is necessary to inquire into our assumption made above that the money supply continues at a rate that maintains the price level at the established point of high relative deviation. This assumption is not necessarily true. On the contrary, rising prices tend to retard the production of monetary metals. Thus the money supply is one of the retarding influences which may effectively put a stop to an upward secondary movement.

Another factor and one we shall discuss first is the productivity of labor. It appears from the data at our disposal that the productivity of labor tends to decline in periods of upward movements of prices and production and rise in other periods. This hypothetical generalization and the data on which it is based merit a close examination.

Most of the available data relate to output and to working force employed. But we have in only one or two cases data on the number of days worked in the year, and in none the number of hours worked per year. Now it may be reasonably supposed that the number of days worked in the year or the number of hours worked during the day are relatively larger in periods of rising prices than in the years of downward movement of production and prices. But the real measure of the productivity of labor is output per man-hour, technical equipment being disregarded. Our figures of output per man would thus underestimate the decline in productivity in periods of rising prices and the rise during periods of falling prices. Even with this unfavorable limitation, the data quite generally support the above proposition.

Let us first take a case in which we have the number of days worked per year.

On Chart 9 illustrating this table the lines for days worked per year and output per day per worker are drawn in compari-

11. Daily Output of Coal per Worker and the Number of Days Worked in the Year, Coal Mines, France [1]

(1847–1902, 1876–81 missing)

Output in index numbers, 1901 taken as 100

Year	Output	Number of Days	Year	Output	Number of Days	Year	Output	Number of Days
1847	76	287	1864	74	288	1886	101	283
1848	69	264	1865	77	283	1887	106	287
1849	74	247	1866	79	286	1888	108	292
1850	79	249	1867	78	286	1889	111	290
1851	73	269	1868	81	281	1890	109	290
1852	74	272	1869	83	281	1891	101	288
1853	78	274	1870	82	288	1892	100	288
1854	72	296	1871	81	286	1893	103	277
1855	72	280	1872	86	292	1894	105	285
1856	72	275	1873	82	295	1895	106	283
1857	69	282	1874	79	295	1896	106	284
1858	70	273	1875	77	295	1897	109	288
1859	?	?				1898	110	290
1860	72	285				1899	109	287
1861	75	279	1882	95	296	1900	106	286
1862	75	290	1883	95	293	1901	100	290
1863	76	283	1884	96	280	1902	98	272
			1885	101	281			

[1] See F. Simiand, *Le Salaire des Ouvriers des Mines en France*. Paris, 1904, tableau A, p. 48.

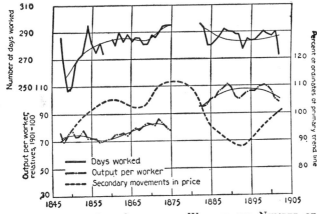

CHART 9. DAILY COAL OUTPUT PER WORKER AND NUMBER OF
DAYS WORKED IN THE YEAR, COAL MINES, FRANCE, 1848–1902

son with the secondary variations in the price of coal (France).
First, it should be remarked that the secondary movements
in the number of days worked are positively correlated with
those in prices. They both rise to the end of the '50s. The
price then declines, the number of days likewise even though
slightly. Again they both reveal the upward movement
towards the end of the '70s, and a long decline thereafter.
The number of days, however, does not show the conspicuous recovery after the '90s that prices show, although even
then the former exhibit a retardation in their decline.

The daily output per worker shows entirely different
movements. During the decade of the '50s, when prices
were rising, it exhibits a definite decline. During the decade
of the '60s it was rising, but prices were falling. In the '80s
and up to the beginning of the '90s output per worker is
rising, but the secondary variations in prices are downward.
The upward movement of prices which followed from the
early '90s seems to have been accompanied by a downward
turn of output per worker. The consideration of the generally rising primary trend in the output series would not
change materially the comparison, and we may definitely
conclude that in this particular case the secondary variations
in output per worker were declining when the secondary
movements in prices were rising and vice versa.

In the next case we have the annual output per worker in the Belgian coal mines for the period 1830–1914. In order to smooth the series we have computed a nine-year moving average, and the data cited are the averages centered on the fifth year.

12. Annual Coal Output per Worker Employed, Metric Tons, Belgium, 1835–1910

Nine-year moving averages

1835	90	1854	123	1873	142	1892	174
1836	92	1855	123	1874	143	1893	172
1837	95	1856	122	1875	144	1894	173
1838	97	1857	121	1876	146	1895	173
1839	99	1858	120	1877	147	1896	174
1840	102	1859	121	1878	150	1897	174
1841	103	1860	123	1879	154	1898	175
1842	105	1861	127	1880	158	1899	174
1843	108	1862	130	1881:	162	1900	173
1844	110	1863	132	1882	165	1901	172
1845	111	1864	134	1883	169	1902	170
1846	113	1865	136	1884	172	1903	169
1847	115	1866	138	1885	174	1904	167
1848	118	1867	142	1886	175	1905	166
1849	120	1868	145	1887	174	1906	166
1850	121	1869	145	1888	174	1907	165
1851	122	1870	144	1889	173	1908	164
1852	121	1871	143	1890	174	1909	163
1853	122	1872	142	1891	174	1910	159

On Chart 10 illustrating this table we have drawn in the secondary variations in prices of coal (Belgium). The series of output has a considerable primary secular movement which has to be recognized in the comparison. To facilitate this, a light line is traced in freehand fashion to represent roughly the line of primary trend. The secondary movements formed by the deviations of the dash line from the light line run generally opposite to the secondary variation in prices. Thus after moving together up to 1840, output rises rapidly to the end of the '40s, while prices decline correspondingly through the major part of that decade. During the '50s prices rise, and the output per worker declines. During the '60s the two series run together, but in the period 1869–75 the price movement rises to a peak, while output again declines. After that the movements are

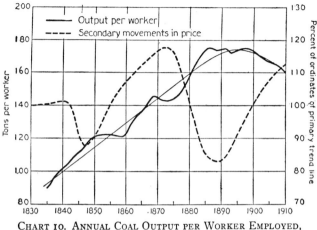

CHART 10. ANNUAL COAL OUTPUT PER WORKER EMPLOYED,
BELGIUM, 1835–1910
Nine-year moving averages

opposed throughout. Output rises at the end of the '80s and prices are declining. Then a decline in the output series is accompanied by a rise in prices.

For Germany we have four similar series of annual output per worker, two of them of particular interest because they represent not extractive but manufacturing industries. All of them, with the exception of that for copper mines, are moving averages, with the periods of nine years for coal and seven for zinc smelting and pig iron production. The data are shown in Table 13, on page 438.

Each one of these series was charted for comparison with the corresponding secondary variations in prices. The results of these comparisons are as follows:

Coal (see Chart 11). In the output of coal we have a considerable primary secular movement. Still the secondary variations are quite clear, and it is also obvious that they move in a direction opposite to that of prices. While prices rose in the early part of the '70s, output declined. With the fall of prices to the first half of the '80s went a considerable rise in output. After that prices recovered and started on an upward movement, but output on the whole declined.

13. Annual Output per Worker, Metric Tons, Four Industries, Germany, 1863–1907

Year	Coal	Copper	Zinc	Pig Iron
1863.................		24.4	10.1	38.5
1864.................	186	26.2	10.3	42.3
1865.................	193	26.8	10.3	49.4
1866.................	198	28.9	10.4	51.2
1867.................	200	30.3	10.5	55.9
1868.................	202	31.9	10.3	59.6
1869.................	203	31.9	10.2	64.0
1870.................	203	33.6	10.4	68.1
1871.................	203	32.8	10.6	71.2
1872.................	204	39.4	10.8	75.6
1873.................	206	41.6	11.0	80.3
1874.................	209	38.4	11.5	85.2
1875.................	213	41.4	12.1	94.5
1876.................	220	43.5	12.8	101.9
1877.................	227	46.6	13.4	109.0
1878.................	234	44.9	13.8	117.3
1879.................	242	43.0	14.1	125.6
1880.................	249	44.8	14.4	132.4
1881.................	255	43.2	14.3	139.5
1882.................	260	43.7	14.4	143.7
1883.................	265	42.8	14.4	148.9
1884.................	270	38.7	14.5	157.2
1885.................	272	38.7	14.5	164.7
1886.................	272	35.0	14.7	170.6
1887.................	272	36.0	14.9	176.3
1888.................	269	36.5	14.9	180.8
1889.................	268	37.7	15.0	186.7
1890.................	267	39.2	15.0	192.6
1891.................	266	38.3	14.9	197.7
1892.................	265	39.0	14.8	203.2
1893.................	264	42.0	14.8	210.6
1894.................	262	42.9	14.6	216.0
1895.................	262	46.4	14.7	223.2
1896.................	262	50.9	14.6	226.2
1897.................	262	48.6	14.6	231.7
1898.................	260	48.6	14.6	234.8
1899.................	259	49.2	14.9	239.9
1900.................	258	48.0	15.2	246.1
1901.................	255	49.0	15.6	254.5
1902.................	255	47.0	16.0	261.0
1903.................	254	47.8	16.3	271.0
1904.................	252	47.2	16.6	276.7
1905.................	249	45.2	16.9	280.6
1906.................	250	43.8	17.1	285.8
1907.................		43.7	17.3	291.9

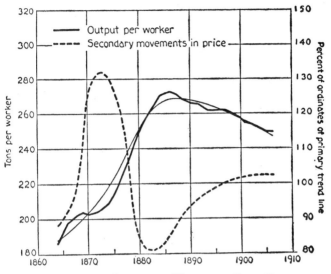

CHART 11. ANNUAL OUTPUT PER WORKER OF COAL, GERMANY,
1864–1906

CHART 12. ANNUAL OUTPUT PER WORKER OF COPPER ORE,
GERMANY, 1860–1910

The series presents a good case for the negative correlation suggested above.

Copper Ore (see Chart 12). In this case we observe on the whole a positive correlation between output per worker and the movements of prices, especially marked in the first half of the series. In the second swing of the secondary variations, however, output starts to recover some five years earlier than prices, and begins to decline about ten years earlier. For these periods then we have opposed movements. The case is, therefore, not entirely unfavorable to the negative correlation considered as the general occurrence.

Zinc Smelting (see Chart 13). Here we have a manufacturing industry and it is rather clear that like most of the

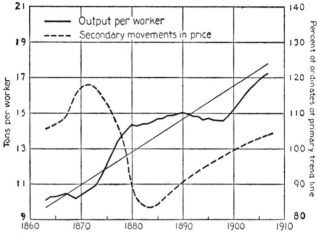

CHART 13. ANNUAL OUTPUT PER WORKER OF ZINC, GERMANY, 1863–1907

cases considered above the secondary movements in the output per worker vary in a direction opposite to that of prices. Output declines in the early '70s and prices rise. Prices decline towards the early '80s while output is rising. Prices moved upward towards the late '90s; output downward. Only during the last six or seven years of the series do output per worker and prices exhibit similar secondary variations.

Pig Iron (see Chart 14). In this case the series of output rises so rapidly it was found advisable to plot it on a log scale. The light line is a freehand curve representing roughly the line of primary trend. A close scrutiny of the chart

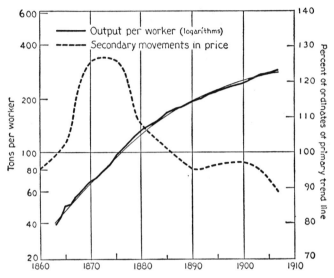

CHART 14. ANNUAL OUTPUT PER WORKER OF PIG IRON, GERMANY, 1863–1905

reveals that here also the secondary movements in output vary in an opposite direction to prices. While output declines towards the early '70s, prices rise. Output rises towards the early '80s, while prices decline. Output declines towards the late '90s, and prices rise up to 1899. After 1900 output moves upward, but prices show a declining secondary movement.

On the whole, the data support the statement that output per worker, either daily or annual, exhibits secondary variations which rise in periods of falling prices and decline in periods of rising prices. The data are, of course, far from exhaustive, but they indicate a high probability of such a relationship.

This establishment of a negative correlation between

secondary variations in prices and output per worker at once raises two questions. First, what are the probable causes of the decline of productivity per worker in periods of upward movement of prices? Second, what are the implications of this relationship in the processes which form the substance of secondary variations in prices and production? Let us consider briefly the first question.

Before we can surmise anything about the causes of the secondary movements in the productivity per worker, we must find out the course of changes in the total number of workers employed. Does this number increase during periods of rising prices or not? What is the relation of the secondary secular movements in working force employed to the movements in prices and production?

In order to answer the question, we can survey the data of the same six series used above (Tables 11, 12, 13). We shall not quote the data for working force employed for their recital would be tedious, and they may be found in the sources cited. We shall simply plot these series on charts and compare them graphically with the corresponding series for prices.

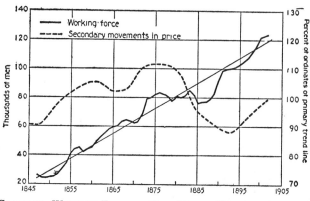

CHART 15. WORKING FORCE IN COAL MINES, FRANCE, 1847–1902

On Chart 15 the index number showing changes in the total working force employed in the French coal mines is compared with the series of secondary variations in coal prices. The series for the working force shows, of course, a steady upward primary trend. But in the deviations from it, the secondary movements are clearly discernible. It is to be seen that these movements show very good positive correlation with the index of prices. The secondary variations in working force and coal prices decline to the end of the '40s and from the beginning of the '50s show a steady rise up to 1875, with a temporary recession in the '60s. After 1875 both series show a declining secondary movement to the end of the '80s followed by an upward variation. The correspondence, on the whole, is clear.

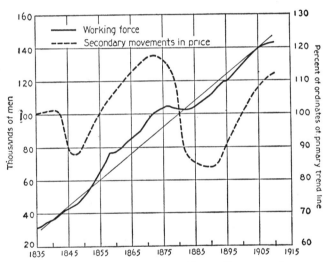

CHART 16. WORKING FORCE IN COAL MINES, BELGIUM, 1835–1910
Nine-years moving averages

On Chart 16 we have the series for total working force employed in the Belgian coal mines compared with the index of secondary variations in the price of coal, Belgium. The thin straight line drawn through the series for the working force is a rough but useful approximation to the line of primary trend and brings out more clearly the secondary variations. Before plotting, the series was smoothed by a nine-year moving average, which items are shown on the chart.

It is obvious that we have here also a case of good positive correlation between the secondary movements in working force employed and those in prices. They both decline to the end of the '40s. They then rise, on the whole continuously, to about 1875. After that date we observe for each a downward movement to about 1890, followed by a recovery to the second half of the 1900–10 decade. The correlation leaves nothing to be desired for its obvious and clear-cut nature.

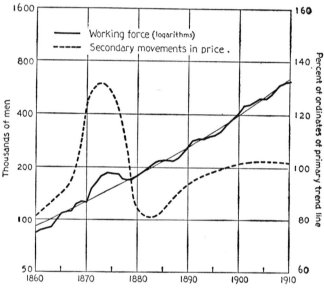

CHART 17. WORKING FORCE IN COAL MINES, GERMANY, 1860–1910

On Chart 17 we present an unsmoothed series showing the working force employed in the German coal mines. The straight line drawn through the series, which is plotted on a log scale, is a first approximation to the line of primary trend. The secondary secular movements thus revealed correspond very well with the secondary variations in the price of coal in Germany. There is in both series a rise towards the first half of the '70s, a decline from there to the middle of the '80s, with a slow recovery thereafter to the end of the first half of the 1900–10 decade. There is again a slight recession in both series in the second half of that decade. Thus correlation in this case is positive and close.

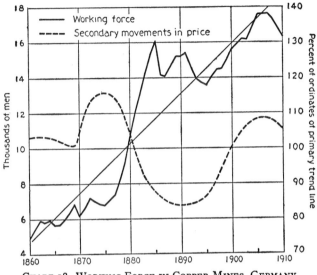

CHART 18. WORKING FORCE IN COPPER MINES, GERMANY, 1860–1910

On Chart 18 we find a somewhat puzzling exhibit. The series showing the working force employed in the German copper mines is compared with the index of secondary variations in the price of copper. During the decade of the '60s both series show declining secondary variations. But prices rise very fast through the first half of the '70s, while the working force continues to decline and rises precipitously only at the end of the '70s and through the first half of the '80s. But precisely during that period the decline in prices is marked. Through the first half of the series we thus have, if anything, a negative correlation. In the second half, the correspondence, however, is positive and fairly good. Both series show an upward movement from the first half of the '90s to about 1906–07, after which they turn downward. On the whole the evidence of this case is conflicting, but it does

indicate that positive correlation between prices and working force employed (in their respective secondary deviations) may be absent during some periods.

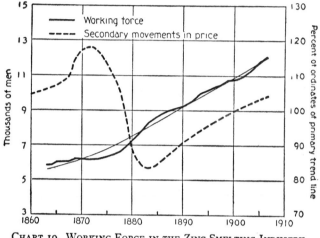

CHART 19. WORKING FORCE IN THE ZINC SMELTING INDUSTRY,
GERMANY, 1863–1907

Chart 19 shows, if anything, a negative correlation
throughout. The data are the number employed in German
zinc smelting and refining establishments. The light line
presents the secondary variations in the price of German
zinc. It is clear that the secondary movements in the
working force employed do not correspond to those in
prices. They decline to the second half of the '70s, while
prices rise to the first half of that decade and decline only
thereafter. The working force series then rises to the second
half of the '80s and declines thereafter to about 1901–02,
while prices rise steadily, beginning about 1884. The reason
for the discrepancy is probably that the secondary variations in production do not follow those in prices, but even
so, this case contradicts the supposition that the movements
in working force and prices are positively correlated.

On Chart 20 we have the series for working force
employed in German blast furnaces (pig iron produc-

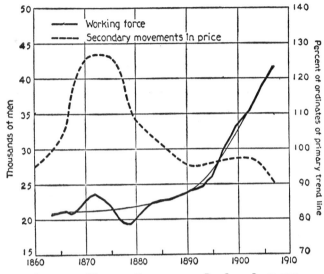

CHART 20. WORKING FORCE IN THE PIG IRON INDUSTRY,
GERMANY, 1863–1908

ing establishments). The primary trend of the series resembles somewhat an equilateral hyperbola. We are, however, interested in the secondary movements, which are fairly clear, once the line of primary trend is roughly indicated. It is to be observed that these secondary variations (the data were smoothed by a seven years moving average) follow rather closely the secondary variations in the corresponding price series. There is in both a rise to about 1873, a decline thereafter (if the first deep trough of a cyclical character in the working force series is disregarded) to the second half of the '80s or the first of the '90s. Then there is again a rise in both series through the '90s that terminates about 1900 in the working force series and about 1901–02 in the price series. From then on both indexes show a declining movement to the end of the period covered.

On the whole, the evidence of this none too large body of data confirms the statement that the number of workers employed tends to exhibit an accelerated growth during periods of rising prices and a retarded growth in times of falling prices. Four cases of the six reveal this good positive correlation, one is doubtful, and one is definitely contrary to the statement. Proof is thus far from overwhelming, and the connection can be accepted only provisionally.

This correlation gives us, however, an inkling as to at least one of the probable causes of the decline of productivity per worker in periods of rising prices. In such periods the number of people drawn into the industry, who find employment in that particular branch of activity, is 'abnormally' large, abnormally, when we conceive the line of the primary trend as the normal or equilibrium level. This employment of an abnormally large body of workers may have certain effects on the productivity per worker:

1. With the number of workers abnormally large their productive capacity may be on the average lower than in times when the smaller forces employed permit selection of the better workers. It is highly probable that during times of continually better employment the percentage of women and minors employed is higher, and that along with the capable male workers the less efficient are employed as well. This absence of rigid selection, which may find its economic justification in the increase of output and greater profits without close regard to individual productivity and costs, is bound to lower the average productive standard of the workers employed.

2. While the periods of rising prices are presumably periods of comparatively greater expansion of equipment, the situation can arise especially in the extractive industries (where there is less room for machinery than in manufacturing), in which there is less equipment per worker employed than in times of falling prices (the general primary trend of equipment per worker being disregarded). But this is only one aspect of unfavorable technical conditions for the workers during periods of rising prices. In extractive industries comparatively poor leads, which do not pay in periods of low prices, are exploited, and the placing of the average worker under comparatively poorer technical conditions accounts for a lower per capita output.

3. As a corollary to this the number of days per year labor is employed tends to increase during periods of rising prices, and the element of fatigue, which is of a cumulative nature, may lower the productivity of the worker.

4. And finally, there are the usual economico-psychological influences. The greater volume of employment during periods of rising prices with the implied opportunities of an easy change of employment renders the worker somewhat independent of his particular job. Furthermore, he may vaguely feel that wage-rates are lagging considerably behind prices and that the changes taking place in the distribution of the national income are unfavorable to him. These circumstances are not conducive to his efficiency and contribute their share in lowering per capita productivity, which seems to accompany the periods of continuously rising prices.

It is apparent that in periods of declining prices these influences have exactly the opposite effect. The body of workers is then comparatively small and presumably better selected. Its very smallness may account for the better technical equipment per worker, not to mention the possibility that the absence of changes and additions to equipment means the absence of disturbances in the technical routine which lower productivity. In the extractive industries only the most productive opportunities are exploited. The number of days worked in the year is less. And with considerable unemployment about him the worker senses the grave necessity of holding his job. The apparent losses of the entrepreneurs and the fall in the cost of living are also conducive to a more satisfied and workman-like mood. These factors all tend to increase productivity per worker in periods of declining prices.

These explanations sound very much like those used in descriptions of cyclical fluctuations to account for the changes in the productivity of labor during periods of prosperity and depression. But all of these influences may just as well be of longer duration as required by the secondary variations than as of shorter as required by the cyclical fluctuations. While the working force employed may expand and contract considerably within the span of the cycle, it may also have longer movements of rise and fall underlying the single cycles. The same consideration obviously applies to the number of days worked in the year. And even the economic psychological influences on the working class, while apprehended by the working men chiefly in their immediate experience in the cycle, may have long duration.[1]

This decline in the productivity of labor being granted, what is its significance for the secondary variations in prices and production?

It is clear that we have here a retarding factor of considerable importance. We have seen above how under our assumption of an initial and substantial rise of prices certain 'forces' are set in motion which tend to prolong this rise indefinitely. We have also seen how this continuous rise of prices occasions an analogous movement in production by arousing entrepreneurs' hopes of prospective profits, thus intensifying the incentive to their type of economic activity. And in this movement of profits with its influence on the various groups of industries and classes is the source of the prolongation of the upward movement in prices and hence in production. Anything, therefore, that serves to cut down profits in spite of an increase in prices will check the influence at the source and eventually put an end to the upward secondary movement.

The fall in the productivity of labor is obviously this type of retarding factor, for with the output per worker declining, although wage-rates may lag behind prices, the time comes when the cost of labor per unit of goods begins to encroach upon the selling price and lowers profits. The force of this factor will be the stronger the further an upward movement has progressed. For as we observed above, the rise of prices tends to slacken then anyway, while the decline in the productivity of labor becomes greater all the time.

The same factor has an opposite effect in times of declining prices. For in that period the continuous interaction of production and prices serves to lower prices continually, lessen profits, and hence diminish production. The rise in

[1] See the article by C. G. DeWolff on the changes in labor policies during the long 'waves,' in the collection *Der Lebendige Marxismus, Festgabe zum 70 Geburtstage* von Karl Kautsky, 1924, pp. 69–70.

the productivity of labor may lower the comparative cost of the commodity, in spite of the fact that in the decline wage-rates lag behind prices. And this influence towards the increase of profits eventually terminates the decline.

Another factor of considerable importance in the processes of secondary variations is the money supply; specifically, the movements in the production of the monetary metals and the flow of these metals into circulation.

We have assumed above that after the initial rise of prices has ceased, the supply of money keeps up with production and maintains prices on the high level already attained. But this is not likely to be the case, at least not during the later phase of an upward movement. For a continuous rise of prices results in a rise in the cost of production of the monetary metals, while these metals themselves, with their price in terms of money fixed, cannot rise in price. In the absence of other changes, a rise of prices initially caused by a greatly increased output of monetary metals and by their flow into the channels of circulation will be checked by a decrease in the output of these metals owing to their higher costs of production.

The available data on the production of gold and on coinage support this view and at the same time suggest one of the factors which may cause a substantial initial rise of prices. When we compare the movements in gold production and new coinage with the generally observed secondary variation in prices and production, we observe that the former rise and decline with considerable precedence over the latter, the difference being from seven to eight years or more. As a result of this lag, we find the secondary movements in gold production and coinage falling most of the period when prices are rising, and rising most of the time when prices are falling.

Of the series available we shall cite only three, one for the world production of gold based on the data of Soetbeer (decennial and quinquennial averages), one for gold coinage in the world, and one for total coinage. The first series is adjusted for the primary trend (a logistic curve) and the items listed are relative deviations:

14. World Output of Gold (Deviations from Trend Line)
Soetbeer Data

1811–20.... 68.2	1851–55... 256.0	1871–75... 102.7	1891–95... 70.9
1821–30.... 56.3	1856–60... 212.7	1876–80... 84.6	1896–1900. 95.0
1831–40.... 53.5	1861–65... 160.6	1881–85... 61.0	1901–05... 101.9
1841–50.... 96.6	1866–70... 139.7	1886–90... 58.3	1906–10... 118.0
			1911–15... 108.7

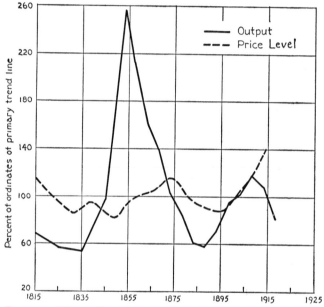

CHART 21. World Gold Output and General Level of Prices,
United Kingdom, 1815–1920
Relative Deviations from the Primary Trend Lines

These deviations from the primary trend line give a very
clear picture of the course of the secondary movements in the
world output of gold. Comparing the latter with the variations in a general price index, such as the Jevons-Sauerbeck
(see Chart 21) for the United Kingdom, we observe a considerable lag of prices behind gold production. Thus gold
output declines up to the decade of the '30s and rises in the
'40s. Prices, however, decline to the end of the '40s. The
gold output rises enormously in the '50s due to gold dis-

coveries in California and Australia but starts to decline almost immediately. Prices are, however, rising until the beginning of the '70s, thus lagging in their downward turn by at least ten years. Rise of gold output starts again in the second half of the '80s with the Transvaal gold discoveries, and the movement continues until the end of the first decade of the twentieth century; the Alaskan discoveries and the application of the scientific method of dredging being mainly responsible for this rise. But prices do not recover generally before 1895, although they do turn upward with gold after the first decade of the new century. Hence, in all cases except the last, the movements in gold output precede by at least 8–10 years those in prices, and even the last case is no exception, as we shall see, in regard to coinage.

If we assume that the increase in gold output is the cause of the initial rise of prices, then the lag in the movement of prices as compared with changes in the output of gold may be due to two circumstances: 1. The current output of gold is hardly significant compared to the stock of the metals already in circulation, therefore, it takes a number of years for an abnormally large output to affect visibly the general price level. 2. This factor of gold supply, together with other factors of a retarding character, must overcome the resistance of the self-perpetuating tendency of a continuous movement of prices and production in one direction. These two circumstances may well delay an initial rise of prices expected as a result of changes in the gold supply.

On the other hand, it should not be assumed that gold production is an independent factor and that its movements are not in turn dependent upon movements in the general price level. It is true that every marked change in gold output is usually connected with the discovery of new mines, apparently an accidental event. But this is not always the case. Thus the Transvaal mines could have had nothing to do with the fact that gold output started to rise in the United States in 1884. And while, of course, such a discovery as that of the California placers at the end of the '40s changes radically the conditions of production and the possibilities of remunerative mining, is it not true that when a continuous decline of prices sets in, the production of gold becomes more and more a paying enterprise and efforts to increase gold output are stimulated? This influence assumes considerable importance, especially in recent times, when with machine methods of gold production, the industry is not dependent on the few rich yields, but has at its disposal the numerous inferior deposits which are commercially profitable by the economies of large-scale machine production. Under such technical conditions the importance of discoveries of an accidental character is greatly diminished and the retroactive effect of a change in the general price level is almost certain to produce corresponding changes in the gold output. These changes, as in the case of the productivity of labor, are in an opposite direction to that of price movements.

These remarks apply to gold output and its influence on prices. But there is the interesting circumstance that not all the gold produced flows into the channels of circulation there to influence prices, for gold also has its commercial uses. The significance of this circumstance is that the upward movement of prices having attained a high level (and gold becoming relatively cheap as coin in terms of other commodities), its flow into circulation may cease, although gold production may still continue to increase owing to possibilities of profitable output. And presumably more and more of it will find commercial uses because of its cheapness.

In this respect it is interesting to cite the figures for gold and total coinage as compared to the output of gold. In Table 15 are given the annual output of gold in the world, the total world gold coinage, and the value of total gold and silver coinage.

The interesting features of the comparative movements of coinage and output of gold are that while gold production continued to rise uninterruptedly to about 1910, gold coinage ceased rising about 1900 and after that year was stable or slightly declining (see Chart 22). The decline would be still more obvious were we to fit a line of primary trend. Gold coinage constituting in value the bulk of the total coinage, the line for the latter also ceases to rise after 1900.

Of course coins are not the only form in which precious

15. Annual Gold Output, Gold Coinage, and Total Coinage,
WORLD, 1873–1913 [1]

Year	Annual Gold Output Millions of Ounces	Gold Coinage Millions of Ounces	Value of Total Coinage Millions of Dollars
1873................	4.654	12.463	379.1
1874................	4.390	6.568	238.7
1875................	4.717	9.481	315.9
1876................	5.016	10.310	339.7
1877................	5.512	9.753	316.0
1878................	5.761	9.113	349.6
1879................	5.262	4.390	195.7
1880................	5.149	7.243	234.3
1881................	4.984	7.112	255.0
1882................	4.934	4.823	210.5
1883................	4.615	5.072	214.1
1884................	4.921	4.810	195.2
1885................	5.246	4.632	221.6
1886................	5.136	4.578	219.5
1887................	5.227	6.047	288.4
1888................	5.331	6.522	269.7
1889................	5.974	8.171	308.3
1890................	5.749	7.220	301.5
1891................	6.320	5.782	257.8
1892................	7.094	8.343	329.8
1893................	7.619	11.243	370.4
1894................	8.764	11.026	341.0
1895................	9.615	11.179	358.0
1896................	9.784	9.477	355.4
1897................	11.420	21.175	605.5
1898................	13.878	19.131	544.8
1899................	14.838	22.548	632.3
1900................	12.315	17.170	540.3
1901................	12.626	12.002	387.0
1902................	14.355	10.663	414.1
1903................	15.853	11.634	452.3
1904................	16.804	22.031	631.0
1905................	18.398	11.898	419.3
1906................	19.411	17.721	421.9
1907................	19.977	19.921	633.6
1908................	21.422	15.829	522.9
1909................	21.965	15.153	426.6
1910................	22.022	22.055	563.8
1911................	22.348	18.002	520.3
1912................	22.549	17.447	532.0
1913................		15.421	497.1

[1] Estimates of the Bureau of the Mint, U.S. Department of the Treasury, Information Respecting U.S. Bonds, Paper Currency and Coinage, and Production of Precious Metals, etc., Washington, 1915.

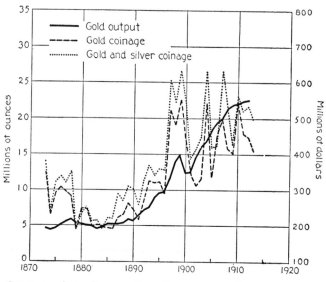

CHART 22. GOLD OUTPUT, GOLD COINAGE, AND GOLD AND SILVER
COINAGE, WORLD, 1873–1913

metals may immediately affect prices. The gold reserves of
the central banks are held both in the form of coin and
bullion, and a cessation of increase in coinage may be
accompanied by a great increase in gold reserves held by
the banks. Still, of the three important central banks of
Europe, only the bank of France shows a considerable increase in reserves after the beginning of the twentieth century. The reserves of the Bank of England are on the
whole stable, if not declining after 1901–02, and those of the
Reichsbank rise, but not to a marked extent.[1] The above
data therefore support the supposition that a larger part
of the output of precious metals is prevented from exercis-
ing an immediate influence on prices during the later phase
of an upward secondary movement.

If, on the whole, the movement of prices has this effect on
gold production and circulation, the lag in the supply of
money is an effective retarding factor in the processes of

[1] See Layton, *loc. cit.*, 1920 edition, pp. 173–74.

secondary variations. For when the initial rise of prices sets in and is carried forward, the conditions of money supply do not remain the same and do not keep pace with the rise of production and prices. On the contrary, the supply tends to decline and eventually results in a rise in the price of credit and means of purchase which will react on profits, or may directly influence prices through the comparative scarcity of money funds.[1]

We have thus far discussed two forces whose retarding influence may account for the termination of either a rising or declining phase of a secondary movement once it has begun and has proceeded for a time: money supply and the productivity of labor. There are possibly other factors which exercise a similar influence, e.g., the movement in stocks of goods. It is quite probable that as time goes on and the secondary variation develops upward, the size of stocks grows and a larger and larger part of the available funds is invested in currently carried stock rather than in improvements in equipment or in the stocks of raw materials. This, if it takes place, retards the self-perpetuating effects that any price increase will have through the change in profits that it brings about. But we possess practically no long-time data on stocks, and this hypothesis must remain a mere guess.

The forces discussed, however, and whose existence seems to be supported by the data, are sufficient to account for a large part of the secondary secular movements. Some of them, as we attempted to show, tend to prolong a once-given price increase, provided this initial increase is long and substantial. And by perpetuating the upward movement of prices they likewise affect production. Other forces act as brakes on this movement in a single direction, for they tend to move contrary to the secondary variations in prices and production.

[1] It is true that in the longer periods of secondary variations there may be a slow change in the reserve rate that would seemingly counteract the growing lack of monetary metals. But the rate of this growth of bank credit 'inflation' should not be above its normal primary trend. If it is, there will be a corresponding rise in the price of credit accommodation and thus call forth another retarding factor which acts through the diminution of the rate of profits.

With this provisional sketch of the mechanism of second-ary secular movements completed we shall discuss the question whether they may be treated as major cycles and their appearance regarded in the same self-perpetuative and self-inductive fashion in which we regard the much shorter cyclical disturbances.

The question of the relative importance of initial causes and of the forces that accelerate or retard a once-given disturbance cannot be solved exactly. The solution depends largely upon the individual investigator's opinion. This does not mean there is no possibility of a rough guess as to the relative significance of these two groups of factors, but being a guess, its results vary with the predilections of the investigators and the emphasis they place on the different aspects of the problem.

We may conceive the secondary secular variations as major cycles, if: (1) the initial disturbances are due to a cause bound to occur fairly regularly or with a rough periodicity; (2) if the processes of exaggeration and retardation are more important than the initial disturbance and the time they take for evoking a rise and a decline fairly equal during the different periods of economic history, so that the cyclical character of these processes would be sufficient to account for secondary variations as major cycles. It seems to us that neither of these propositions is true. The initial causes of the secondary movements, whether a change in the output of precious metals or in the supply of commodities, need not periodically recur although there is a suggestion of the retroactive influence of price rise on the output and use of gold. Nor are the forces called into play of great significance unless the initial disturbance assumed is of considerable magnitude. The secondary variations are thus not major cycles but rather specific, historical occurrences. But this is merely a rough statement approaching a guess in its uncertainty. The length of time covered by the series is too short to be able to draw conclusions on this point with any certainty.

The above account of the nature and mechanism of the secondary variations is necessarily brief. We started by citing some concrete features of the secondary variations in prices and production, their correlation, the precedence of one movement over the other, their average duration. We then attempted to explain why it is that, granted an upward secondary movement in prices, we may expect an analogous movement in production. We proceeded to investigate whether there are any forces that would prolong a price and production increase beyond the initial rise. And having found these forces we instituted a search for the retarding factors. We thus obtained a description of processes very similar to the current conception of cyclical fluctuations. But we have in conclusion expressed the opinion that on the basis of existing data we must not conceive the secondary deviations as major cycles.

Throughout, the exposition emphasized those elements usually omitted in explanations of the causes of long-time changes in the price level. Hence the possible overemphasis on the 'cyclical' elements and the omission of many other factors. But this is due to a comparative lack of data and previous investigations. That the discussion is thus incomplete goes without saying.

APPENDIX A

Note on the Studies of Major Cycles

The long-time movements in production and prices which we have called secondary secular variations were noticed and commented upon by economists long ago. Jevons, in attempting to prove the ten-year cycles, pointed out the protracted movements of the price level that underlay them.[1] These movements of the price level and their influence on production were discussed at length by H. Dennis, Layton, and others. Most of the writers upon business cycles recognize the existence of such movements, although they do not go into detailed description of their nature and influence (Lescure, Aftalion, Lenoir, Spiethoff, Cassel).

Not long ago the theory was developed that these protracted movements form a succession of gigantic cycles, no less periodic and no less inherent to the growth of the capitalistic system than the shorter oscillations of either seven to ten or three to four years' dura-

---

[1] *Investigations in Currency and Finance*, chap. III; *The Variations of Prices and the Value of Currency since 1782*, pp. 119–50, esp. pp. 129–30.

tion. Reasonably enough, this hypothesis was put forward mostly by Marxian socialists (or economists in contact with the latter), i.e., by students whose main interest was in the development and perturbations of the capitalistic system, and who were apt to notice clearly the numerous social implications of the changes in the rate of industrial growth.

The first statement [1] of this hypothesis, as far as we could ascertain, was in an extended article by J. Fedder (van Gelderen) entitled, '*Springvloed Beschouwingen over industrielle ontwikkeling en prijsbeweging*' in *De Nieuwe Tijd* (a socialist publication), 1913, pages 253–77, 369–84, 445–64. After presenting the theory of cyclical fluctuations in the usual Marxian form, the author of the article surveys the prices for England, United States, Belgium, Hungary, and Germany (all beginning with 1850) and comes to the following conclusion: 'Besides the average ten-year cycles in the price level, the price curves exhibit a longer wave motion, which covers several decades in its up and down variations.

'A common direction is apparent in all the curves:

one period of rising   1850–73,
   "   "   " falling   1873–95,
   "   "   " rising   1896 — to date.' (Page 268.)

And having surveyed the movements in the decennial averages of the Sauerbeck index numbers, Fedder says: 'It is clear that a movement of so general a character cannot be due to local or accidental factors. Rather we have here a phenomenon as much inherent to the capitalistic system as other changes in the space of economic life. The symptoms of an expansion period of an industrial cycle are the same that mark the period of springflood (1850–73; 1896–1911). Both arise from the mechanism of the process of capitalistic reproduction' (page 269).

The author then discusses the periods indicated above, showing

---

[1] In his article 'Commercial Crises and Sunspots,' p. 1 (see *Investigations in Currency and Finance*, London, 1884) W. S. Jevons mentions Hyde Clarke as one of the early writers who recognized the periodicity of crises. He quoted from Clarke's paper entitled 'Physical Economy — a Preliminary Inquiry into the Physical Laws Governing the Periods of Famines and Panics' (1847, *Railway Register*) as follows: 'Still thinking that the interval was an interval of about ten years I was during the present famine, led to look for a larger period, which would contain the smaller periods, and as the present famine and distress seemed particularly severe, my attention was directed to the famine so strongly felt during the French Revolution. This gave a period of about fifty-four years.' (Jevons, pp. 222–23.) It is interesting to notice that the period thus indicated, namely, from 1793 to 1847, coincides pretty closely with the dates indicated by the later students of long cycles.

how the rate of development was particularly high during 1850–73, how after that date the picture changed, the countries surrounded themselves with high tariff walls in order to exploit better the internal markets, and reached out for colonies as an additional outlet for their output. Then gold discoveries and the extraordinary development of the electric industries ushered in another springflood period, just as the iron, steel, and transport industries ushered in the preceding one.

The reflection of these periods in production, exchange, trade, interest rates, and the money market is then studied. Fedder is handicapped, however, by the absence of a technique which would permit him to differentiate between what we call the primary and the secondary secular movements. He establishes, nevertheless, the acceleration of industrial output and of the volume of trade, as well as the other phenomena which exhibit the content of a secondary secular variation.

A 'springflood' period, once started, bears the seeds of self-destruction. The end of the period comes because (1) the acceleration of production and trade cannot go beyond the point of saturation of the markets to which the highly developed capitalistic countries export. And this moment is hastened by the industrialization of the importing countries. (2) The production of raw materials, whether organic or inorganic, cannot keep pace with that of finished products. Summing up the theory in a nutshell, the major cycles form a periodic change in capitalistic development, a periodic change whose function is to bring about in the expansion of the capitalistic form of economic life a proper distribution of productive forces (labor and capital) over a greater number of countries, that heretofore were outside of the circle of closely bound national economies.

This exposition of the article serves to show how the explanation of major cycles was modeled upon that of the shorter oscillations, and how entirely different such a presentation is from one in which the movements are treated as due to the accidental circumstances of gold discoveries or some fundamental technical change. Later studies of a similar type served to broaden the statistical basis of the generalization and to increase the number of social implications, mentioned only casually by Fedder. These studies did not appear, however, until after the World War.

In his long speech to the third Communistic International Congress, Trotsky, not being aware of the existence of this article in Dutch, made a curious use of the idea. Referring to a chart of economic development for 138 years (beginning with 1776) published in a Sunday *Times* he notes five periods of acceleration and retardation. These changes 'form a process of adaptation, of equilibration.

When the capitalistic system in a country reaches a saturation point of its market, it has to think of other markets. It will depend upon great historical events — crises, revolutions, etc., whether the period will become one of accelerated growth, stability, or decline. This is a cardinal trait of the process of capitalistic development.'[1] He then goes on to show that on the eve of the war the world was moving into one of these protracted periods of decline, and a depression postponed by the war was now on the horizon with dire consequences to the world's capitalistic system. The whole phenomenon of these major cycles was, however, confused with the line of primary movements as was revealed by some of Trotsky's subsequent writings.

In a study in Russian by N. D. Kondratieff, which appeared in 1922 under the title *The World Economy and its Conjunctures During and After the War*, Vologda, the idea of major cycles was clearly formulated, the author being aware apparently of the existence of the articles by Fedder. On page 242 he says: 'The dynamics [the movement] of the world conjuncture is rhythmical. . . . We have to distinguish two main kinds of cycles: a big cycle that covers about fifty years, and a short industrial cycle covering usually from eight to eleven years.' Beyond this simple statement and an indication of the dates of the big cycles that have taken place through the nineteenth century and later, there is not much discussion of the phenomenon, although a forecast is made that the year 1920 forms a turning point in a big cycle, the beginning of a period of protracted 'depressed conjunctures.'

In 1924, in the collection *Der Lebendige Marxismus, Festgabe zum 70 Geburtstage* von Karl Kautsky, there appeared an interesting article by de Wolff, entitled *Prosperitäts- und Depressionsperioden* (pages 13–43). The author, a compatriot of Fedder, follows in the wake of the latter, repeats in brief some of Fedder's conclusions, but adds some interesting observations of his own. Indicating that in the 'springflood' periods prices are on the whole rising and during 'ebbtide' periods declining, he adds: 'The duration of all these periods is equal, namely, to two cycles and a prosperity or depression period, the former for a 'springflood,' the latter for an 'ebbtide' (page 24). Since during the period of observation (the author begins with 1825) the duration of the cycles was getting smaller, there being on the whole three of ten years, three of eight years, and one of seven, the computed duration of the long periods is 25, 23, 21, and 19 years respectively. This in de Wolff's opinion accords closely with the showing of the data.

---

[1] See *Proceedings* of the Third Communist International (in Russian), June–July, 1921, p. 22.

Tugan Baranowski had already pointed out that the respective duration of prosperity and depression changes with a change in the movement of the general price level. This is as it should be, according to de Wolff, but if we take a whole major cycle, the years of depression and the years of prosperity ought to be equal in number, different as they will be in the two long up and down periods. Another 'polarity' between the latter is that in 'springflood' we have increased production — relatively lower productivity; in 'ebb-tide' — smaller output, and relatively higher productivity. As a proof and illustration the data of Simiand on the French coal mines are used.

De Wolff has rather interesting suggestions concerning the social implications of these long periods of rise and fall. During the 'springflood' periods there is comparatively little unemployment, and the workers are fairly well off economically. The policies of the labor organizations through such periods will thus tend to confine themselves to peaceful economic achievements. But during the periods of decline there is more unemployment, the unions are not rich, and the radical policies of a revolutionary character tend to prevail. Wars, and the possibility of wars are also affected by these changes in the rate of development. They tend to appear at the peak of a 'springflood' period, when the rapid pace of growth stimulates a search for colonies and the size of their material surplus inclines the nations to be more belligerent than usual.

The most complete treatment of long cycles, as far as empirical content goes, is in the latest articles by N. D. Kondratieff, who applies the modern methods of statistical technique to the analysis of time series, and having analyzed a number of these, attempts to form generalizations concerning technical and social changes accompanying the long oscillations. The results of his study were first published in the Russian periodical, *The Problems of Economic Conditions* (supplement to the *Monthly Economic Bulletin of the Conjuncture Institute*), vol. I, issue I, Moscow, 1925, pp. 28–79, and then in a condensed form in his article '*Die Lange Wellen der Konjunktur*,' *Archiv f. Socialwissenschaft u. Socialpolitik*, vol. 56, heft 3, December, 1926, pp. 573–609.

Kondratieff starts with a distinction between three kinds of cycles: the long ones of about fifty years' duration, middle ones of seven to ten, and short ones of three to four years. He goes on to establish the existence of the long cycles either by indicating them in series, where the primary secular movement (prices) is not significant, or by eliminating the primary trend line and showing the existence of the long cycles in the deviations smoothed with a nine years moving average. The series, whenever available, are taken from 1770 on.

Prices of commodities, consoles and rentes, money, wages, volume of foreign trade, commodity volume of output are investigated, and the existence of similar up and down movements demonstrated. The dates of the major cycles revealed are as follows: first cycle — rise: 1780–90 to 1810–17, decline: 1810–17 to 1844–51; second cycle — rise: 1844–51 to 1870–75, decline: 1870–75 to 1890–96; third cycle — rise: 1890–96 to 1914–20, decline: 1914–20 and on. The real character of these major movements is attested by the numerous and important changes accompanying them: (1) they influence the respective duration of prosperity and depression; (2) agriculture suffers especially during such a major decline; (3) during the declining phase a number of inventions, technical improvements, and discoveries are being made, which are utilized in the next rise; (4) gold output grows through the early periods of a rising phase, and more countries are drawn into the orbit of the world economy, especially colonies; (5) at the peak of such a long wave great social catastrophes and wars usually take place. These statements are all empirical observations, and in no way reveal the causes of the long cycles.

The nature of the data, in Kondratieff's opinion, makes the cyclical character of these long movements highly probable. Their variation is not any greater than that of the middle cycles. They cannot be distinguished from the latter on the ground that they are due to extraneous circumstances such as wars, inventions, gold discoveries, or the acquisition of new lands. These events are in themselves strongly conditioned by economic factors, and the long cycles are as inherent to the life of a capitalistic economy as the shorter ones. Kondratieff's is the latest statement of the hypothesis concerning the existence of long cycles.

The purpose of this brief note was to give the list of studies dealing with this interesting problem, and a brief summary of their content, for they seem less well known than the discussions of long-time price movements, such as those of H. Dennis, Layton, Hobson, and others. In the chapter itself we have shown a hesitancy to accept this notion of the secondary secular movements as periodic cycles, our main ground for it being an absence of factors that would explain the periodicity. It is to be noted that Kondratieff himself does not point out such causative factors either. On the other hand, the data seem to be too scanty (only two complete 'cycles' are in the series) for an empirical generalization to be of great weight. We do not have, as with cyclical fluctuations, from sixteen to thirty repetitions of the same phenomenon (in its most cardinal traits), so comparison with the latter as to variability in duration is out of place. Moreover, while having neither great argumentative support nor significant proof in the data, the hypothesis concerning the existence of long cycles if taken as a guide would not permit a flexible determination of the secular variations which we have grouped as secondary. For these reasons we hesitated to accept this hypothesis even as a working guide in our statistical analysis.

———

Since this chapter was written, a new theory of secondary movements was proposed by Dr. Charles Wardwell (see his *An Investigation of Economic Data for Major Cycles*, Philadelphia, 1927).

Dr. Wardwell conceives the secondary secular movements as major cycles of a duration of about fifteen years or less. His explanatory hypothesis is as follows: we start with a business cycle in the trough of a major cycle: the depression is severe, the excessive fixed equipment is wiped out by the preceding secondary downward movement, and the business community has learned a lesson of caution. In the following business cycle (number one) there will be little over-investment in fixed capital and the depression will be mild. But after this successful survival of cycle number one, the business community emboldened, and ready to expand with little or no over-investment in fixed capital, will plunge heavily, and the prosperity of cycle number two will be high above the primary trend. A depression will follow, but it will not wipe out the excessive fixed capital investment and the whole cycle number three will be characterized by a milder prosperity and lower level of activity, the business enterprises living down the results of overexpansion. With cycle number three we enter the declining phase of the major cycle, which brings us back to our starting point. In this manner the major cycle is explained by a cumulation of optimism manifested in a fixed investment policy, and the result is a protracted wave of moderation.

This theory draws attention to an important factor in the ordinary business cycle whose influence extends beyond the duration of the cycle itself; that is, the fixed investment. If we can conceive a cumulation of optimism in the fixed investment policy, everything else is explained. But one may doubt whether these forces of pessimism or optimism can account for the protracted movements underlying business cycles. We tend to think of these psychological factors as accompanying the changes in business conditions rather than as causing them. It still must be explained how in cycle number two the business community finds it possible to expand its investments in fixed capital to an excessive amount when, according to the assumptions, we start at the end of a protracted depression and in cycle number one both prosperity and depression are equally mild, and no surplus funds are available above the usual reserves to stimulate expansion. We still need some stimuli whether 'outside or immanent' to explain this long wave of optimism, which on the whole is gradual and protracted.

We may remark that our data do not indicate any precedence of secondary movements in producers' goods over consumers' goods, a time discrepancy used by Dr. Wardwell as a test of his hypothesis.

In 1928 there appeared in Russian a discussion of the whole problem of major cycles, which contains a report by Kondratieff and a counter reply by D. T. Oparin.[1] Here Kondratieff develops a theory to account for the appearance of the prolonged swings. They seem to him to be essentially cycles of expansion and contraction in the growth of the basic capital equipment of a country.[2] The entire book presents an interesting summary of arguments for and against recognition of the fifty-year cycles.

In a recent extensive article by Kondratieff in the *Archiv. f. Social wissenchaft und Socialpolitik*, r. 60, heft I, pp. 1–85, a study of the major cycles in agricultural prices and manufactured commodities is set forth.

APPENDIX B

COMPARATIVE AMPLITUDE OF SECONDARY SECULAR MOVEMENTS IN INDUSTRIES PRODUCING PRODUCERS' AND CONSUMERS' GOODS

The two groups of commodities distinguished here are divided not by their proximity to the ultimate consumer, but as to whether the commodity by and large will be eventually used by immediate consumers or by business establishments. It is the distinction between wheat and pig iron, and not between wheat and bread. For all our series refer to commodities rather far removed from the finished product ready for immediate consumption.

Grouping the series for the United States on this basis and recording the average size of a secondary movement item (as a relative deviation from the primary trend taken as 100) we obtain the following picture:

16. AVERAGE DEVIATION (SECONDARY MOVEMENTS), CONSUMERS' AND PRODUCERS' GOODS, PRODUCTION SERIES, UNITED STATES

Producers' Goods		Consumers' Goods	
Portland Cement, 1880–1924	25.0	Imports of Silk, 1864–1924	10.6
Steel, 1865–1924	16.3	Anthracite Coal, 1825–1924	9.9
Petroleum, 1861–1924	12.9	Wheat, 1866–1924	6.9
Zinc, 1880–1924	8.2	Cotton, 1866–1924	6.2
Lead, 1873–1924	8.0	Corn, 1866–1924	5.3
Pig Iron, 1854–1924	7.7	Consumption of Cotton,	
Copper, 1880–1924	5.7	1870–1924	4.6
Bituminous Coal, 1840–1924	4.2	Salt, 1880–1924	4.2
Locomotives, 1835–1923	16.8	Potatoes, 1866–1924	3.6

[1] *Major Cycles of Conjuncture*, Moscow, Ranion.   [2] *Op. cit.*, p. 72.

We see that by and large it is true that the industries producing consumers' goods exhibit secondary variations of a considerably milder kind than the producers' goods branches. But the statement cannot be interpreted in the sense that every industry in the producers' goods group is fluctuating more than any branch among the consumers' goods. The comparison by groups stands, but when we consider single industries other factors may influence the size of the secondary variations and disturb the relationship.

For this reason the comparison for other countries is not very significant, since there we find only one or at most two industries of consumers' goods in each. In Germany we have wheat as over against the coal-metal group. The average deviation for the former is 3.7, while for the latter it varies from 4.2 in the case of copper to 9.6 in the case of steel. In France we find wheat and salt having the average deviation (secondary movements) 2.3 and 2.5 respectively, while for the industries producing producers' goods it varies from 2.7 (petroleum imports) to 12.6 (steel). Both cases support the statement made. Only in the United Kingdom do we find a different picture. There imports of cotton and imports of tea show average deviations of 7.9 and 5.8 respectively, while that for coal is 2.9, for pig iron 3.4, for steel 4.2, and for tonnage cleared 6.8. The exaggerated deviation in the case of cotton imports is largely due to the influence of the wars of 1812 and 1860 and to the fact that cotton is more a producers' good in the United Kingdom than elsewhere, but the case of tea imports finds no such grounds of explanation.

CHAPTER V

RAPIDITY OF GROWTH AND AMPLITUDE OF FLUCTUATIONS — STATISTICAL TEST

WE are now ready to examine the connection between the primary trend line and the deviations from it. Stated specifically, the question is: Do we get larger relative deviations from the trend line when the underlying trend is moving rapidly than when it is moving slowly? If we try to answer this question only by means of the general economic knowledge at our disposal, an affirmative answer is likely.

In order, however, to have our data yield the answer to this question we must select two measures, one representing the rapidity of growth, the other the violence of the deviations or fluctuations. The most suitable measure of growth is the average percentage rate of increase over a given period of time. Taken from two different types of curves, there may be some difference in the representative character of this average, but hardly enough, we believe, to disturb the validity of the comparison. As a measure of the violence of fluctuations the average relative deviation may be taken, when necessary, in terms of the trend as 100. The average deviation is selected, because it is easiest to obtain, and there are no reasons for preferring the standard deviation.

We have distinguished three components in our series: the primary secular movements, the secondary secular movements, and the cyclical fluctuations. We can, therefore, study the following sets of relationships: (a) between primary secular movements and the total deviations from the primary trend lines, (b) between primary secular movements and the secondary secular movements, (c) between primary secular movements and the cyclical fluctuations, (d) between secondary secular movements and the cyclical fluctuations.

We shall study the first three of these sets by a comparison of average rate of increase with average deviation, while in the fourth only average deviations will be compared.

The comparison is made by ranking, i.e., a certain group is ranked first by the average rate of increase, then by the average relative deviations, and the ranks compared. When necessary, the coefficient of rank-correlation is computed.

1. Rate of Percentage Increase and Average Deviation from Secular Trend Lines

Ranking of Various Industries, United States

Industry and Period Covered	Rate of Increase	Total Deviations		Secondary Secular Movements		Cyclical Fluctuations	
		Average Value	Rank	Average Value	Rank	Average Value	Rank
Portland Cement, 1880–1924	18.8	27.0	1	25.0	1	7.2	7
Steel, 1865–1924	13.1	21.5	2	16.3	2	12.7	1
Petroleum, 1861–1924	8.8	17.5	3	12.9	3	9.5	4
Imports of Gold, 1864–1924	8.4	16.3	4	10.6	4	11.0	3
Anthracite Coal, 1825–1924	7.2	13.0	6	9.9	5	7.0	9
Zinc, 1880–1924	6.9	11.3	7	8.2	6	7.1	8
Copper, 1880–1924	6.5	11.3	8	5.7	9	9.3	5
Bituminous Coal, 1840–1924	6.3	9.1	10	4.2	12	7.5	6
Pig Iron, 1854–1924	6.2	15.7	5	7.7	8	11.7	2
Salt, 1880–1924	5.3	7.4	12	4.2	11	5.2	12
Consumption of Cotton, 1870–1924	4.7	8.0	11	4.6	10	6.7	10
Lead, 1873–1924	4.3	10.3	9	8.0	7	5.6	11
Cotton Crops, 1866–1924	2.9	11.7		6.2			
Wheat Crops, 1866–1924	2.5	11.2		6.9			
Potato Crops, 1866–1924	2.5	12.7		3.6			
Corn Crops, 1866–1924	2.1	11.0		5.3			

The correlation is first considered within homogeneous groups, i.e., various industries within one country and various countries under one industry. Only after these comparisons are completed is an attempt made to bring all the data together.

Let us begin the comparisons within the separate countries. For this the United States offers the best example.

In the table on page 469 all the industries are included except the series for the production of locomotives, which gives exaggerated relative deviations since it is for an individual enterprise. The evidence presented by the table concerning the four sets of relationships listed above appears to be as follows:

(a) For the rapidity of primary trend growth and the total deviations from the primary trend line, the correlation for all 16 items is not very close, although fairly significant. The rank coefficient yields .606.[1] But when we inquire more closely into the individual ranking, the main cause of the discrepancies, where they appear, seems to lie in grouping together the industrial and agricultural branches, for the latter are the lowest on the scale of rapidity of development but quite high on the scale of average deviations. In the second ranking the agricultural branches are excluded, which leaves only twelve industries. The correlation then is much higher, the coefficient being .874.

(b) The correlation of primary secular movements and secondary movements is also fairly high. The coefficient for all sixteen series including agriculture is .791. The same coefficient in the correlation of total deviations yields only .606. The improvement here is evidently due to the fact that the secondary deviations in agriculture are not magnified as the total deviations are by the peculiar nature of the agricultural cycles. Still, even in this case the agricultural group yields larger deviations. If we eliminate it, the coefficient becomes .832, in this instance less than the coefficient for the correlation of total deviations.

[1] Coefficients here and below computed by the formula:

$$\rho = 1 - \frac{6 \, \Sigma \, D^2}{n \, (n^2 - 1)}$$

where D = difference in rank and n = number of pairs.

The lower coefficient in the correlation of secondary movements with the rate of growth of the primary trend indicates that in the total deviations there is present a factor which is also connected with the rapidity of growth of the underlying primary trend and which makes for a lower volume of secondary variations than required by the primary secular movement involved. We shall see that in most of the other cases there is the same difference between the corresponding coefficients, thus giving a general indication of the influence of another factor.

(c) In the correlation of cyclical fluctuations and the primary trend it is important to study the single discrepancies in rank, for they reveal the other factors at work.

The most important discrepancies are in pig iron, portland cement, and anthracite coal. In pig iron the development is comparatively slow, but the cycles are of considerable magnitude. This may be safely attributed to the industry's position in the industrial system of the country. In the steel industry, which occupies a similar position in the productive system, the development happens to be very rapid, hence there is no discrepancy in ranks between the rate of increase and the average deviation. In portland cement the growth is very rapid, but the cycles are comparatively mild. This is hardly due to the position of the industry in the productive system, but may be due to the concentrated and organized character of the industry, where an effective combination has existed from the beginning. That this factor of combination is of considerable importance in the determination of the amplitude of cyclical fluctuations, we shall have occasion later to observe. In the case of the anthracite coal industry we also have considerable development with comparatively mild cycles. This may be due to the fact that the industry produces mainly consumers' goods and to its organized character during the last thirty years.

The rank coefficient of correlation for these twelve cases is .57. The same coefficient for secondary variations and rate of increase is .83, and for the correlation of total deviations with the rate of increase .88. This shows that the connection between the amplitude of the cyclical fluctuations and the rate of increase is considerably weaker than that between the amplitude of secondary variations and the underlying primary trend; no doubt because the numerous factors which may disturb this connection are of much greater force in the shorter cyclical fluctuations than in their influence on the long-drawn-out secondary variations.

(d) In studying the connection between cyclical fluctuations and secondary secular movements we are interested not only in the absolute magnitude of the correlation but also in the question whether or not this connection is closer than that between the cyclical fluctuations and the rate of increase of the underlying primary trend. Were it closer, it would indicate that some of the factors which cause a disturbance of the positive connection of cyclical fluctuations with the underlying rate of increase also set up a similar disturbance in the amplitude of secondary movements. Were the degree of connection lower it would indicate that the factors disturbing the secondary movements-primary trend correlation are different from those disturbing the cycles-primary trend relations, and that these two factors are to a large extent competitive. It would thus indicate that we have large cycles with comparatively small secondary movements and that there is a group of forces that disturbs the positive connection in accordance with the general expectation developed above.

In the case of the United States the important discrepancies in rank are for pig iron, bituminous coal, and portland cement. We encounter again the same exceptions met in the two tables above, without their self-cancellation. The coefficient for the group (rank) is .43 as over against .57 for cycles-primary trend and as compared to the much larger ones for the other comparisons.

To summarize the case for the United States:

(1) All four sets of relationships have revealed a substantial degree of positive correlation. The rank coefficient varied from .88 in the highest to .43 in the lowest.

(2) The highest correlation was observed between the rate of increase and the total deviations from the primary trend line, the lowest between secondary secular movements and cyclical fluctuations.

Let us now extend these comparisons to other countries, excluding as we did above the agricultural branches. First let us take the United Kingdom.

2. Rate of Percentage Increase and Average Deviation from Secular Trend Lines

Ranking of Various Industries, United Kingdom

Industry and Period Covered	Rate of Increase	Total Deviations		Secondary Secular Movements		Cyclical Fluctuations	
		Average Value	Rank	Average Value	Rank	Average Value	Rank
Steel Output, 1875–1914 ..	6.3	9.6	2	4.2	4	9.4	2
Tonnage cleared, 1815–1913	3.9	7.3	3	6.8	2	3.7	4
Imports of Cotton, 1781– 1913.................	3.3	14.7	1	7.9	1	11.4	1
Coal Output, 1854–1913...	2.5	4.2	6	2.9	6	2.8	5
Consumption of Tea, 1850– 1920.................	2.4	6.9	4	5.8	3	2.3	6
Pig Iron Output, 1854–1913	2.0	6.9	5	3.4	5	6.2	3

(*a*) The rate of increase — total deviations correlation in this case is apparent, for the ranks by the average deviations are 6, 4, 5, in the lower half. The coefficient is .657.

(*b*) The correlation is rather low between the secondary variations and the rate of growth. The coefficient is .371, while in case (*a*) it was .657. The omission of the cyclical element considerably lowers the degree of connection between the deviations and the underlying primary trend. In rank there are large discrepancies in the cotton, steel, iron, and coal series.

(*c*) In the primary growth-cyclical fluctuations comparison, the marked discrepancies are in pig iron, tonnage, and cotton imports. In pig iron we have, as in the United States, a comparatively slow growth with rather violent cyclical fluctuations. In the case of cotton imports we have a similar relation to be explained by the fluctuations in import data as compared with indexes of production or consumption. In the case of tonnage cleared we have rapid growth, but comparatively mild cyclical fluctuations. This may be due to two factors: (1) tonnage cleared does not reflect the actual volume of goods transported, for tonnage measures the carrying capacity of ships cleared rather than the actual freight. The fluctuations in carrying capacity might be milder than those in volume carried, because the ships may be only partially loaded during slack times and overloaded during prosperous times; (2) the series includes a volume of economic activity of a much wider scope than practically any other, and hence might show milder fluctuations, since most of the other series are the comparatively variable producers' goods branches. We see in this comparison the same factors disturbing the connection, whose similar disturbing influence we observed in the comparison for the United States.

The rank coefficient of correlation for this group is .43, i.e., fairly low. It is, however, higher than the analogous coefficient for secondary movements and the underlying rate of increase.

(d) In the secondary movements-cyclical fluctuations comparison, the imports of cotton (exception observed under (c)), does cancel out, but the discrepancy in rank in the other series has remained. As a result, the coefficient for the group is .37 as compared with .43 for cycles-primary trend.

The conclusions for the United Kingdom series is, therefore, the same as for the United States, except that throughout the former shows a lower degree of correlation than the latter.

We shall now consider Belgium, Germany, and France in the order named:

3. RATE OF PERCENTAGE INCREASE AND AVERAGE DEVIATION FROM SECULAR TREND LINES

Ranking of Various Industries, Belgium

Industry and Period Covered	Rate of Increase	Total Deviations		Secondary Secular Movements		Cyclical Fluctuations	
		Average Value	Rank	Average Value	Rank	Average Value	Rank
Steel Output, 1880–1913.	10.8	15.9	1	7.2	2	11.4	1
Pig Iron, 1850–1913.....	4.6	13.6	2	8.4	1	10.2	2
Zinc, 1845–1913.........	4.2	6.3	3	6.6	3	3.3	3
Coal, 1831–1913.........	2.8	3.9	4	2.0	4	3.3	4

For Belgium we have only four series but the correlation is high for all four relationships. It is perfect (1.0) for (*a*), 0.8 for (*b*), perfect again for (*c*) and .8 for (*d*). We cannot, owing to the small number of cases, compare the closeness of correlation in the four sets of relationships. But the high coefficients indicate the existence of a positive correlation in all.

4. RATE OF PERCENTAGE INCREASE AND AVERAGE DEVIATION FROM SECULAR TREND LINES

Ranking of Various Industries, Germany

Industry and Period Covered	Rate of Increase	Total Deviations		Secondary Secular Movements		Cyclical Fluctuations	
		Average Value	Rank	Average Value	Rank	Average Value	Rank
Steel, 1879–1914..........	10.2	12.0	I	9.6	I	5.0	2
Pig Iron Consumption, 1860–1913..............	5.5	9.0	2	5.5	4	6.9	I
Coal, 1860–1914..........	5.0	7.4	4	6.5	3	3.0	5
Zinc, 1845–1914..........	3.4	7.6	3	6.6	2	3.5	4
Copper, 1880–1913.......	2.3	5.6	5	4.2	5	4.2	3
Wheat Crops, 1878–1914..	2.0			3.7	6		

(*a*) The rate of increase-total deviations correlation here is nearly perfect. It would be but slightly disturbed by the addition of wheat, which would rank sixth in the rate of increase and fifth in the average deviation. For the five series, the coefficient is .900.

(*b*) With the inclusion of wheat the number of series is six. The coefficient is .77, i.e., fairly high, but lower than for the total deviations. The addition of wheat only strengthens the connection, for without it the coefficient would be .600.

(*c*) Rate of increase-cyclical fluctuations. Pig iron is here again above its rank in the amplitude of fluctuations. The more important discrepancies are, however, in coal and copper. The coal industry in spite of its comparatively rapid development had rather mild cyclical fluctuations, while in the case of copper the relationship is the reverse. The mildness of the cycles in coal may be a result of the extremely efficient organization of the industry in the Rheinisch Westphalian Syndicate, while the copper disturbances may have been accelerated by the international character of the copper market. But this is pretty much a matter of conjecture.

The rank coefficient for the whole group is .5, showing a considerable but not high degree of correlation. Here again in the case of cyclical fluctuations we have a much lower correlation with the underlying rate of increase than in the case of either secondary movements or of total deviations.

(d) Secondary secular movements-cyclical fluctuations. In this group the coefficient is .1, as over against .5 and more in the other comparisons. The main reason is that the difference in the organization of the industries that would account for a low average deviation in the cyclical fluctuations in the coal industry has no such effect on the amplitude of the secondary movements. On the contrary, this mildness of the cycles might have intensified the secondary variations, as may be surmised by comparing the latter for pig iron and coal.

On the whole, the case of Germany supports fully the generalizations suggested in the comparisons for the United States and the United Kingdom. The degree of correlation between the secular movements (rapidity of growth) and amplitude of deviations is rather high. This positive correlation is highest in the rate of increase-total deviations case

5. RATE OF PERCENTAGE INCREASE AND AVERAGE DEVIATION FROM SECULAR TREND LINES

Ranking of Various Industries, France

Industry and Period Covered	Rate of Increase	Total Deviations		Secondary Secular Movements		Cyclical Fluctuations	
		Average Value	Rank	Average Value	Rank	Average Value	Rank
Steel, 1870–1913.........	7.2	14.2	2	12.6	1	6.5	4
Consumption of Petroleum 1866–1913.............	6.9	8.3	5	2.7	5	7.5	2
Zinc Production, 1870–1913................	4.8	15.4	1	10.0	2	8.1	1
Coal Output, 1811–1913..	4.1	6.5	6	4.1	4	5.0	5
Pig Iron Output, 1824–1913................	3.2	13.5	3	9.4	3	7.0	3
Salt Output, 1872–1913...	2.1	9.5	4	2.5	6		
Wheat, 1815–1913.......	0.47			2.3	7		

and lowest in the secondary movements-cyclical fluctuations relationship.

France. (*a*) Rate of increase — total deviations. This is the only case (of the five cited) where the correlation is insignificant.

The most important single discrepancy in ranks is in consumption of petroleum, which ranks second in the rate of increase and fifth in the average deviation. This may be owing to the fact that it is a consumption series, although we had consumption series in all the comparisons above without disturbing the correlation. The rank coefficient in this case is .257.

(*b*) Rate of increase — secondary movements. This is the only case where the elimination of the cyclical element raises the coefficient considerably. It is .75 for the comparison.

(*c*) Rate of increase-cyclical fluctuations. Here pig iron as in all the other cases is higher in rank in amplitude of fluctuations than one would expect from its rate of increase. There is a noticeable discrepancy in the case of steel, where rapid growth is combined with mild cyclical fluctuations. The reasons for this discrepancy as well as for the comparatively large variability in zinc are matters for conjecture.

The coefficient for this group is .10, indicating hardly any correlation. Again the cyclical fluctuations show a looser connection with the underlying primary trend than either the secondary movements or the total deviations.

(*d*) Secondary secular movements — cyclical fluctuations. In this case there is no correlation at all. The rank coefficient yields 0.0.

To sum up: we find that our tentative generalizations for the United States assume a more general significance. It is advisable to study the items of each table separately rather than to rely upon the value of the rank coefficients of correlation, which are unreliable for a small number of cases. A number of such coefficients may, however, form the basis for a significant statement. Before we go on to the next group of cases, let us present all the coefficients in the following table:

RANK COEFFICIENTS OF CORRELATION, VARIOUS INDUSTRIES
WITHIN EACH COUNTRY

		A Primary Trend-Total Devia-tions	B Primary Trend-Secondary Secular Movements	C Primary Trend-Cycles	D Secondary Secular Trend-Cycles
United States........	12 series.....	.88	.83	.57	.43
United Kingdom......	6 series.....	.66	.37	.43	.37
Germany.............	6 series.....	.90	.60	.50	.10
France..............	7–5 series.....	.26	.75	.10	.00
Belgium.............	4 series.....	1.00	.80	1.00	.80

While these results support the tentative generalizations suggested above, they are far from being overwhelming evidence. The more reason, therefore, to proceed with the other comparisons possible, viz., those for the various national branches of the same industry.

6. RATE OF PERCENTAGE INCREASE AND AVERAGE DEVIATION FROM SECULAR TREND LINES

Ranking of Various Countries, Coal Output

Country and Period Covered	Rate of In-crease	Total Deviations		Secondary Secular Movements		Cyclical Fluctuations	
		Aver-age Value	Rank	Aver-age Value	Rank	Aver-age Value	Rank
United States, 1840–1924....	6.3	9.1	1	4.2	2	7.5	1
Germany, 1860–1914........	5.0	7.4	2	6.5	1	3.0	4
France, 1811–1913..........	4.1	6.5	3	4.1	3	5.0	2
Belgium, 1834–1913........	2.8	3.9	5	2.0	5	3.3	3
United Kingdom, 1854–1913	2.5	4.2	4	2.9	4	2.8	5

(a) Rate of increase and total deviations. The correlation is rather close, the rank coefficient being .90.

(b) Rate of increase and secondary secular movements. For this group the correlation is still close, the coefficient being .80.

(c) Rate of increase and cyclical fluctuations. In the comparisons involving different national branches of the same industry we are eliminating a number of the factors mentioned as causes disturbing the connection sought for. But new factors come in, mainly the national differences which bear upon the amplitude of cyclical fluctuations. These national differences are found in the extent to which industries are centralized and unified as well as in numerous other factors such as the banking system, business habits, etc.

The outstanding discrepancy is Germany, where there is very rapid growth with mild cycles. As suggested above, this may be attributed to the extreme development of combinations and their effective stabilizing influence. The coefficient for the group is .7, slightly smaller than that for the secondary movements.

(*d*) Secondary secular movements and cyclical fluctuations. Here the correlation drops to an insignificant figure, the coefficient being 0.2.

7. RATE OF PERCENTAGE INCREASE AND AVERAGE DEVIATION
FROM SECULAR TREND LINES

Ranking of Various Countries, Pig Iron Output

Country and Period Covered	Rate of Increase	Total Deviations		Secondary Secular Movements		Cyclical Fluctuations	
		Average Value	Rank	Average Value	Rank	Average Value	Rank
United States, 1854–1924...	6.2	15.7	I	7.7	3	11.7	I
Germany, 1860–1913......	5.5	9.0	4	5.5	4	6.9	4
Belgium, 1850–1913.......	4.6	13.6	2	8.4	2	10.2	2
France, 1824–1913........	3.2	13.5	3	9.4	I	7.0	3
United Kingdom, 1854–1913	2.0	6.9	5	3.4	5	6.2	5

(*a*) The most important single discrepancy is for Germany, where we have again a consumption series. The rank coefficient for the five cases is .700.

(*b*) Besides Germany, there is a discrepancy in rank for France and the United States. As a result, the coefficient is 0.1.

(*c*) In this comparison, as in the case of coal, Germany combines rapid development with mild cyclical fluctuations. The coefficient for this group is .7, larger than that shown by the comparison of secondary movements and equal to that for total deviations.

(*d*) In this case, owing to the mild character of both cycles and secondary movements in Germany, the correlation is fairly good. The coefficient is 0.6.

8. Rate of Percentage Increase and Average Deviation from Secular Trend Lines

Ranking of Various Countries, Steel Output

Country and Period Covered	Rate of Increase	Total Deviations		Secondary Secular Movements		Cyclical Fluctuations	
		Average Value	Rank	Average Value	Rank	Average Value	Rank
United States, 1865–1924...	13.1	21.5	1	16.3	1	12.7	1
Belgium, 1880–1913........	10.8	15.9	2	7.2	4	11.4	2
Germany, 1879–1914.......	10.2	12.0	4	9.6	3	5.0	5
France, 1879–1913.........	7.2	14.2	3	12.6	2	6.5	4
United Kingdom, 1875–1914	6.3	9.6	5	4.2	5	9.4	3

The coefficients of correlation for this group of series for our well-established four sets of comparisons are (a) .90, (b) .60, (c) .60, (d) .20. We have in this case, unlike the two preceding, a confirmation of the generalizations suggested above, viz., with the significant degree of positive correlation manifested, the lowest (and rather insignificant) is in the secondary movements-cyclical fluctuations connection, the highest is the rate of increase-total deviations pair.

The important exceptions under comparison (c) include again Germany and the United Kingdom; the cyclical fluctuations being lower in the former than one would expect from its rate of growth and higher in the latter. We may surmise that this is due to the difference in the national organization of the industry, a very important disturbing factor in international comparisons of the connection between rapidity of growth and violence of cyclical oscillations.

In Table 9 we find a somewhat similar degree of correlation, although the small number of cases lowers the value of the comparison. The coefficients are: for (a) .80, for (b) .60, for (c) .60, for (d) 1.00. The high coefficient for the last group is something of a surprise, but the comparative size of the first three coefficients supports our tentative statements.

No significant discrepancies can be noted, due partly to the small number of cases. Germany, however, again shows

9. Rate of Percentage Increase and Average Deviation
from Secular Trend Lines

Ranking of Various Countries, Zinc Output

Country and Period Covered	Rate of In- crease	Total Deviations		Secondary Secular Movements		Cyclical Fluctuations	
		Aver- age Value	Rank	Aver- age Value	Rank	Aver- age Value	Rank
United States, 1880–1924..	6.9	11.3	2	8.2	2	7.1	2
France, 1870–1913........	4.8	15.4	1	10.0	1	8.1	1
Belgium, 1845–1913......	4.2	6.3	4	6.6	4	3.3	4
Germany, 1845–1914......	3.4	7.6	3	6.6	3	3.5	3

a consistently lower rank in its deviations from the trend
lines.

The showing of the group of copper industries is likewise
marked by one exception:

10. Rate of Percentage Increase and Average Deviation
from Secular Trend Lines

Ranking of Various Countries, Copper Output

Country and Period Covered	Rate of In- crease	Total Deviations		Secondary Secular Movements		Cyclical Fluctuations	
		Aver- age Value	Rank	Aver- age Value	Rank	Aver- age Value	Rank
Canada, 1881–1914.....	12.4	15.7	1	10.2	1	11.3	1
United States, 1880–1914	7.9	6.3	3	3.3	4	9.3	2
Japan, 1883–1914......	5.8	7.0	2	4.3	2	5.3	3
Germany, 1880–1913....	2.3	5.6	4	4.2	3	4.2	4

The rank coefficients in their order for this group are:
(a) .80, (b) .40, (c) 1.00, (d) .40. The high value for group (c)
is probably fortuitous, due possibly to the coincidence that
Germany, a country distinguished by the mild character
of its cyclical fluctuations, happens also to be at the bottom
in rank for the rate of increase. This yielded the perfect
correlation for relation (c). On the other hand, the low
correlation for (b), due to the mildness of the secondary
movements in the United States series, may have its explanation in the fact that the United States was hardly affected

by the Secretan Syndicate activities, and was later enjoying the steadying influence of its own combine.

With this exception (c), we have again the highest showing for the (a) comparison, i.e., between rate of increase and total deviations.

The comparison for wheat includes more countries, and presents especial interest since it is the only one dealing with an agricultural branch of production (see Table 11).

11. Rate of Percentage Increase and Average Deviation from Secular Trend Lines

Ranking of Various Countries, Wheat Crops

Country and Period Covered	Rate of In-crease	Total Deviations		Secondary Secular Movements		Cyclical Fluctuations	
		Average Value	Rank	Average Value	Rank	Average Value	Rank
Argentine, 1881–1914...	6.3	23.0	1	12.5	2	17.4	2
Australia, 1875–1914....	3.9	22.5	2	14.4	1	18.4	1
United States, 1866–1914	2.9	11.4	3	7.8	3	8.8	4
Japan, 1877–1914......	2.6	8.8	5	2.5	5	7.1	5
Germany, 1878–1914....	2.0	7.6	6	3.7	4	5.9	6
France, 1871–1913......	0.47	9.6	4	2.3	6	9.7	3

The rank coefficients of correlation in their order are: (a) .83, (b) .89, (c) .60, (d) .60. All these coefficients are fairly high, indicating that agricultural activity does not eliminate the influence of growth on the amplitude of the shorter oscillations. It is only when the agricultural branches of activity are included with the others that the difference in the factors influencing variability is obscured.

The total deviations show a lower coefficient than the secondary secular movements probably because of some disturbing factor influencing the amplitude of the cyclical fluctuations. In the comparison (c) we find an important discrepancy in the case of France. The high amplitude of fluctuations in its crops may possibly be ascribed to the less intensive character of its wheat culture, less than for Germany, Japan, or the United States.

The international comparisons may now be summarized in a convenient table giving the computed rank coefficients.

Warning should be given against taking the value of any of them as significant. What is significant is their cumulative bearing.

RANK COEFFICIENT OF CORRELATION BETWEEN RATE OF INCREASE AND DEVIATIONS FROM TREND LINES

Various National Branches of Each Industry

		A	B	C	D
Coal.......... 5 series.....	.90	.80	.70	.20
Pig Iron........ 5 series.....	.70	.10	.70	.60
Steel.......... 5 series.....	.90	.60	.60	.20
Zinc.......... 4 series.....	.80	.60	.60	1.00
Copper........ 4 series.....	.80	.40	1.00	.40
Wheat........ 6 series.....	.83	.89	.60	.60

Again it is group A which maintains a consistently high degree of correlation, its lowest being .70, its highest .90. The groups B and C show approximately the same degree of correlation, while group D shows the largest number of insignificant measures. By and large then the comparison of different national branches of the same industry supports the conclusion arrived at in the study of the different national groups including various industries.

We may now compute what for some purposes are the most significant and reliable coefficients of rank correlation, namely, those derived from all the series used in our different group comparisons. Excluding agriculture, we obtain the following values:[1]

Comparison (a).......... 35 series.......... 0.72
Comparison (b).......... 35 series.......... 0.60
Comparison (c).......... 34 series.......... 0.59
Comparison (d).......... 34 series.......... 0.51

[1] For the same distributions we have computed the Pearsonian coefficient of correlation r. The value of this was then as follows: (a) .81; (b) 0.80; (c) 0.48; (d) 0.41. The discrepancy in value between this set of (r) coefficients and the rank coefficients is due to the influence of large deviations on the Pearsonian coefficient. The coincidence of these large deviations gave a high value in (a) and (b), and the absence of their concurrence a low value in (c) and (d). It is our opinion that in the present case the rank coefficients are more representative of the degree of concurrence than the more sensitive r.

It is apparent that these coefficients support fully the tentative statements made above, namely:

(1) There exists significant positive correlation between the rapidity of primary growth and the deviations from both the primary and the secondary trend lines. If the series shows rapid growth, the secondary secular movements and the cyclical fluctuations which it manifests are likely to be of greater magnitude.

(2) The closest degree of correlation exists between the total deviations from the primary trend lines and the latter's rate of growth. For the secondary secular movements and the rate of increase, the closeness of connection diminishes appreciably. It diminishes still more when we measure the correlation between 'pure' cyclical fluctuations and the rate of increase. This suggests (1) that in a number of cases mild secondary secular movements are associated with rather violent cyclical fluctuations and vice versa; (2) that in the case of cycles there are a number of factors operative which disturb the connection sought for. In commenting upon the above tables we suggested some of these factors.

(3) The lowest degree of connection, although on the whole still significant, exists between the amplitude of secondary secular movements and cyclical fluctuations.

It must also be noticed that for the comparisons type (c) and (d) the 'international' groups, i.e., comparisons of various national branches of the same industry show higher coefficients than the intra-country comparisons of various industries. This leads to two further suggestions:

(4) The factors that disturb the primary trend-cyclical fluctuations relationship have more to do with differences among industries within one and the same country than with national differences among branches of the same industry.

(5) Certain national conditions which are conducive to milder cycles (less intense than those we would expect from the rate of underlying growth) contribute also to mild secondary movements.

Another study of the amplitude of deviations from the trend lines is possible. Being interesting for itself, it also

offers an additional test for some of the tentative generali-
ations just formulated. This is a study of the changes in
amplitude with the passage of time within the same indus-
ry and in the same country.

For this purpose we may divide the whole period covered
by each series into two parts, and compute the average value
of deviations for each. Before we can compare them, one
correction is necessary. For the whole period covered by
he series the average value of the relative deviations from
he trend lines is 100 (the trend being expressed as 100),
but it may not be so for the separate halves. Actually it is
very near that value, but it is advisable to divide the average
leviation for each half by the average value of the trend
tem for this half. The values thus computed (average
leviation over the average of the trend for the half) are
presented in Table 12.

The growth as described by the line of primary trend
hould be faster during the earlier period and slower during
he later. If this generalization is true, then we ought to
observe a diminution in the size of the average deviation.
Of course, there may be a number of other factors besides
he retardation in growth that would account for the diminu-
ion of the average deviation. But still it would constitute
at least a partial proof.

The results of the tabulation by the three groups of
deviations from trend lines may be described as follows:

1. *Total Deviations.* For the United States series, when
aken for their original periods, in 11 cases out of 17 the
average deviation diminished in the second period as compared with the first. In inspecting the cases that do not
reveal this tendency, we perceive the disturbing effects of
he World War. Recomputing the six series not yielding results in agreement with the other, by excluding the decade
1915–24, we find in three of the six cases the results reversed.
In these three cases the new periods were given in the table.

Altogether 14 cases out of 17 conformed to the expecta-
ion. The three exceptions were cotton crops, bituminous
coal, and pig iron.

For the series covering other countries, only three cases
out of the 28 surveyed show an increase in the average

12. Average Deviation from Secular Trend Lines for First and Second Half of Each Period Covered

Various Series — All Countries

Series	Period Covered		Total Deviations Average Value		Secondary Movements Average Value		Cyclical Fluctuations Average Value	
	I Half	II Half	I	II	I	II	I	II
United States								
Wheat Crops........	1866–1894	1895–1924	12.3	10.5	8.9	5.2	9.0	8.5
Corn Crops.........	1866–1894	1895–1924	13.1	8.9	7.4	3.3	10.3	8.7
Potato Crops	1866–1894	1895–1924	13.8	11.6	3.0	4.1	13.1	11.8
Cotton Crops.......	1866–1894	1895–1924	10.3	12.9	5.5 *a*	4.4 *a*	9.2	11.4
A. Coal Output	1825–1874	1875–1924	17.4	8.5	13.4	6.0	8.0	5.9
B. Coal Output	1840–1881	1882–1924	8.2	10.0	2.7	5.9	8.3	6.7
Petroleum Output...	1861–1892	1893–1924	23.2	10.6	17.5	7.8	13.2	5.3
Pig Iron Output.....	1854–1888	1889–1924	15.7	16.0	8.3 *a*	7.4 *a*	11.3 *a*	10.1 *a*
Steel Production.....	1865–1894	1895–1924	26.9	15.7	25.0	7.2	12.6 *a*	11.8 *a*
Portland Cement....	1880–1901	1902–1924	28.3	25.8	24.9	25.2	9.0	5.5
Copper Output......	1880–1896	1897–1914	8.8	4.1	4.5	2.3	6.9	4.3
Zinc Output	1880–1896	1897–1914	7.0	5.5	5.3	3.9	5.7	5.4
Lead Output........	1873–1893	1894–1914	11.1 *b*	9.4 *b*	9.4	6.6	5.6	4.6
Salt Output *c*........	1880–1896	1897–1914	7.2	6.1	5.0	3.4	3.7	6.7
Imports of Silk......	1864–1895	1895–1924	18.8	13.4	10.9	10.5	12.8	6.7
Consumption of Cotton..........	1870–1896	1897–1924	8.2	7.6	5.0	4.3	6.5	9.1
Locomotives Produced...........	1825–1878	1879–1923	36.3	32.8	18.7	14.8	28.5	30.0
United Kingdom								
Coal Output........	1854–1883	1884–1914	4.7	3.7	3.2	2.6	3.1	2.6
Pig Iron Output.....	1854–1883	1884–1913	7.5	6.1	3.8	2.9	6.8	5.5
Steel Output........	1875–1894	1895–1914	12.2	6.8	3.6	4.8	11.8	6.9
Tonnage Cleared	1815–1863	1864–1913	8.6	6.0	7.9	5.8	4.9	2.5
Imports of Cotton...	1781–1846	1847–1913	18.5	11.2	10.1	5.8	14.5	8.5
Consumption of Tea..............	1850–1884	1885–1920	10.3	3.8	9.7	2.3	2.2	2.4

a Computation brought up to 1914 only, and the two periods changed accordingly.
b 1873–1898, 1899–1924 for total deviations.
c 1880–1901, 1902–1924 for secondary movements and cyclical fluctuations.

TABLE 12 (*continued*)

Series	Period Covered		Total Deviations Average Value		Secondary Movements Average Value		Cyclical Fluctuations Average Value	
	I Half	II Half	I	II	I	II	I	II
GERMANY								
Wheat Crops........	1878–1896	1897–1914	7.7	6.9	4.7	2.7	5.9	6.0
Coal Output........	1860–1886	1887–1914	7.4	7.2	6.6	6.5	3.1	2.8
Pig Iron Output.....	1860–1886	1887–1913	11.8	6.0	8.4	2.4	8.3	5.4
Steel Output........	1879–1895	1896–1913	15.3	9.3	10.6	8.7	6.3	3.8
Copper Output......	1880–1896	1897–1913	7.3	3.7	5.0	3.3	5.2	3.1
Zinc Output	1845–1878	1879–1913	10.0	5.4	8.2	5.1	5.0	2.0
FRANCE								
Wheat Crops........	1871–1891	1892–1913	11.2	7.9	1.6 ^{d}	3.0 ^{d}	9.0 ^{d}	10.4 ^{d}
Coal Output........	1811–1861	1862–1913	7.7	5.5	4.5	3.8	6.3	3.6
Petroleum Output...	1866–1889	1890–1913	9.4	7.2	2.5	2.9	9.2	5.9
Pig Iron Output.....	1824–1868	1869–1913	14.0	11.7	10.2	8.2	7.4	6.8
Steel Output........	1870–1891	1892–1913	19.0	9.1	18.3	6.5	8.1	4.8
Zinc Production.....	1870–1891	1892–1913	21.6	9.1	15.3	4.7	10.9	5.5
Salt Output.........	1872–1892	1893–1913	9.2	9.7	2.1	2.8	8.1	9.4
BELGIUM								
Coal Output........	1831–1871	1872–1913	4.5	3.3	2.9	1.2	3.5	3.0
Pig Iron Output.....	1850–1882	1883–1913	14.1	12.8	9.0	7.6	12.5	8.9
Steel Output........	1880–1896	1897–1913	20.0	11.7	9.9	4.8	13.4	9.6
Zinc Output........	1845–1878	1879–1913	7.1	5.5	8.6	4.6	4.8	1.9
JAPAN								
Wheat Crops........	1877–1895	1896–1914	8.1	10.1	2.8	2.2	7.0	7.3
Copper Output......	1883–1898	1899–1914	7.2	6.5	5.3	3.2	5.1	5.5
ARGENTINE								
Wheat..............	1881–1897	1898–1914	26.4	20.2	15.9	9.5	18.6	16.9
AUSTRALIA								
Wheat..............	1875–1894	1895–1914	18.1	27.3	12.2	17.6	15.9	20.8
CANADA								
Copper.............	1881–1897	1898–1914	16.7	14.8	11.7	8.7	10.4	12.3

^{d} 1815–1863, 1864–1913 for secondary movements and cyclical fluctuations.

deviation in the latter half of the period as compared with the earlier one. The other 25 cases all confirm our expectation of a diminution with the passage of time in the violence of fluctuations around the line of primary trend. Added to the United States we have a total of 45 series, of which 39, or about 87 per cent, confirm our expectation.

2. *Secondary Secular Movements.* In the 17 cases for the United States only three show an increased average deviation in the later half. The other 14 indicate a diminution in the size of secondary variations as time passes and as the industry slackens in its rate of growth.

In the series covering other countries only four of the 28 reveal an increase in the average size of secondary movements in the later half as compared with the earlier one. With the inclusion of American data we have a total of 45 cases, of which 38, or about 84 per cent, confirm our expectation.

3. *Cyclical Fluctuations.* Of the 17 series for the United States, 13 show a diminution in the average deviation in the second period and four show an increase. It must be remarked, however, that some cases which first showed an increasing average deviation showed the opposite when we eliminated the period of the World War. The remaining cases in the table which show an increasing size of cyclical fluctuations would be unaffected even though the last decade were eliminated.

Of the 28 series outside the United States series, 7 show an increasing size of cyclical fluctuations. It is interesting that in nearly all of these the second period begins about the '90s and covers the rise up to the end of the series. This is also true of wheat, cotton (the war period excluded), consumption of cotton, and salt for the United States. Together with the United States exceptions we have a total of 12 cases out of 45 showing no diminution in the size of cyclical fluctuations from one period to the other.

The number of exceptions here is greater than in the two similar comparisons above. A partial explanation of this may be sought for in the fact that the second period usually has a greater number of rising secondary variations than the first, for many of the second periods start from the second half of the '90s, i.e., exactly at the beginning of an upward secondary movement. This prevalence of rising secondary variations in the second period may very well cancel the decline in the rate of increase of the underlying trend, so that the combined secular movements continue to grow at an undiminished rate. Such a circumstance may account for a number of exceptions larger than in the comparisons of the same two periods for secondary variations (deviations) or the total deviations.

Another interesting observation about these exceptions is that a number of them are found in agricultural series. Of the twelve exceptions, five are in wheat and cotton crops. Now the total number of agricultural series used is nine, and we have more than half which fail to show any decline in the size of cyclical fluctuations with the passage of time. Small as the number of series is, it is indicative of the fact that there is generally no such diminution in the violence of oscillations in agricultural activity as there is in industrial activity and trade, and that the decrease in the rate of growth does not have the same influence there.

The data as they stand indicate, however, that in about 75 per cent of the cases the size of cyclical fluctuations does diminish with the passage of time, and relying upon other evidence at our disposal we may assert that the diminution in the rate of growth was probably one of the contributing factors. The good showing in this comparison as contrasted with the others (those for inter- and intra-country), is due to the elimination of most of the disturbing factors, since we are taking one and the same industry in a particular country.

The data at our disposal permit us to go further and study the connection between the amplitude of production and price cycles and of production and price secondary secular movements. We may also study the duration of cyclical fluctuations, and observe the bearing of secular movements upon it. But the first topic has no definite relevance to our main subject — that of the connection between long-time movements and cyclical fluctuations, and the second cannot be investigated very confidently by means of our data, since the determination of the duration of cycles from annual series is rather arbitrary. Besides, preliminary reflections disclose a considerable number of factors other than the rate of growth which determine duration of cycles within the various industries and countries, while the processes of growth themselves do not necessarily exercise any preponderant influence. Computations and comparisons carried through in an analogous method to those above revealed no significant correlation between rapidity of growth and duration of the cyclical oscillations. The only significant result relevant to our topic is the possible influence of cyclical duration on the amplitude of the underlying secondary secular movements, a topic we shall discuss briefly in the next chapter.[1]

We confined the present discussion, therefore, only to the demonstration of the evidence of our data on the subject of the influence which primary growth exercises upon the amplitude of shorter oscillations. The main conclusion is that rapid growth is associated usually with a higher amplitude of both secondary secular movements and cyclical fluc-

---

[1] An interesting connection between the duration of business cycles of a country and the long-time growth of its industries is suggested by the fact that at different periods of time it is different industries that are the 'leaders' in the current business fluctuations. After an industry has reached a considerable size, and before in its process of growth it has reached the stability of a comparatively small rate of secular expansion, it is likely to be the 'leader,' since its comparatively rapid growth and its size make it a most important factor in the economic state of the country. Thus, e.g., the textile industries were undoubtedly the leaders in Great Britain during the first half of the nineteenth century, to be superseded by railroads, iron, and steel. Likewise, in the United States there was the same succession, followed to the end of the nineteenth century by the electric industries, and in the recent decades by automobiles and radio. It may be then suggested that the period of 'gestation,' i.e., the duration of the productive process, in the 'leader' industry is of direct influence on the duration of the business cycle in the country. Thus, the era of the textile industry leadership was characterized by comparatively short swings, while the decades when railroad construction was the leading activity were marked by rather long cyclical fluctuations. Thus, the succession of industries in the center of the economic life of the country, arising from peculiarities of technical progress, might easily explain the variations in the duration of business cycles. However, for lack of space we cannot pursue this hypothesis to any considerable extent.

tuations. This conclusion, with the supplementary, more specific suggestions, calls for further evidence from our general knowledge of the relevant fields. It is essential to formulate the reasons which lead us to expect the existence of such a connection. To this discussion we shall devote the following chapter.

APPENDIX

Formulæ for Computation of the Average Percentage Rate of Increase

Logistic Curve   The equation used being

$$y = \frac{L}{1 \cdot 10^{a-bx}} \quad \text{where } L \text{ is a constant,}$$

the percentage rate of increase is then expressed as $\dfrac{1}{y}\dfrac{dy}{dx}$

It is equal:

$$\frac{1}{y}\frac{dy}{dx} = \frac{b \, 10^{a-bx} \log_e 10}{1 + 10^{a-bx}}$$

For a definite period of time the total percentage rate of increase is

$$\int \frac{1}{y}\frac{dy}{dx} = \int \frac{b \, 10^{a-bx} \log_e 10}{1 + 10^{a-bx}} = \underbrace{-\log_e (1 + 10^{a-bx})}_{(a)} + C =$$

$$\log_e \frac{1}{1 + 10^{a-bx}} + C$$

Taking the expression (a), substituting in it the two points of time, and subtracting the later from the earlier one obtains the total sum of percentage increases for the period. Dividing the result by the number of x units, one obtains the average rate of percentage increase.

Gompertz Curve

The equation used is: $y = Ce^{A(1-R^x)} \ (R<1)$

The percentage rate of increase is then:

$$\frac{1}{y}\frac{dy}{dx} = -AR^x \log R; \quad \int \frac{1}{y}\frac{dy}{dx} = \int -AR^x \log R$$

$$= -AR^x + C \quad \text{Thus} \quad \int_o^h = A\,(-R^h + R^o).$$

To transfer this to the common log base multiply by 2.302585.

CHAPTER VI

RAPIDITY OF GROWTH AND AMPLITUDE OF FLUCTUATIONS — THE RATIONALE

The influence of the rate of growth upon amplitude of secondary secular movements. The probable reasons for it. The influence of cycle-duration upon the amplitude of secondary secular movements — argument and test.

The influence of the rate of growth upon cyclical fluctuations. The support from business cycles theories. The uncertain character of the latter.

Brief presentation of arguments. Theories which find in industrial growth the source of cyclical fluctuations. Factors determining uncertainty and the secular changes in them. The factor of emotional contagion. The disparity between savings and investments. The disparity between volume of output and volume of purchasing power disbursed. Other factors.

Can there be cycles without secular movements?

The influence of secondary secular movements upon cyclical fluctuations.

In trying to account for the existence of a connection between rapidity of growth and amplitude of deviations from the trend it is best to distinguish and discuss separately: (a) the influence of primary growth upon the amplitude of secondary secular movements; (b) the influence of primary growth upon the amplitude of cyclical fluctuations. Discussion of the first topic will perforce be brief, for as yet we know but little of the exact nature of the phenomena underlying the long swings of the secondary movements. A more extensive treatment of the second topic is possible and we shall draw upon the numerous business cycle theories for suggestions which may help us to establish the rationale of the correlation found in our previous comparisons.

There is something very reasonable in the statement that wherever we observe rapid growth, we expect rather considerable fluctuations around the 'normal.' In an attempt to put one's finger on this reasonableness, in an attempt to specify this vague general knowledge of economic reality which gives rise to the expectation, one finds a basis in the conception of an identity of economic forces that make for the growth of industry with those that make for its fluctuations. A process of industrial growth is a manifestation of men's economic activity, motivated mainly by desire for profit and the accumulation of wealth, whatever the final urges may be which underlie these obvious motives. Rapid growth may thus be conceived as a vigorous response by these human economic forces to a given situation. But with a vigorous response in one direction, presumably there is an observable reaction to all sorts of disturbing influences. If under certain circumstances it is possible for economic forces to increase an industry's output by so many per cent, the actions of these forces may be said to be in the nature of a vigorous response to existing stimuli. And it is but natural to expect that there will be just as vigorous a reaction to any disturbance which may set in.

More specifically, the greater responsiveness of rapidly growing industries, and we are speaking here of the secondary secular movements, can be accounted for by two groups of factors: (a) by the fact that a rapid rate of growth implies rapid change; (b) by the circumstance that rapidly growing industries have comparatively ample funds for large relative expansion (i.e., expansion measured in percentages of current output). Whenever we have a rapidly growing industry as compared with one slowly growing, we have a situation of comparatively rapid change on the one hand and comparatively slow on the other. But change in the conditions of economic life, as it takes place in our era, always means uncertainty. No matter how certain the prospect of successful growth in the long run, any change which it involves unsettles old conditions and creates new ones. To expand always involves uncertainty, but in a young industry this is doubly true. An industry can grow very rapidly when it is young, i.e., when it begins to extend to new markets and when its technical changes are rather numerous. Hence, a process of rapid growth always implies changing conditions, and takes place amidst rapidly changing factors. It thus calls for economic activity unafraid to make rapid adjustments and prepared to take on new risks in spite of the comparative uncertainty involved in the continuous expansion.

Obviously any disturbing factor which appears under these conditions exercises an exaggerated influence upon the economic forces affecting a rapidly growing industry. The prevailing conditions of uncertainty create a threatening outlook and the reaction is pronounced. If the disturbing factor is in the human economic forces themselves (e.g., psychological contagion), its influence will be comparatively stronger because of the peculiar mode of economic activity or response, which assumes a sort of specific behavior pattern adapted to the peculiar circumstances of rapid change. A slowly growing industry, on the other hand, presents conditions of greater stability and attracts that type of economic individual who prefers these conditions, thus giving rise to a somewhat different reaction pattern.

Hence the economic feature of pronounced change accompanying rapid growth is the general uncertainty for every individual enterprise and a consequent readaptation in the general mode of business activity. It might seem that this applies only to those shorter changes embraced by cyclical fluctuations. It might appear that only in these does the difference in the 'speculativeness' of business men result in a significantly different response to an otherwise similar profit stimulus. But in so far as a secondary movement is a net resultant of the single cyclical fluctuations, where the disproportion (of a continuous character) between the phases creates a long upward or downward movement, this disproportion will be the greater the more violent is the response of the group of business men concerned during the prolonged initial rise or fall, and the resulting secondary movement will form a greater positive or negative deviation.

But besides the economic aspect of the great change implied in rapid growth, there is the purely technical phase, which as an essential base for the economic changes merits separate consideration. It was shown in Chapter I that rapid growth of an industry is usually connected with a high rate of technical changes, and that in a young and rapidly growing industry the field open for such technical changes is comparatively wider than in one old and stable.

The acceleration of entrepreneurial activity during the periods of rising secondary movements will have then greater expansion possibilities in a young than in an old industry. A rapidly growing industry may have the comparative advantage of still greater profits because of the economic efficiency of the technical changes introduced, while an older and less rapidly growing industry will have to content itself with that increase of profits which is connected with shifts in the national distribution.

The other factor, the greater availability of free funds for expansion, is equally applicable to the cyclical and to the secondary secular movements. That an industry growing rapidly, i.e., comparatively faster than most of the other branches of productive activity, is *ipso facto* small as compared to these was pointed out in Chapter I. It was also shown that its flow of profits compared to the capital·invested is larger. Now this greater availability of free funds facilitates a greater relative expansion whenever stimulated by changing conditions. And the consequent overstocking is proportionately larger. Likewise factors tending to an opposite turn of affairs will be more pronounced in this rapidly growing, more changeable, and speculative industry.

To these considerations must be added the difference between the groups of consumers' and producers' goods. We have set forth the reasons which give rise to milder secondary variations in the one group than in the other. At the same time most of the consumers' goods branches have a rate of growth smaller than those for producers' goods. There is thus a roundabout connection between rate of growth and size of secondary variations which may operate as a subsidiary factor. But it should be noticed that in the few cases when the branches producing consumers' goods display a high rate of growth they also display rather considerable secondary movements.

The explanation of the above connection runs in essentially the same terms as that between total deviations and the underlying rate of growth. At the same time, as we have seen above, the former correlation is significantly lower than the latter. Evidently in a number of cases cyclical fluctuations of a considerable magnitude accompany comparatively mild secondary secular movements and vice versa. Is there any reason to suppose that these two groups of changes are competitive in the sense that where we find violent cycles we should expect mild secondary variations and vice versa?

As we have seen just now the reasoning points the other way. With violent cyclical fluctuations, the tempo of business activity is rather fast, the consequent maladjustment considerable, hence the resulting secondary movement ought to be larger. What is it that may bring about mild secondary variations with considerable cyclical fluctuations?

As a preliminary suggestion the length of the cycle may be mentioned. If we have a continuously acting disturbance and two industries in which for some reason or other the length of a cyclical fluctuation is quite different, which of the two industries will better and more fully reflect the continuously acting cause? Probably the industry of the shorter cycles, for there the swings of cyclical character would not be long enough to disturb considerably the more prolonged influence, and what is ·more, it would not affect it in its cumulative effects. On the other hand, a cycle of considerable length will interrupt the whole movement and modify the effects of a prolonged rise or fall, preventing it from having any considerable cumulative influence. If for example we have a secondary movement continuing for 22 years and a cycle continuing for 10 to 11 years, the five or six years of a depression coming during the 10–12 years of an upward secondary secular swing will considerably reduce any cumulative effects which this swing may have gathered. If, on the other hand, we have short cycles of three to five years' duration, the influence of the given prolonged rise in prices will be of a greater effect for its influence will cumulate more steadily. Thus we have the possibility of a considerable cyclical fluctuation accompanying a rather mild secondary movement because of the length of the cycle.

Unfortunately, we are unable to test this suggestion except in the crudest manner. We may inspect the tables in the previous chapter that give the correlation of rate of increase and amplitude of secondary secular movements, and wherever there is a marked discrepancy in rank, the duration of the cycles in the corresponding series may be considered. We need not give the tables of average duration of cycles, but when necessary we shall state their specific values.

Looking then at Table 1 of Chapter V, comparison (b), we find the rank in amplitude appreciably smaller than the rank in the rate of increase in the following series: copper, bituminous coal, and salt. But precisely these three series show the longest cycles as compared with the others for the United States (locomotive output excluded). The average duration of a cycle in these industries is in the order mentioned: 4.7, 5.2, and 5.3 years. On the other hand, the series that show a rank in amplitude greater than the rank by rate of increase are: lead, cotton crops, wheat crops, and corn crops. With the exception of lead, which shows a cycle of considerable duration, the other three series are in the lower half of the column giving the different durations in descending order.

Of course this factor of cycle duration is not always active, for the amplitude of the secondary movements is affected by other influences. The case of lead in the United States forms an exception. In other countries we find cases which point to the probable influence of the duration of the cycles, and other cases which do not reveal this influence. In the United Kingdom the important discrepancies in rank (between rate of increase and size of secondary variations) are in steel, coal, imports of cotton, and consumption of tea. In steel and coal the rank by size is smaller than the rank by rate of increase, and these two series show the longest cycles in the country. In cotton imports the situation is reversed, its cycle is the shortest in the country. The case of tea is not so decisive. Its rank by size is higher than its rank by rate of increase. But while the duration of its cycle is in the lower half of the series for the United Kingdom, it is absolutely fairly large.

In the case of Germany we have two important discrepancies: pig iron and zinc. In pig iron the somewhat small size of secondary variations is explained by the extreme length of the cycle. But in zinc we have considerable secondary variations, while the length of the cycle is also considerable.

In the case of France, however, both cases contradict our

hypothesis. The consumption of petroleum shows comparatively insignificant secondary variations, but its cycle is the shortest. Pig iron shows considerable secondary variations and a long cycle. For Belgium we have no serious discrepancies in rank. For the European countries then, four cases support our hypothesis and at least three do not show the expected influence of length of cycles. It is only in the United States where the number of series is considerable that the expected influence is unmistakable.

This evidence of course is not highly convincing. It does lend, however, partial support to the hypothesis formulated above, a hypothesis that is otherwise 'reasonable,' i.e., which has some basis in the body of our accepted knowledge.

In the attempt to explain why there is a definite connection between rapidity of growth and amplitude of cyclical fluctuations, the extensive writings on the nature and causes of cyclical fluctuations should offer some assistance. The trouble is that most of these are schematic descriptions of the influence of one or two causative factors in hypothetically stable conditions, and we are left to surmise the changes that would take place in these factors if conditions pursued the course laid down by industrial growth.

But our knowledge of industrial growth is quite incomplete. We have emphasized some of its characteristics, but we have left untouched the problem of long-time changes in a number of economic institutions. If cyclical variations are considered to be caused by the functioning of these uninvestigated institutions, we would be unable to conclude anything concerning the effect of long-time movements on business fluctuations. The following tentative outline of these effects is, therefore, necessarily incomplete. In presenting it we have drawn upon only those business cycle theories which deal with factors that seem to us subject to the definite influence of secular movements. But of course all economic institutions are shaped and modified by the long-time movements, and the omission of some from the discussion should be regarded as a confession of ignorance rather than as an assertion of lack of connection with processes of growth.

With these qualifications stated, we may outline the

reasons which lead us to suppose the existence of a definite relation between secular movements and the cyclical fluctuations.[1]

I. Innovations, Progress, and the Cyclical Fluctuations

There are at least two theories which stress the processes of growth and progress themselves as the main cause of cyclical fluctuations.

Joseph Schumpeter ascribes the appearance of cyclical fluctuations to the activity of entrepreneurs of the dynamic type. These innovators tend to act in waves, in a unison of an innovating urge and its subsidence. This revolutionary activity of the one or the few arouses similar action by economic men of the more passive and meeker types. Crisis and depression follow because after the innovations are carried through, the data on which the active business men plan their actions have been modified by these innovations and a period of readjustment becomes necessary.

It is clear that if the activity resulting in progress and growth is responsible for the cyclical fluctuations, the faster and more appreciable the growth, the larger should be the amplitude of the wave-like fluctuations engendered. If the relative increase in the volume of production attained by the entrepreneurs is considerable, the data on which both they and the 'static' men plan their activity will be distorted and the subsequent decline should be both longer and more pronounced.

This connection may be made clearer by taking Schumpeter's definition of the period of depression as a time during which a process of 'statization' takes place. Depression means really a cessation of innovating activity, keeping production on the level attained in the preceding period of innovations. Maintaining production on a given level is a decline only in comparison with the preceding and succeeding periods of rise. But the greater the increases in production during the innovating periods, the greater the decline which

[1] For the summaries of the theories used in the exposition see W. C. Mitchell, *Business Cycles, The Problem and Its Setting*, chap. I. New York, 1927.

appears in the level periods, the periods of 'statization.' If we thus postulate a period of rapid growth, with its high rate of innovations, the resulting fluctuations in prosperity and depression are more pronounced than otherwise.[1]

Another presentation of cyclical fluctuations as a consequence of economic development is that of Vogel. Vogel points out how extremely difficult it is for industries, which usually grow at different rates, to keep their moving equilibrium in the face of various disturbances.

In this connection it is interesting to note some of the results obtained from a study of the rates of increase in various industries.[2] The results indicate that as time passes and the rate of increase diminishes, the difference between the rates of increase in the different industries diminishes as well. In other words, a closer integration of industries takes place as far as the rapidity of their growth is concerned. Of course one does not know whether the equilibrium should be measured in absolute terms, in units of commodities, or in terms of the relative rate of change. But since we measure the cycle in terms of relative deviations, one may suppose that the moving equilibrium to which Vogel refers is to be imagined statistically as a process of concurrent gradual change in the rate of growth of the different industries.

Accepting this definition of an equilibrium, we can see that this equilibrium changes more rapidly in the early periods of growth of industries than in the later. For there is a transition from a wide divergence of rates of increase to one much narrower, and the narrower this divergence in growth the smaller the possibility for change of this equilibrium. This process of integration of an industrial system proceeds more rapidly and to a greater extent during the early periods of growth of a national system than later, when a certain degree of integration is achieved. If the difficulty of maintaining the equilibrium in face of disturbing circumstances is due mainly to its complexity when industries grow at different

[1] This interpretation of Schumpeter's theory is to be taken as a brief summary rather than as a precise formulation. Our purpose in this chapter is not so much to give an authentic exposition, as to use each theory as a point of departure for our reasoning.

[2] Not included in the text for lack of space.

rates, the nearer such an equilibrium is to stable conditions, the less the disturbance created by the accidental, outside circumstances.

This suggestion is not at all so formal logically as it may seem at first glance. It goes without saying that in a country where the industries grow rapidly and at varying rates the possibility of continuous adjustment is much smaller than in an older country where industries approach the maximum level. But one must remember not only the difficulties of adaptation to conditions of rapid growth, but also the fact that in its development the economic system is gradually evolving certain organizations which help to integrate it and to overcome maladjustments due to differences in the rate of growth. One may again recall that organization into trusts, cartels, or business associations presupposes a preceding development of small enterprises into larger ones and a stabilization of the whole process of productive activity, that comes only after the rate of technical change has already abated. Taking into account these secondary manifestations of a process of development one is impressed by the truth of the statement that a decline in the rate of increase helps to maintain the equilibrium within the system, and that the disturbances in the moving equilibrium tend to be milder the slower the growth.

As an interesting corollary we might notice that this discussion of the general equilibrium within an economic system or a set of industries likewise refers to the partial equilibrium of a given industry with the others. Whenever we have a rapidly growing industry, we have simultaneously a rapid diminution of the discrepancy between the rate of growth of this industry and that of the others. In so far, therefore, as cyclical fluctuations in the given industry are caused by disturbances of the equilibrium between it and the rest of the system, this diminution in the discrepancy, this slowing up in the movement of the equilibrium level is, according to this theory, bound to result in an increasing mildness of these fluctuations. Thus we see that the forces in industrial growth set up cyclical fluctuations of a magnitude corresponding to the rapidity of progress, and as a consequence wherever we have a rapidly rising secular movement in production, the cyclical fluctuations should be of considerable magnitude.

But the same relation also holds true for the price cycles, for the dynamic entrepreneurs not only increase production but also prices of commodities which they purchase in order to carry their projects through. And likewise disparities in the rate of growth cause not only over- and under-production, but also corresponding wavelike movements in prices. The greater the magnitude of production cycles, the larger the amplitude of the price cycles. This relationship will be considered in fuller detail below, in the discussion of long-time changes in the factor of uncertainty which bears upon the problem at hand.

II. UNCERTAINTY AND THE EMOTIONAL FACTOR

A. *Uncertainty.* Some theories describe the business cycle chiefly as a result of the uncertainty on the part of producers and middlemen concerning the conditions which will prevail in the market when they are ready to dispose of their goods (Hardy). Formulated thus, the theory is vague. Indeed in a more specific description of the processes by which such uncertainty results in business cycles, we see that the main explanation lies in the concerted, competitive action of business men in response to misleading signs of price changes or of changes in orders. We may then ask of what influence are economic development, growth, or long-time change in general on the way business men respond to such changes as stimuli? If we consider an industry in various phases of its historical development, may we expect a greater relative exaggeration in response to a given price stimulus in the earlier stages of rapid growth than in the later stages of slower growth?

The factors, which arouse an exaggerated response to such a stimulus, can be listed in the following groups: (1) the ease of response. This includes the availability of means, relative to the 'normal' size of the entrepreneurs' activity; the readiness of the entrepreneur himself to venture into new activity on the basis of this condition, this being confined to psychological, 'irrational' grounds only; (2) the economic reasons for the response. This includes the prospective profits from the transactions to be consummated. Besides these factors determining the *initial* response, there are a number of others, such as the length of the production period, banking policy, organization, etc., which would determine the duration and in part the intensity of the whole cyclical phase into which this initial response will develop.

It is easy to see that both in the factors that make for an easier response and in those that justify it from the point of view of economic 'reasonableness' there is a predominance of those characteristics of early and rapid development. Business men are more liable under conditions of a rapidly growing, rapidly changing industry to overshoot the mark than in a well-established industry. We have mentioned more than once the two factors that account for this: (1) the greater degree of change in a rapidly growing industry; (2) the larger comparative size of funds for expansion.

Besides these factors there are two others of importance: In a rapidly changing industry further expansion may have additional economic reasons, for it holds out to the entrepreneur the benefits of increasing returns. When the industry grows rapidly, presumably the individual enterprise does also (except where there are limiting conditions as in agriculture). In the early periods, while technical progress is reaching the stage where methods are being standardized, there is usually a period where increase in the size of the producing units is a source of great economies. This source recedes to the background, once the maximum technically efficient size is achieved.

The second point refers to the effects of decline in the rate of growth. The economies of large-scale production becoming apparent and effective at a certain point in an industry's development results for most industries in the taking over by a comparatively small number of large-scale enterprises of the bulk of output. In a few industries we find effective combinations and even dominance by one corporation. But even where this does not take place, there frequently occurs a diminution in the number of independent units within any industry. Leaving out of consideration the iron and steel branches, which in most of the countries we have surveyed are at present dominated by effective trusts or cartels, there has been a diminution of independent enterprises in other metals such as copper, lead, zinc. This decline in the number of enterprises in the field reduces the exaggerating influence of competition. And while this factor may work the other way, for in the very early days of an industry the number of pioneers is small, this period is very limited, and is characterized by elements making for speculative activity.[1]

These two factors, in addition to the others mentioned above, make it quite clear why, generally speaking, the relative disturbance in industrial activity which takes place in response to a given price stimulus (increase) is larger in the faster growing industries than in the slower. This granted for the positive phase of a production cycle, it is equally apparent for the declining phases whose intensity is largely determined by the degree of exaggeration represented by the phase of prosperity. The higher the latter, the more intense may we expect the depression to be. Hence the factors in a rapidly growing industry which make for a quick and strong response to a rise in prices will eventually, in the unfolding of the processes constituting the cyclical fluctuations, lead to a depression more intense than would otherwise prevail.

An effect of the same significance results for the fluctuations in prices. Given an initial price rise, one of the sources of the prolongation of this rise is that business enterprises expand their production in order to supply the existing demand, and in this expansion increase their demand for raw materials and labor, thus raising the prices for these factors. This rise in prices of the means of production under conditions where the demand for the commodity is still unsatisfied tends to drive the price beyond the initial rise.

Evidently this secondary effect is the stronger, the greater the response of the given branch of production to the initial price rise. If this response is vigorous, the rise in prices of the related commodities will be pronounced, and the effect on the price of the initial commodity the larger. Hence, the conditions which call forth a considerable response in a branch of production to a given rise in price intensify the corresponding phase (and thus the next phase) of the price cycle.

[1] Cf. building, oil, gold, automobile booms.

This statement is subject, however, to a qualification which gives it much less definite bearing than would seem at first glance. We have remarked above that a rapidly growing industry tends to be rather small in size in comparison to other, more slowly growing industries. It must also be noticed that a large part of the raw materials are demanded by nearly all of the industries. The demand, therefore, registered by rapidly growing industries tends to be small as compared with the demand of the other, slower growing industries. The price-raising effect of the exaggerated response on the part of the rapidly growing industries is, therefore, likely to be rather limited by the comparatively small size of the demand.

B. *The Emotional Factor.* According to some economists (notably Pigou) cyclical fluctuations are largely due to waves of buoyancy and depression, of optimism and pessimism, both 'erroneous.' The causes making for such a simultaneous (for most business men) recurrence of these psychological waves are: first, a measure of psychological dependence which binds together the business community, and second, the fact that the error of optimism on the part of one group of business men creates a justification for some improved expectation on the part of other groups.

In this explanation we see the factor to which we have briefly referred several times as being appreciably influenced by the conditions implied in the rate of growth. We shall now consider the latter in connection with the two factors indicated as making for emotional waves.

The closeness of psychological interdependence is contingent to a large extent upon the degree to which business men in the community allow 'irrational' elements to sway them in the determination of their business activity. The more irrational the latter, the more is the business man susceptible to the influence of imitation and psychological contagion. Compare, e.g., the activity of an amateur or even professional stock exchange speculator with a producer of such a staple and organized market commodity as portland cement. The former is much more readily influenced by feelings of optimism or pessimism generated in his fellow-traders than the latter. But the degree of irrationality in business men's behavior depends upon the uncertainty of the business. The more fixed and routine the latter, the more certain it is, the less is there room for irrational influences, and the susceptibility to outside psychological influences is reduced, with a lower degree of purely 'psychological' interdependence in the community.

This psychological dependence rests, therefore, largely upon the element of uncertainty in the activity of the business men. And, to follow up this line of conjecture, we find that the dependence occurs in two ways. First, in any immediate situation, the greater the uncertainty and the more conspicuous the absence of factors dominating the situation and pointing definitely one way or another, the more will the action of business men be subject to guesses based largely on feelings, the greater will be the 'watching' of one group by another, and the more marked will be the action of the 'psychological' interdependence. And, second, the same influence may be of a long-range kind. In an industry, which, for some reason or other, exhibits considerable fluctuations and rapidly changing conditions, there will be a general disposition on the part of business men engaged therein to be more sensitive to passing influences, to be more inclined to judge on 'irrational' grounds, because the rational ones, in view of rapid change, rarely afford the possibility of satisfactory decisions. In such conditions of frequency of change, where there are considerable fluctuations in the volume of business and profits, there is more place for uncertainty and irrationality, and the attitude and decisions of the business community are an adjustment to the situation. There is a more speculative character about this activity, there is a greater readiness to respond to any change, there is a closer contact among the members of the community, and closer bonds of 'psychological' interdependence. It is quite possible that there is a process of selection among business men, in the sense that only those inclined to the more speculative activity, only those who are predisposed to this activity of deciding and risking in quickly changing conditions will enter the corresponding branch of business activity and help to perpetuate these conditions, until in the process of economic and technical development the industry reaches the point of comparative stability, and the need of the moment is not for pioneer industrialists and innovators, but for close-fisted, exacting managers who will introduce standard methods both in the internal organization of the business enterprise and in its outside market activities.

This has a definite bearing on the second factor also, on the justification that an optimistic error on the part of one group creates higher expectations on the part of others. For one thing, the larger the optimistic error displayed by the other group, the more prevalent it is, the greater is the justification for acting upon the changed expectations. And we have just seen how psychological errors arise out of uncertainty and conditions changing with the rate of development and growth. But again it might be suggested that basing one's activity upon the optimistic errors of others is in itself a speculative way of acting as compared with planning based upon careful estimates of demand and supply. Acting upon the basis of the performance of a part of the community is really speculating. And the degree to which such a 'justification' becomes effective in determining other people's activity depends then upon the general character of this activity, upon the degree to which it is shaped by objective data, guesswork, or an inclination to follow very closely occurrences in the market. Here again, the potency of the justification created by other men's economic activity depends largely upon the whole congeries of circumstances that make business action more or less speculative, i.e., upon the factor of uncertainty.

We see therefore that the emotional factor in cyclical fluctuations is only one specific force among those that exercise their influence through the uncertainty in economic life. The differential aspects of this force depend largely upon the differences in the degree of uncertainty existing. And these latter, as shown at length above, are associated quite definitely with changes implied in the process of growth and development, or with differences associated with varying rates of the underlying increase.

III. SAVINGS — INVESTMENTS

By some economists business cycles are treated as a result of maladjustment between the flow of savings and investments and the demand of the business community for new capital. We shall discuss two variants of this theory in their bearing upon the problem at hand. The first variant (by Tugan Baranovski) stresses the comparatively even rate at which some incomes are received and the comparative steadiness with which they go to form a loan-fund, and the much more fluctuating rate at which business men draw upon this loan-fund in order to further their enterprises. This rate at which the loan-fund grows serves as a 'brake' upon the greater expansive proclivities of the business men's investing activities. But while it does so during the prosperity phase, during depression the accumulation of loan-funds forms a continuously growing stimulus which finally breaks down the temporary reluctance of the business community to make any further commitments.

This being the origin of cyclical fluctuations, what are the factors which determine the variations in duration and amplitude? We may surmise as follows: (1) Since it is the stable incomes that largely contribute to the stability of the loan fund, which serves as a check both on the expansive and on the contractive tendencies in the capital investment activity, the smaller the relative share of these stable incomes, the less effective will be the check, and the more intense and drawn out will be the periods of both prosperity and depression. (2) The greater an industry's dependence upon this stable loan fund, the more effective will be the check. For if an industry can subsidize itself very largely from its own earnings, then even though it may have recourse to other sources for funds, it is able to keep on investing at an ever-increasing rate for a longer time, or more comparatively to its present size, than when it relies largely upon credit obtained from banks or credit markets in general.

Our scant knowledge of the processes of growth of an industrial system does not permit any confident statement as to what happens to the relative share of stable incomes in the whole body of a growing national economy. But some hypotheses may be suggested concerning each separate industry.

Within every industry, in the process of development and slowing up of the rate of change, there usually take place the following correlated changes: (1) an increase in security and stability; (2) a shift of emphasis from the frequent improvements in technique in the early periods to problems of better organization, management, etc. In those industries whose early periods belong to the nineteenth century there was also, (3) a shift from personal individual ownership to the corporate form. In the industries now in their early periods the corporate form, brought in by financial interests from the older industries, exists from the start.

The probable consequence of these developments may be stated as follows. With the increase of security, development of corporate management, and growth in the size of the economic unit, there is greater opportunity for capital investments by means of bond issues. While the industry is rapidly developing, while changes are considerable, it does not present a field for investment offering secure returns. It is only with greater stabilization of the processes, with records of past performance, that a much greater part of the total capital can be derived from bonded securities. The development of large units increasing the necessity and prevalence of shareholding finance has also increased the total bondholding as well as the holding of more variable investment securities. When combinations spread and the corresponding financial reorganizations took place, nearly all the actual investment was bonded.

Both the shift of emphasis to problems of organization and management and the development of the corporate form with huge units predominant in many branches of industry seem to have led to an increase in the proportionate number of salaried personnel as over against the body of wage-earners, or rather as over against the total economically employed population. The emphasis on questions of management induced the development of considerable subsidiary apparatus which could deal with these problems. The growth of huge corporations called for people and an organization that would replace the omnipresent eye of the old-time personal owner. Within each single industry as it develops and enters the phase of technical stability there seems to be an increase in the number of people not engaged in the production process itself.

While this may be true of a single industry, it is not necessarily applicable to a national economic system as a whole. The increase of bonded capital may take place. But any increase in the salaried force may be more than counterbalanced by the appearance of new industries and by the process of progressive organization, so that the proportional share of people with fluctuating incomes may not be diminishing at all. On the other hand, there are such circumstances to be considered as the increase in the forces devoted to final distribution of goods, i.e., to retail trade. On the whole, the problem within the realm of this particular question is well-nigh indeterminable.

In reference to the other question, that of the dependence of an industry upon the common loan-fund, we are hardly in better position. In the very first stages of any industry it is almost wholly dependent upon the common sources of capital supply. This early pioneering stage having passed, the profit returns yielded by such an industry relative to its current output are on the whole much higher than in the later stages of comparatively greater stability. But while this supply of its own means is increasing, the relative capital needs of the industry are also larger than in the later stages. Whether a greater part of these needs can be satisfied out of its own profits in the early periods of growth as compared with the later remains doubtful.

This indeterminateness is, however, a result of our omission of another factor which determines the availability to an industry of funds from the common loan-fund: that is, prospective profits. If an industry in its early periods of growth earns more relatively to its current output and capital than in the later stages, it has also a larger loan-fund available, one which varies considerably with the changes in the profit prospects of the industry. The rosier those prospects are generally, the smaller the retarding power of the loan fund as a brake. For aided by its own profits and future prospects of greater ones, a rapidly growing industry is liable to be checked at a much later and higher stage of its period of prosperity than an industry having no such advantages of

profitable technical changes and which is liable to feel the
stresses and strains of a period of prosperity much more
quickly.

The consideration of the profit element brings us to the
other variant of the savings-investment theory, that of J. A.
Hobson. According to Hobson it is the automatic savings of
the wealthy classes, especially great during periods of prosperity, that help to swell the capital investment beyond the
exact proportion of current income which can be reinvested
in accordance with the existing arts of production and cus-
tomary foresight. It is this automatic over-reinvestment that
accounts for the crisis and depression, which in its lowering
of the incomes of the richer classes cuts down the amount of
reinvestment and helps to restore the balance.

If the cyclical fluctuations are thus a result of too much
automatic reinvestment, the force of the disturbance depends
largely on the relative size to which such automatic reinvestment is possible, i.e., on the size of profits which are the source
of the reinvested funds. The larger those profits, the larger
will be the share left over for reinvestment. The subsequent
depression will be the stronger, the larger the preceding over-
investment.

Of course the deduction is not so obvious as that. For Mr.
Hobson speaks of a rate of reinvestment that is reasonable
under existing circumstances, i.e., that part of current income
which has to be put into capital to provide for maximum
consumption during the near future. It is quite possible that
the circumstances that give rise to comparatively larger profits in rapidly growing industries necessitate a higher rate
of reinvestment to make reasonable provision for the future.
The expected greater growth of the industry does form a
basis for larger capital needs to supply the future maximum
consumption. It may be pointed out, however, that this additional reinvestment is unlikely to be directed to branches
of industry where such increase would be justified by the
growth of future consumption in connection with the rapid
increase of the branch concerned. On the contrary, the
larger profits are likely to be reinvested in the same industry,
and thus contribute to a more acute overproduction than

would have been possible in a slower growing, less profitable branch of production.

The general consideration of the processes of saving and investment thus leaves a slight balance in favor of establishing definitely a positive correlation between rapidity of growth and the amplitude and duration of cyclical fluctuations. The suggestions developed indicate that where growth takes place, the accompanying conditions allow a more considerable overproduction and presumably a longer duration of the period of expansion than in industries marked by slow growth and greater stability.

IV. PRODUCTION-FLOW OF CONSUMERS' INCOMES

We take up this group of theories immediately after the savings-investment group, because some variants of the former make use of the same differences in the flow of incomes used by the latter. Thus May and Lederer point to the stability of consumers' incomes as compared to the movement of prices of commodities. As a result of this disproportion there is a lack of purchasing power in the hands of consumers to buy the current output, while during depression the purchasing power, if it declines at all, does so to a much smaller degree than production. The exhaustion of the stocks of goods that follows prepares the ground for the coming revival.

Now this stability of the flow in some of the consumers' incomes was pointed out by Tugan Baranovski, although he was referring only to the salaried classes, bondholders, and landlords while May and Lederer emphasize the comparative stability of wages. This raises the question as to the long time changes in the stability of wages. There can hardly be any suggestion of an immediate influence of the decline in the rate of growth upon the stability of wages. Although if one turns to economic history and recalls the slowing up in growth that came in the wake of the Industrial Revolution, one may see that as compared with the times of transition from hand labor to machine performance, compared with the periods when the introduction of machines was creating a relative oversupply of labor, the later times reveal much more stable employment. For under the conditions when Marx's statement about the reserve army of labor was truer than ever, business men had the opportunity to contract and expand their commitments with labor at will. It was only later with industry achieving a fairly stable level of technical conditions, with the supply of labor adjusted to the long-run demand, and with the formation of a class of skilled, valuable laborers that the variability in employment and wages tended to become less.

Of greater importance, however, are the developments in social organization which make for increasing stability in employment and wages. One of the most important factors is the development of strong labor organizations which through a series of restrictive and aggressive measures keep the supply of labor from exceeding demand and put the laborer in a strong bargaining position in relation to his employer. This sets up limits to the employers' freedom in varying his demand schedules as far as labor is concerned, and makes him less adaptable to the varying business conditions than he might wish. And there is no doubt that one of the main purposes of labor organizations in their wage and employment policies is to stabilize conditions so as to prevent the numberless evils consequent upon unemployment.

This development is in no way a direct consequence of the diminution in the rate of growth which we found to be a characteristic feature within specific production branches. At the same time this subsidence of technical change, which in many cases really means the gradual and complete consummation of the industrial revolution, is to a large extent a necessary foundation, an underlying change which permits the much more perceptible evolution in social and economic organization. Of course, the latter is not fully explained by the former, for like any other social phenomenon it has a host of contributing factors. There is, however, a very strong presumption that the purely industrial development with its corresponding gradual stability is a *sine qua non*, and hence one of the most important factors in the determination of these changes in economic institutions.

A much more elaborate variant of the production-flow of incomes theory is presented by the Pollak Foundation group. The main source of cyclical fluctuations lies, according to this variant, in the failure of business enterprises to pay out the full values received for their product, with a consequent diminution in consumer purchasing power. Now this failure is due to the fact that under modern conditions a thriving enterprise must provide for expansion, and it achieves this by distributing only a part of its profits as dividends. But the consumers themselves are saving, too, and thus divert the income needed to sustain the demand for consumers' goods into demand for equipment. A somewhat similar view is developed by P. W. Martin, according to whom any diversion of buying power from goods to capital creates a deficiency of purchasing power.

It may be noticed that both these variants associate the lack of purchasing power with its diversion to purposes of expansion and growth. This lack becomes a necessary accompaniment to any process of increase and growth. The circumstances which prevent this insufficiency from becoming immediately apparent and causing a depression is the length of the production process and the fact that the purchasing power is for a time disbursed before the products from which it is derived appear on the market. The amplitude and duration of the fluctuations would then presumably depend: (1) upon the degree or rate of expansion undertaken; (2) upon the duration of the processes of production, and thus upon the period of time between disbursements of wages and the appearance on the market of the final product.

It seems reasonable to suppose that the faster the increase in output and the relatively larger the expansion, the more intense will be the fluctuations. For on one hand, this greater expansion will mean a relatively larger volume of purchasing power disbursed without a counterpart on the market, and on the other, after a series of reciprocal influences has taken place, the surplus will begin to be felt on the market, and the lack of purchasing power will be the greater, the larger the initial expansion.

This has unlimited application only to an industrial system in its entirety and not to a specific industry. For in the latter the failure to distribute the full money value of the output does not react immediately on the industry itself, so that a comparatively greater failure in one industry does not necessarily mean that this industry is going to be the main sufferer. But on the other hand, the larger the expansion undertaken by an industry the more it is likely to feel the generally prevailing lack of purchasing power after a time. So there is some reason to think that the connection between rate of expansion and the intensity of the resulting cyclical fluctuations prevails also for a single industry.

V. PROFITS AND THE BUSINESS CYCLE

The theory of Veblen and Lescure points out that any increase in prospective profits serves as a basis for credit extension and expansion, because prospective profits mean an increased capitalization of the value of the enterprise, which in turn means an increase in forms of collateral for the extension of credit. Hence a given price increase, arousing hopes for increased profits, is likely to initiate a prolonged period of cumulative expansion. This latter comes to an end when the increased cost of production and the high prices of goods cause a decline in demand, a fall in profits, and a still greater decline in prospective profits, which endangers the existing credit structure and calls for contraction.

Since, according to this theory, anticipated earning capacity is one of the most important factors, and since this anticipated earning capacity varies with the state of an industry in the process of growth (as we have pointed out above in connection with Hardy's theory), this explanation makes cyclical fluctuations partly dependent upon the process of development. For where, thanks to technical changes, expansion promises besides the given price increase also the benefits of increasing returns, prospective earnings are larger, and the resulting expansion of credit considerable.

It must be noticed that Veblen himself takes account of the rapidity of technical changes, although he seems to consider the rate of change a constant quantity. He points out that under modern conditions of technical changes the period of depression tends to perpetuate itself because the newly built enterprises producing at lower costs are able to lower prices and thus tend to prolong the price decline. Periods of prosperity are episodes, soon turning into the normal state of depression.

If we now introduce the conception that the rate of technical changes diminishes with the process of development, the conclusions for the dynamics of business cycles would seem to be as follows: The periods of depression ought to be more severe in the early periods of development, or in industries where the rate of growth is rapid, as compared with those where it is slow. With the slowing up in the rate of technical change, we may expect an increasing mildness in the depressions. On the other hand, the prosperity period ought to be magnified in a state of rapid technical change, for such change postpones to a certain extent the time when rising costs result in higher prices and declining demand.

This reasoning arrives at the conclusion which we have seen verified in the analysis of the data: that with the diminution in rapidity of growth the amplitude of cyclical fluctuations tends to diminish. This diminution of amplitude was seen to be connected with corresponding changes in rapidity of growth. Thus the Veblen-Lescure theory gives support to some of the hypotheses developed above.

This brings to an end the suggestions as to the connection of amplitude and duration of cyclical fluctuations with the rate of growth. We have omitted in the discussion a number of factors determining the cyclical movements. We have not discussed the influence of the weather cycle, although it may be said in passing that the diminished rôle of agriculture in the body of a growing national economy and the development of higher technical cultures within the weather-afflicted branches of production tend to diminish the cyclical fluctuations in general business. We have omitted the factor of maladjustment between producers' goods and consumers' goods groups of industries, between distributive trades and production. We have not touched at all upon the question of banking and interest rates in the business cycles. We know next to nothing of the bearing of long-time changes on these factors, and we must leave our discussion incomplete. The influence of some of these forces may obscure the influence of the primary secular movements as we have seen time and again in the statistical analysis of the preceding chapter.

With this recognition of its limitations, we may summarize our discussion as follows:

The main reason for the connection between the cyclical fluctuations and the process of development is that both are manifestations of the economic activity of business men within the modern economic system. Conditions of rapid development, namely, the possibility and availability of numerous technical changes, a comparatively high rate of profits, a comparative availability of funds for expansion, conditions of uncertainty, and the secondary phenomena invariably associated with these, induce comparatively violent business cycles.

But this relationship may be modified by the influence of other factors. The most important of these is the peculiar connection between different branches of economic activity, when arranged in order of productive dependence of one upon the other and in relation to the demand of ultimate consumers. The difference in amplitude which arises in this connection as well as the difference in duration (which has its source in the varying length of the process of 'gestation') may cut across the difference in amplitude and duration as determined by the rate of growth. In the case of the size of business cycles, it lowers the correlation with the rate of increase; in the case of duration, it may render it wholly nil.

This all concerns production cycles. The price cycles, of course, have a definite correlation with the production cycles both in length and intensity. For in the processes of business cycles it is the consecutive interaction of production and prices that accounts for the bulk of the phenomena. And a production cycle of a definite amplitude and duration relatively to others being given, there is the expectation that the price cycle will occupy the same rank in respect to the other price cycles. This correlation is, however, subject to disturbances by factors which may affect differently the price and production cycles, such as trust regulation, the international character of prices as compared with the domestic run of production, and others.

These conclusions shed light on the question raised by some of the business-cycle theories, viz., whether or not progress is the cause of cyclical fluctuations. If this statement is understood in the sense that development and growth determine to a considerable extent the form of cyclical fluctuations, this, in the light of the discussion above, is quite true. But the theories mentioned make progress or developments a *sine qua non* for the existence of business cycles. Is such a point of view acceptable?

It is, of course, idle to speculate whether cyclical fluctuations would have occurred were there no development and increase at all, for in actual experience, in the complete phenomenon of economic activity they present two inseparable aspects of one and the same set of actions. But at the same time it should be noted that we have at least one group of factors of equal significance, which could possibly account for the appearance of cyclical fluctuations even were there no long-time increase in the volume of economic activity. The difference in variability between production of producers' and consumers' goods, wholesale and retail trade, would probably still persist, and aided by the stimulating effects of credit extension and banking policy would still be a possible source of cyclical fluctuations.

The whole question is, however, fictitious in so far as we are unable to pursue the vast ramifications of a process of growth and development. We have seen that rapidity of growth is by no means the only factor which accounts for or influences cyclical fluctuations, and that is all we can know in our observation of these phenomena. Unlike the natural sciences, we cannot isolate factor after factor and observe the unavoidable, residual concomitant which we may call the cause of the event.

Another set of factors which may disturb the relationship between cyclical fluctuations and the rate of growth may be summarily called the factors of business organization. They are not mentioned by business cycle theorists, because the latter take for granted most of the elements of the modern economic system and point out only those which are the undoubted sources of the cyclical fluctuations. But while these factors are in no sense a source of business cycles, they exercise an undoubted influence on the latter as on many other phenomena of economic life. They may be responsible for differences in the size of cycles among different industries or among different national branches of the same industry impossible of explanation by other factors.

One of the most important influences within this group is the difference in the spread of trusts and combinations among industries or countries. While in a way dependent upon the general process of development, for successful combinations can hardly be formed while the productive technique is still in flux and the number of individual enterprises large, there are other factors which determine the formation of these organizations. Thus while in iron and steel we may have a successful combination, in the old and established cotton industry, already on the slow grade of development, a successful combination has yet to appear. These differences, possible among different industries within one country, are still more frequent among different national branches of the same industry. For here there come into play all the numerous circumstances which characterize one national economic system in all its difference from that of another.

Economic life and economic activity do not take place in a vacuum. They are part and parcel of the total social life of a national community, and are influenced not only by the underlying geographical, technical, and natural factors, but also by the various aspects of the spiritual life of a society. These spiritual influences are clearly reflected in the economic institutions, those crystallized habits of the business community, and these institutions are the forms which mould the current business activity in its ebb and flow.

Cyclical fluctuations are subject to these numerous national influences, and no doubt the rapidity of growth plays a prominent part. But after all, rapidity of growth is only one and a rather formal attribute of a process of development. Could we describe all or at least most of the changes which in actual life constitute a process of development, we would include a number of the specifically national factors as determinants and the correlation of these with cyclical fluctuations would be more complete.

But we have chosen only a few of the general features of the process of development, which seem to us the most important. And when we correlate these traits with those of cyclical fluctuations, a phenomenon which in the shortness of its period is highly complicated and whose attributes (such as the intensity and duration) reflect many more variables than the measure of the rate of increase, we obtain a correlation lowered because of the excluded factors, viz., the differences between one national economy and another.

There remains but little to add concerning the influence of secondary movements on cyclical fluctuations. This influence may be considered from two aspects. First, the secondary variations imply a certain movement of the general price level, and thus exercise an immediate influence on the course of cyclical fluctuations. Second, the secondary movements imply certain changes in the influence of forces that make for the primary movements, and in this way likewise affect the business cycle.

The general movement of the price level has, of course, an immediate reflection in the run of cyclical fluctuations, because prices are the guide of business men in their activity, and because of the fact that under the peculiar conditions of the present day economic system consecutive changes in prices have a great effect on profits. We are entering here a familiar field, and shall only mention our previous discussion. A rising price level implies greater profits to the entrepreneurs and promotes a longer duration of any price rise occasioned by other factors. Its immediate effect is, then, to prolong the period of prosperity and shorten the period of depression. On the total duration or intensity of the cycle the general movement of the price level can evidently have no effect, except through its influence on other forces which affect the processes of growth.

The two main groups of effects of the secondary movements are: (1) The changes in the distribution of incomes; i.e , the increase in the relative share of the entrepreneurs and the decrease in the relative share of the workers and recipients of stable incomes. This has a direct bearing on business cycles from the point of view of those theories which emphasize the discrepancies in the flow of production and consumers' incomes or investment and saving. For an increase in the relative share of the entrepreneurs magnifies this discrepancy and tends to enhance the amplitude and duration of business cycles. On the other hand, in times of declining secular trends, stable incomes presumably exercise a pronounced checking influence and prevent the prosperity phase of the cycle from going very high or continuing for very long.

(2) The other group of effects is connected with the influence that the shift in the relative distribution of the national income has on the productive activity directed by entrepreneurs. We have seen how the secondary variations in production may be conceived to a large extent as reflections of the secondary movements in prices. But secondary secular movements in production are nothing more than accelerations and retardations in the rate of growth, i.e., acceleration and retardation in the influence of the factors which make for growth. To this extent they are variations also in the factors whose influence on the cyclical fluctuations we have tried to establish. And if rapid growth has a corresponding reflection in the amplitude and duration of cyclical fluctuations, so likewise must the acceleration in the rate of growth which we call the upward secondary movement. The declining secondary variation must also exercise a corresponding influence on the measures of cyclical fluctuations.

Thus both groups of effects, the one concerned with the immediate influence in the relative distribution, and the other with the influence of the factors of growth, suggest a definite dependence of cyclical fluctuations upon the direction of the secondary movements. With rising secondary movements the cycles ought to be getting longer and their size greater, with declining secondary variations the cycles ought to be milder and shorter.

But there are numerous factors that may cut across this dependence, and obscure it entirely. It must be remembered that secondary variations are accelerations and retardations of a rate of growth that is itself changing, and the size of the latter change in comparison with the change involved in secondary movements is so considerable that in most cases its influence is of greater significance than the variations within it. It must also be remembered that the influence of any factor of growth is obstructed by the effects of other factors, so that the influences of variations in the general tendency of the rate of growth to decline could hardly be perceptible. And it must finally be recollected that the length of cycles, determined mostly by other factors than those connected with the processes of development influence the size of the secondary variations, and may cut across the opposite influence of secondary variations on the length of cycles. If the duration of cyclical fluctuations is considerable, the amplitude of the secondary variations and hence their influence seems to be small. These complicating influences account for the fact that the actual analysis does not reveal any close dependence of business cycles in their total duration and amplitude upon the direction of secondary movements. It is possible that in a more intensive and careful investigation the isolation of the factors would be more successful and statistical tests of this dependence could be devised.

We are at the end of our investigation, although our results concerning the interrelations of the groups of phenomena studied are far from complete. But the limits of the investigation and the volume of data, as well as the methods of treatment, hardly permit any further refinement in the present connection. And although in our attempt to answer a number of questions, we have raised many others, this seems to be the inevitable fate of any work searching among the complicated interdependence of factors which constitute our economic world.

Before concluding the argument, however, it would be interesting from the point of view of economic theory to seek the significance of the methods used and the result attained. In attempting this, we forsake, of course, the ground of our investigation, place ourselves outside and survey it as objectively as we can, in order to arrive at some conclusion as to its place in the development of the science and the possibilities which it opens. This is to a large extent the expression of personal opinion, supported as it is by our conception of the development of the science and the tasks before it. A few concluding paragraphs will be devoted to the presentation of these opinions.

CONCLUDING NOTES

The present status of the problem of long-time movements in economic theory.

Survey of the path traced in this study. Brief summary of the conclusions. The limitations of the study.

The theoretical significance of the investigation. Possibilities of future development in economic theory. The present state of theoretical economics. The probable future of dynamic theory.

THE treatment of problems connected with long-time development has suffered a curious evolution, from its conspicuous place in economic theory of the early classical days to its almost complete present neglect. The secular movements of economic phenomena received their full share of attention by the classical and the socialist schools, slight as the empirical basis of their generalizations may have been. In the reaction from the universalism and oversimplifications of these generalizations, the marginal utility and the mathematical schools definitely limited their scope to the consideration of static problems. And not even in its latest developments does equilibrium economics attempt to consider the really dynamic elements of economic life, mainly because no inductive knowledge of a general and measurable kind has been available. The specific studies by the adherents of the Historical School did not furnish this knowledge, for they dealt mainly with qualitative changes, and yielded no definite, general conclusions as to the dynamics within the modern business economy itself.

While pure economic theory thus confined itself to a consideration of the static equilibrium, economic changes brought to the fore new phenomena which cried for investigation, if only in their most general aspects. Business cycles aroused more attention than formerly as their rough regularity and their consequences became more and more apparent. The growth of trusts, changes in labor organizations, new types of behavior on the part of business men, a more inductive approach within the science itself — all occasioned extended discussions of economic phenomena which seemingly had no relation with the immutable self-contained static system. For these phenomena were themselves ever-changing features of economic development.

The current general discussions in the field of economic science thus contain side by side with an exposition, descriptive or mathematical, of stable market equilibrium, chapters (quite frequently in ordered mechanical sequence) on the phenomena that condition the operation of the immutable equilibrium system. To what degree these phenomena are important, and what is their general course of development is not known, hence their influence upon the static market scheme is likewise unknown. We have in consequence two somewhat incommensurable parts in the general science of economics, one reading in terms of an absolute, independent static system, the other dealing with changing and developing phenomena which have apparently no uniformity or sequence in their appearance that could be welded with the discussion of the static system into a unified system of economics. In the light of this situation, of what potential significance are the statistical methods of analysis adopted in our study and the few results of varying certainty we have obtained?

The investigation was based upon the recognition that the curve fitting method of describing secular movements can be used to determine whether or not the long-time development in different branches of economic activity followed in the past similar courses — courses which would reveal certain broad characteristics of the process of development. The most essential hypothetical characteristics were derived from a general survey which suggested the tendency of industries to exhibit a declining rate of growth. This feature limited the choice of curves. From those which express this decline in the rate of percentage increase, we have chosen the simple logistic and the simple Gompertz curves as the most suitable.

The statistical analysis of the data revealed that these curves, chiefly the logistic, yielded suitable descriptions of the long-time movements in production or volume of business activity for a number of branches in the five most important industrial countries. With few exceptions, the series were taken for as long a period as they were available, and none was for a period shorter than 30 to 40 years. Technically speaking, the curves formed good fits as far as these long periods were concerned, and fulfilled the expectation that the statistical data would show a rough similarity in the course of development.

The most important part of this statistical generalization is the decline in the rate of increase. It is quite possible that other curves having the same property would yield generally good fits, although the logistic and the Gompertz curves used have the advantage of simplicity and sound logic. Chapter I dealt mostly with the factor of technical change, for this influence was considered the most important. But the discussion of the growth processes does not result in a complete theory of economic development. In this lies its weakness, but also the source of future possibilities.

It was further shown that in the deviations from the logistic and the Gompertz curves, i.e., from the lines of the primary trend, there are movements extending over a considerable period of time, movements which seem to reflect corresponding variations in the general level of prices. The discussion which followed attempted to indicate the mechanism by which such changes in prices are reflected in the rapidity of industrial development, and how once a prolonged rise of prices has set in, some of the peculiar responses of factors within the industrial system might account for the continuation of this increase until opposing factors become forceful enough to stop it. While the movements in prices are the most important influence on the secondary secular variations in production, there are others, such as wars, cardinal inventions, or discoveries, and occasionally a powerful trust policy.

The primary and secondary secular movements are the two quite different component parts of the complex total phenomenon called the secular changes. The primary secular movement exercises considerable influence both upon the secondary variations and upon the cycles, more marked in the former than the latter. The faster the rate of growth in the underlying primary trend line, the greater is the amplitude of the secondary variations and of the cyclical fluctuations. In the latter, however, there are so many complicating influences that the connection with the primary secular movements is not at all direct. The secondary secular variations are of considerable influence on the respective duration of the separate phases of prosperity and depression within the cycle. On the other hand, the total duration of the cycle, which depends on factors other than the secular movements, is in its turn of considerable influence on the amplitude of the secondary variations. All these rather involved interrelations may vary for different industries, and their explanatory limitations ought always to be kept in mind.

These, very briefly, are the most important results of our investigation. Their potential significance lies in the two parts of the task essayed: (1) in the attempt to establish an inductive generalization concerning the course of economic development; (2) in the attempt to show what influence this general course of development has upon the shorter changes in time.

The first part of the task is, as we have pointed out, quite incomplete. In Chapter VI, where an attempt was made to work out analytically the possible influence of secular movements on business cycles, we were handicapped by the lack of knowledge of the total process of development. We had to consider the factor of technical change as the chief influence underlying the general characteristics of a constantly retarded growth.

But there are other components of the total process of development. The consideration of these other strands, the separate phenomena that stand out as products of recent growth, suggests that the somewhat formal characteristics of the general curve of secular movements could be used as a die in which to cast most of the facts and interrelations of the complex economic reality. For with this general retardation of growth there go not only important shifts in the character of the industrial technique, but also changes in the relation between labor and capital, changes in the distributive process, in the character of the market, in the type of business organization, and in the respective rôles of industry and agriculture.

Let us take, for example, the change in relations between labor and capital which accompanies the slowing down in the rate of technical progress and the expansion of an industry. In the early periods of an industry's growth, with the rapidity of technical change and introduction of new machinery, there is a great lack of experienced workers and a possible oversupply of the inexperienced, especially if this growth marks a revolution within an old industry. The main task of the entrepreneur in regard to labor is to further its efficiency in the handling of the new technique, to break down its resistance, and to allow the worker free rein in his adjustment. As conditions become more stable, with keener competition and smaller profit margins the problems of scientific management arise. The old type of management which left the worker to make his own individual adjustment to the tools and machines is no longer suitable. Now these changes in the status of the workers within the plant are of considerable importance, and it is a part of that development whose technical changes are the underlying current, and the logistic curve of output a formal expression. One may speculate upon the importance of these same elements in growth of trade-union organizations and other correlated changes.

Another example is the development of trusts. It is fairly well established that effective combinations cannot appear until (1) the industrial technique is stabilized; (2) the development of the industry results in the control of the bulk of its output by a few dominant concerns. And the larger the relative proportion of overhead costs the more intense the economic motives for ceasing competition. But overhead costs are a product of the technical growth of an industry, as are the decline in the number of industrial enterprises affected and the stabilization of industrial technique. Trusts can attain significance only in a certain stage of the process of industrial development, and after all they are only an extreme manifestation of the disappearance of the spirit of effective and unlimited competition which comes with the growth of an industry from turbulent beginnings to the stable conditions of a greatly retarded increase.

One could go on multiplying the examples of the profound influence of the processes of development on these component elements of the economic system and seek definite connection with the traits we have discussed. And if these elements are so affected, a complete unfolding of the process of development along the general lines indicated would include not only the technical but all the manifold social and economic changes accompanying it. Such an analytic description would provide the structure of the new dynamic economics.

One must not minimize its difficulties. Even if the inductive generalization suggested in the essay were accepted as characterizing the course of economic development, it applies only to each single industry. The question of what happens to the interrelations of certain parts of the system is not thereby solved, although a step towards the general description is made. It will require a vast amount of additional statistical investigation as well as a deeper study of the history of every industry to be able to develop this first and feeble attempt at a general description into a complete theory of economic development.

But even if the latter were realized, the analysis of economic change would still be incomplete. It is true that such a theory of development will include in its range all phenomena discussed in economic science. Production, distribution, exchange, and consumption, in all their numerous subdivisions, will be treated there, for every part of a national economic system is developing and undergoing long-time changes. But these long-time changes do not exhaust all the manifestations and interrelations of economic phenomena.

The other parts of the general theory of economic change will be covered by the study of secondary secular variations and cyclical fluctuations. Especially in the latter, stimulated by the numerous special investigations of the cyclical problem, there will come under consideration a number of factors and of interrelations which are of no marked significance in the long-time development. The connection of supply and demand, production and prices, labor and capital, will appear in a new light, conditioned by a new group of facts, whose influence is too short to matter very much in the theory of general development.

One visualizes the dynamic theory of economics arising from the long vision of a statistician and the penetration of a theoretical analyst, framing a complete account of economic reality as it presents itself to our eye. It will give us a complete account of why and how economic phenomena are as they are, and what brought them to the form in which we conceive them. We shall know not only the current state of economic reality, but the more or less stable sequences and interrelations which underlie its changes. The stability of these interrelations will be only relative. The process of long-time movement would seem a condition of stability of those factors which come prominently into play in the cyclical fluctuations. But the interesting part in the study of these conditions would be not to show them in their stability, where their composition becomes a matter of conjecture, but in their movement and flux where the hypotheses concerning their mechanism and forces can be tested. If we have a theory of economic changes in their different, discernible types we shall have a complete and general theory of dynamic economics.

THE END

APPENDIX

The tables which follow (pages 332–531) present all the statistical material which underlies the charts in Chapter III. The headings of columns are uniform for all the tables, while each table bears the number of the chart which illustrates it.

The column headings are as follows:

    I. The original data.

    II. The ordinates of the line of primary trend.

    III. The relative deviations of the original data from the ordinates of the primary trend line, the latter taken as 100.

    IV. The ordinate of the line of secondary secular movements (smoothed moving average of column III).

    V. The relative deviations of column III from column IV, the items of the latter taken as 100.

At the bottom of each table are given: (1) the source of the original data; (2) the equation of the primary trend line, the unit of x and the date of origin; (3) the period for which the moving average of column III was taken. The latter item should not be considered of great importance, since the actual moving average served only as a help in smoothing and in a few cases the final smoothed line deviated from it considerably.

TABLE I. WHEAT CROPS, UNITED STATES, 1866–1924

Columns I and II in millions of bushels

	I	II	III	IV	V
1866..........	152.0	205.5	74.0	95.0	77.9
1867..........	212.4		98.7	95.4	103.5
1868..........	224.0		99.5	95.8	103.9
1869..........	260.1		110.6	96.3	114.8
1870..........	235.9	245.0	96.3	96.8	99.5
1871..........	230.7		90.0	97.3	92.5
1872..........	250.0		93.4	97.8	95.5
1873..........	281.3		100.8	98.5	102.3
1874..........	308.1		106.0	99.6	106.4
1875..........	292.1	302.1	96.7	101.7	95.1
1876..........	289.4		91.9	107.0	85.9
1877..........	364.2		111.1	115.4	96.3
1878..........	420.1		123.4	123.8	99.7
1879..........	496.4		140.5	125.0	112.4
1880..........	498.6	366.3	136.1	124.7	109.2
1881..........	383.3		100.8	121.5	83.0
1882..........	504.2		128.0	115.3	111.0
1883..........	421.1		103.2	109.3	94.4
1884..........	512.8		121.6	104.8	116.0
1885..........	357.1	435.7	82.0	100.3	81.8
1886..........	457.2		101.6	96.0	105.8
1887..........	456.3		98.2	91.8	107.0
1888..........	415.9		86.8	89.4	97.1
1889..........	434.4		88.0	88.5	99.4
1890..........	378.1	507.9	74.4	88.2	84.4
1891..........	584.5		111.9	88.6	126.3
1892..........	528.0		98.4	89.4	110.1
1893..........	427.6		77.6	90.8	85.5
1894..........	516.5		91.3	92.8	98.4
1895..........	569.5	580.0	98.2	95.8	102.5
1896..........	544.2		91.6	99.4	92.2
1897..........	610.3		100.4	102.3	98.1
1898..........	772.2		124.2	105.2	118.1
1899..........	636.1		100.1	106.2	94.3
1900..........	602.7	649.2	92.8	106.2	87.4
1901..........	788.6		119.1	105.5	112.9
1902..........	724.8		107.4	103.5	103.8
1903..........	663.9		96.6	100.6	96.0
1904..........	596.9		85.2	97.9	87.0

TABLE I (*continued*)

	I	II	III	IV	V
1905..........	726.8	713.1	101.9	95.2	107.0
1906..........	756.8		104.5	93.0	112.4
1907..........	638.0		86.7	91.0	95.3
1908..........	644.7		86.3	89.0	97.0
1909..........	700.4		92.3	87.3	105.7
1910..........	635.1	769.9	82.5	85.9	96.0
1911..........	621.3		79.7	85.5	93.2
1912..........	730.3		92.5	90.0	102.8
1913..........	763.4		95.5	97.0	98.5
1914..........	891.0		110.1	100.1	110.0
1915..........	1025.8	818.9	125.3	100.8	124.3
1916..........	636.3		76.9	101.2	76.0
1917..........	636.7		76.2	101.2	75.3
1918..........	921.4		109.2	101.1	108.0
1919..........	968.0		113.6	100.6	112.9
1920..........	833.0	860.0	96.9	100.1	96.8
1921..........	814.9		94.0	98.3	95.6
1922..........	867.6		99.3	96.3	103.1
1923..........	797.4		90.6	94.3	96.1
1924..........	862.6		97.3	92.4	105.3
1925..........		893.6			

Source of data: *Yearbook of the U.S. Department of Agriculture*: 1920, pp. 550–51; 1922, p. 583; 1925, p. 743.

Equation of the primary trend line:

$$y = \frac{1012.8}{1 + 10^{0.49609 - 0.12464\,x}}$$

x in units of 5 years, origin at 1870.

Column IV: smoothed moving average of 7 years.

TABLE 1a. WHEAT, DECEMBER FARM PRICES, UNITED STATES, 1866–1915

Columns I and II in cents per bushel
Prices for 1866–78 deflated to gold basis

	I	II	III	IV	V
1866	108.4		108.4	90.0	120.4
1867	105.1		107.1	90.7	118.1
1868	77.7	96.2	80.8	91.5	88.3
1869	57.5		60.8	92.4	65.8
1870	82.1		88.3	93.4	94.5
1871	102.5		112.1	94.6	118.5
1872	99.1		110.2	96.1	114.7
1873	94.0	88.4	106.3	97.8	108.7
1874	77.6		89.1	99.6	89.5
1875	77.9		90.8	101.4	89.5
1876	86.9		102.7	104.0	98.7
1877	100.9		121.0	108.5	111.5
1878	76.5	82.2	93.0	115.5	80.5
1879	110.6		136.0	121.2	112.2
1880	95.1		118.3	122.5	96.6
1881	119.2		149.9	122.5	133.2
1882	88.4		112.5	119.0	94.5
1883	91.1	77.7	117.2	111.0	105.6
1884	64.5		83.7	97.0	86.3
1885	77.1		100.8	94.0	107.2
1886	68.7		90.5	95.0	95.3
1887	68.1		90.4	100.0	90.4
1888	92.6	74.8	123.8	104.8	118.1
1889	69.5		93.3	104.5	89.3
1890	83.3		112.3	102.0	110.1
1891	83.4		112.9	97.0	116.4
1892	62.2		84.5	88.0	96.0
1893	53.5	73.4	72.8	82.0	88.8
1894	48.9		66.4	82.0	81.0
1895	50.3		68.1	82.8	82.2
1896	71.7		96.6	83.7	115.4
1897	80.9		108.6	84.8	128.1
1898	58.2	74.8	77.8	86.2	90.3
1899	58.6		78.0	88.0	88.6
1900	62.0		82.1	90.0	91.2
1901	62.6		82.5	92.2	89.5
1902	63.0		82.6	94.6	87.3
1903	69.5	76.7	90.6	97.4	93.0
1904	92.4		119.4	99.9	119.5

TABLE 1a (*continued*)

	I	II	III	IV	V
1905	74.6		95.5	102.0	93.6
1906	66.2		84.0	103.8	80.9
1907	86.5		108.8	105.0	103.6
1908	92.2	80.2	115.0	105.6	108.9
1909	98.4		121.2	105.9	114.4
1910	88.3		107.4	105.8	101.5
1911	87.4		106.2	105.7	100.5
1912	76.0		90.2	105.5	85.5
1913	79.9	85.4	93.6	105.2	89.0
1914	98.6		114.0	104.9	108.7
1915	91.9	87.6	104.9	104.6	100.3

Source of data: *Yearbook of the U.S. Department of Agriculture*: 1920, pp. 550–51; 1925, p. 743.

Equation of the primary trend line:

$$y = 105.60 - 10.214\,x + 0.809\,x^2$$

x in units of 5 years, origin at 1863.

Column IV: smoothed moving average of 7 years.

TABLE 2. CORN CROPS, UNITED STATES, 1866–1924

Columns I and II in millions of bushels

	I	II	III	IV	V
1865.........		898.6			
1866.........	867.9		93.4	85.0	109.9
1867.........	768.3		80.0	86.2	92.8
1868.........	906.5		91.4	87.5	104.5
1869.........	874.3		85.5	88.9	96.2
1870.........	1094.3	1054.3	103.8	90.4	114.8
1871.........	991.9		91.1	91.9	99.1
1872.........	1092.7		97.3	93.6	104.0
1873.........	932.3		80.6	95.4	84.5
1874.........	850.1		71.3	97.4	73.2
1875.........	1321.1	1226.1	107.8	99.5	108.3
1876.........	1283.8		101.6	102.5	99.1
1877.........	1342.6		103.2	105.4	97.9
1878.........	1388.2		103.8	106.8	97.2
1879.........	1823.2		132.6	107.4	123.5
1880.........	1717.4	1412.3	121.6	107.7	112.9
1881.........	1194.9		82.3	107.8	76.3
1882.........	1617.0		108.4	107.8	100.6
1883.........	1551.1		101.3	107.6	94.1
1884.........	1795.5		114.3	107.2	106.6
1885.........	1936.2	1610.3	120.2	106.6	112.8
1886.........	1665.4		100.8	105.6	95.5
1887.........	1456.2		86.0	104.2	82.5
1888.........	1987.8		114.6	102.2	112.1
1889.........	1998.7		112.6	99.5	113.2
1890.........	1460.4	1816.3	80.4	96.5	83.3
1891.........	2055.8		110.6	92.7	119.3
1892.........	1713.7		90.2	87.9	102.6
1893.........	1707.6		87.9	87.0	101.0
1894.........	1339.7		67.5	87.8	76.9
1895.........	2311.0	2026.3	114.1	92.6	123 2
1896.........	2503.5		121.1	98.9	122.4
1897.........	2144.6		101.7	101.9	99.8
1898.........	2261.1		105.1	103.6	101.4
1899.........	2454.6		111.9	104.7	106.9
1900.........	2505.1	2234.9	112.1	105.4	106.4
1901.........	1613.5		70.9	106.0	66.9
1902.........	2619.5		113.1	106.4	106.2
1903.........	2346.9		99.6	106.7	93.3
1904.........	2528.7		105.5	106.8	98.8

TABLE 2 (*continued*)

	I	II	III	IV	V
1905.........	2748.9	2438.3	112.7	106.7	105.6
1906.........	2897.7		117.0	106.2	110.2
1907.........	2512.1		99.8	105.4	94.6
1908.........	2545.0		99.6	104.4	95.4
1909.........	2572.3		99.2	103.3	96.0
1910.........	2886.3	2632.2	109.7	102.3	107.2
1911.........	2531.5		94.9	101.3	93.7
1912.........	3124.7		115.5	100.4	115.0
1913.........	2447.0		89.3	99.6	89.7
1914.........	2672.8		96.2	99.0	97.2
1915.........	2994.8	2813.1	106.5	98.4	108.2
1916.........	2566.9		90.2	97.9	92.1
1917.........	3065.2		106.4	97.5	109.1
1918.........	2502.7		85.0	97.2	87.4
1919.........	2811.3		95.5	97.9	97.6
1920.........	3208.6	2978.8	107.7	98.7	109.1
1921.........	3068.6		102.0	98.7	103.3
1922.........	2906.0		95.6	98.7	96.9
1923.........	3053.6		99.5	98.7	100.8
1924.........	2312.7		74.6	98.7	75.6
1925.........		3128.0			

Source of data: *Yearbook of the U.S. Department of Agriculture*: 1920, pp. 537-38; 1925, p. 788.

Equation of the primary trend line:

$$y = \frac{3971.2}{1 + 10^{0.53391 - 0.09193\,x}}$$

x in units of 5 years, origin at 1865.

Column IV: smoothed moving average of 7 years.

TABLE 2a. CORN, DECEMBER FARM PRICES, UNITED STATES, 1866–1915

Columns I and II in cents per bushel
1866–78 deflated to gold basis

	I	II	III	IV	V
1866	33.7		76.1	86.2	88.3
1867	41.5		96.0	87.4	109.8
1868	33.5	42.24	79.3	88.7	89.4
1869	45.0		108.5	90.1	120.4
1870	43.0		105.5	91.6	115.2
1871	38.8		97.0	93.2	104.1
1872	31.4		80.0	95.0	84.2
1873	38.9	38.53	101.0	96.9	104.2
1874	52.5		138.0	98.9	139.5
1875	31.9		84.9	101.0	84.1
1876	30.5		82.2	103.3	79.6
1877	33.2		90.6	106.1	85.4
1878	31.3	36.17	86.5	109.4	79.1
1879	37.1		103.2	113.1	91.2
1880	39.6		110.7	118.1	93.7
1881	63.6		178.9	119.7	149.5
1882	48.5		137.2	119.5	114.8
1883	42.4	35.16	120.6	116.6	103.4
1884	35.7		101.4	109.1	92.9
1885	32.8		92.9	104.1	89.2
1886	36.6		103.5	104.3	99.2
1887	44.4		125.3	105.0	119.3
1888	34.1	35.50	96.1	105.8	90.8
1889	27.4		76.5	106.3	72.0
1890	50.0		138.2	106.4	129.9
1891	39.7		108.7	106.2	102.4
1892	38.8		105.3	105.4	99.9
1893	35.9	37.20	96.5	104.1	92.7
1894	45.1		119.3	102.1	116.8
1895	25.0		65.1	90.1	72.3
1896	21.3		54.6	75.6	72.2
1897	26.0		65.6	76.1	86.2
1898	28.4	40.25	70.6	78.6	89.8
1899	29.9		72.7	82.6	88.0
1900	35.1		83.6	87.1	96.0
1901	60.1		140.1	90.9	154.1
1902	40.1		91.6	94.1	97.3
1903	42.1	44.65	94.3	96.1	98.1
1904	43.7		95.4	97.8	97.5

TABLE 2a (*continued*)

	I	II	III	IV	V
1905.............	40.8		86.9	99.1	87.7
1906.............	39.3		81.7	100.1	81.6
1907.............	50.9		103.4	101.0	102.4
1908.............	60.0	50.40	119.0	101.8	116.9
1909.............	58.6		113.1	102.5	110.3
1910.............	48.0		90.2	103.1	87.5
1911.............	61.8		113.1	103.3	109.5
1912.............	48.7		86.8	103.4	83.9
1913.............	69.1	57.50	120.2	103.4	116.2
1914.............	64.4		108.8	103.3	105.3
1915.............	57.5	60.78	94.6	103.2	91.7

Source of data: *Yearbook of the U.S. Department of Agriculture*: 1920, pp. 537–38; 1922, p. 571; 1925, p. 788.

Equation of the primary trend line:

$$y = 47.305 - 5.741 \, x + 0.676 \, x^2$$

x in units of 5 years, origin at 1863.

Column IV: smoothed moving average of 7 years.

TABLE 3. POTATO CROPS, UNITED STATES, 1866–1924

Columns I and II in millions of bushels

	I	II	III	IV	V
1865..........		96.8			
1866..........	107.2		107.1	101.7	105.3
1867..........	97.8		94.6	101.4	93.3
1868..........	106.1		99.4	101.1	98.3
1869..........	133.9		121.7	100.8	120.7
1870..........	114.8	113.4	101.2	100.6	100.6
1871..........	120.5		102.9	100.4	102.5
1872..........	113.5		94.0	100.2	93.8
1873..........	106.1		85.2	100.1	85.1
1874..........	106.0		82.6	100.0	82.6
1875..........	166.9	132.2	126.3	101.0	125.0
1876..........	124.8		91.5	103.1	88.7
1877..........	170.1		121.0	104.2	116.1
1878..........	124.1		85.6	104.8	81.7
1879..........	181.6		121.7	105.0	115.9
1880..........	167.7	153.5	109.3	105.1	104.0
1881..........	109.1		69.0	104.9	65.8
1882..........	171.0		105.0	104.5	100.5
1883..........	208.2		124.2	103.0	120.6
1884..........	190.6		110.6	101.1	109.4
1885..........	175.0	177.2	98.8	98.7	100.1
1886..........	168.1		92.2	96.5	95.5
1887..........	134.1		71.5	95.0	75.3
1888..........	202.4		105.0	94.2	111.5
1889..........	201.2		101.6	94.3	107.7
1890..........	150.5	203.4	74.0	94.5	78.3
1891..........	256.1		122.5	95.1	128.9
1892..........	164.5		76.6	95.7	80.0
1893..........	195.0		88.4	96.3	91.8
1894..........	183.8		81.3	96.7	84.1
1895..........	317.1	232.0	136.7	96.8	141.2
1896..........	271.8		114.2	96.7	118.1
1897..........	191.0		78.2	96.2	81.3
1898..........	218.8		87.4	95.2	91.8
1899..........	260.3		101.4	93.5	108.4
1900..........	247.8	262.8	94.3	92.3	102.2
1901..........	198.6		73.7	92.2	79.9
1902..........	293.9		106.6	97.1	109.8
1903..........	262.1		92.8	99.7	93.1
1904..........	352.3		122.0	102.0	119.6

TABLE 3 (*continued*)

	I	II	III	IV	V
1905..........	278.9	295.4	94.4	103.5	91.2
1906..........	331.7		109.8	104.3	105.3
1907..........	323.0		104.5	104.8	99.7
1908..........	302.0		95.6	105.0	91.0
1909..........	394.6		122.3	105.1	116.4
1910..........	349.0	329.5	105.9	105.1	100.8
1911..........	292.7		87.0	104.9	82.9
1912..........	420.6		122.4	104.6	117.0
1913..........	331.5		94.6	104.0	91.0
1914..........	409.9		114.6	103.2	111.0
1915..........	359.7	364.7	98.6	102.0	96.7
1916..........	287.0		77.2	100.4	76.9
1917..........	442.1		116.7	98.5	118.5
1918..........	411.9		106.7	94.8	112.6
1919..........	322.9		82.1	94.5	86.9
1920..........	403.3	400.2	100.8	95.0	106.1
1921..........	361.7		88.8	97.3	91.3
1922..........	453.4		109.4	101.0	108.3
1923..........	416.1		98.7	105.0	94.0
1924..........	425.3		99.2	109.0	91.0
1925..........		435.6			

Source of data: *Yearbook of the U.S. Department of Agriculture*: 1920, p. 616; 1925, p. 913.

Equation of the primary trend line:

$$y = \frac{780.5}{1 + 10^{0.76961-0.07918\,x}}$$

x in units of 5 years, origin at 1870.

Column IV: smoothed moving average of 7 years.

TABLE 3a. POTATOES, DECEMBER FARM PRICES, UNITED
STATES, 1866–1915

Columns I and II in cents per bushel
1866–78 deflated to gold basis

	I	II	III	IV	V
1866.........	33.6		72.2	86.0	84.0
1867.........	47.7		102.5	88.2	116.2
1868.........	42.5	46.54	91.3	91.0	100.3
1869.........	32.3		69.3	94.2	73.6
1870.........	56.5		121.1	97.6	124.1
1871.........	48.2		103.2	101.2	102.0
1872.........	47.6		101.8	104.3	97.6
1873.........	57.3	46.83	122.4	106.0	115.5
1874.........	55.3		117.8	107.0	110.1
1875.........	29.9		63.5	107.8	58.9
1876.........	55.5		117.6	108.5	108.4
1877.........	41.7		88.2	109.1	80.8
1878.........	57.9	47.42	122.1	109.5	111.5
1879.........	43.6		91.6	109.8	83.4
1880.........	48.3		101.1	109.9	92.0
1881.........	91.0		189.7	109.9	172.6
1882.........	55.7		115.7	108.5	106.6
1883.........	42.2	48.32	87.3	105.0	83.1
1884.........	39.6		81.6	101.2	80.6
1885.........	44.7		91.6	100.8	90.9
1886.........	46.7		95.2	101.3	94.0
1887.........	68.2		138.4	101.9	135.8
1888.........	40.2	49.51	81.2	102.5	79.2
1889.........	35.4		71.1	103.0	69.0
1890.........	75.3		150.3	103.2	145.6
1891.........	35.6		70.6	103.0	68.5
1892.........	65.5		129.2	102.0	126.7
1893.........	58.4	51.00	114.5	97.5	117.4
1894.........	52.8		102.8	90.0	114.2
1895.........	26.2		50.7	85.0	59.6
1896.........	29.0		55.7	86.5	64.4
1897.........	54.2		103.4	88.1	117.4
1898.........	41.5	52.79	78.6	90.1	87.2
1899.........	39.7		74.6	92.0	81.1
1900.........	42.3		78.9	93.9	84.0
1901.........	76.3		141.2	95.7	147.5
1902.........	46.9		86.1	97.2	88.6
1903.........	60.9	54.88	111.0	98.5	112.7
1904.........	44.8		80.9	99.6	81.2

TABLE 3a (*continued*)

	I	II	III	IV	V
1905.........	61.1		109.4	100.6	108.7
1906.........	50.6		89.8	101.5	88.5
1907.........	61.3		107.9	102.2	105.6
1908.........	69.7	57.28	121.7	102.7	118.5
1909.........	54.2		93.8	102.9	91.2
1910.........	55.7		95.5	103.0	92.7
1911.........	79.9		135.7	103.0	131.7
1912.........	50.5		85.0	102.7	82.8
1913.........	68.7	59.96	114.6	101.7	112.7
1914.........	48.7		80.4	99.7	80.6
1915.........	61.7	61.16	100.9	97.2	103.8

Source of data: *Yearbook of the U.S. Department of Agriculture*: 1920, p. 616; 1925, p. 913.

Equation of the primary trend line:

$$y = 46.55 - 0.158\,x + 0.150\,x^2$$

x in units of 5 years, origin at 1863.

Column IV: smoothed moving average of 7 years.

TABLE 4. COTTON CROPS, UNITED STATES, 1866–1924

Columns I and II in thousands of bales

	I	II	III	IV	V
1865.........		2,299			
1866.........	1,750		71.1	83.0	85.7
1867.........	2,340		89.1	87.0	102.4
1868.........	2,380		85.2	90.5	94.1
1869.........	3,012		101.9	93.9	108.5
1870.........	3,800	3,122	121.7	97.5	124.8
1871.........	2,553		76.8	100.1	76.7
1872.........	3,920		111.2	102.4	108.6
1873.........	3,683		98.8	104.6	94.5
1874.........	3,941		100.3	106.2	94.4
1875.........	5,123	4,132	124.0	107.4	115.5
1876.........	4,438		101.7	108.2	94.0
1877.........	4,370		95.0	108.6	87.5
1878.........	5,244		108.5	108.6	99.9
1879.........	5,755		113.6	108.3	104.9
1880.........	6,343	5,301	119.7	107.4	111.5
1881.........	5,456		98.2	106.2	92.5
1882.........	6,957		119.8	104.5	114.6
1883.........	5,701		94.1	102.2	92.1
1884.........	5,682		90.0	99.7	90.3
1885.........	6,575	6,569	100.1	98.5	101.6
1886.........	6,446		94.5	97.9	96.5
1887.........	7,020		99.1	97.6	101.5
1888.........	6,941		94.6	97.3	97.2
1889.........	7,473		98.4	97.1	101.3
1890.........	8,674	7,850	110.5	96.9	114.0
1891.........	9,018		111.5	96.7	115.3
1892.........	6,664		80.0	96.6	82.8
1893.........	7,493		87.4	96.5	90.6
1894.........	9,476		107.5	96.6	111.3
1895.........	7,161	9,054	79.1	97.2	81.4
1896.........	8,533		92.1	97.9	94.1
1897.........	10,898		115.0	98.6	116.6
1898.........	11,189		115.5	99.4	116.2
1899.........	9,345		94.3	100.2	94.1
1900.........	10,123	10,112	100.1	101.0	99.1
1901.........	9,510		92.4	101.8	90.8
1902.........	10,631		101.6	102.6	99.0
1903.........	9,851		92.6	103.4	89.6
1904.........	13,438		124.3	104.3	119.2

TABLE 4 (*continued*)

	I	II	III	IV	V
1905.........	10,575	10,988	96.2	105.3	91.4
1906.........	13,274		119.3	106.4	112.1
1907.........	11,107		98.6	107.6	91.6
1908.........	13,242		116.1	109.1	106.4
1909.........	10,005		86.7	110.9	78.2
1910.........	11,609	11,678	99.4	112.1	88.7
1911.........	15,693		133.2	112.5	118.4
1912.........	13,703		115.3	112.3	102.7
1913.........	14,156		118.0	110.7	106.6
1914.........	16,135		133.4	108.5	122.9
1915.........	11,192	12,201	91.7	105.6	86.8
1916.........	11,450		93.3	102.5	91.0
1917.........	11,302		91.5	98.2	93.2
1918.........	12,041		96.9	92.5	104.8
1919.........	11,421		91.3	90.3	101.1
1920.........	13,440	12,585	106.8	88.5	120.7
1921.........	7,954		62.9	87.0	72.3
1922.........	9,762		76.9	85.5	89.9
1923.........	10,140		79.5	84.5	94.1
1924.........	13,628		106.4	83.5	127.4
1925.........		12,862			

Source of data: *Yearbook of the U.S. Department of Agriculture*: 1920, p. 637; 1925, p. 952.
Equation of the primary trend line:

$$y = \frac{13,498}{1 + 10^{0.52152 - 0.16611\,x}}$$

x in units of 5 years, origin at 1870.

Column IV: smoothed moving average of 7 years.

TABLE 4a. PRICES OF RAW COTTON — UPLAND
MIDDLING, NEW YORK, 1866–1915

Relatives, 1913 = 100
1866–78 deflated to gold basis

	I	II	III	IV	V
1866........	234.4		135.9	107.2	126.8
1867........	130.1		78.7	105.8	74.4
1868........	160.0	158.05	101.2	104.2	97.1
1869........	172.8		113.7	102.4	111.0
1870........	122.7		84.1	100.6	83.6
1871........	147.7		105.6	98.8	106.9
1872........	−139.5		104.2	96.8	107.6
1873........	135.0	127.83	105.6	94.0	112.3
1874........	116.4		94.6	91.6	103.3
1875........	95.4		80.8	89.2	90.6
1876........	82.3		72.6	87.2	83.3
1877........	88.8		81.9	87.6	93.5
1878........	88.5	103.61	85.4	89.7	95.2
1879........	86.7		86.7	92.8	93.4
1880........	96.1		99.8	96.0	104.0
1881........	97.8		105.6	99.2	106.5
1882........	+95.5		107.3	102.4	104.8
1883........	88.8	85.38	104.0	106.4	97.7
1884........	84.6		102.0	108.8	93.7
1885........	84.1		104.5	110.4	94.7
1886........	79.4		101.8	111.4	91.4
1887........	79.4		105.0	111.8	.93.9
1888........	87.2	73.15	119.2	112.0	106.4
1889........	90.9		126.4	111.7	113.2
1890........	86.7		122.7	110.3	111.2
1891........	67.3		97.0	105.4	92.0
1892........	60.1		88.2	98.9	89.2
1893........	65.1	66.91	97.3	92.5	105.2
1894........	54.7		81.8	88.4	92.5
1895........	57.1		85.5	85.1	100.5
1896........	61.9		92.7	82.4	112.5
1897........	55.9		83.8	82.2	101.9
1898........	46.7	66.67	70.0	84.4	82.9
1899........	51.4		75.8	88.2	85.9
1900........	75.1		108.9	93.6	116.3
1901........	67.5		96.3	101.5	94.9
1902........	69.8		97.9	107.0	91.5
1903........	87.9	72.43	121.4	108.1	112.3
1904........	94.6		126.5	108.7	116.4

TABLE 4a (continued)

	I	II	III	IV	V
1905.........	74.7		96.8	108.9	88.9
1906.........	86.2		108.5	109.0	99.5
1907.........	92.9		113.5	108.9	104.2
1908.........	81.8	84.18	97.2	108.6	89.5
1909.........	94.7		107.9	108.0	99.9
1910.........	118.2		129.5	107.2	120.8
1911.........	102.0		107.6	105.6	101.9
1912.........	89.9		91.4	99.0	92.3
1913.........	100.0	101.93	98.1	90.0	109.0
1914.........	94.6		88.7	84.5	105.0
1915.........	79.4	111.42	71.3	80.0	89.1

Sources of data: Up to 1892, October of each year, Aldrich Senate Report, *On Wholesale Prices, Wages and Transportation*, 1893, part II, p. 11; from 1892, annual averages, U.S. Bureau of Labor Statistics, Bulletin no. 390, pp. 50–51.

Equation of the primary trend line:

$$y = 194.27 - 39.214\,x + 2.998\,x^2$$

x in units of 5 years, origin at 1863.

Column IV: smoothed moving average of 7 years up to 1893, 5 years average from 1893.

TABLE 5. ANTHRACITE COAL OUTPUT, UNITED STATES, 1825–1924

Columns I and II in thousands of short tons

	I	II	III	IV	V
1825.......	43	80.8	53.2	56.0	95.0
1826.......	59		59.8	59.0	101.4
1827.......	78		64.6	62.0	104.2
1828.......	95		64.3	67.0	96.0
1829.......	138		76.4	76.0	100.5
1830.......	215	220.6	97.5	87.0	112.1
1831.......	218		83.0	101.6	81.7
1832.......	448		143.2	119.5	119.8
1833.......	601		161.4	124.7	129.4
1834.......	464		85.7	126.4	67.8
1835.......	691	526.5	131.2	126.8	103.5
1836.......	843		137.5	125.0	110.0
1837.......	1,071		150.1	117.6	127.6
1838.......	910		109.6	112.2	97.7
1839.......	1,008		104.4	107.3	97.3
1840.......	967	1,122.6	86.1	102.5	84.0
1841.......	1,182		92.3	99.4	92.9
1842.......	1,366		93.5	99.4	94.1
1843.......	1,557		93.4	101.9	91.7
1844.......	2,009		105.6	107.0	98.7
1845.......	2,480	2,170.4	114.3	112.3	101.8
1846.......	2,888		118.7	116.3	102.1
1847.......	3,551		130.2	119.6	108.9
1848.......	3,806		130.3	121.6	107.2
1849.......	3,995		116.6	123.0	94.8
1850.......	4,138	3,839.7	107.8	124.1	86.9
1851.......	5,481		129.3	124.8	103.6
1852.......	6,152		131.4	125.2	105.0
1853.......	6,400		123.8	125.2	98.9
1854.......	7,395		129.6	124.8	103.8
1855.......	8,142	6,300.4	129.2	122.9	105.1
1856.......	8,535		124.4	118.4	105.1
1857.......	8,187		109.4	112.6	97.2
1858.......	8,426		103.3	108.0	95.6
1859.......	9,620		108.3	103.0	105.1
1860.......	8,116	9,683.7	83.8	99.4	84.3
1861.......	9,800		94.0	97.6	96.3
1862.......	9,695		104.1	96.6	107.8
1863.......	11,785		97.3	96.2	101.1
1864.......	12,539		96.0	96.0	100.0

TABLE 5 (*continued*)

	I	II	III	IV	V
1865.......	11,892	14,064.3	84.6	96.0	88.1
1866.......	15,651		104.3	96.0	108.6
1867.......	16,002		99.9	96.0	104.1
1868.......	17,003		99.6	96.1	103.6
1869.......	17,083		93.7	96.1	97.5
1870.......	15,664	19,445.0	80.6	96.2	83.8
1871.......	19,342		93.8	96.2	97.5
1872.......	24,233		111.4	96.2	115.8
1873.......	26,153		113.6	96.1	118.2
1874.......	24,819		103.4	95.6	108.2
1875.......	22,486	25,758.2	87.3	94.3	92.6
1876.......	22,793		84.3	91.0	92.6
1877.......	25,660		90.4	86.8	104.1
1878.......	21,690		72.7	86.3	84.2
1879.......	30,208		96.4	87.7	109.9
1880.......	28,650	32,878.5	87.1	91.0	95.7
1881.......	31,920		93.0	93.3	99.7
1882.......	35,121		98.1	94.7	103.6
1883.......	38,457		103.0	95.8	107.5
1884.......	37,157		95.4	96.4	99.0
1885.......	38,336	40,638.0	94.3	96.8	97.4
1886.......	39,035		92.5	97.2	95.2
1887.......	42,088		96.1	97.6	98.5
1888.......	46,620		102.7	97.8	105.0
1889.......	45,547		96.7	98.0	98.7
1890.......	46,469	48,845.0	95.1	98.0	97.0
1891.......	50,665		100.4	98.0	102.5
1892.......	52,473		100.8	97.8	103.1
1893.......	53,968		100.4	97.3	103.2
1894.......	51,921		93.5	96.5	96.9
1895.......	57,999	57,300.0	101.2	95.6	105.9
1896.......	54,346		92.3	94.6	97.6
1897.......	52,612		86.9	93.3	93.1
1898.......	53,383		85.7	90.6	94.6
1899.......	60,418		94.3	88.9	106.1
1900.......	57,368	65,823.3	87.1	89.2	97.6
1901.......	67,472		100.1	90.8	110.2
1902.......	41,374		59.9	92.5	64.8
1903.......	74,607		105.4	94.5	111.5
1904.......	73,157		101.0	96.8	104.3

Table 5 (*continued*)

	I	II	III	IV	V
1905.......	77,660	74,233.3	104.6	99.5	105.1
1906.......	71,282		94.1	101.4	92.8
1907.......	85,604		110.6	102.6	107.8
1908.......	83,269		105.3	103.3	101.9
1909.......	81,070		100.4	103.6	96.9
1910.......	84,485	82,406.0	102.5	103.5	99.0
1911.......	90,464		107.8	103.3	104.4
1912.......	84,362		98.7	102.9	95.9
1913.......	91,525		105.1	102.4	102.6
1914.......	90,822		102.5	101.7	100.8
1915.......	88,995	90,226.0	98.6	100.9	97.7
1916.......	87,578		95.6	100.0	95.6
1917.......	99,612		104.6	98.8	105.9
1918.......	98,826		104.5	97.2	107.5
1919.......	88,092		91.7	94.4	97.1
1920.......	89,598	97,614.0	91.8	89.6	102.5
1921.......	90,473		91.4	85.0	107.5
1922.......	54,683		55.8	83.1	67.1
1923.......	93,339		91.4	85.0	107.5
1924.......	87,927	103,180.0	85.2	88.4	96.4

Sources of data: Up to 1911, *Mineral Resources of the United States,* 1911, part II, p. 27; 1911–18, *Mineral Resources of the United States,* 1918, part II, pp. 710–11; 1919–24, *Yearbook of Commerce,* 1924, p. 168; 1925, p. 253.

Equation of the primary trend line:

$$\log y = 1.61429 + 3.60011 \, (1 - 0.38209^x)$$

x in units of 34 years, origin at 1823.

Column IV: smoothed moving average of 7 years.

TABLE 5a. ANTHRACITE COAL, STOVE, WHOLESALE
PRICES, UNITED STATES, 1840–1915

Relatives, 1913 = 100
1862–78 deflated to gold basis

	I	II	III	IV	V
1840..........	85.7		111.3	96.0	115.9
1841..........	76.2		99.2	92.5	107.2
1842..........	85.7	76.61	111.9	90.0	124.3
1843..........	57.1		74.7	88.5	84.4
1844..........	66.6		87.3	88.0	99.2
1845..........	71.4		93.7	88.3	106.1
1846..........	76.2		101.5	89.0	114.0
1847..........	69.0	75.91	90.9	90.0	101.0
1848..........	64.3		84.8	91.3	92.9
1849..........	68.5		90.4	93.0	97.2
1850..........	63.8		84.3	94.7	89.0
1851..........	61.9		81.9	97.5	84.0
1852..........	70.4	75.50	93.2	100.4	92.8
1853..........	75.2		99.6	103.8	96.0
1854..........	92.3		122.3	104.6	116.9
1855..........	100.9		133.8	105.7	126.6
1856..........	89.5		118.7	106.2	111.8
1857..........	80.9	75.37	107.3	106.0	101.2
1858..........	70.4		93.4	105.4	88.6
1859..........	70.4		93.3	104.4	89.4
1860..........	73.3		97.1	103.6	93.7
1861..........	73.3		97.1	103.5	93.8
1862..........	61.4	75.52	81.3	104.2	78.0
1863..........	85.3		112.8	105.5	106.9
1864..........	96.0		126.8	107.3	118.2
1865..........	84.8		111.9	109.0	102.7
1866..........	101.4		133.6	110.3	121.1
1867..........	72.4	75.97	95.3	111.5	85.5
1868..........	64.7		85.0	112.3	75.7
1869..........	102.4		134.3	112.8	119.1
1870..........	86.1		112.7	113.0	99.7
1871..........	98.0		128.0	113.0	113.3
1872..........	70.3	76.70	91.7	112.5	81.5
1873..........	88.7		115.3	111.8	103.1
1874..........	99.2		128.7	108.5	118.6
1875..........	96.0		124.2	104.5	118.9
1876..........	93.0		120.0	96.0	125.0
1877..........	40.0	77.71	51.5	78.0	66.0
1878..........	78.9		101.2	77.0	131.4
1879..........	51.7		66.1	84.0	78.7

TABLE 5a (*continued*)

	I	II	III	IV	V
1880............	78.1		99.5	90.7	109.7
1881............	77.1		97.9	91.8	106.6
1882............	79.0	79.01	100.0	92.9	107.6
1883............	81.9		103.3	93.8	110.1
1884............	80.9		101.6	94.4	107.6
1885............	73.3		91.7	94.6	96.9
1886............	63.8		79.5	94.6	84.0
1887............	76.2	80.59	94.6	94.5	100.1
1888............	78.1		96.5	94.2	102.4
1889............	80.0		98.4	93.6	105.1
1890............	73.3		89.7	92.8	96.7
1891............	76.2		92.8	91.9	101.0
1892............	82.1	82.46	99.6	91.0	109.5
1893............	82.8		99.9	90.1	110.9
1894............	71.1		85.3	89.2	95.6
1895............	61.8		73.8	88.6	83.3
1896............	75.0		89.1	88.3	100.9
1897............	79.3	84.62	93.7	88.9	105.4
1898............	75.0		88.1	90.7	97.1
1899............	73.2		85.5	93.2	91.7
1900............	77.9		90.5	96.0	94.3
1901............	85.4		98.6	98.5	100.1
1902............	88.2	87.07	101.3	100.6	100.7
1903............	95.3		108.8	102.3	106.4
1904............	95.3		108.1	103.4	104.5
1905............	95.3		107.3	104.4	102.8
1906............	96.1		107.7	105.0	102.6
1907............	95.3	89.80	106.1	105.5	100.6
1908............	95.3		105.4	105.8	99.6
1909............	95.2		104.6	105.9	98.8
1910............	95.2		103.9	105.9	98.1
1911............	95.0		103.0	105.8	97.4
1912............	99.4	92.81	107.1	105.5	101.5
1913............	100.0		107.0	105.2	101.7
1914............	100.0		106.2	104.6	101.5
1915............	99.7		105.2	103.9	101.3

Sources of data: Up to 1891, *Aldrich Report*, part II, p. 177; from 1891, U.S. Bureau of Labor Statistics, Bulletin no. 390, pp. 126–27 (New York, Tidewater).

Equation of the primary trend line:
$$y = 77.60 - 1.131\,x + 0.1434\,x^2$$

x in units of 5 years, origin at 1837.

Column IV: smoothed moving average of 9 years.

TABLE 6. BITUMINOUS COAL OUTPUT, UNITED STATES,
1840–1924

Columns I and II in thousands of short tons

	I	II	III	IV	V
1840........	1,103	1,048	105.2	98.5	106.8
1841........	1,109		94.2	99.0	95.2
1842........	1,244		95.3	99.3	96.0
1843........	1,504		104.7	99.5	105.2
1844........	1,672		106.8	99.7	107.1
1845........	1,830	1,696	107.9	99.9	108.0
1846........	1,978		103.8	100.6	103.2
1847........	1,735		82.1	101.2	81.1
1848........	1,968		84.7	101.8	83.2
1849........	2,453		96.8	102.4	94.5
1850........	2,880	2,744	105.0	102.3	102.6
1851........	3,253		105.5	101.6	103.8
1852........	3,665		107.2	100.7	106.5
1853........	4,170		111.0	99.9	111.1
1854........	4,582		111.9	99.4	112.6
1855........	4,785	4,434	107.9	99.0	109.0
1856........	5,012		100.7	98.6	102.1
1857........	5,154		93.3	98.2	95.0
1858........	5,548		91.5	97.9	93.5
1859........	6,013		91.0	97.6	93.2
1860........	6,494	7,154	90.8	97.3	93.3
1861........	6,688		83.3	96.9	86.0
1862........	7,791		87.6	96.5	90.8
1863........	9,534		97.6	96.0	101.7
1864........	11,067		104.0	96.6	107.7
1865........	11,900	11,509	103.4	98.5	105.0
1866........	13,352		103.5	100.8	102.7
1867........	14,722		103.1	102.0	101.1
1868........	15,859		101.2	103.0	98.3
1869........	15,821		92.7	103.6	89.5
1870........	17,371	18,448	94.2	104.1	90.5
1871........	27,543		133.5	104.5	127.8
1872........	27,220		119.3	104.8	113.8
1873........	31,450		125.8	105.1	119.7
1874........	27,787		102.2	105.3	97.1

TABLE 6 (*continued*)

	I	II	III	IV	V
1875........	29,863	29,373	101.7	105.4	96.5
1876........	30,487		93.1	105.5	88.2
1877........	34,841		96.4	105.5	91.4
1878........	36,246		91.7	105.4	87.0
1879........	37,898		88.3	105.2	83.9
1880........	42,832	46,303	92.5	105.0	88.1
1881........	53,961		104.9	104.7	100.2
1882........	68,430		121.0	104.4	115.9
1883........	77,251		125.3	104.1	120.4
1884........	82,999		124.3	103.7	119.9
1885........	72,824	71,876	101.3	103.3	98.1
1886........	74,645		94.1	102.9	91.4
1887........	88,562		102.1	102.3	99.8
1888........	102,040		108.4	101.4	106.9
1889........	95,683		94.2	100.0	94.2
1890........	111,302	109,023	102.1	98.0	104.2
1891........	117,901		98.9	95.6	103.5
1892........	126,857		98.0	92.9	105.5
1893........	128,385		91.9	89.8	102.3
1894........	118,820		79.3	84.2	94.2
1895........	135,118	160,125	84.4	81.2	104.0
1896........	137,640		79.5	81.0	98.1
1897........	147,618		79.3	82.2	96.5
1898........	166,594		83.6	85.5	97.8
1899........	193,323		91.1	90.0	101.2
1900........	212,316	225,304	94.2	93.0	101.3
1901........	225,828		93.9	96.0	97.8
1902........	260,217		101.8	98.8	103.0
1903........	282,749		104.5	100.5	104.0
1904........	278,660		97.5	101.9	95.7
1905........	315,063	300,918	104.7	103.0	101.7
1906........	342,875		108.3	104.0	104.1
1907........	394,759		118.8	104.8	113.4
1908........	332,574		95.5	105.3	90.7
1909........	379,744		104.4	105.8	98.7
1910........	417,111	379,537	109.9	105.9	103.8
1911........	405,907		103.0	105.7	97.4
1912........	450,105		110.2	105.5	104.5
1913........	478,435		113.1	105.3	107.4
1914........	422,704		96.5	104.9	92.0

TABLE 6 (*continued*)

	I	II	III	IV	V
1915.......	442,624	452,519	97.8	104.0	94.0
1916.......	502,520		108.1	103.0	105.0
1917.......	551,791		115.7	102.0	113.4
1918.......	579,386		118.5	100.8	117.1
1919.......	465,860		92.9	99.6	93.3
1920.......	568,667	513,459	110.7	98.0	113.0
1921.......	415,922		79.6	96.0	82.9
1922.......	422,268		79.4	94.0	84.5
1923.......	564,565		104.3	92.0	113.4
1924.......	483,687		87.8	89.5	98.1
1925.......		560,014			

Sources of data: *Mineral Resources of the United States*: 1911, part II, p. 27; 1918, part II, pp. 710–11.   *Yearbook of Commerce*, 1925, p. 253.

Equation of the primary trend line:

$$y = \frac{655,928}{1 + 10^{1.95757 - 0.20953\,x}}$$

x in units of 5 years, origin at 1860.

Column IV: smoothed moving average of 9 years.

TABLE 6a. BITUMINOUS COAL, WHOLESALE PRICES, UNITED STATES, 1857–1915

Relatives, 1913 = 100
1862–78 deflated to gold basis

	I	II	III	IV	V
1857........	174.6	185.24	94.3	98.1	96.1
1858........	186.3		102.2	93.1	109.8
1859........	136.6	179.30	76.2	88.6	86.0
1860........	158.3		89.6	87.4	102.5
1861........	142.8		82.1	89.8	91.4
1862........	167.2		97.7	92.4	105.7
1863........	160.4		94.2	95.9	99.3
1864........	152.2	165.70	91.9	99.6	92.3
1865........	162.9		99.8	103.1	96.8
1866........	203.9		126.8	106.4	119.2
1867........	168.5		106.5	109.4	97.4
1868........	150.1		·96.3	112.0	86.0
1869........	169.3	153.34	110.4	113.6	97.2
1870........	168.8		111.7	114.5	97.6
1871........	173.6		116.6	115.0	101.4
1872........	176.8		120.5	115.1	104.7
1873........	192.4		133.2	115.1	115.7
1874........	185.6	142.22	130.5	115.0	113.5
1875........	162.1		115.6	114.6	100.8
1876........	135.7		98.1	113.8	86.2
1877........	132.0		96.9	112.8	85.9
1878........	130.1		96.9	111.6	86.8
1879........	139.0	132.34	105.0	109.6	95.8
1880........	159.9		122.4	107.4	114.0
1881........	155.2		120.4	105.0	114.7
1882........	141.3		111.1	101.3	109.7
1883........	138.2		110.2	97.4	113.1
1884........	108.7	123.70	87.9	93.5	94.0
1885........	99.3		81.2	89.1	91.1
1886........	97.8		81.0	87.4	92.7
1887........	105.6		88.5	86.3	102.5
1888........	99.3		84.3	85.8	98.3
1889........	96.2	116.31	82.7	85.4	96.8
1890........	97.8		85.0	85.1	99.9
1891........	99.3		87.2	84.8	102.8
1892........	96.0		85.2	84.5	100.8
1893........	96.6		86.7	84.0	103.2
1894........	89.6	110.16	81.3	83.9	96.9

TABLE 6a (*continued*)

	I	II	III	IV	V
1895........	92.1		84.4	83.6	101.0
1896........	87.2		80.6	83.3	96.8
1897........	79.9		74.5	83.1	89.7
1898........	71.2		67.0	83.0	80.7
1899........	88.4	105.25	84.0	86.6	97.0
1900........	95.2		91.1	92.6	98.4
1901........	95.8		92.3	101.6	90.8
1902........	132.9		129.0	104.5	123.4
1903........	145.3		142.0	105.2	135.0
1904........	104.6	101.58	103.0	105.2	97.9
1905........	103.1		102.0	105.0	97.1
1906........	102.3		101.7	104.7	97.1
1907........	106.0		105.9	104.4	101.4
1908........	100.8		101.2	104.0	97.3
1909........	99.9	99.15	100.8	103.6	97.3
1910........	99.8		100.1	103.2	97.9
1911........	98.9		100.2	102.7	97.6
1912........	102.3		103.9	102.2	101.7
1913........	100.0		101.8	101.8	100.0
1914........	100.0	97.97	102.1	101.4	100.7
1915........	95.0	97.98	97.0	101.0	96.0

Sources of data: Up to 1891, July of each year, *Aldrich Report*, part II, p. 178; from 1891, annual averages, U.S. Bureau of Labor Statistics, Bulletin no. 390, pp. 130–31 (Georges Creek 1890–1912, Pocahontas 1913–15).

Equation of the primary trend line:

$$y = 194.15 - 15.467\,x + 0.621\,x^2$$

x in units of 5 years, origin at 1854.

Column IV: smoothed moving average of 9 years.

TABLE 7. CRUDE PETROLEUM OUTPUT, UNITED STATES, 1860–1924

Columns I and II in thousands of barrels

	I	II	III	IV	V
1860........	500	2,375			
1861........	2,114		80.0	79.6	100.5
1862........	3,057		105.0	79.6	131.9
1863........	2,611		82.1	79.7	103.0
1864........	2,116		61.4	79.8	76.9
1865........	2,498	3,719	67.2	79.9	84.1
1866........	3,598		87.0	80.2	108.5
1867........	3,347		73.4	80.6	91.1
1868........	3,646		73.2	81.4	89.9
1869........	4,215		78.1	82.6	94.6
1870........	5,261	5,821	90.4	84.4	107.1
1871........	5,205		80.3	87.0	92.3
1872........	6,293		88.2	92.5	95.4
1873........	9,894		126.9	99.3	127.8
1874........	10,927		129.3	108.0	119.7
1875........	8,788	9,111	96.5	117.0	82.5
1876........	9,133		90.1	126.4	71.3
1877........	13,350		119.5	132.5	90.2
1878........	15,397		126.2	134.8	93.6
1879........	19,914		150.6	135.6	111.1
1880........	26,286	14,256	184.4	136.0	135.6
1881........	27,661		174.4	135.4	128.8
1882........	30,350		173.7	133.0	130.8
1883........	23,450		122.9	129.5	94.9
1884........	24,218		117.1	120.5	97.2
1885........	21,859	22,293	98.1	111.0	88.4
1886........	28,065		113.2	106.0	106.8
1887........	28,283		103.6	104.2	99.4
1888........	27,612		92.6	104.9	88.3
1889........	35,164		108.8	108.5	100.3
1890........	45,824	34,837	131.5	110.4	119.1
1891........	54,293		140.1	111.0	126.2
1892........	50,515		118.4	110.0	107.6
1893........	48,431		104.0	107.5	96.7
1894........	49,345		97.8	104.9	93.2
1895........	52,892	54,380	97.3	100.0	97.3
1896........	60,960		100.8	95.5	105.5
1897........	60,476		90.9	91.6	99.2
1898........	55,364		76.3	88.9	85.8
1899........	57,071		72.6	87.0	83.4

TABLE 7 (*continued*)

	I	II	III	IV	V
1900.....	63,621	84,718	75.1	86.0	87.3
1901.....	69,389		73.7	86.5	85.2
1902.....	88,767		85.8	88.2	97.3
1903.....	100,461		89.0	90.8	98.0
1904.....	117,081		95.8	93.7	102.2
1905.....	134,718	131,618	102.4	96.0	106.7
1906.....	126,494		86.6	97.6	88.7
1907.....	160,095		103.5	98.6	105.0
1908.....	178,527		102.1	99.0	103.1
1909.....	183,171		96.8	98.9	97.9
1910.....	209,557	203,602	102.9	98.3	104.7
1911.....	220,449		97.8	96.8	101.0
1912.....	222,935		90.1	95.1	94.7
1913.....	248,446		92.3	93.1	99.1
1914.....	265,763		94.6	91.0	104.0
1915.....	281,104	312,870	89.8	89.5	100.3
1916.....	300,767		87.1	88.2	98.8
1917.....	335,316		88.7	88.0	100.8
1918.....	335,928		81.8	88.5	92.4
1919.....	378,372		85.3	89.4	95.4
1920.....	442,929	476,051	93.0	91.0	102.2
1921.....	472,183		90.2	96.0	94.0
1922.....	557,531		97.6	101.0	96.6
1923.....	732,407		118.4	107.0	110.7
1924.....	713,940		107.2	112.0	95.7
1925.....		713,709			

Sources of data: *Mineral Resources of the United States*, 1918, part II, p. 1144.   *Yearbook of Commerce*, 1925, p. 271.

Equation of the primary trend line:

$$y = \frac{6,060,606}{1 + 10^{3.01705-0.19477\,x}}$$

x in units of 5 years, origin at 1870.

Column IV: smoothed moving average of 11 years up to 1902, 5 years average from 1902.

TABLE 7a. PRICES OF CRUDE PETROLEUM, UNITED
STATES, 1862–1916

Relatives, 1913 = 100
1862–78 deflated to gold basis

	I	II	III	IV	V
1862........	63.8		63.0	101.8	61.9
1863........	102.0		105.8	102.4	103.3
1864........	124.1	91.5	135.7	102.9	131.9
1865........	100.7		115.4	103.3	111.7
1866........	77.4		93.1	103.7	89.8
1867........	52.3		66.3	103.9	63.8
1868........	77.4		103.5	103.9	99.6
1869........	83.2	70.6	117.9	103.4	114.0
1870........	74.8		110.1	102.8	107.1
1871........	80.8		126.0	102.0	123.5
1872........	70.0		114.9	100.9	113.9
1873........	50.1		86.8	99.7	87.1
1874........	38.9	54.5	71.4	97.8	73.0
1875........	41.9		80.4	94.7	84.9
1876........	51.8		104.0	92.2	112.8
1877........	50.6		106.6	90.6	117.7
1878........	42.7		94.5	89.6	105.5
1879........	37.3	42.8	87.1	88.7	98.2
1880........	34.9		84.7	88.1	96.2
1881........	30.7		77.6	88.1	88.1
1882........	28.9		76.2	88.2	86.4
1883........	33.7		92.8	88.6	104.7
1884........	31.3	34.7	90.3	89.0	101.5
1885........	34.9		101.7	89.4	113.8
1886........	28.9		85.0	89.6	94.9
1887........	28.3		84.1	89.8	93.7
1888........	29.5		88.6	89.9	98.5
1889........	35.2	33.0	106.8	89.9	119.9
1890........	35.4		106.2	89.9	118.4
1891........	27.3		81.1	89.9	90.2
1892........	22.7		66.7	90.6	73.6
1893........	26.1		75.9	101.0	75.1
1894........	34.2	34.7	98.6	107.3	91.9
1895........	55.4		154.0	110.8	139.0
1896........	48.1		129.3	113.1	114.3
1897........	32.1		83.5	114.7	72.8
1898........	37.2		93.7	116.1	80.7
1899........	52.8	41.0	128.9	117.3	109.9

TABLE 7a (*continued*)

	I	II	III	IV	V
1900........	55.2		128.1	118.1	108.5
1901........	49.4		109.2	118.5	92.2
1902........	50.5		106.6	118.8	89.7
1903........	64.8		130.9	118.8	110.2
1904........	66.4	51.6	128.6	118.6	108.4
1905........	56.5		103.4	117.9	87.7
1906........	65.2		113.0	116.2	97.2
1907........	70.8		116.6	111.6	104.5
1908........	72.7		114.0	105.0	108.6
1909........	67.9	66.8	101.7	97.8	104.0
1910........	54.9		78.1	94.0	83.1
1911........	53.1		71.9	92.4	77.8
1912........	64.3		83.1	91.2	91.1
1913........	100.0		123.6	90.2	137.0
1914........	78.2	84.4	92.6	89.3	103.7
1915........	62.4		69.6	88.5	78.6
1916........	101.4		106.9	87.8	121.8

Sources of data: Up to 1893, July of each year, *Aldrich Report*, part IV, pp. 1835–36 (crude, barreled); from 1893 annual averages, U.S. Bureau of Labor Statistics, Bulletin no. 390, pp. 134–35 (Pennsylvania).

Equation of the primary trend line:

$$y = 116.15 - 27.256\,x + 2.232\,x^2$$

x in units of 5 years, origin at 1859.

Column IV: smoothed moving average of 7 years up to 1893, 5 years average from 1893.

TABLE 8. OUTPUT OF PIG IRON, UNITED STATES,
1854–1924

Columns I and II in thousands of long tons

	I	II	III	IV	V
1854.........	657		136.6	138.0	99.0
1855.........	700	517	135.4	129.0	105.0
1856.........	789		139.6	120.0	116.3
1857.........	713		115.7	111.0	104.2
1858.........	630		94.5	105.0	90.0
1859.........	751		104.6	100.0	104.6
1860.........	821	769	106.8	95.0	112.4
1861.........	653		77.5	90.0	85.2
1862.........	703		76.7	86.0	89.2
1863.........	846		85.4	85.5	99.9
1864.........	1,014		95.2	86.0	110.8
1865.........	832	1,140	73.0	88.5	82.5
1866.........	1,206		96.6	92.0	105.0
1867.........	1,305		96.2	95.5	100.7
1868.........	1,431		97.6	98.5	99.1
1869.........	1,711		108.6	101.0	107.5
1870.........	1,665	1,684	98.9	102.1	96.9
1871.........	1,707		92.7	102.3	90.6
1872.........	2,549		127.4	100.5	126.8
1873.........	2,561		118.7	97.2	122.1
1874.........	2,401		103.7	95.7	108.4
1875.........	2,024	2,475	81.8	94.2	86.8
1876.........	1,869		69.2	92.7	74.6
1877.........	2,067		70.6	92.4	76.4
1878.........	2,301		72.9	92.7	78.6
1879.........	2,742		81.1	93.2	87.0
1880.........	3,835	3,610	106.2	93.8	113.2
1881.........	4,144		105.5	94.5	111.6
1882.........	4,623		108.8	95.5	113.9
1883.........	4,596		100.6	96.9	103.8
1884.........	4,098		83.8	99.3	84.4
1885.........	4,045	5,209	77.7	101.0	76.9
1886.........	5,683		100.6	101.2	99.4
1887.........	6,417		105.4	101.3	104.0
1888.........	6,490		99.4	101.1	98.3
1889.........	7,604		109.2	100.9	108.2
1890.........	9,203	7,404	124.3	99.9	124.4
1891.........	8,280		103.7	97.5	106.4
1892.........	9,157		106.9	93.7	114.1
1893.........	7,125		77.9	88.7	87.8
1894.........	6,657		68.4	86.1	79.4

TABLE 8 (*continued*)

	I	II	III	IV	V
1895.........	9,446	10,312	91.6	85.2	107.5
1896.........	8,623		78.1	86.2	90.6
1897.........	9,653		81.9	89.0	92.0
1898.........	11,774		94.0	93.3	100.8
1899.........	13,621		102.8	97.2	105.8
1900.........	13,789	13,991	98.6	101.2	97.4
1901.........	15,878		106.8	104.5	102.2
1902.........	17,821		113.2	106.2	106.6
1903.........	18,009		108.3	108.0	100.3
1904.........	16,497		94.3	109.1	86.4
1905.........	22,992	18,381	125.1	109.8	113.9
1906.........	25,307		130.7	110.4	118.4
1907.........	25,781		126.8	110.6	114.6
1908.........	15,936		74.8	110.9	67.4
1909.........	25,795		115.7	111.1	104.1
1910.........	27,304	23,268	117.3	111.1	105.6
1911.........	23,650		97.4	111.0	87.7
1912.........	29,727		117.6	110.9	106.0
1913.........	30,966		117.8	110.8	106.3
1914.........	23,332		85.5	110.4	77.4
1915.........	29,916	28,306	105.7	109.8	96.3
1916.........	39,435		134.8	108.8	123.9
1917.........	38,621		127.8	106.8	119.7
1918.........	39,055		125.2	105.4	118.8
1919.........	31,015		96.5	102.5	94.1
1920.........	36,926	33,104	111.6	98.8	113.0
1921.........	16,688		49.2	94.5	52.1
1922.........	27,220		78.2	91.3	85.7
1923.........	40,361		113.2	90.0	125.8
1924.........	31,406		86.1	89.6	96.1

Sources of data: *Mineral Resources of the United States*, 1918, part I, p. 566 (data of the American Iron and Steel Institute).   *Yearbook of Commerce*, 1925, p. 333.

Equation of the primary trend line:

$$y = \frac{50,403}{1 + 10^{1.80987 - 0.17431\,x}}$$

x in units of 5 years, origin at 1860

Column IV: smoothed moving average of 11 years.

TABLE 8a. PRICES OF PIG IRON, NO. 1, FOUNDRY,
UNITED STATES, 1854–1915

Columns I and II in dollars per ton
1862–78 deflated to gold basis

	I	II	III	IV	V
1854..........	36.88		122.5	105.0	116.7
1855..........	27.75		93.2	97.8	95.3
1856..........	27.18	29.47	92.2	92.5	99.7
1857..........	26.34		90.3	87.8	102.8
1858..........	22.19		76.6	83.7	91.5
1859..........	23.33		81.7	79.8	102.4
1860..........	22.70		80.4	78.4	102.6
1861..........	20.26	27.92	72.6	78.8	92.1
1862..........	21.12		76.5	86.0	89.0
1863..........	24.28		88.9	93.6	95.0
1864..........	29.14		107.8	101.2	106.5
1865..........	29.31		109.6	108.0	101.5
1866..........	33.26	26.45	125.7	114.0	110.2
1867..........	31.91		122.0	119.4	102.2
1868..........	28.10		108.6	123.0	88.2
1869..........	30.54		119.3	126.0	94.7
1870..........	28.91		114.2	127.2	89.8
1871..........	31.40	25.04	125.4	127.3	98.5
1872..........	43.56		175.9	126.6	138.9
1873..........	37.61		153.5	124.9	122.9
1874..........	27.14		112.1	119.0	94.2
1875..........	22.21		92.7	111.0	83.5
1876..........	19.88	23.68	84.0	97.0	86.6
1877..........	18.07		77.2	94.3	81.9
1878..........	17.42		75.2	94.6	79.5
1879..........	21.72		94.9	97.1	97.7
1880..........	28.48		125.9	100.6	125.1
1881..........	25.17	22.37	112.5	102.3	110.0
1882..........	25.77		114.0	102.8	110.9
1883..........	22.42		102.6	102.6	100.0
1884..........	19.81		91.7	101.6	90.3
1885..........	17.99		84.2	99.6	84.5
1886..........	18.71	21.11	88.6	97.1	91.2
1887..........	20.93		100.3	94.6	106.0
1888..........	18.88		91.5	92.1	99.3
1889..........	17.76		87.1	89.6	97.2

TABLE 8a (*continued*)

	I	II	III	IV	V
1890..........	18.41		91.4	87.0	105.1
1891..........	17.52	19.91	88.0	83.4	105.5
1892..........	15.75		80.0	77.8	102.8
1893..........	14.52		74.7	73.2	102.0
1894..........	12.66		65.9	69.4	95.0
1895..........	13.10		69.0	67.6	102.1
1896..........	12.95	18.77	69.0	70.7	97.6
1897..........	12.10		65.2	77.0	84.7
1898..........	11.66		63.6	85.0	74.8
1899..........	19.36		106.9	93.5	114.3
1900..........	19.98		111.7	99.6	112.2
1901..........	15.87	17.68	89.8	105.0	85.5
1902..........	22.19		127.0	108.8	116.7
1903..........	19.92		115.4	111.9	103.1
1904..........	15.57		91.3	113.7	80.3
1905..........	17.88		106.0	114.6	92.5
1906..........	20.98	16.66	125.9	115.0	109.5
1907..........	23.89		145.1	115.1	126.1
1908..........	17.70		108.9	115.0	94.7
1909..........	17.81		110.9	114.0	97.3
1910..........	17.36		109.4	111.9	97.8
1911..........	15.71	15.68	100.2	109.8	91.3
1912..........	16.56		106.9	107.5	99.4
1913..........	17.07		111.5	104.5	106.7
1914..........	14.94		98.7	102.5	96.3
1915..........	15.94		106.6	101.5	105.0

Sources of data: J. M. Swank, *History of the Manufacture of Iron in All Ages*, Philadelphia, 1892, p. 514. U.S. Bureau of Labor Statistics, Bulletin no. 390, pp. 138–39 (for 1914–15, spliced from the basic).

Equation of the primary trend line:

$$y = 31.07 - 1.6269 x + 0.285 x^2$$

x in units of 5 years, origin at 1851.

Column IV: smoothed moving average of 7 years.

TABLE 9. CRUDE STEEL PRODUCTION, UNITED STATES,
1865–1924

Columns I and II in thousands of long tons

	I	II	III	IV	V
1865........	14	21.9	63.9	50.0	127.8
1866........	17		58.1	52.0	111.7
1867........	20		51.2	55.0	93.1
1868........	27		51.7	58.7	88.1
1869........	31		44.5	63.2	70.4
1870........	69	88.9	77.6	67.8	114.5
1871........	73		64.2	74.2	86.5
1872........	143		98.5	81.7	120.6
1873........	199		107.4	101.5	105.8
1874........	216		91.2	115.8	78.8
1875........	390	291.7	133.7	124.8	107.1
1876........	533		148.1	131.6	112.5
1877........	570		131.5	136.5	96.3
1878........	732		137.0	139.6	98.1
1879........	935		138.7	141.0	98.4
1880........	1,247	802.1	155.5	141.5	109.9
1881........	1,588		166.2	141.3	117.6
1882........	1,737		152.7	139.8	109.2
1883........	1,674		123.7	135.7	91.2
1884........	1,551		96.3	129.0	74.7
1885........	1,712	1,862.7	91.9	121.8	75.5
1886........	2,563		118.8	116.2	102.2
1887........	3,339		133.8	111.5	120.0
1888........	2,899		101.4	107.1	94.7
1889........	3,386		101.3	103.1	98.3
1890........	4,277	3,778	113.2	99.4	113.6
1891........	3,904		98.3	95.7	102.7
1892........	4,928		101.9	92.1	110.6
1893........	4,020		73.5	88.5	83.1
1894........	4,412		71.3	85.7	83.2
1895........	6,115	6,848	89.3	84.3	105.9
1896........	5,282		69.5	84.8	82.0
1897........	7,157		85.0	87.9	96.7
1898........	8,933		95.7	91.9	104.1
1899........	10,640		102.7	95.6	107.4
1900........	10,188	11,280	90.3	98.4	91.8
1901........	13,474		109.5	100.7	108.7
1902........	14,947		111.4	102.1	109.1
1903........	14,535		99.3	103.8	95.7
1904........	13,860		86.9	104.6	83.1

TABLE 9 (*continued*)

	I	II	III	IV	V
1905........	20,024	17,154	116.7	104.8	111.4
1906........	23,398		126.7	104.7	121.0
1907........	23,363		117.6	104.3	112.8
1908........	14,023		65.5	103.5	63.3
1909........	23,955		104.3	102.0	102.3
1910........	26,095	24,350	107.2	99.4	107.8
1911........	23,676		91.6	96.7	94.7
1912........	31,251		113.9	100.0	113.9
1913........	31,301		107.5	103.5	103.9
1914........	23,513		76.1	104.0	73.2
1915........	32,151	32,564	98.7	104.3	94.6
1916........	42,774		124.4	104.1	119.5
1917........	45,061		124.4	103.0	120.8
1918........	44,462		116.4	100.5	115.8
1919........	34,671		86.1	97.0	88.8
1920........	42,133	42,018	100.3	92.4	108.6
1921........	19,784		45.1	86.0	52.4
1922........	35,603		77.7	81.5	95.3
1923........	44,944		93.8	76.3	122.9
1924........	37,932	49,921	76.0	72.2	105.3

Sources of data: *Mineral Resources of the United States*, 1918, part II, p. 576.   *Yearbook of Commerce*, 1925, p. 338.

Equation of the primary trend line:

$$\log y = 1.20426 + 3.984512 \ (1 - 0.497456^x)$$

x in units of 20 years, origin at 1864.

Column IV: smoothed moving average of 7 years.

TABLE 9a. PRICE OF STEEL RAILS (BESSEMER), UNITED
STATES, 1867–1924

Columns I and II in dollars per ton
1867–78 deflated to gold basis

	I	II	III	IV	V
1867.........	120.18		109.9	108.0	101.8
1868.........	113.49	104.23	108.9	107.7	101.1
1869.........	99.45		99.9	106.9	93.5
1870.........	92.87		98.0	106.0	92.5
1871.........	91.74	90.04	101.9	104.9	97.1
1872.........	99.68		116.2	103.6	112.2
1873.........	105.92		130.0	101.2	128.5
1874.........	84.73	77.17	109.8	97.9	112.2
1875.........	59.81		81.6	95.1	85.8
1876.........	53.09		76.4	93.0	82.2
1877.........	43.45	65.64	66.2	91.3	72.5
1878.........	41.66		66.9	89.6	74.7
1879.........	48.25		82.0	88.7	92.4
1880.........	67.50	55.43	121.8	87.9	138.6
1881.........	61.13		116.5	87.1	133.8
1882.........	48.50		97.9	86.5	113.2
1883.........	37.75	46.56	81.1	86.3	94.0
1884.........	30.75		69.8	86.3	80.9
1885.........	28.50		68.6	86.4	79.4
1886.........	34.50	39.01	88.4	87.2	101.4
1887.........	37.08		100.4	88.5	113.4
1888.........	29.83		85.6	90.3	94.8
1889.........	29.25	32.79	86.2	92.0	93.7
1890.........	31.78		102.0	93.7	108.9
1891.........	29.92		101.3	95.5	106.1
1892.........	30.00	27.90	107.5	97.6	110.1
1893.........	28.12		105.3	99.7	105.6
1894.........	24.00		94.0	101.9	92.2
1895.........	24.33	24.34	100.0	104.0	96.2
1896.........	28.00		118.7	106.6	111.4
1897.........	18.75		82.1	109.7	74.8
1898.........	17.62	22.11	79.7	113.1	70.5
1899.........	28.12		128.9	118.2	109.1
1900.........	32.29		150.1	124.0	121.0
1901.........	27.33	21.21	128.9	127.0	101.5
1902.........	28.00		131.1	128.0	102.4
1903.........	28.00		130.3	128.0	101.8
1904.........	28.00	21.63	129.4	127.3	101.6

TABLE 9a (*continued*)

	I	II	III	IV	V
1905.........	28.00		126.1	125.8	100.2
1906.........	28.00		122.8	122.6	100.2
1907.........	28.00	22.39	119.7	118.4	101.1
1908.........	28.00		114.7	114.2	100.4
1909.........	28.00		110.1	109.7	100.4
1910.........	28.00	26.47	105.8	105.0	100.8
1911.........	28.00		100.2	100.1	100.1
1912.........	28.00		95.2	95.5	99.7
1913.........	28.00	30.90	90.6	93.0	97.4
1914.........	28.00		85.3	92.8	91.9
1915.........	28.00		80.6	95.3	84.6
1916.........	31.33	36.63	85.5	98.3	87.0
1917.........	38.00		97.5	100.3	97.2
1918.........	54.00		130.6	100.8	129.6
1919.........	47.26	43.70	108.1	100.6	107.5
1920.........	51.83		111.4	98.9	112.6
1921.........	44.04		89.8	93.7	95.8
1922.........	40.69	52.10	78.1	84.7	92.2
1923.........	43.00		77.3	78.8	98.1
1924.........	43.00		73.0	74.3	98.3
1925.........		61.83			

Sources of data: Up to 1890, *Mineral Industry* (ed. by R. P. Rothwell), 1892, p. 285; from 1890, U.S. Bureau of Labor Statistics, Bulletin no. 390, pp. 146–47.

Equation of the primary trend line:

$$y = 119.75 - 16 \cdot 186\,x + 0 \cdot 6645\,x^2$$

x in units of 3 years, origin at 1865.

Column IV: smoothed moving average of 7 years.

TABLE 10. PORTLAND CEMENT PRODUCTION, UNITED
STATES, 1880–1924

Columns I and II in thousands of barrels

	I	II	III	IV	V
1880......	42	36.9	113.7	121.0	94.0
1881......	60		120.9	118.0	102.5
1882......	85	62.4	136.3	114.6	119.9
1883......	90		103.3	109.4	94.4
1884......	100		89.4	103.8	84.5
1885......	150	136.8	109.6	98.4	111.4
1886......	150		81.6	92.8	87.9
1887......	250	231.0	108.3	87.4	123.9
1888......	250		77.5	82.0	94.5
1889......	300		72.4	76.6	94.5
1890......	335	506.0	66.2	70.6	93.8
1891......	455		67.0	64.6	103.7
1892......	547	852.8	64.1	60.6	105.8
1893......	591		49.7	57.3	86.7
1894......	799		52.4	57.0	91.9
1895......	990	1,859.2	53.2	61.6	86.4
1896......	1,543		62.1	67.9	91.5
1897......	2,678	3,113.5	86.0	78.0	110.3
1898......	3,692		85.9	90.0	95.4
1899......	5,652		103.0	109.4	94.1
1900......	8,482	6,667.6	127.2	124.2	102.4
1901......	12,711		144.7	138.0	104.9
1902......	17,231	10,900.8	158.1	147.6	107.1
1903......	22,343		152.9	152.8	100.1
1904......	26,506		144.6	155.6	92.9
1905......	35,247	22,041.7	159.9	156.6	102.1
1906......	46,463		166.5	151.8	109.7
1907......	48,785	33,775.5	144.4	143.6	100.6
1908......	51,073		121.7	136.2	89.4
1909......	64,991		129.8	130.2	99.7
1910......	76,550	58,294.0	131.3	123.2	106.6
1911......	78,529		115.7	116.2	99.6
1912......	82,438	77,497.6	106.3	108.0	98.4
1913......	92,097		106.3	99.0	107.4
1914......	88,230		103.3	91.6	112.8

TABLE 10 (*continued*)

	I	II	III	IV	V
1915......	85,915	104,766.0	82.0	84.8	96.7
1916......	91,521		81.8	78.2	104.6
1917......	92,814	119,069.4	78.0	71.6	108.9
1918......	71,082		57.4	65.8	87.2
1919......	80,778		62.8	67.3	93.3
1920......	100,023	133,461.0	74.9	72.5	103.4
1921......	98,842		72.6	79.5	91.3
1922......	114,790	139,003.9	82.6	87.0	94.9
1923......	137,460		97.7	93.8	104.2
1924......	149,358		96.8	99.4	97.4
1925......		144,106.8			

Sources of data: *Mineral Resources of the United States*: 1908, part II, p. 446; 1917, part II, p. 350. *Yearbook of Commerce*, 1925, p. 324.

Equation of the primary trend line:

$$y = \frac{148,481}{1 + 10^{3.60421 - 0.56912\,x}}$$

x in units of 5 years, origin at 1880.

Column IV: smoothed moving average of 5 years.

TABLE 10a. PORTLAND CEMENT, FACTORY PRICES, UNITED STATES, 1881–1924

Columns I and II in dollars per barrel

	I	II	III	IV	V
1881............	2.50		99.6	90.7	109.8
1882............	2.01	2.40	83.7	91.5	91.5
1883............	2.15		93.5	92.5	101.1
1884............	2.10		95.5	93.7	101.9
1885............	1.95		92.9	95.3	97.5
1886............	1.95		97.5	97.6	99.9
1887............	1.95	1.91	102.1	100.1	102.0
1888............	1.95		106.6	103.5	103.0
1889............	1.67		95.4	108.0	88.3
1890............	2.09		125.1	120.5	103.8
1891............	2.13		133.1	125.0	106.5
1892............	2.11	1.53	137.8	126.1	109.3
1893............	1.91		129.9	126.3	102.9
1894............	1.73		122.6	126.3	97.1
1895............	1.60		117.6	125.8	93.5
1896............	1.57		119.8	123.2	97.2
1897............	1.61	1.26	127.8	120.0	106.5
1898............	1.62		132.8	116.0	114.5
1899............	1.43		120.9	112.5	107.5
1900............	1.09		94.0	109.3	86.0
1901............	.99		87.6	105.5	83.0
1902............	1.21	1.10	110.0	102.1	107.7
1903............	1.24		113.8	99.5	114.4
1904............	.88		81.5	97.1	83.9
1905............	.94		87.9	94.7	92.8
1906............	1.13		106.6	92.1	115.7
1907............	1.11	1.05	105.7	89.5	118.1
1908............	.85		80.2	86.8	92.4
1909............	.81		76.0	84.6	89.8
1910............	.89		82.5	82.4	100.1
1911............	.84		77.4	80.4	96.3
1912............	.81	1.10	73.9	79.2	93.3
1913............	1.00		88.9	81.3	109.3
1914............	.93		79.3	85.0	93.3

TABLE 10a (*continued*)

	I	II	III	IV	V
1915.............	.86		72.3	91.7	78.8
1916.............	1.10		90.4	98.5	91.8
1917.............	1.35	1.26	107.5	105.3	102.1
1918.............	1.60		121.8	113.3	107.5
1919.............	1.71		125.1	120.1	104.2
1920.............	2.02		143.3	122.0	117.5
1921.............	1.89		128.6	121.3	106.0
1922.............	1.76	1.53	115.0	117.5	97.9
1923.............	1.90		117.3	113.8	103.1
1924.............	1.81		105.9	111.5	95.0

Sources of data: *Mineral Resources of the United States*, 1917, part II, p. 358; *Yearbook of Commerce*, 1925, p. 324.

Equation of the primary trend line:

$$y = 2.99 - 0.6469\,x + 0.0538\,x^2$$

x in units of 5 years, origin at 1877.

Column IV: smoothed moving average of 7 years.

TABLE 11. COPPER PRODUCTION, SMELTER, DOMESTIC
ORE, UNITED STATES, 1880–1924

Columns I and II in thousands of long tons

	I	II	III	IV	V
1880	27.0	36.9	73.1	84.3	86.7
1881	32.0		75.3	86.0	87.6
1882	40.5		84.3	89.0	94.7
1883	51.6		96.0	92.0	104.3
1884	64.7		108.9	96.8	112.5
1885	74.1	65.1	113.8	100.9	112.8
1886	70.4		94.9	102.8	92.3
1887	81.0		97.1	103.4	93.9
1888	101.1		109.2	103.4	105.6
1889	101.2		99.4	103.1	96.4
1890	116.0	111.0	104.4	102.8	101.6
1891	126.8		101.6	102.3	99.3
1892	154.0		111.2	101.8	109.2
1893	147.0		96.4	101.2	95.3
1894	158.1		94.9	100.7	94.2
1895	169.9	180.1	94.3	100.1	94.2
1896	205.4		103.5	99.6	103.9
1897	220.6		101.7	99.0	102.7
1898	235.1		99.9	98.3	101.6
1899	253.9		100.0	97.8	102.2
1900	270.6	272.4	99.3	97.4	102.0
1901	268.8		91.6	97.3	94.1
1902	294.4		93.6	97.4	96.1
1903	311.6		92.9	97.6	95.2
1904	362.7		101.7	97.9	103.9
1905	402.6	377.7	106.6	98.5	108.2
1906	409.8		103.0	99.2	103.8
1907	387.9		92.8	100.0	92.8
1908	420.8		96.0	100.7	95.3
1909	487.9		106.5	101.4	105.0
1910	482.2	478.0	100.9	102.1	98.8
1911	489.8		99.1	103.0	96.2
1912	555.0		108.8	103.9	104.7
1913	546.7		103.9	104.5	99.4
1914	513.4		94.7	107.0	88.5

TABLE II (*continued*)

	I	II	III	IV	V
1915............	619.6	558.6	110.9	116.0	95.6
1916............	860.6		151.0	123.0	122.8
1917............	842.0		145.0	122.0	118.9
1918............	852.0		143.8	115.0	125.0
1919............	574.3		95.1	104.0	91.4
1920............	539.8	615.2	87.7	95.0	92.3
1921............	225.7		36.3	90.0	40.3
1922............	424.2		67.4	87.0	77.5
1923............	640.6		100.6	84.0	119.8
1924............	729.6		113.3	82.5	137.3
1925............		650.9			

Sources of data: *Statistical Abstract of the United States*, 1923, p. 829; *Yearbook of Commerce*, 1925, p. 353.

Equation of the primary trend line:

$$y = \frac{699.5}{1 + 10^{0.98900 - 0.26460\,x}}$$

x in units of 5 years, origin at 1885.

Column IV: smoothed moving average of 7 years.

TABLE 11a. PRICES OF COPPER INGOTS, UNITED STATES, 1876–1915

Relatives, 1913 = 100
1873–78 deflated to gold basis

	I	II	III	IV	V
1876..........	141.7		102.1	99.6	102.5
1877..........	126.8		94.7	99.7	95.0
1878..........	117.5	128.92	91.1	99.8	91.3
1879..........	108.1		86.4	99.9	86.5
1880..........	144.6		119.3	100.0	119.3
1881..........	131.0		111.7	100.1	111.6
1882..........	−139.5		123.0	100.2	122.8
1883..........	+122.5	109.54	111.8	100.3	111.5
1884..........	102.1		95.7	100.4	95.3
1885..........	75.7		72.9	100.5	72.5
1886..........	81.7		80.9	100.5	80.5
1887..........	81.7		83.2	100.5	82.8
1888..........	120.0	95.39	125.8	100.5	125.2
1889..........	119.2		127.4	100.1	127.3
1890..........	97.9		106.6	99.5	107.1
1891..........	81.1		90.1	96.0	93.9
1892..........	71.7		81.2	92.5	87.8
1893..........	67.9	86.48	78.5	90.0	87.2
1894..........	58.9		68.7	89.4	76.8
1895..........	66.8		78.6	90.1	87.2
1896..........	68.2		80.9	92.2	87.7
1897..........	70.4		84.3	95.8	88.0
1898..........	74.2	82.80	89.6	99.0	90.5
1899..........	109.9		132.2	102.0	129.6
1900..........	103.3		123.8	104.9	118.0
1901..........	104.9		125.3	107.5	116.6
1902..........	74.6		88.8	108.9	81.5
1903..........	85.1	84.36	100.9	109.9	91.8
1904..........	81.5		95.1	110.4	86.1

TABLE 11a (continued)

	I	II	III	IV	V
1905..........	98.0		112.6	110.6	101.8
1906..........	121.9		137.8	110.6	124.6
1907..........	132.1		147.1	110.3	133.4
1908..........	84.8	91.15	93.0	109.3	85.1
1909..........	83.3		89.0	105.1	84.7
1910..........	82.1		85.6	99.4	86.2
1911..........	79.3		80.6	93.7	86.0
1912..........	104.4		103.6	93.0	111.4
1913..........	100.0	103.17	96.9	93.2	104.0
1914..........	85.1		79.8	98.5	81.0
1915..........	109.7		99.7	103.0	96.0

Sources of data: Up to 1891, July of each year, *Aldrich Report*, part I, p. 40; from 1891, annual averages, U.S. Bureau of Labor Statistics, Bulletin no. 390, pp. 150–51 (Lake Copper up to 1907, electrolytic from 1907).

Equation of the primary trend line:

$$y = 153.53 - 27.228\,x + 2.6167\,x^2$$

x in units of 5 years, origin at 1873.

Column IV: smoothed moving average of 9 years.

TABLE 12. REFINED LEAD OUTPUT, DOMESTIC ORE,
UNITED STATES, 1872–1924

Columns I and II in thousands of short tons

	I	II	III	IV	V
1872...........	25.9	63.4			
1873...........	42.5		63.3	66.0	95.9
1874...........	52.1		73.5	72.5	101.4
1875...........	59.6		79.8	79.0	101.0
1876...........	64.1		81.7	85.5	96.1
1877...........	81.9	82.3	99.5	92.0	108.2
1878...........	91.1		104.8	98.7	106.1
1879...........	92.8		101.4	105.3	96.3
1880...........	97.8		101.7	110.8	91.8
1881...........	117.1		116.1	112.8	102.9
1882...........	132.9	105.6	125.9	114.4	110.1
1883...........	144.0		129.4	114.6	112.9
1884...........	139.9		119.6	114.4	104.5
1885...........	129.4		105.5	113.6	92.9
1886...........	130.6		101.6	110.2	92.2
1887...........	145.7	134.3	108.5	104.7	103.6
1888...........	151.9		107.6	102.3	105.2
1889...........	156.4		105.5	100.8	104.7
1890...........	143.6		92.5	99.4	93.1
1891...........	178.6		106.2	98.1	108.3
1892...........	173.3	169.2	102.4	96.8	105.8
1893...........	164.0		92.3	95.6	96.5
1894...........	162.7		87.5	94.6	92.5
1895...........	170.0		87.4	94.4	92.6
1896...........	188.0		92.7	94.9	97.7
1897...........	212.0	211.3	100.3	96.0	104.5
1898...........	222.0		100.3	98.2	102.1
1899...........	210.5		91.0	100.6	90.5
1900...........	270.8		112.2	102.6	109.4
1901...........	270.7		107.6	103.6	103.9
1902...........	270.0	261.6	103.2	104.4	98.9
1903...........	282.0		103.1	104.8	98.4
1904...........	307.0		107.6	105.0	102.5
1905...........	307.5		103.4	104.9	98.6
1906...........	336.2		108.7	104.6	103.9
1907...........	352.4	321.2	109.7	104.0	105.5
1908...........	311.7		93.0	103.3	90.0
1909...........	352.8		101.0	102.4	98.6

TABLE 12 (*continued*)

	I	II	III	IV	V
1910...........	375.4		103.4	102.0	101.4
1911...........	392.0		103.9	102.4	101.5
1912...........	392.5	391.3	100.3	104.7	95.8
1913...........	411.9		101.1	109.0	92.8
1914...........	512.8		121.0	110.8	109.2
1915...........	507.0		115.1	111.2	103.5
1916...........	552.2		120.9	110.8	109.1
1917...........	548.4	473.2	115.9	107.0	108.1
1918...........	539.9		109.7	100.0	109.7
1919...........	424.4		83.1	91.5	90.8
1920...........	476.8		90.0	85.0	105.9
1921...........	398.2		72.7	84.0	86.5
1922...........	468.7	567.9	82.5	85.7	96.3
1923...........	543.8		92.2	88.0	104.8
1924...........	566.4	611.4	92.6	88.6	104.5

Sources of data: *Statistical Abstract of the United States*, 1923, p. 829; *Yearbook of Commerce*, 1925, p. 359.

Equation of the primary trend line:
$$\log y = 1.80237 + 2.93597(1 - 0.87525^x)$$

x in units of 17 years, origin at 1872.

Column IV: smoothed moving average of 7 years.

TABLE 12a. PRICES OF PIG LEAD, UNITED STATES, 1870–1914

Relatives, 1913 = 100
1870–78 deflated to gold basis

	I	II	III	IV	V
1870..........	132.5		101.6	112.0	90.7
1871..........	135.1		105.8	112.5	94.1
1872..........	143.2	125.00	114.6	112.8	101.6
1873..........	140.0		114.0	113.0	100.9
1874..........	129.6		107.5	112.9	95.2
1875..........	137.6		116.3	112.2	103.7
1876..........	141.7		122.0	107.5	113.5
1877..........	120.9	113.92	106.1	99.0	107.2
1878..........	66.9		59.6	93.1	64.0
1879..........	90.4		81.9	92.7	88.3
1880..........	107.3		98.7	93.1	106.0
1881..........	101.7		95.1	93.6	101.6
1882..........	110.7	105.23	105.2	94.1	111.8
1883..........	99.4		95.6	94.7	101.0
1884..........	81.4		79.3	95.4	83.1
1885..........	89.3		88.0	96.1	91.6
1886..........	110.7		110.5	96.7	114.3
1887..........	100.6	98.90	101.7	97.3	104.5
1888..........	88.1		89.8	97.5	92.1
1889..........	+91.5		94.0	97.6	96.3
1890..........	100.0		103.6	96.9	106.9
1891..........	99.3		103.7	94.7	109.5
1892..........	93.9	94.96	98.9	92.1	107.4
1893..........	85.0		89.8	89.5	100.3
1894..........	75.2		79.7	87.0	91.6
1895..........	74.1		78.8	85.5	92.2
1896..........	68.2		72.8	86.2	84.5
1897..........	81.4	93.39	87.2	90.0	96.9
1898..........	86.4		92.4	97.0	95.3
1899..........	101.8		108.6	100.3	108.3
1900..........	101.1		107.7	102.9	104.7
1901..........	99.5		105.8	105.4	100.4
1902..........	93.4	94.20	99.2	107.9	91.9
1903..........	97.3		102.6	110.1	93.2
1904..........	100.7		105.5	111.7	94.4

TABLE 12a (*continued*)

	I	II	III	IV	V
1905..........	108.9		113.3	112.1	101.1
1906..........	133.6		138.1	112.1	123.2
1907..........	125.5	97.39	128.9	111.9	115.2
1908..........	95.9		97.4	110.9	87.8
1909..........	97.5		97.9	106.0	92.4
1910..........	101.8		101.1	97.7	103.5
1911..........	101.1		99.3	95.7	104.4
1912..........	100.7	102.95	97.8	95.4	104.7
1913..........	100.0		95.7	91.9	104.1
1914..........	88.4		83.3	90.0	92.6

Sources of data: Up to 1892, July of each year, *Aldrich Report*, part II, p. 192 (New York Shipping and Commercial List); from 1892, annual averages, U.S. Bureau of Labor Statistics, Bulletin no. 390, pp. 150–51.

Equation of the primary trend line:

$$y = 138.43 - 14.6447\,x + 1.1888\,x^2$$

x in units of 5 years, origin at 1867.

Column IV: smoothed moving average of 7 years.

TABLE 13. CRUDE ZINC OUTPUT, DOMESTIC ORE,
UNITED STATES, 1880–1924

Columns I and II in thousands of short tons

	I	II	III	IV	V
1880...........	23.2	29.2	79.7	91.4	87.2
1881...........	n.d.			92.2	
1882...........	33.8		98.3	93.1	105.6
1883...........	36.8		99.7	94.0	106.0
1884...........	38.5		97.4	95.0	102.5
1885...........	40.7	43.3	94.0	96.0	97.9
1886...........	42.6		90.7	97.1	93.4
1887...........	50.3		99.2	98.4	100.8
1888...........	55.9		102.7	101.3	101.4
1889...........	58.9		101.3	105.1	96.4
1890...........	63.7	63.4	100.5	106.9	94.0
1891...........	80.9		117.9	107.0	110.2
1892...........	87.3		118.2	106.0	111.5
1893...........	78.8		99.7	102.4	97.4
1894...........	75.3		89.4	96.8	92.4
1895...........	89.7	91.6	98.0	93.1	105.3
1896...........	81.5		82.5	93.7	88.0
1897...........	100.0		94.3	95.7	98.5
1898...........	115.4		101.9	97.4	104.6
1899...........	129.1		107.0	99.1	108.0
1900...........	123.9	130.6	94.9	100.5	94.4
1901...........	140.8		100.2	101.9	98.3
1902...........	156.9		104.3	103.0	101.3
1903...........	159.2		99.2	103.7	95.7
1904...........	186.7 *		109.5	104.0	105.3
1905...........	203.8 *	183.9	110.8	103.9	106.6
1906...........	199.7		101.3	102.7	98.6
1907...........	223.7		107.8	101.6	106.1
1908...........	190.7		85.0	100.5	84.6
1909...........	230.2		96.8	101.6	95.3
1910...........	252.5	256.0	98.6	103.1	95.6
1911...........	271.6		99.0	104.9	94.4
1912...........	323.9		110.9	107.0	103.6
1913...........	337.3		108.6	110.0	98.7
1914...........	343.4		104.6	116.0	90.2

*Including small amounts of foreign ore.

TABLE 13 (*continued*)

	I	II	III	IV	V
1915..........	458.1	352.4	130.0	126.0	103.2
1916..........	564.3		150.0	130.0	115.4
1917..........	584.6		146.1	128.5	113.7
1918..........	492.4		116.0	118.0	98.3
1919..........	452.3		100.9	98.0	103.0
1920....... ..	450.0	486.7	92.5	83.0	111.4
1921..........	198.2		37.7	74.0	50.9
1922..........	353.3		62.7	75.0	83.6
1923..........	508.3		84.4	78.0	108.2
1924..........	515.8	640.5	80.5	84.0	95.8

Sources of data: *Mineral Resources of the United States*, 1918, part I, p. 1028. *Yearbook of Commerce*, 1925, p. 363.

Equation of the primary trend line:

$$\log y = 4.42449 + 4.96677(1 - 0.89907^x)$$

x in units of 15 years, origin at 1875.

Column IV: smoothed moving average of 5 years.

TABLE 13a. PRICES OF ZINC, UNITED STATES, 1870–1914

Columns I and II in cents per pound
1870–78 deflated to gold basis

	I	II	III	IV	V
1870	6.1		90.1	107.1	84.2
1871	6.3		96.0	106.9	89.8
1872	6.2	6.35	97.6	106.7	91.5
1873	7.6		122.9	106.4	115.6
1874	6.3		104.7	105.7	99.1
1875	6.4		109.3	104.6	104.5
1876	6.5		114.3	102.3	111.7
1877	5.6	5.52	101.4	99.5	101.9
1878	4.4		81.4	97.0	83.9
1879	4.5		85.2	95.1	89.6
1880	5.2		101.6	94.1	108.0
1881	4.9		97.1	94.0	103.3
1882	4.9	4.93	99.5	94.4	105.4
1883	4.5		92.7	95.1	97.5
1884	4.6		96.3	95.8	100.5
1885	4.2		89.3	96.9	92.2
1886	4.4		95.0	98.5	96.4
1887	4.5	4.56	98.7	101.5	97.2
1888	4.4		96.7	103.2	93.7
1889	4.8		104.6	103.9	100.7
1890	5.5		121.3	104.0	116.7
1891	5.0		110.5	102.8	107.5
1892	4.7	4.52	104.1	99.5	104.6
1893	4.1		90.8	96.4	94.2
1894	3.6		79.8	93.3	85.5
1895	3.6		79.8	92.5	86.3
1896	4.0		88.8	93.5	95.0
1897	4.2	4.51	93.2	95.5	97.6
1898	4.5		98.5	97.5	101.0
1899	5.9		127.4	99.9	127.5
1900	4.4		93.7	101.7	92.2
1901	4.1		86.2	103.5	83.3
1902	4.9	4.82	101.6	104.6	97.1
1903	5.6		113.6	105.1	108.1
1904	5.2		103.2	105.3	98.0

TABLE 13a (*continued*)

	I	II	III	IV	V
1905............	5.9		114.6	105.2	108.9
1906............	6.2		117.9	104.8	112.5
1907............	6.2	5.37	115.5	103.9	111.2
1908............	4.8		87.0	102.6	84.8
1909............	5.5		97.1	100.8	96.3
1910............	5.6		96.2	98.4	97.8
1911............	5.8		97.0	95.5	101.6
1912............	7.1	6.14	115.6	93.3	123.9
1913............	5.8		91.5	91.4	100.1
1914............	5.3		81.0	90.1	89.9

Sources of data: Up to 1891, July of each year, Spelter, *Aldrich Report*, part II, p. 213 (New York Shipping and Commercial List); from 1891, annual averages, U.S. Bureau of Labor Statistics, Bulletin no. 390, pp. 154–55 (zinc-slab).

Equation of the primary trend line:
$$y = 7.405 - 1.1689\,x + 0.11426\,x^2$$

x in units of 5 years, origin at 1867.

Column IV: smoothed moving average of 7 years.

TABLE 14. SALT OUTPUT, UNITED STATES, 1880-1924
Columns I and II in thousands of barrels

	I	II	III	IV	V
1880..........	5,961	4,932	120.9	111.0	108.9
1881..........	6,200		115.5	109.5	105.5
1882..........	6,412		110.5	107.5	102.8
1883..........	6,192		99.3	105.0	94.6
1884..........	6,515		97.7	102.5	95.3
1885..........	7,039	7,107	99.0	99.3	99.7
1886..........	7,707		100.0	96.8	103.3
1887..........	8,003		96.2	94.5	101.8
1888..........	8,056		90.3	92.2	97.9
1889..........	8,006		84.1	90.8	92.6
1890..........	8,777	10,128	86.7	90.7	95.6
1891..........	9,988		91.4	91.3	100.1
1892..........	11,699		99.7	92.5	107.8
1893..........	11,897		94.9	93.9	101.1
1894..........	12,968		97.2	95.5	101.8
1895..........	13,670	14,152	96.6	97.0	99.6
1896..........	13,851		91.3	98.5	92.7
1897..........	15,973		98.6	99.7	98.9
1898..........	17,613		102.3	100.9	101.4
1899..........	19,709		108.0	101.6	106.3
1900..........	20,869	19,270	108.3	101.7	106.5
1901..........	20,567		100.3	101.3	99.0
1902..........	23,849		109.8	100.8	108.9
1903..........	18,968		82.6	100.3	82.4
1904..........	22,030		91.1	99.8	91.3
1905..........	25,966	25,415	102.2	99.2	103.0
1906..........	28,172		105.1	98.7	106.5
1907..........	29,704		105.4	98.0	107.6
1908..........	28,822		97.5	97.3	100.2
1909..........	30,108		97.4	96.5	100.9
1910..........	30,306	32,304	93.8	95.7	98.0
1911..........	31,184		92.4	94.5	97.8
1912..........	33,325		94.8	93.7	101.2
1913..........	34,399		94.0	96.5	97.4
1914..........	34,805		91.5	100.0	91.5

TABLE 14 (*continued*)

	I	II	III	IV	V
1915..........	38,231	39,452	96.9	104.5	92.7
1916..........	45,449		111.3	105.7	105.3
1917..........	49,844		118.1	105.9	111.5
1918..........	51,705		118.7	105.6	112.4
1919..........	49,164		109.4	104.9	104.3
1920..........	48,857	46,301	105.5	104.0	101.4
1921..........	35,580		74.9	101.0	74.2
1922..........	48,520		99.6	97.8	101.8
1923..........	52,219		104.5	94.6	110.5
1924..........	48,594		95.0	91.4	103.9
1925..........		52,382			

Sources of data: *Mineral Resources of the United States*: 1900, p. 836; 1910, p. 769; *Statistical Abstract of the United States*: 1923, p. 831; 1924, p. 715.

Equation of the primary trend line:

$$y = \frac{71,265}{1 + 10^{0.95560 - 0.17484\,x}}$$

x in units of 5 years, origin at 1885.

Column IV: smoothed moving average of 7 years.

TABLE 14a. SALT, WHOLESALE PRICES, UNITED STATES, 1875–1915

Relatives, 1913 = 100
1875–78 deflated to gold basis

	I	II	III	IV	V
1875.........	145.6		119.6	106.0	112.8
1876.........	96.4		82.3	104.7	78.6
1877.........	97.0		86.1	103.5	83.2
1878.........	88.4		81.7	102.5	79.7
1879.........	149.4	103.71	144.0	101.7	141.6
1880.........	89.7		89.4	100.9	88.6
1881.........	89.7		92.6	100.3	92.3
1882.........	89.7		96.0	100.0	96.0
1883.........	89.7		99.6	100.0	99.6
1884.........	89.7	86.66	103.5	100.1	102.4
1885.........	83.6		99.0	100.3	98.7
1886.........	77.7		94.7	100.6	94.1
1887.........	77.7		97.5	100.9	96.6
1888.........	77.7		100.4	101.2	99.2
1889.........	77.7	75.07	103.5	101.6	101.9
1890.........	77.7		105.2	102.1	103.0
1891.........	77.7		107.1	102.3	104.7
1892.........	74.3		104.1	102.2	101.9
1893.........	68.8		98.1	101.6	96.6
1894.........	70.5	68.90	102.3	99.9	102.4
1895.........	68.8		100.1	97.4	102.8
1896.........	61.0		88.9	97.3	91.4
1897.........	64.8		94.6	101.8	92.9
1898.........	65.2		95.4	102.7	92.9
1899.........	62.4	68.19	91.5	103.0	88.8
1900.........	98.1		141.9	103.2	137.5
1901.........	84.0		119.9	102.9	116.5
1902.........	62.4		87.9	102.4	85.8
1903.........	60.2		83.6	100.5	83.2
1904.........	75.5	72.92	103.5	97.8	105.8
1905.........	74.0		98.7	96.5	102.3
1906.........	70.0		90.9	95.4	95.3
1907.........	77.8		98.5	94.4	104.3
1908.........	77.0		95.0	93.6	101.5
1909.........	80.1	83.10	96.4	94.4	102.1

TABLE 14a (*continued*)

	I	II	III	IV	V
1910.........	74.0		85.8	95.5	89.8
1911.........	81.1		90.8	96.9	93.7
1912.........	96.8		104.7	98.4	106.4
1913.........	100.0		104.6	99.9	104.7
1914.........	100.0	98.72	101.3	101.7	99.6
1915.........	104.9		102.1	103.5	98.8

Sources of data: Up to 1893, *Aldrich Report*, part II, p. 99 (fine, boiled); from 1893, U.S. Bureau of Labor Statistics, Bulletin no. 390. pp. 94–95 (American).

Equation of the primary trend line:

$$y = 126.20 - 25.213\,x + 2.7222\,x^2$$

x in units of 5 years, origin at 1874.

Column IV: smoothed moving average of 7 years.

TABLE 15. CONSUMPTION OF COTTON BY TEXTILE MILLS,
UNITED STATES, 1870–1924

Columns I and II in thousands of bales

	I	II	III	IV	V
1870..........	797	960.8	83.0	102.9	80.7
1871..........	1,163		114.8	103.3	111.1
1872..........	1,097		103.0	103.7	99.3
1873..........	1,201		107.5	104.1	103.3
1874..........	1,320		112.7	104.6	107.7
1875..........	1,201	1,224.0	98.1	105.1	93.3
1876..........	1,354		105.0	105.6	99.4
1877..........	1,429		105.5	106.1	99.4
1878..........	1,496		105.4	106.7	98.8
1879..........	1,561		105.1	107.3	97.9
1880..........	1,570	1,549.9	101.3	107.7	94.1
1881..........	1,938		118.9	107.8	110.3
1882..........	1,964		114.9	107.6	106.8
1883..........	2,072		115.9	107.1	108.2
1884..........	1,877		100.5	105.8	95.0
1885..........	1,753	1,947.8	90.0	104.7	86.0
1886..........	2,162		105.8	103.6	102.1
1887..........	2,088		97.6	102.5	95.2
1888..........	2,261		101.2	101.2	100.0
1889..........	2,270		97.5	99.9	97.6
1890..........	2,518	2,425.8	103.8	98.6	105.3
1891..........	2,640		104.0	97.3	106.9
1892..........	2,856		107.7	95.9	112.3
1893..........	2,375		86.0	93.8	91.7
1894..........	2,291		79.7	91.8	86.8
1895..........	2,871	2,988.6	96.1	91.0	105.6
1896..........	2,505		80.3	91.4	87.9
1897..........	2,792		85.7	93.2	92.0
1898..........	3,465		102.6	95.2	107.8
1899..........	3,632		103.6	97.1	106.7
1900..........	3,873	3,636.0	106.5	98.3	108.3
1901..........	3,547		93.8	99.1	94.7
1902..........	4,083		104.0	99.6	104.4
1903..........	3,924		96.4	99.9	96.5
1904..........	3,935		93.3	100.1	93.2
1905..........	4,279	4,360.8	98.1	100.1	98.0
1906..........	4,909		108.6	100.0	108.6
1907..........	4,985		106.6	99.7	106.9
1908..........	4,539		93.9	99.3	94.6
1909..........	5,241		105.0	98.6	106.5

TABLE 15 (*continued*)

	I	II	III	IV	V
1910..........	4,799	5,148.4	93.2	98.0	95.1
1911..........	4,705		88.5	97.9	90.4
1912..........	5,368		97.9	99.1	98.8
1913..........	5,786		102.5	101.0	101.5
1914..........	5,885		101.3	103.9	97.5
1915..........	6,009	5,977.2	100.5	107.0	93.9
1916..........	7,278		118.4	107.8	109.8
1917..........	7,658		121.3	107.8	112.5
1918..........	7,685		118.5	105.9	111.9
1919..........	6,224		93.6	100.0	93.6
1920..........	6,762	6,819.4	99.2	93.1	106.6
1921..........	5,409		77.5	90.0	86.1
1922..........	6,549		91.6	88.0	104.1
1923..........	7,312		100.1	86.3	115.9
1924..........	6,218		83.1	85.0	97.8
1925..........		7,646.1			

Sources of data: *Statistical Abstract of the United States*, 1923, p. 834; *Yearbook of Commerce*, 1925, p. 430.

Equation of the primary trend line:

$$y = \frac{12,744.1}{1 + 10^{0.97367 - 0.11497\,x}}$$

x in units of 5 years, origin at 1875.

Column IV: smoothed moving average of 7 years.

TABLE 15a. COTTON TEXTILES, WHOLESALE PRICES,
UNITED STATES, 1866–1915

Relatives, 1913 = 100
1866–78 deflated to gold basis

	I	II	III	IV	V
1866..........	294.7		166.6	130.0	128.2
1867..........	216.0		126.3	114.0	110.8
1868..........	137.3		83.2	104.5	79.6
1869..........	154.2	159.23	96.8	100.8	96.0
1870..........	171.1		110.9	99.0	112.0
1871..........	150.3		100.6	98.0	102.7
1872..........	154.0		106.7	97.2	109.8
1873..........	149.9		107.5	96.7	111.2
1874..........	137.5	134.48	102.2	96.4	106.0
1875..........	117.7		90.2	96.2	93.8
1876..........	109.1		86.3	96.0	89.9
1877..........	106.4		86.9	95.9	90.6
1878..........	101.8		86.0	95.9	89.7
1879..........	93.1	114.42	81.4	95.9	84.9
1880..........	110.7		99.4	96.0	103.5
1881..........	106.8		98.6	96.1	102.6
1882..........	108.7		103.3	96.3	107.3
1883..........	103.1		100.9	96.5	104.6
1884..........	94.6	99.06	95.5	96.7	98.8
1885..........	88.4		91.2	96.9	94.1
1886..........	85.1		89.8	97.1	92.5
1887..........	88.3		95.3	97.4	97.8
1888..........	92.1		101.7	97.7	104.1
1889..........	91.3	88.39	103.3	97.9	105.5
1890..........	88.6		101.6	98.1	103.6
1891..........	78.0		90.7	98.2	92.4
1892..........	89.9		106.0	98.0	108.2
1893..........	86.2		103.1	96.8	106.5
1894..........	72.9	82.41	88.5	94.6	93.6
1895..........	75.9		92.4	87.4	105.7
1896..........	68.4		83.5	83.8	99.6
1897..........	66.0		80.9	83.1	97.3
1898..........	54.6		67.1	83.7	80.2
1899..........	72.4	81.13	89.2	87.0	102.5

TABLE 15a (*continued*)

	I	II	III	IV	V
1900..........	81.7		99.9	90.3	110.6
1901..........	74.8		90.7	93.7	96.8
1902..........	82.0		98.6	97.1	101.5
1903..........	85.4		101.9	100.5	101.4
1904..........	88.3	84.54	104.4	104.0	100.4
1905..........	82.8		96.1	107.5	89.4
1906..........	96.0		109.4	109.3	100.1
1907..........	126.0		140.9	110.0	128.1
1908..........	88.9		97.7	109.7	89.1
1909..........	95.2	92.64	102.8	108.4	94.8
1910..........	101.6		106.7	101.6	105.0
1911..........	92.6		94.7	97.6	97.0
1912..........	101.1		100.8	95.1	106.0
1913..........	100.0		97.2	93.4	104.1
1914..........	88.1	105.43	83.6	92.4	90.5
1915..........	83.5		76.7	91.4	83.9

Sources of data: Up to 1890, *Aldrich Report*, part I, p. 79 (textile group of 7 price series); from 1890, U.S. Bureau of Labor Statistics, Bulletin no. 390, pp. 112–13 (price of print-cloth).

Equation of the primary trend line:

$$y = 188.67 - 31.79\,x + 2.346\,x^2$$

x in units of 5 years, origin at 1864.

Column IV: smoothed moving average of 9 years up to 1890, 5 years moving average from 1890.

TABLE 16. IMPORTS OF RAW SILK, UNITED STATES,
1864–1924

(Fiscal years)

Columns I and II in thousands of pounds

	I	II	III	IV	V
1864..........	408	318	128.3	105.0	122.2
1865..........	288		78.3	105.0	74.6
1866..........	568		134.3	105.0	127.9
1867..........	492		101.3	104.8	96.7
1868..........	512		91.7	104.6	87.7
1869..........	720	641	112.3	104.0	108.0
1870..........	584		80.3	103.2	77.8
1871..........	1,100		133.1	102.0	130.5
1872..........	1,064		113.3	99.7	113.6
1873..........	1,159		108.7	96.0	113.2
1874..........	795	1,211	65.7	90.3	72.8
1875..........	1,102		80.9	83.0	97.5
1876..........	1,355		88.9	80.1	111.0
1877..........	1,186		69.5	80.2	86.7
1878..........	1,183		61.8	84.9	72.8
1879..........	1,890	2,150	87.9	92.0	95.5
1880..........	2,562		107.4	101.0	106.2
1881..........	2,790		105.3	109.2	96.4
1882..........	3,549		120.8	117.3	103.0
1883..........	4,731		145.0	122.5	118.4
1884..........	4,285	3,620	118.4	125.7	94.2
1885..........	4,309		108.6	127.4	85.2
1886..........	6,818		156.6	127.1	123.2
1887..........	6,028		126.3	124.7	101.3
1888..........	6,370		121.6	121.0	100.5
1889..........	6,645	5,743	115.7	116.5	99.3
1890..........	7,510		119.7	111.4	107.5
1891..........	6,267		91.5	104.5	87.6
1892..........	8,834		118.3	99.6	118.8
1893..........	8,497		104.2	95.5	109.1
1894..........	5,902	8,903	66.3	91.9	72.1
1895..........	9,316		96.8	89.0	108.8
1896..........	9,364		90.1	87.1	103.4
1897..........	7,993		71.1	86.1	81.4
1898..........	12,088		99.6	85.7	116.2
1899..........	11,250	13,120	85.8	85.6	100.2

TABLE 16 (*continued*)

	I	II	III	IV	V
1900..........	13,074		92.9	85.7	108.4
1901..........	10,406		69.0	85.8	80.4
1902..........	14,235		87.9	86.0	102.2
1903..........	15,271		87.9	86.3	101.9
1904..........	16,723	18,639	89.7	86.6	103.6
1905..........	22,357		112.5	87.0	129.3
1906..........	17,352		82.0	87.4	93.8
1907..........	18,744		83.1	87.8	94.6
1908..........	16,662		69.3	88.3	78.5
1909..........	25,188	25,622	98.3	89.0	110.4
1910..........	23,457		86.4	90.0	96.0
1911..........	26,666		92.7	91.2	101.6
1912..........	26,585		87.3	93.0	93.9
1913..........	32,102		99.5	95.0	104.7
1914..........	34,546	34,189	101.0	97.4	103.7
1915..........	31,053		86.2	99.5	86.6
1916..........	41,925		110.5	101.4	109.0
1917..........	40,351		100.9	103.2	97.8
1918..........	43,681		103.7	105.0	98.8
1919 *........	55,522	44,393	125.1	106.6	117.4
1920..........	39,660		85.2	108.0	78.9
1921..........	52,332		107.4	109.4	98.2
1922..........	58,467		114.3	110.6	103.3
1923...	61,954		115.5	111.6	103.6
1924..........	60,603	56,255	107.7	112.5	95.8

* Calendar years beginning with 1919.

Sources of data: *Statistical Abstract of the United States*, 1919, p. 794. *Yearbook of Commerce*, 1925, p. 456.

Equation of the primary trend line:
$$\log y = 2.50258 + 3.23934(1 - 0.67398^x)$$

x in units of 20 years, origin at 1864.

Column IV: smoothed moving average of 7 years.

TABLE 16a PRICES OF RAW SILK, UNITED STATES, 1860–1914

Relatives, 1913 = 100
1862–78 deflated to gold basis

	I	II	III	IV	V
1860..........	304.2		131.3	100.0	131.3
1861..........	224.2		98.0	96.5	101.6
1862..........	212.1	225.92	93.9	93.0	101.0
1863..........	132.4		59.4	92.0	64.6
1864..........	126.1		57.3	92.8	61.7
1865..........	203.6		93.7	94.2	99.5
1866..........	210.3		98.0	97.0	101.0
1867..........	214.4	211.67	101.3	101.0	100.3
1868..........	263.7		126.3	107.8	117.2
1869..........	204.7		99.4	112.0	88.8
1870..........	243.8		120.0	114.9	104.4
1871..........	215.0		107.3	116.3	92.3
1872..........	270.7	197.60	137.0	117.2	116.9
1873..........	246.3		126.4	117.7	107.4
1874..........	187.1		97.4	118.1	82.5
1875..........	188.1		99.4	118.3	84.0
1876..........	301.2		161.5	118.3	136.5
1877..........	214.1	183.71	116.5	117.5	99.1
1878..........	157.9		87.3	114.0	76.6
1879..........	200.1		112.3	110.0	102.1
1880..........	192.1		109.5	107.0	102.3
1881..........	200.1		115.8	104.5	110.8
1882..........	176.1	170.01	103.6	102.8	100.8
1883..........	168.1		100.5	101.2	99.3
1884..........	160.1		97.3	100.0	97.3
1885..........	144.1		89.0	98.9	90.0
1886..........	144.1		90.5	97.5	92.8
1887..........	160.1	156.49	102.3	96.0	106.6
1888..........	144.1		93.7	94.4	99.3
1889..........	160.1		105.9	92.8	114.1
1890..........	144.1		97.0	91.0	106.6
1891..........	110.2		75.5	88.0	85.8
1892..........	118.9	143.24	83.0	84.0	98.8
1893..........	124.8		88.8	79.0	112.4
1894..........	92.4		67.0	74.0	90.5

TABLE 16a (*continued*)

	I	II	III	IV	V
1895..........	104.0		76.8	74.0	103.8
1896..........	93.6		70.5	75.9	92.9
1897..........	95.2	130.09	73.2	78.2	93.6
1898..........	99.9		78.4	80.5	97.4
1899..........	121.1		97.0	83.2	116.6
1900..........	114.5		93.6	86.5	108.2
1901..........	96.5		80.6	89.5	90.1
1902..........	105.0	117.11	89.7	92.5	97.0
1903..........	113.6		99.2	96.0	103.3
1904..........	100.1		89.4	99.5	89.8
1905..........	109.7		100.3	103.0	97.4
1906..........	114.4		107.1	106.2	100.8
1907..........	139.0	104.28	133.3	108.0	123.4
1908..........	106.9		105.1	108.3	97.0
1909..........	105.5		106.3	108.5	98.0
1910..........	96.8		100.1	108.2	92.5
1911..........	95.4		102.3	107.9	94.8
1912..........	94.7	91.70	103.3	107.5	96.1
1913..........	100.0		112.1	107.0	104.8
1914..........	101.5	86.72	117.0	106.c	110.4

Sources of data: Up to 1890, *Aldrich Report*, part IV, p. 1835 (Italian raw silk); from 1890, U.S. Bureau of Labor Statistics, Bulletin no. 390, pp. 124–25 (Japanese, Kansai no. 1).

Equation of the primary trend line:

$$y = 254.14 - 20.711\,x + 0.5232\,x^2$$

x in units of 5 years, origin at 1857.

Column IV: smoothed moving average of 7 years.

TABLE 17. BANK CLEARINGS, NEW YORK CITY, DEFLATED, 1875–1923

Relatives, Average for 1890–99 = 100

	I	II	III	IV	V
1875..........	61.8	64.47	95.9	114.0	84.1
1876..........	55.9		83.2	114.6	72.6
1877..........	62.7		89.8	114.9	78.2
1878..........	65.7		90.7	115.2	78.7
1879..........	73.5		97.8	115.3	84.8
1880..........	101.3	77.76	130.3	115.0	113.3
1881..........	127.4		157.6	114.2	138.0
1882..........	119.0		141.9	113.0	125.6
1883..........	105.6		121.5	111.1	109.4
1884..........	92.9		103.2	108.1	95.5
1885..........	71.7	93.07	77.0	101.5	75.9
1886..........	96.0		99.5	93.5	106.3
1887..........	98.9		98.9	89.0	111.1
1888..........	85.3		82.4	85.0	96.9
1889..........	97.4		91.0	82.0	111.0
1890..........	104.0	110.40	94.2	78.8	119.5
1891..........	92.8		81.3	75.5	107.7
1892..........	101.6		86.0	72.0	119.4
1893..........	95.1		78.0	68.9	113.2
1894..........	69.7		55.3	66.6	83.0
1895..........	81.3	129.67	62.7	65.4	95.9
1896..........	85.7		64.3	67.1	95.8
1897..........	91.5		66.3	75.2	88.2
1898..........	116.4		81.8	84.0	97.4
1899..........	160.7		109.8	97.0	113.2
1900..........	141.6	150.66	94.0	109.0	86.2
1901..........	207.3		133.6	114.3	116.9
1902..........	196.0		122.8	117.0	104.2
1903..........	183.5		111.8	119.0	93.9
1904..........	152.6		90.5	120.3	75.2
1905..........	232.1	173.00	134.2	120.8	111.1
1906..........	252.9		142.3	120.8	117.8
1907..........	221.8		121.7	120.2	101.2
1908..........	171.3		91.7	116.8	78.5
1909..........	221.1		115.4	111.8	103.2
1910..........	221.4	196.22	112.8	105.8	106.6
1911..........	199.4		99.2	100.9	98.3
1912..........	202.4		98.5	96.3	102.3
1913..........	203.3		96.6	93.4	103.4
1914..........	184.1		85.6	96.2	89.0

TABLE 17 (*continued*)

	I	II	III	IV	V
1915..........	182.8	219.75	83.2	99.0	84.0
1916..........	262.9		117.2	100.3	116.8
1917..........	268.7		117.3	100.9	116.3
1918..........	220.5		94.3	101.0	93.4
1919..........	239.2		100.3	100.8	99.5
1920..........	245.4	243.00	101.0	100.3	100.7
1921..........	237.5		96.0	99.6	96.4
1922..........	259.9		103.2	98.8	104.5
1923..........	245.7	265.41 (1925)	95.8	98.0	97.8

Source of data: Collected by F. R. Macaulay, National Bureau of Economic Research, Inc.

Equation of the primary trend line:

$$y = \frac{417.35}{1 + 10^{0.64019 - 0.09805\,x}}$$

x in units of 5 years, origin at 1880.

Column IV: smoothed moving average of 5 years.

TABLE 18. BANK CLEARINGS, BOSTON, DEFLATED,
1875–1923

Relatives, Average for 1890–99 = 100

	I	II	III	IV	V
1875..........	43.2	39.8	108.5	105.0	103.3
1876..........	41.3		95.8	104.7	91.5
1877..........	44.0		94.6	104.4	90.6
1878..........	45.2		90.6	104.0	87.1
1879..........	54.6		102.4	103.6	98.8
1880..........	63.4	56.7	111.8	103.2	108.3
1881..........	77.6		128.7	102.8	125.2
1882..........	65.0		101.7	102.3	99.4
1883..........	64.5		95.4	101.8	93.7
1884..........	61.6		86.4	101.2	85.4
1885..........	69.1	75.0	92.1	100.6	91.6
1886..........	82.3		104.8	100.0	104.8
1887..........	87.0		106.1	99.3	106.8
1888..........	85.5		100.0	98.6	101.5
1889..........	93.5		105.2	97.8	107.6
1890..........	99.0	92.3	107.3	96.8	110.8
1891..........	90.6		95.2	95.7	99.5
1892..........	97.9		99.9	94.2	106.1
1893..........	88.4		87.7	92.2	95.1
1894..........	83.5		80.6	89.0	90.6
1895..........	95.7	106.4	89.9	85.6	105.0
1896..........	91.8		84.6	88.5	95.6
1897..........	104.0		94.0	97.5	96.4
1898..........	110.7		98.2	103.9	94.5
1899..........	138.7		120.9	106.5	113.5
1900..........	117.7	116.7	100.9	107.6	93.8
1901..........	134.4		113.8	107.8	105.6
1902..........	127.0		106.3	107.4	99.0
1903..........	121.7		100.7	106.8	94.3
1904..........	118.6		97.0	106.2	91.3
1905..........	135.1	123.6	109.3	105.5	103.6
1906..........	142.0		114.1	104.6	109.1
1907..........	132.3		105.5	103.5	101.9
1908..........	119.4		94.5	102.1	92.6
1909..........	131.4		103.4	100.5	102.9

TABLE 18 (*continued*)

	I	II	III	VI	V
1910...........	125.2	**127.9**	97.9	98.6	99.3
1911...........	125.8		97.9	96.6	111.3
1912...........	131.2		101.6	94.8	107.2
1913...........	117.5		90.7	93.1	97.4
1914...........	107.7		82.8	92.8	89.2
1915...........	116.1	130.6	88.9	94.0	94.6
1916...........	134.3		102.6	95.4	107.5
1917...........	131.0		99.8	96.9	103.0
1918...........	138.1		105.0	98.2	106.9
1919...........	139.4		105.8	99.5	106.3
1920...........	127.9	132.1	96.8	100.7	96.1
1921...........	116.6		88.1	101.8	86.5
1922...........	130.8		98.6	102.8	95.9
1923...........	154.5		116.3	103.8	112.0

Source of data: Collected by F. R. Macaulay, National Bureau of Economic Research, Inc.

Equation of the primary trend line:

$$y = \frac{134.4}{1 + 10^{0.13660 - 0.23886\,x}}$$

x in units of 5 years, origin at 1880.

Column IV: smoothed moving average of 5 years.

TABLE 19. BANK CLEARINGS, CHICAGO, DEFLATED,
1875–1923

Relatives, average for 1890–99 = 100

	I	II	III	IV	V
1875..........	21.8	21.3	102.3	88.0	116.3
1876..........	20.9		88.2	89.2	98.9
1877..........	20.5		78.5	90.4	86.8
1878..........	20.6		72.3	91.9	78.7
1879..........	26.8		86.7	93.8	92.4
1880..........	34.3	33.4	102.7	96.4	106.5
1881..........	43.0		116.5	99.1	117.6
1882..........	44.1		109.2	100.8	108.3
1883..........	48.3		110.0	101.8	108.1
1884..........	44.9		94.5	102.4	92.3
1885..........	47.9	51.1	93.7	102.8	91.1
1886..........	54.6		97.7	103.0	94.9
1887..........	61.4		101.2	103.2	98.1
1888..........	63.7		95.6	103.2	92.6
1889..........	69.0		97.9	103.0	95.0
1890..........	82.4	75.4	109.3	102.7	106.4
1891..........	88.6		108.6	102.2	106.3
1892..........	104.8		119.4	101.5	117.6
1893..........	94.2		100.2	99.8	100.4
1894..........	90.5		90.3	96.5	93.6
1895..........	96.8	106.5	90.9	93.0	97.7
1896..........	93.9		82.7	90.6	91.3
1897..........	97.3		80.6	90.2	89.4
1898..........	117.4		91.9	92.5	99.4
1899..........	135.0		100.0	95.7	104.5
1900..........	135.1	142.2	95.0	98.0	96.9
1901..........	152.1		101.8	99.5	102.3
1902..........	160.4		102.4	100.8	101.6
1903..........	168.5		102.7	101.8	100.9
1904..........	167.6		97.8	102.7	95.2
1905..........	186.7	178.6	104.5	103.4	101.1
1906..........	196.2		105.9	104.0	101.8
1907..........	205.0		106.9	104.5	102.3
1908..........	201.1		101.4	104.8	96.8
1909..........	223.8		109.2	104.9	104.1

TABLE 19 (*continued*)

	I	II	III	IV	V
1910............	219.3	211.6	103.6	105.0	98.7
1911............	219.1		101.0	104.9	96.3
1912............	234.6		105.5	104.7	100.8
1913............	242.7		106.5	104.4	102.0
1914............	234.6		100.6	103.8	96.9
1915............	237.5	238.5	99.6	103.2	96.5
1916............	267.3		110.2	102.4	107.6
1917............	269.4		109.3	101.3	107.9
1918............	238.7		95.3	99.5	95.8
1919............	241.4		94.9	94.7	100.2
1920............	231.6	258.5	89.6	92.3	97.1
1921............	220.4		84.3	91.7	91.9
1922............	249.0		94.3	92.3	102.2
1923............	259.6		97.3	93.1	104.5

Source of data: Collected by F. R. Macaulay, National Bureau of Economic Research, Inc.

Equation of the primary trend line:

$$y = \frac{297.4}{1 + 10^{0.89838 - 0.21504\,x}}$$

x in units of 5 years, origin at 1880.

Column IV: smoothed moving average of 5 years.

TABLE 20. BANK CLEARINGS, PHILADELPHIA,
DEFLATED, 1875–1923

Relatives, average for 1890–99 = 100

	I	II	III	IV	V
1875..........	44.7	47.2	94.7	87.4	108.4
1876..........	46.6		94.5	88.3	107.0
1877..........	40.5		78.6	89.6	87.7
1878..........	38.0		70.8	92.0	77.0
1879..........	58.5		104.7	96.6	108.4
1880..........	63.5	58.1	109.3	102.3	106.8
1881..........	70.4		116.0	105.1	110.4
1882..........	70.3		111.1	106.8	104.0
1883..........	72.9		110.6	108.1	102.3
1884..........	67.7		98.7	109.2	90.4
1885..........	66.6	71.3	93.4	110.2	84.8
1886..........	82.8		111.3	111.2	100.1
1887..........	89.6		115.6	111.8	103.4
1888..........	87.4		108.4	112.0	96.8
1889..........	100.9		120.4	111.9	107.6
1890..........	101.3	87.0	116.4	110.8	105.1
1891..........	88.8		97.9	107.8	90.8
1892..........	105.4		111.7	99.3	112.5
1893..........	92.9		94.7	93.5	101.3
1894..........	87.0		85.5	91.0	94.0
1895..........	101.1	105.6	95.7	89.7	106.7
1896..........	91.2		83.0	89.1	93.2
1897..........	105.9		92.7	90.2	102.8
1898..........	105.9		89.2	92.8	96.1
1899..........	133.2		108.2	98.8	109.5
1900..........	126.0	127.5	98.8	103.0	95.9
1901..........	145.6		109.9	105.7	104.0
1902..........	152.3		111.1	107.2	103.6
1903..........	149.5		104.8	107.8	97.2
1904..........	146.0		98.8	107.8	91.7
1905..........	173.0	152.9	113.2	107.2	105.6
1906..........	185.1		116.7	103.8	112.4
1907..........	164.7		100.2	98.4	101.8
1908..........	136.5		80.2	93.2	86.1
1909..........	154.6		87.9	88.8	99.0

TABLE 20 (*continued*)

	I	II	III	IV	V
1910	164.1	181.7	90.7	86.4	105.0
1911	164.1		87.2	84.9	102.7
1912	168.9		86.8	84.3	103.0
1913	174.5		86.8	84.2	103.1
1914	160.4		77.3	86.7	89.2
1915	176.2	214.0	82.3	91.5	89.9
1916	230.9		104.4	94.9	110.0
1917	251.5		110.2	97.4	113.1
1918	246.1		104.5	99.3	105.2
1919	243.3		100.4	100.8	99.6
1920	241.2	249.8	96.6	102.0	94.7
1921	234.9		91.1	103.1	88.4
1922	270.5		101.7	104.0	97.8
1923	278.9		101.8	104.6	97.3

Source of data: Collected by F. R. Macaulay, National Bureau of Economic Research, Inc.

Equation of the primary trend line:

$$y = \frac{748.39}{1 + 10^{1.07486 - 0.38735\,x}}$$

x in units of 20 years, origin at 1880.

Column IV: smoothed moving average of 5 years.

TABLE 21. BANK CLEARINGS, ST. LOUIS, DEFLATED, 1875–1921

Relatives, average for 1890–99 = 100

	I	II	III	IV	V
1875..........	39.7	35.0	113.4	104.0	109.9
1876..........	37.5		99.7	104.6	95.3
1877..........	37.2		92.5	104.8	88.3
1878..........	39.1		91.4	105.0	87.0
1879..........	45.7		100.7	105.1	95.8
1880..........	54.1	48.1	112.5	105.1	107.0
1881..........	61.1		118.6	104.8	113.2
1882..........	61.7		112.4	104.3	107.8
1883..........	63.8		109.4	103.6	105.6
1884..........	59.8		96.8	102.6	94.3
1885..........	60.2	65.3	92.2	101.3	91.0
1886..........	65.3		93.8	99.8	94.0
1887..........	71.0		96.1	98.3	97.8
1888..........	69.5		88.8	96.5	92.0
1889..........	77.4		93.5	94.9	98.5
1890..........	86.4	87.1	99.2	93.2	106.4
1891..........	86.8		93.9	91.4	102.7
1892..........	96.4		98.7	89.7	110.0
1893..........	87.9		85.3	88.0	96.9
1894..........	90.8		83.8	86.5	96.9
1895..........	100.1	113.8	88.0	85.7	102.7
1896..........	94.5		78.8	85.8	91.8
1897..........	111.5		88.4	87.5	101.0
1898..........	118.7		89.7	91.3	98.2
1899..........	128.3		92.6	96.0	96.5
1900..........	128.7	144.9	88.8	101.5	87.5
1901..........	170.8		112.6	105.9	106.3
1902..........	183.7		115.8	108.3	106.9
1903..........	181.8		109.8	109.6	100.2
1904..........	199.7		115.8	109.9	105.4
1905..........	204.8	179.3	114.2	109.5	104.2
1906..........	202.6		108.1	108.9	99.3
1907..........	206.0		106.5	108.1	98.5
1908..........	200.0		99.7	107.1	93.1
1909..........	214.4		103.1	106.0	97.3

TABLE 21 (*continued*)

	I	II	III	IV	V
1910..........	225.0	215.1	104.6	104.9	99.7
1911..........	232.9		104.9	103.8	101.1
1912..........	270.8		118.2	102.7	115.1
1913..........	239.6		101.5	101.5	100.0
1914..........	222.9		91.7	100.3	91.4
1915..........	233.6	250.1	93.4	99.1	94.2
1916..........	268.2		104.5	97.7	106.9
1917..........	288.3		109.6	96.1	114.0
1918..........	276.8		102.7	94.3	108.9
1919..........	223.0		80.8	92.5	87.4
1920..........	269.9	282.5	95.5	90.6	105.4
1921..........	212.3		73.8	88.4	83.5

Source of data: Collected by F. R. Macaulay, National Bureau of Economic Research, Inc.

Equation of the primary trend line:

$$y = \frac{404.6}{1 + 10^{1.02361 - 0.61623\,x}}$$

x in units of 20 years, origin at 1875.

Column IV: smoothed moving average of 7 years.

TABLE 17–21a. CARL SNYDER'S INDEX OF GENERAL
PRICE LEVEL, UNITED STATES, 1875–1914

Relatives, average for 1890–99 = 100

	I	II	III	IV	V
1875.........	114.9		101.4	96.0	105.6
1876.........	109.4		98.3	96.4	102.0
1877.........	105.3	109.23	96.4	96.9	99.5
1878.........	97.1		90.0	97.5	92.3
1879.........	97.1		91.2	98.3	92.8
1880.........	104.0		98.9	99.2	99.7
1881.........	108.1		104.2	100.8	103.4
1882.........	110.8	102.44	108.2	102.4	105.7
1883.........	108.1		106.2	102.7	103.4
1884.........	104.0		102.9	102.8	100.1
1885.........	99.9		99.5	102.8	96.7
1886.........	98.5		98.8	102.8	96.1
1887.........	99.9	99.05	100.9	102.7	98.2
1888.........	102.6		103.6	102.6	101.0
1889.........	101.2		102.2	102.4	99.8
1890.........	102.6		103.6	102.2	101.4
1891.........	104.0		105.0	101.8	103.2
1892.........	101.2	99.07	102.1	101.1	101.0
1893.........	102.6		102.9	100.3	102.6
1894.........	98.5		98.1	98.8	99.3
1895.........	98.5		97.4	97.6	99.8
1896.........	97.1		95.4	96.6	98.8
1897.........	97.1	102.48	94.8	96.2	98.5
1898.........	97.1		93.5	96.2	97.2
1899.........	101.2		96.2	96.4	99.8
1900.........	104.0		97.6	96.7	100.9
1901.........	105.3		97.6	97.1	100.5
1902.........	108.1	109.29	98.9	97.5	101.4
1903.........	109.4		98.3	98.0	100.3
1904.........	110.8		97.7	98.5	99.2
1905.........	112.2		97.2	99.0	98.2
1906.........	116.3		99.0	99.5	99.5
1907.........	121.8	119.51	101.9	100.1	101.8
1908.........	121.8		99.7	100.7	99.0
1909.........	127.2		101.8	101.2	100.6

TABLE 17–21a (*continued*)

	I	II	III	IV	V
1910..........	131.3		102.8	101.4	101.4
1911..........	131.3		100.7	101.3	99.4
1912..........	135.4	133.13	101.7	101.1	100.6
1913..........	136.8		101.1	100.9	100.2
1914..........	138.2		98.8	100.6	98.2

Source of data: *Journal of the American Statistical Association*, June, 1924, p. 195.

Equation of the primary trend line:

$$y = 119.42 - 11.8911\,x + 1.7006\,x^2$$

x in units of 5 years, origin at 1872.

Column IV: smoothed moving average of 7 years.

TABLE 22. NUMBER OF LOCOMOTIVES PRODUCED,
BALDWIN WORKS, 1835–1923

	I	II	III	IV	V
1835..........	14	13.1	106.9	159.0	67.2
1836..........	40		278.7	153.0	182.2
1837..........	40		256.2	145.0	176.7
1838..........	23		136.2	135.0	100.9
1839..........	26		143.3	122.0	117.5
1840..........	9	19.4	46.4	101.0	45.9
1841..........	8		37.6	76.0	49.5
1842..........	14		60.6	71.0	85.4
1843..........	12		48.1	72.5	66.3
1844..........	22		82.2	78.4	104.8
1845..........	27	28.7	94.1	84.0	111.9
1846..........	42		133.6	88.4	151.1
1847..........	39		114.2	92.1	124.0
1848..........	20		54.2	93.9	57.7
1849..........	30		75.8	94.8	80.0
1850..........	37	42.4	87.3	95.4	91.5
1851..........	50		107.8	95.6	112.8
1852..........	59		117.2	95.5	122.7
1853..........	60		110.4	95.0	116.2
1854..........	62		106.2	93.4	113.7
1855..........	47	62.5	75.2	88.0	85.6
1856..........	59		86.4	82.5	104.7
1857..........	66		89.1	76.0	117.2
1858..........	33		41.2	70.2	58.7
1859..........	70		81.7	68.5	119.3
1860..........	83	91.6	90.6	68.5	132.3
1861..........	40		40.0	70.9	56.4
1862..........	75		69.3	74.2	93.4
1863..........	96		82.3	77.9	105.6
1864..........	130		103.9	82.4	126.1
1865..........	115	133.6	86.1	88.4	96.4
1866..........	118		81.1	95.3	85.1
1867..........	127		80.7	103.0	78.3
1868..........	124		73.3	111.7	65.6
1869..........	235		129.7	116.3	111.5

TABLE 22 (*continued*)

	I	II	III	IV	V
1870	280	193.1	145.0	117.8	123.1
1871	331		158.0	118.3	133.6
1872	422		186.6	118.2	157.9
1873	437		180.0	117.5	153.2
1874	205		79.1	116.4	68.0
1875	130	275.9	47.1	115.0	40.9
1876	232		77.7	113.4	68.5
1877	185		57.6	111.8	51.5
1878	292		85.1	110.2	77.2
1879	298		81.6	108.6	75.1
1880	517	388.0	133.2	107.1	124.4
1881	554		132.3	105.0	125.3
1882	563		126.2	104.1	121.2
1883	557		117.2	102.7	114.1
1884	429		84.1	101.2	83.1
1885	242	533.6	45.4	99.5	45.6
1886	550		96.5	97.6	98.9
1887	653		107.7	95.7	112.5
1888	737		114.9	93.6	122.8
1889	827		121.9	91.2	133.7
1890	946	714.2	132.5	88.6	149.5
1891	899		118.9	86.0	138.3
1892	731		91.6	82.2	111.4
1893	772		91.9	78.0	117.8
1894	313		35.5	73.2	48.5
1895	401	924.8	43.4	74.0	58.6
1896	547		56.4	76.5	73.7
1897	501		49.3	80.4	61.3
1898	755		71.0	85.9	82.7
1899	901		81.3	93.0	87.4
1900	1217	1153.8	105.5	101.0	104.5
1901	1375		114.5	114.0	100.4
1902	1533		123.0	119.4	103.0
1903	2022		156.5	127.3	122.9
1904	1485		110.9	128.0	86.6
1905	2250	1384.6	162.5	127.6	127.4
1906	2666		186.7	126.7	146.6
1907	2655		180.5	125.0	144.4
1908	617		40.7	121.0	33.6
1909	1024		65.8	110.0	59.8

TABLE 22 (*continued*)

	I	II	III	IV	V
1910...........	1675	1599.9	104.6	84.5	123.8
1911...........	1606		98.0	81.5	120.2
1912...........	1618		96.5	82.0	117.7
1913...........	2061		120.3	86.0	139.9
1914...........	804		46.0	95.0	48.4
1915...........	867	1787.0	43.5	114.0	38.2
1916...........	1989		109.4	125.0	87.5
1917...........	2737		148.1	127.5	115.7
1918...........	3580		190.5	128.0	148.8
1919...........	1722		90.2	127.0	71.0
1920...........	1534	1939.8	78.2	124.0	63.1
1921...........	969		49.4	116.0	42.6
1922...........	684		34.4	102.0	33.7
1923...........	1696		84.3	87.0	96.9

Source of data: *History of Baldwin Locomotive Works*, 1832–1923, Philadelphia, 1927; collected by W. L. Thorp, National Bureau of Economic Research, Inc.

Equation of the primary trend line:

$$y = \frac{2354}{1 + 10^{\,2.08738 - 0.34392\,x}}$$

x in units of 10 years, origin at 1840.

Column IV: smoothed moving average of **7 years**.

TABLE 23. COAL OUTPUT, UNITED KINGDOM, 1854–1914

Columns I and II in thousands of tons

	I	II	III	IV	V
1854........	64,666		105.4	95.4	110.5
1855........	61,453	64,886	94.7	96.1	98.5
1856........	66,645		99.0	96.8	102.3
1857........	65,395		93.7	97.5	96.1
1858........	65,009		91.3	98.2	93.0
1859........	71,980		97.7	99.0	98.7
1860........	80,043	77,089	103.8	99.8	104.0
1861........	83,635		104.7	100.6	104.1
1862........	81,638		98.8	101.4	97.4
1863........	86,292		101.2	102.2	99.0
1864........	92,788		105.2	103.0	102.1
1865........	98,151	90,980	107.9	103.8	104.0
1866........	101,631		108.0	104.5	103.4
1867........	104,500		107.5	105.0	102.4
1868........	103,141		102.7	105.5	97.3
1869........	107,428		103.8	105.8	98.1
1870........	110,431	106,564	103.6	106.0	97.6
1871........	117,352		106.6	105.8	100.8
1872........	123,497		108.8	105.6	103.1
1873........	127,017		108.6	105.2	103.2
1874........	125,068		103.9	104.8	99.1
1875........	131,367	123,775	106.1	104.4	101.6
1876........	133,345		104.6	104.0	100.6
1877........	134,611		102.6	103.5	99.1
1878........	132,655		98.3	103.0	95.4
1879........	134,008		96.6	102.5	94.2
1880........	146,819	142,450	103.1	101.9	101.2
1881........	154,184		105.3	101.3	103.9
1882........	156,500		104.1	100.7	103.4
1883........	163,737		106.1	100.1	106.0
1884........	160,758		101.5	99.5	102.0
1885........	159,351	162,332	98.2	98.9	99.3
1886........	157,518		95.0	98.4	96.5
1887........	162,120		95.8	97.9	97.9
1888........	169,935		98.4	97.4	101.0
1889........	176,917		102.5	96.8	105.8

TABLE 23 (continued)

	I	II	III	IV	V
1890.......	181,614	179,746	101.0	96.4	104.8
1891.......	185,479		100.4	95.9	104.7
1892.......	181,787		95.9	95.4	100.5
1893.......	164,326		84.5	95.1	88.9
1894.......	188,278		94.4	94.9	99.5
1895.......	189,661	204,261	92.9	94.9	97.9
1896.......	195,361		93.7	95.0	98.6
1897.......	202,130		95.0	95.1	99.9
1898.......	202,055		93.1	95.3	97.7
1899.......	220,095		99.5	95.7	104.0
1900.......	225,181	225,437	99.9	96.2	103.8
1901.......	219,047		95.4	96.8	98.6
1902.......	227,095		97.2	97.4	99.8
1903.......	230,334		96.8	98.0	98.8
1904.......	232,428		96.0	98.5	97.5
1905.......	236,129	246,107	95.9	98.9	97.0
1906.......	251,068		100.4	99.3	101.1
1907.......	267,831		105.4	99.7	105.7
1908.......	261,529		101.3	100.1	101.2
1909.......	263,774		100.7	100.5	100.2
1910.......	264,433	265,991	99.4	100.9	98.5
1911.......	271,879		100.8	101.0	99.8
1912.......	260,416		95.2	100.9	94.3
1913.......	287,430		103.7	100.5	103.2
1914.......	265,664		94.6	100.0	94.6
1915.......		284,614			

Source of data: W. Page (editor), *Commerce and Industry*, vol. II, Tables of Statistics for the British Empire from 1815, London, 1919, pp. 180–81.

Equation of the primary trend line:

$$y = \frac{407,664}{1 + 10^{0.63227 - 0.45293\,x}}$$

x in units of 25 years, origin at 1860.

Column IV: smoothed moving average of 13 years.

TABLE 23a. Export Prices of Coal, United Kingdom, 1854–1913

Columns I and II in shillings per ton

	I	II	III	IV	V
1854.........	9.87		98.4	91.7	107.3
1855.........	9.83		98.0	91.7	106.9
1856.........	9.61		95.8	91.8	104.4
1857.........	9.52	10.039	94.8	92.1	102.9
1858.........	9.33		92.9	92.4	100.5
1859.........	9.33		92.8	92.8	100.0
1860.........	9.06		90.0	93.2	96.6
1861.........	9.19		91.2	93.6	97.4
1862.........	9.05	10.081	89.8	94.0	95.5
1863.........	9.00		89.2	94.5	94.4
1864.........	9.48		93.8	95.0	98.7
1865.........	9.69		95.7	95.5	100.2
1866.........	10.29		101.5	96.2	105.5
1867.........	10.39	10.152	102.3	97.0	105.5
1868.........	9.92		97.5	98.9	98.6
1869.........	9.62		94.4	103.0	91.7
1870.........	9.64		94.4	113.0	83.5
1871.........	9.80		95.8	121.0	79.2
1872.........	15.83	10.252	154.4	125.0	123.5
1873.........	20.90		203.3	126.9	160.2
1874.........	17.21		162.0	126.9	131.6
1875.........	13.28		128.6	126.0	102.1
1876.........	10.93		105.5	123.3	85.6
1877.........	10.17	10.382	98.0	113.7	86.2
1878.........	9.46		90.8	102.7	88.4
1879.........	8.77		84.0	95.1	88.3
1880.........	8.95		85.4	90.0	94.9
1881.........	8.97		85.4	87.5	97.6
1882.........	9.14	10.541	86.7	85.6	101.3
1883.........	9.35		88.4	84.1	105.1
1884.........	9.29		87.5	84.0	104.2
1885.........	8.95		84.0	84.0	100.0
1886.........	8.45		79.0	84.0	94.0
1887.........	8.32	10.730	77.5	89.0	89.1
1888.........	8.41		78.1	90.5	86.3
1889.........	10.21		94.4	91.5	103.2

TABLE 23a (*continued*)

	I	II	III	IV	V
1890..........	12.62		116.2	92.5	125.6
1891..........	12.16		111.5	93.5	119.3
1892..........	11.04	10.949	100.8	94.4	106.8
1893..........	9.90		90.0	95.3	94.4
1894..........	10.5ɔ		95.0	96.1	91.9
1895..........	9.33		84.1	96.9	86.8
1896..........	8.85		79.4	97.6	81.4
1897..........	8.98	11.196	80.2	98.2	81.7
1898..........	9.92		88.2	98.8	89.3
1899..........	10.72		94.8	99.4	95.4
1900..........	16.75		147.4	100.0	147.4
1901..........	13.86		121.4	100.5	120.8
1902..........	12.29	11.473	107.1	100.9	106.1
1903..........	11.70		101.4	101.3	100.1
1904..........	11.13		96.0	101.7	94.4
1905..........	10.56		90.6	102.0	88.8
1906..........	10.90		93.0	102.2	91.0
1907..........	12.75	11.780	108.2	102.4	105.7
1908..........	12.77		107.8	102.6	105.1
1909..........	11.30		94.8	102.7	92.3
1910..........	11.72		97.8	102.7	95.2
1911..........	11.43		94.9	102.7	92.4
1912..........	12.70	12.116	104.8	102.7	102.0
1913..........	13.94		114.4	102.5	111.6

Source of data: A. Sauerbeck 'On Prices of Commodities and the Precious Metals,' *Journal of the Royal Statistical Society*, September, 1886, vol. 49, p. 639, and subsequent issues.

Equation of the primary trend line:

$$y = 10.027 - 0.00267x + 0.01473x^2$$

x in units of 5 years, origin at 1852.

Column IV: smoothed moving average of 13 years.

TABLE 24. PIG IRON PRODUCTION, UNITED KINGDOM, 1788–1913

Columns I and II in thousands of tons

	I	II	III	IV	V
1788.......	68	54	127.0		
1796.......	125	90	139.2		
1806.......	244	172	141.6		
1818.......	325	374	86.8		
1820.......	368	420	87.6		
1823.......	455	453	100.4		
1825.......	581	575	101.1		
1827.......	691	658	104.8		
1828.......	703	700	100.5		
1830.......	677	783	86.5		
1833.......	700	947	73.9		
1836.......	1,000	1,128	88.6		
1839.......	1,249	1,340	93.2		
1840.......	1,396	1,412	98.9	85.9	115.1
1842.......	1,099	1,591	69.1	87.0	79.4
1843.......	1,215	1,681	72.3	88.1	82.1
1844.......	2,000	1,771	112.9	89.2	126.6
1845.......	1,512	1,861	81.3	90.7	89.6
1847.......	2,000	2,081	96.1	94.0	102.2
1850.......	2,249	2,412	93.3	100.6	92.7
1852.......	2,701	2,674	101.0	103.0	98.1
1854.......	3,070	2,935	104.6	104.2	100.4
1855.......	3,218	3,066	105.0	104.5	100.5
1856.......	3,586		111.6	104.5	106.8
1857.......	3,659		108.9	104.3	104.5
1858.......	3,456		98.5	103.9	94.8
1859.......	3,713		101.5	103.4	98.2
1860.......	3,827	3,806	100.5	102.7	97.9
1861.......	3,712		93.6	101.6	92.2
1362.......	3,944		95.6	99.8	95.8
1863.......	4,510		105.2	98.4	106.9
1864.......	4,768		106.9	98.2	108.8
1865.......	4,819	4,607	104.7	99.1	105.7
1866.......	4,524		94.8	100.8	94.0
1867.......	4,761		96.5	102.6	94.1
1868.......	4,970		83.1	103.7	80.2
1869.......	5,446		103.5	104.4	99.1

TABLE 24 (*continued*)

	I	II	III	IV	V
1870.......	5,964	5,426	109.9	104.8	104.9
1871.......	6,627		118.6	105.1	112.9
1872.......	6,742		117.4	105.2	111.6
1873.......	6,566		111.2	105.3	105.6
1874.......	5,991		98.8	105.4	93.7
1875.......	6,365	6,222	102.3	105.4	97.1
1876.......	6,556		102.9	105.4	97.6
1877.......	6,609		101.4	105.4	96.3
1878.......	5,381		95.8	105.3	91.0
1879.......	5,995		88.1	105.1	83.8
1880.......	7,749	6,955	111.4	104.9	106.2
1881.......	8,144		115.0	104.7	109.8
1882.......	8,587		119.0	104.4	114.0
1883.......	8,529		116.2	104.1	111.7
1884.......	7,812		104.6	103.6	101.0
1885.......	7,415	7,599	97.6	103.0	94.8
1886.......	7,010		91.0	102.3	89.0
1887.......	7,560		96.8	99.7	97.1
1888.......	7,999		101.1	97.5	103.7
1889.......	8,323		103.8	95.6	108.6
1890.......	7,904	8,124	97.3	94.2	103.3
1891.......	7,406		90.1	93.4	96.5
1892.......	6,709		80.8	93.2	86.7
1893.......	6,977		83.1	93.3	89.1
1894.......	7,427		87.5	93.7	93.4
1895.......	7,703	8,579	89.8	94.2	95.3
1896.......	8,660		100.2	94.8	105.7
1897.......	8,797		101.0	95.6	105.7
1898.......	8,610		98.1	96.4	101.8
1899.......	9,422		106.5	97.3	109.5
1900.......	8,960	8,925	100.4	98.1	102.4
1901.......	7,929		88.3	98.8	89.4
1902.......	8,680		96.1	99.5	96.6
1903.......	8,935		98.3	100.2	98.1
1904.......	8,693		95.1	100.9	94.3
1905.......	9,608	9,192	104.5	101.5	103.0
1906.......	10,184		110.3	101.9	108.2
1907.......	10,114		109.1	102.0	107.0
1908.......	9,056		97.3	102.0	95.4
1909.......	9,532		101.9	101.9	100.0

TABLE 24 (*continued*)

	I	II	III	IV	V
1910......	10,012	9,394	106.6	101.6	104.9
1911......	9,527		101.1	101.2	99.9
1912......	8,752		92.5	100.7	91.9
1913......	10,260		108.1	100.1	108.0
1914......	8,924				
1915......		9,544			

Source of data: T. M. Swank, *Iron in All Ages*, p. 252; corrected by W. Page, *loc. cit.*, p. 180.

Equation of the primary trend line:

$$y = \frac{9951.2}{1 + 10^{1.21216 - 0.28690\,x}}$$

x in units of 10 years, origin at 1825.

Column IV: smoothed moving average of 11 years.

TABLE 24a. PRICES OF PIG IRON, UNITED KINGDOM, 1782–1913

Relatives, 1782 = 100

	I	II	III	IV	V
1782.............	100		90.1	79.6	113.2
1783.............	97		88.1	76.0	115.9
1784.............	72	109.19	65.9	73.2	90.0
1785.............	67		61.9	71.0	87.2
1786.............	84		78.2	69.8	112.0
1787.............	72		67.6	70.8	95.5
1788.............	73		69.1	72.8	94.9
1789.............	78	104.70	74.5	75.5	98.7
1790.............	76		73.2	78.5	93.2
1791.............	92		89.4	81.7	109.4
1792.............	92		90.1	85.0	106.0
1793.............	91		89.9	88.7	101.4
1794.............	94	100.34	93.7	93.5	100.2
1795.............	86		86.4	101.4	85.2
1796.............	101		102.3	112.4	91.0
1797.............	124		126.6	120.8	104.8
1798.............	127		130.8	125.4	104.3
1799.............	126	96.32	130.8	127.8	102.3
1800.............	115		120.5	129.3	93.2
1801.............	139		147.0	130.1	113.0
1802.............	119		127.0	130.6	97.2
1803.............	118		127.1	130.9	97.1
1804.............	116	91.96	126.1	131.0	96.3
1805.............	118		129.4	130.9	98.9
1806.............	123		136.0	130.6	104.1
1807.............	116		129.3	129.7	99.7
1808.............	113		127.1	127.7	99.5
1809.............	114	88.18	129.3	124.3	104.0
1810.............	99		113.3	120.3	94.2
1811.............	106		122.5	113.4	108.0
1812.............	88		102.7	105.0	97.8
1813.............	81		95.4	100.0	95.4
1814.............	77	84.06	91.6	94.6	96.8
1815.............	81		97.2	93.0	104.5
1816.............	71		86.0	98.8	87.0
1817.............	78		95.4	104.1	91.6
1818.............	98		120.9	107.6	112.4
1819.............	104	80.28	129.5	110.4	117.3

TABLE 24a (*continued*)

	I	II	III	IV	V
1820............	95		119.4	112.6	106.0
1821............	82		104.0	114.4	90.9
1822............	74		94.7	115.8	81.8
1823............	78		100.8	116.6	86.5
1824............	94	76.62	122.7	117.0	104.9
1825............	114		150.2	116.8	128.6
1826............	..100		133.0	116.0	114.7
1827............	86		115.4	114.7	100.6
1828............	80		108.4	113.2	95.8
1829............	72	73.10	98.5	111.7	88.2
1830............	66		91.1	110.1	82.7
1831............	63		87.8	108.4	81.0
1832............	61		85.9	106.4	80.7
1833............	65		92.4	104.3	88.6
1834............	65	69.68	93.3	102.2	91.3
1835............	64		92.7	100.2	92.6
1836............	86		125.8	98.1	128.2
1837............	74		109.3	96.2	113.6
1838............	77		114.9	94.4	121.7
1839............	77	66.39	116.0	92.7	125.1
1840............	63		95.8	91.0	105.3
1841............	61		93.7	89.3	104.9
1842............	51		79.1	87.6	90.3
1843............	43		67.4	86.1	78.3
1844............	43	63.20	68.0	84.7	80.3
1845............	59		94.3	83.4	113.1
1846............	60		96.8	82.2	117.8
1847............	60		97.8	81.3	120.3
1848............	47		77.4	80.4	96.2
1849............	40	60.14	66.5	79.5	83.6
1850............	37		62.1	78.6	79.0
1851............	36		61.1	77.8	78.6
1852............	40		68.5	77.9	87.9
1853............	53		91.7	78.0	117.6
1854............	60	57.21	104.9	78.1	134.3
1855............	51		90.0	78.2	115.1
1856............	55		98.1	78.3	125.3
1857............	51		91.9	78.4	117.2
1858............	46		83.7	78.5	106.6
1859............	42	54.39	77.2	78.6	98.2

TABLE 24a (*continued*)

	I	II	III	IV	V
1860............	40		74.3	78.8	94.3
1861............	37		69.4	79.1	87.7
1862............	35		66.3	79.4	83.5
1863............	37		70.9	79.8	88.8
1864............	44	51.68	85.1	80.4	105.8
1865............	39		76.2	81.6	93.4
1866............	46		90.8	84.0	108.1
1867............	42		83.8	89.5	93.6
1868............	41		82.6	99.9	82.7
1869............	42	49.11	85.5	106.0	80.7
1870............	44		90.5	108.8	83.2
1871............	47		97.7	110.3	88.6
1872............	74		155.4	110.8	140.3
1873............	85		180 4	111.1	162.4
1874............	66	46.64	141.5	111.0	127.5
1875............	52		112.6	110.8	101.6
1876............	46		100.7	110.0	91.5
1877............	42		92.9	108.8	85.4
1878............	36		80.4	105.0	76.6
1879............	37	44.30	83.5	95.0	87.9
1880............	42		95.8	88.4	108.4
1881............	37		85.3	86.0	99.2
1882............	39		90.8	84.5	107.5
1883............	37		87.0	83.5	104.2
1884............	32	42.07	76.1	82.8	91.9
1885............	31		74.4	82.3	90.4
1886............	30		72.8	82.2	88.6
1887............	31		76.0	82.7	91.9
1888............	31		76.8	83.6	91.9
1889............	38	39.96	95.1	84.9	112.0
1890............	39		98.6	86.4	114.1
1891............	36		91.9	88.2	104.2
1892............	33		85.1	90.8	93.7
1893............	32		83.4	94.0	88.7
1894............	32	37.98	84.3	97.5	86.5
1895............	32		85.1	103.0	82.6
1896............	34		91.3	108.5	84.1
1897............	34		92.8	114.0	81.4
1898............	36		98.9	118.8	83.2
1899............	47	36.11	130.2	121.0	107.6

TABLE 24a (*continued*)

	I	II	III	IV	V
1900............	55		153.8	123.0	125.0
1901............	41		115.8	124.0	93.4
1902............	40		141.1	125.5	90.9
1903............	40		115.2	127.0	90.7
1904............	39	34.37	113.5	128.0	88.7
1905............	42		123.4	129.5	95.3
1906............	46		136.5	131.4	103.9
1907............	48		143.8	133.3	107.9
1908............	43		130.1	135.2	96.2
1909............	42	32.74	128.3	137.1	93.6
1910............	42		129.4	139.0	93.1
1911............	41		127.4	140.9	90.4
1912............	48		150.5	142.8	105.4
1913............	50		158.1	144.7	109.3

Source of data: Up to 1866, W. S. Jevons, *Investigations in Currency and Finance*, London, 1884, pp. 146–47; from 1866, A. Sauerbeck, *loc. cit.*

Equation of the primary trend line:
$$y = 113.80 - 4.662x + 0.05955\ x^2$$

x in units of 5 years, origin at 1779.

Column IV: smoothed moving average of 5 years up to 1816, 11 years from 1816.

TABLE 25. STEEL PRODUCTION, UNITED KINGDOM, 1875–1914

Columns I and II in thousands of tons

	I	II	III	IV	V
1875............	724	713	101.5	97.4	104.2
1876............	852		101.5	97.7	103.9
1877............	905		94.0	98.1	95.8
1878............	1,118		102.8	98.7	104.2
1879............	1,030		84.9	99.6	85.2
1880............	1,321	1,381	95.7	100.8	94.9
1881............	1,809		116.7	102.1	114.3
1882............	2,246		130.7	104.1	125.6
1883............	2,042		108.3	106.6	101.6
1884............	1,892		92.1	109.6	84.0
1885............	2,202	2,247	98.0	111.2	88.1
1886............	2,403		98.5	111.0	88.7
1887............	3,197		121.5	108.6	111.9
1888............	3,775		133.6	105.7	126.4
1889............	3,605		119.4	103.5	115.4
1890	3,637	3,213	113.2	101.6	111.4
1891............	3,208		94.1	99.8	94.3
1892............	2,967		82.4	98.2	83.9
1893............	2,983		78.5	96.4	81.4
1894............	3,200		80.1	94.6	86.1
1895............	3,312	4,177	79.3	93.0	85.3
1896............	4,306		98.8	91.8	107.6
1897............	4,560		100.5	91.4	110.0
1898............	4,639		98.2	91.9	106.9
1899............	4,933		101.2	92.6	109.3
1900............	4,901	5,061	96.8	93.3	103.8
1901............	4,897		93.8	94.0	99.8
1902............	4,909		91.3	94.8	96.3
1903............	5,034		90.9	95.6	95.1
1904............	5,027		88.3	96.4	91.6
1905............	5,812	5,824	99.8	97.2	102.7
1906............	6,462		108.5	98.1	110.6
1907............	6,523		107.2	99.0	108.3
1908............	5,296		85.2	100.0	85.2
1909............	5,882		92.7	101.0	91.7

TABLE 25 (*continued*)

	I	II	III	IV	V
1910.............	6,374	6,454	98.8	102.1	96.8
1911.............	6,462		98.5	103.2	95.4
1912.............	6,796		102.0	104.4	97.7
1913.............	7,664		113.2	105.6	107.2
1914.............	7,835		113.9	106.9	106.5
1915.............		6,879			

Source of data: W. Page, *loc. cit.*, p. 181.

Equation of the primary trend line:

$$\log y = 2.37880 + 1.59045\,(1 - 0.38825^x)$$

x in units of 15 years, origin at 1870.

Column IV: smoothed moving average of 11 years.

TABLE 26. TONNAGE OF SHIPS CLEARED, PORTS OF THE UNITED KINGDOM, 1815–1913

Columns I and II in thousands of tons

	I	II	III	IV	V
1815..........	2,150	1,593	135.0	119.0	113.4
1816..........	1,739		103.9	116.5	89.2
1817..........	1,999		113.9	114.0	99.9
1818..........	2,450		133.4	111.5	119.6
1819..........	2,119		110.5	109.0	101.4
1820..........	1,983	1,999	99.2	106.8	92.9
1821..........	1,872		89.1	104.6	85.2
1822..........	1,997		90.7	102.7	88.3
1823..........	2,111		91.6	100.8	90.9
1824..........	2,404		99.9	98.9	101.0
1825..........	2,699	2,508	107.6	97.0	110.9
1826..........	2,430		92.2	95.4	96.6
1827..........	2,656		96.2	93.9	102.4
1828..........	2,615		90.5	92.4	97.9
1829..........	2,793		92.6	91.0	101.8
1830..........	2,861	3,143	91.0	89.6	101.6
1831..........	3,197		96.8	88.3	109.6
1832..........	2,880		83.2	87.1	95.5
1833..........	3,003		83.0	86.0	96.5
1834..........	3,149		83.4	85.0	98.1
1835..........	3,325	3,935	84.5	84.0	100.6
1836..........	3,567		86.3	84.3	102.4
1837..........	3,584		82.8	84.9	97.5
1838..........	4,099		90.6	85.8	105.6
1839..........	4,495		95.2	87.0	109.4
1840..........	4,782	4,916	97.3	88.5	109.9
1841..........	4,762		92.3	90.0	102.6
1842..........	4,627		85.6	91.5	93.6
1843..........	4,977		88.1	92.8	94.9
1844..........	5,297		89.9	94.1	95.5
1845..........	6,032	6,139	98.3	95.4	103.0
1846..........	6,315		98.1	96.6	101.6
1847..........	7,083		105.1	97.8	107.5
1848..........	6,781		96.3	98.9	97.4
1849..........	7,084		96.5	100.0	96.5
1850..........	7,405	7,645	96.9	101.1	95.8
1851..........	8,108		101.2	102.2	99.0
1852..........	8,243		98.3	103.3	95.2
1853..........	9,447		107.9	104.4	103.4
1854..........	9,508		104.2	105.5	98.8

TABLE 26 (*continued*)

	I	II	III	IV	V
1855.........	9,538	9,497	100.4	106.5	94.3
1856.........	11,036		110.9	107.3	103.4
1857.........	11,704		112.5	107.7	104.5
1858.........	11,348		104.5	107.8	96.9
1859.........	11,682		103.3	106.8	96.7
1860.........	12,517	11,758	106.5	105.7	100.8
1861.........	13,416		109.0	104.6	104.2
1862.........	13,444		104.6	103.8	100.8
1863.........	13,483		100.6	103.2	97.5
1864.........	13,689		98.1	102.8	95.4
1865.........	14,579	14,500	100.5	102.6	98.0
1866.........	15,650		103.2	102.8	100.4
1867.........	16,417		103.8	103.3	100.5
1868.........	17,058		103.5	104.6	98.9
1869.........	17,712		103.3	106.0	97.5
1870.........	18,527	17,798	104.1	107.4	96.9
1871.........	21,068		113.5	108.7	104.4
1872.........	21,486		111.2	109.4	101.6
1873.........	22,575		112.4	109.9	102.3
1874.........	23,060		110.6	110.2	100.4
1875.........	23,584	21,722	108.6	110.4	98.4
1876.........	25,718		113.6	110.4	102.9
1877.........	25,910		109.9	110.5	99.5
1878.........	26,301		107.4	110.4	97.3
1879.........	26,683		105.0	110.3	95.2
1880.........	29,663	26,335	112.6	110.0	102.4
1881.........	29,431		107.4	109.4	98.2
1882.........	31,172		109.5	108.0	101.4
1883.........	32,857		111.2	106.6	104.3
1884.........	32,584		106.4	105.0	101.3
1885.........	32,419	31,679	102.3	103.4	98.9
1886.........	31,805		96.7	101.7	95.1
1887.........	32,984		96.7	100.0	96.7
1888.........	34,566		97.8	98.6	99.2
1889.........	36,366		99.5	97.2	102.4
1890.........	37,448	37,767	99.2	95.8	103.5
1891.........	37,954		97.0	94.4	102.8
1892.........	38,194		94.3	93.0	101.4
1893.........	37,491		89.5	91.9	97.4
1894.........	40,718		94.2	91.8	102.6

TABLE 26 (*continued*)

	I	II	III	IV	V
1895............	40,537	44,571	90.9	91.9	98.9
1896..........	42,985		93.3	92.1	101.3
1897..........	45,276		95.2	92.3	103.1
1898..........	45,839		93.5	92.6	101.0
1899..........	48,907		96.8	93.0	104.1
1900..........	49,301	52,015	94.8	93.4	101.5
1901..........	48,299		90.1	93.9	96.0
1902..........	49,821		90.3	94.5	95.6
1903..........	52,529		92.5	95.1	97.3
1904..........	54,064		92.6	95.8	96.7
1905..........	56,417	59,974	94.1	96.7	97.3
1906..........	60,509		98.2	97.6	100.6
1907..........	67,031		105.9	98.8	107.2
1908..........	65,977		101.6	100.0	101.6
1909..........	66,958		100.5	101.2	99.3
1910..........	67,370	68,265	98.7	102.6	96.2
1911..........	69,745		99.7	104.2	95.7
1912..........	76,266		106.5	106.0	100.5
1913..........	82,661		112.7	107.5	104.8
1915..........		76,695			

Source of data: W. Page, *loc. cit.*, pp. 162–63.

Equation of the primary trend line:

$$y = \frac{152,161}{1 + 10^{1.85934-0.09998\,x}}$$

x in units of 5 years, origin at 1820.

Column IV: smoothed moving average of 7 years.

TABLE 26a. INDEX OF THE GENERAL LEVEL OF PRICES,
UNITED KINGDOM, 1782–1914

Relatives, 1782 = 100

	I	II	III	IV	V
1782............	100		87.3	84.5	103.3
1783............	100		87.6	82.8	105.8
1784............	93	113.80	81.7	81.4	100.4
1785............	90		79.4	80.0	99.2
1786............	85		75.2	78.7	95.6
1787............	87		76.4	77.6	98.5
1788............	87		77.6	77.2	100.5
1789............	85	111.74	76.1	78.3	97.2
1790............	87		78.2	80.1	97.6
1791............	89		80.3	82.7	97.1
1792............	93		84.2	86.0	97.9
1793............	99		90.0	90.4	99.6
1794............	98	109.64	89.4	95.3	93.8
1795............	117		107.1	100.5	106.6
1796............	125		114.9	106.0	108.4
1797............	110		101.5	110.7	91.7
1798............	118		109.3	113.8	96.0
1799............	130	107.51	120.9	115.6	104.6
1800............	141		131.7	117.0	112.6
1801............	140		131.3	118.3	111.0
1802............	110		103.6	119.2	86.9
1803............	125		118.2	120.1	98.4
1804............	119	105.35	113.0	121.1	93.3
1805............	132		125.8	122.7	102.5
1806............	130		124.4	128.0	97.2
1807............	129		124.0	131.6	94.2
1808............	145		140.0	132.7	105.5
1809............	157	103.16	152.2	133.0	114.4
1810............	142		138.2	132.4	104.4
1811............	136		133.0	130.5	101.9
1812............	121		118.8	126.0	94.3
1813............	115		113.4	121.4	93.4
1814............	114	100.92	113.0	116.8	96.7
1815............	109		108.5	114.0	95.2
1816............	91		91.0	111.6	81.5
1817............	117		117.5	109.4	107.4
1818............	132		133.2	107.4	124.0
1819............	112	98.66	113.5	105.4	107.7

TABLE 26a (*continued*)

	I	II	III	IV	V
1820............	103		104.9	103.4	101.4
1821............	94		96.2	101.4	94.9
1822............	88		90.5	99.4	91.0
1823............	89		91.9	97.4	94.4
1824............	88	96.36	91.3	95.7	95.4
1825............	103		107.4	94.0	114.3
1826............	90		94.3	92.3	102.4
1827............	90		94.8	90.8	104.4
1828............	81		85.7	89.5	95.8
1829............	79	94.03	84.0	88.2	95.2
1830............	81		86.6	86.9	99.7
1831............	82		88.1	85.9	102.6
1832............	78		84.2	86.0	97.9
1833............	75		81.4	86.9	93.7
1834............	78	91.66	85.1	88.2	96.5
1835............	80		87.7	89.8	97.7
1836............	86		94.8	91.7	103.4
1837............	84		93.1	93.5	99.6
1838............	84		93.6	94.4	99.2
1839............	92	89.26	103.1	94.4	109.2
1840............	87		98.0	93.0	105.4
1841............	85		96.3	91.4	105.4
1842............	75		85.4	89.4	95.5
1843............	71		81.3	87.5	92.9
1844............	69	86.82	79.5	85.9	92.5
1845............	74		85.7	84.6	101.3
1846............	74		86.2	83.3	103.5
1847............	78		91.4	82.5	110.8
1848............	68		80.1	81.8	97.9
1849............	64	84.35	75.9	81.5	93.1
1850............	64		76.3	82.0	93.0
1851............	66		79.2	84.1	94.2
1852............	65		78.5	86.8	90.4
1853............	74		89.9	90.0	99.9
1854............	83	81.85	101.4	92.5	109.6
1855............	80		98.3	94.6	103.9
1856............	82		101.4	96.4	105.2
1857............	85		105.8	97.8	108.2
1858............	76		95.2	98.9	96.3
1859............	77	79.31	97.1	99.8	97.3

TABLE 26a (*continued*)

	I	II	III	IV	V
1860	79		100.3	100.6	99.7
1861	78		99.6	101.4	98.2
1862	79		101.6	102.1	99.5
1863	78		101.0	102.9	98.2
1864	78	76.73	101.7	103.7	98.1
1865	78		102.3	104.6	97.8
1866	83		109.7	105.5	104.0
1867	81		107.8	106.5	101.2
1868	81		108.5	107.9	100.6
1869	80	74.13	107.9	110.0	98.1
1870	78		106.0	112.7	94.1
1871	81		110.9	113.9	97.4
1872	89		122.7	114.4	107.3
1873	90		125.0	114.6	109.1
1874	83	71.48	116.1	114.3	101.6
1875	78		109.9	113.2	97.1
1876	77		109.3	111.2	98.3
1877	77		110.2	108.0	102.0
1878	71		102.4	105.0	97.5
1879	68	68.81	98.8	102.9	96.0
1880	72		105.5	101.0	104.5
1881	69		101.9	99.1	102.8
1882	68		101.2	97.5	103.8
1883	67		100.5	96.0	104.7
1884	62	66.10	93.8	94.7	99.0
1885	59		90.0	93.6	96.2
1886	56		86.2	92.6	93.1
1887	55		85.3	91.6	93.1
1888	57		89.2	90.7	98.3
1889	59	63.35	93.1	89.9	103.6
1890	59		93.9	89.3	105.1
1891	59		94.8	88.8	106.8
1892	55		89.2	88.4	100.9
1893	55		90.0	87.9	102.4
1894	51	60.57	84.2	87.6	96.1
1895	51		85.0	87.6	97.0
1896	50		84.1	88.6	94.9
1897	51		86.6	90.8	95.4
1898	52		87.6	93.1	94.1
1899	55	57.76	95.2	95.4	99.8

TABLE 26a (*continued*)

	I	II	III	IV	V
1900............	61		106.7	97.9	109.0
1901............	57		100.7	100.3	100.4
1902............	56		99.9	102.9	97.1
1903............	56		100.9	105.5	95.6
1904............	57	54.91	103.8	107.8	96.3
1905............	59		108.6	110.2	98.5
1906............	63		117.2	112.9	103.8
1907............	65		122.2	115.6	105.7
1908............	59		112.1	118.6	94.5
1909............	60	52.03	115.3	121.8	94.7
1910............	64		124.4	124.9	99.6
1911............	65		127.8	128.9	99.1
1912............	69		137.2	132.9	103.2
1913............	69		138.8	136.9	101.4
1914............	70	49.12	142.5	140.9	101.1

Sources of data: Up to 1866, W. S. Jevons, *Investigations in Currency and Finance*, pp. 144–45; from 1866, A. Sauerbeck, *loc. cit.*

Equation of the primary trend line:

$$y = 115.82 - 2.008\,x + 0.017\,x^2$$

x in units of 5 years, origin at 1779.

Column IV: smoothed moving average of 7 years.

TABLE 27. IMPORTS OF RAW COTTON, UNITED KINGDOM,
1781–1914

Columns I and II in thousands of pounds, 1781–1830, in millions of
pounds, 1831–1913

	I	II	III	IV	V
1780.....		13,809			
1781.....	5,199		35.1	56.0	62.7
1782.....	11,828		74.9	62.0	120.8
1783.....	9,736		58.0	69.0	84.1
1784.....	11,482		64.6	76.4	84.6
1785.....	18,400	18,749	98.1	87.0	112.8
1786.....	19,475		97.0	96.6	100.4
1787.....	23,250		108.5	102.4	106.0
1788.....	20,467		89.9	108.0	83.2
1789.....	32,576		135.2	111.0	121.8
1790.....	31,448	25,435	123.6	112.0	110.4
1791.....	28,707		105.4	111.7	94.4
1792.....	34,907		120.2	101.0	119.0
1793.....	19,041		61.7	91.0	67.8
1794... .	24,359		74.6	83.0	89.9
1795.....	26,401	34,465	76.6	76.0	100.8
1796.....	32,126		87.1	72.8	119.6
1797.....	23,354		59.4	84.0	70.7
1798.....	31,881		76.3	93.0	82.0
1799.....	43,379		98.2	99.0	99.2
1800.....	56,011	46,620	120.1	101.6	118.2
1801.....	56,004		112.3	102.0	110.1
1802.....	60,346		113.5	101.7	111.6
1803.....	53,812		95.4	101.1	94.4
1804.....	61,867		103.7	100.2	103.5
1805.....	59,682	62,946	94.8	99.3	95.5
1806.....	58,176		86.4	97.8	88.3
1807.....	74,925		104.6	96.1	108.8
1808.....	43,606		57.4	94.0	61.1
1809.....	92,812		115.5	91.3	126.5
1810.....	132,489	84,737	156.4	88.6	176.5
1811.....	91,577		101.2	85.5	118.4
1812.....	63,026		65.5	82.4	79.5
1813.....	50,966		49.9	76.6	65.1
1814.....	60,060		55.7	77.1	71.5
1815.....	100,709	113,635	88.6	83.6	106.0
1816.....	95,281		78.6	90.0	87.3
1817.....	126,304		98.0	93.0	105.4
1818.....	178,746		131.0	94.5	138.6
1819.....	151,153		104.9	95.2	110.2

TABLE 27 (*continued*)

	I	II	III	IV	V
1820.....	151,673	151,636	100.0	95.7	104.5
1821.....	132,537		82.1	96.1	85.4
1822.....	142,838		83.3	96.4	86.4
1823.....	191,403		105.6	96.7	109.2
1824.....	149,380		78.1	97.0	80.5
1825.....	228,005	201,034	113.4	97.3	116.5
1826.....	177,607		83.1	97.5	85.2
1827.....	272,449		120.4	97.8	123.1
1828.....	227,761		95.3	98.1	97.1
1829.....	222,767		88.5	98.4	89.9
1830.....	263,961	264,276	99.9	98.7	101.2
1831.....	288.7		103.0	99.0	104.0
1832.....	286.8		96.9	99.5	97.4
1833.....	303.7		97.3	100.4	96.9
1834.....	326.9		99.7	103.0	96.8
1835.....	363.7	343.7	105.8	105.4	100.4
1836.....	407.0		112.1	108.0	103.8
1837.....	407.3		106.4	110.1	96.6
1838.....	507.9		126.3	111.7	113.1
1839.....	389.4		92.3	113.3	81.5
1840.....	592.5	441.2	134.3	114.9	116.9
1841.....	488.0		105.1	116.4	90.3
1842.....	531.8		109.1	117.3	93.0
1843.....	673.2		131.8	117.2	112.5
1844.....	646.1		121.0	114.6	105.6
1845.....	722.0	557.2	129.6	109.4	118.5
1846.....	467.9		80.1	104.6	76.6
1847.....	474.7		77.7	100.2	77.5
1848.....	713.0		111.9	100.3	111.6
1849.....	755.5		113.8	103.5	110.0
1850.....	663.6	690.8	96.1	106.3	90.4
1851.....	757.4		105.1	108.1	97.2
1852.....	929.8		123.9	109.8	112.8
1853.....	895.3		114.8	111.0	103.4
1854.....	887.3		109.6	112.0	97.9
1855.....	891.8	838.4	106.4	112.9	94.2
1856.....	1,023.9		117.7	113.7	103.5
1857.....	969.3		107.6	114.2	94.2
1858.....	1,034.3		111.0	114.7	96.8
1859.....	1,226.0		127.3	114.5	111.2

TABLE 27 (*continued*)

	I	II	III	IV	V
1860.....	1,390.9	994.5	139.9	114.1	122.6
1861.....	1,257.0		122.5	107.0	114.5
1862.....	524.0		49.5	95.5	51.8
1863.....	669.6		61.5	94.8	64.9
1864.....	893.3		79.7	95.4	83.5
1865.....	978.0	1,152.2	84.9	97.0	87.5
1866.....	1,377.1		116.5	100.0	116.5
1867.....	1,262.9		104.1	103.8	100.3
1868.....	1,328.8		106.9	105.1	101.7
1869.....	1,221.6		95.9	106.1	90.4
1870.....	1,339.4	1,304.0	102.7	106.6	96.3
1871.....	1,778.1		133.5	106.8	125.0
1872.....	1,408.8		103.6	106.9	96.9
1873.....	1,527.6		110.1	106.8	103.1
1874.....	1,566.9		110.8	106.2	104.3
1875.....	1,492.4	1,443.8	103.4	103.2	100.2
1876.....	1,487.9		101.3	100.6	100.7
1877.....	1,355.3		90.8	99.4	91.3
1878.....	1,340.4		88.3	99.0	89.2
1879.....	1,469.4		95.3	99.9	95.4
1880.....	1,628.7	1,567.3	103.9	100.6	103.3
1881.....	1,679.1		105.7	101.2	104.4
1882.....	1,784.1		110.9	101.7	109.0
1883.....	1,734.3		106.4	102.2	104.1
1884.....	1,749.2		105.9	102.6	103.2
1885.....	1,425.8	1,672.3	85.3	103.0	82.8
1886.....	1,715.0		101.5	103.4	98.2
1887.....	1,791.4		104.9	103.6	101.3
1888.....	1,731.8		100.4	103.8	96.7
1889.....	1,937.5		111.2	104.0	106.9
1890.....	1,793.5	1,759.0	102.0	103.9	98.2
1891.....	1,994.9		112.5	103.5	108.7
1892.....	1,775.2		99.3	101.6	97.7
1893.....	1,416.8		78.7	97.8	80.5
1894.....	1,778.1		98.5	96.6	102.0
1895.....	1,757.0	1,828.6	96.1	96.0	100.1
1896.....	1,754.9		95.4	95.7	99.7
1897.....	1,724.2		93.2	95.7	97.4
1898.....	2,128.5		114.4	95.9	119.3
1899.....	1,626.2		86.9	96.2	90.3

TABLE 27 (*continued*)

	I	II	III	IV	V
1900.....	1,760.2	1,883.3	93.5	96.7	96.7
1901.....	1,829.7		96.7	97.7	99.0
1902.....	1,816.7		95.6	99.2	96.4
1903.....	1,793.1		93.9	101.5	92.5
1904.....	1,954.9		102.0	103.8	98.3
1905.....	2,203.6	1,925.7	114.4	106.1	107.8
1906.....	2,007.4		103.9	108.5	95.8
1907.....	2,386.9		123.1	110.8	111.1
1908.....	2,060.7		105.9	112.6	94.0
1909.....	2,188.8		112.1	114.5	97.9
1910.....	1,972.7	1,958.4	100.7	115.8	87.0
1911.....	2,207.1		112.4	116.8	96.2
1912.....	2,805.8		142.6	117.8	121.1
1913.....	2,174.3		110.2	118.8	92.8
1915.....		1,982.5			

Sources of data: E. Baines, *History of the Cotton Manufactures in Great Britain*, London, 1835, pp. 109, 111, 215, 347. W. Page (editor), *Commerce and Industry*, Tables of Statistics for the British Empire from 1815, pp. 140–41.

Equation of the primary trend line:

$$y = \frac{2,053,610}{1 + 10^{1.76779-0.13388\,x}}$$

x in units of 5 years, origin at 1795.

Column IV: smoothed moving average of 7 years.

TABLE 27a. PRICES OF RAW COTTON, UNITED KINGDOM, 1782–1913

Relatives, 1782 = 100

	I	II	III	IV	V
1782............	100		95.1	86.9	109.4
1783............	102		98.2	85.4	115.0
1784............	61	102.71	59.4	83.9	70.8
1785............	84		82.7	82.4	100.4
1786............	86		85.7	81.0	105.8
1787............	91		91.7	79.6	115.2
1788............	96		97.9	78.2	125.2
1789............	57	96.86	58.8	76.9	76.5
1790............	66		68.9	76.2	90.4
1791............	64		67.7	77.5	87.4
1792............	81		86.7	80.3	108.0
1793............	76		82.3	84.7	97.2
1794..........	68	91.24	74.5	91.2	81.7
1795............	79		87.6	101.0	86.7
1796............	115		129.1	115.6	111.7
1797............	92		104.5	136.0	76.8
1798............	139		159.9	142.5	112.2
1799............	204	85.86	237.6	144.0	165.0
1800............	116		136.7	142.0	96.3
1801............	114		136.0	137.8	98.7
1802............	94		113.6	132.5	85.7
1803............	86		105.2	127.7	82.4
1804............	86	80.71	106.6	123.0	86.7
1805............	100		125.4	120.0	104.5
1806............	93		118.1	117.0	100.9
1807............	85		109.3	114.0	95.9
1808............	105		136.8	112.0	122.1
1809............	103	75.79	135.9	110.0	123.5
1810............	86		114.9	108.2	106.2
1811............	66		89.3	107.9	82.8
1812............	70		95.9	112.5	85.2
1813............	83		115.2	128.5	128.6
1814............	111	71.10	156.1	133.3	117.1
1815............	94		133.9	135.3	99.0
1816............	87		125.5	135.5	92.6
1817............	110		160.7	132.3	121.5
1818............	106		156.9	125.0	125.5
1819............	67	66.65	100.5	107.4	93.6

TABLE 27a (*continued*)

	I	II	III	IV	V
1820............	61		92.7	95.4	97.2
1821............	53		81.6	89.4	91.3
1822............	47		73.3	85.0	86.2
1823............	46		72.7	80.8	90.0
1824............	48	62.43	76.9	77.1	99.7
1825............	63		102.2	73.5	139.0
1826............	40		65.8	70.1	93.9
1827............	38		63.3	66.8	94.8
1828............	34		57.4	64.0	89.7
1829............	41	58.44	70.2	62.5	112.3
1830............	36		62.4	64.5	96.7
1831............	33		58.0	69.5	83.5
1832............	35		62.3	75.0	83.1
1833............	43		77.6	79.4	97.7
1834............	48	54.69	87.8	82.7	106.2
1835............	55		101.9	83.9	121.5
1836............	53		99.5	84.0	118.5
1837............	40		76.1	82.9	91.8
1838............	38		73.3	80.1	91.5
1839............	41	51.16	80.1	77.0	104.0
1840............	36		71.3	72.8	97.9
1841............	37		74.2	68.0	109.1
1842............	31		63.0	64.5	97.7
1843............	27		55.6	61.0	91.1
1844............	27	47.87	56.4	58.3	96.7
1845............	24		50.8	55.8	91.0
1846............	28		60.0	54.8	109.5
1847............	29		63.0	55.2	114.1
1848............	21		46.2	56.2	82.2
1849............	23	44.81	51.3	57.5	89.2
1850............	32		72.3	58.9	122.8
1851............	27		61.8	60.4	102.3
1852............	25		58.0	62.1	93.4
1853............	24		56.4	63.9	88.3
1854............	24	41.99	57.2	66.0	86.7
1855............	26		62.7	68.6	91.4
1856............	30		73.3	71.6	102.4
1857............	36		89.0	75.4	118.0
1858............	32		80.2	79.8	100.5
1859............	33	39.40	83.8	86.0	97.4

TABLE 27a (*continued*)

	I	II	III	IV	V
1860..........	30		77.1	125.0	61.7
1861..........	39		101.4	175.0	57.9
1862..........	82		215.9	201.0	107.4
1863..........	117		311.9	213.0	146.4
1864..........	128	37.04	345.6	220.0	157.1
1865..........	77		210.3	221.2	95.1
1866..........	72		199.0	216.0	92.1
1867..........	51		142.7	190.4	75.0
1868..........	49		138.7	158.0	87.8
1869..........	57	34.91	163.3	145.0	112.6
1870..........	46		133.2	140.6	95.1
1871..........	40		117.1	134.2	87.3
1872..........	49		145.1	127.5	113.8
1873..........	46		137.8	119.5	115.3
1874..........	37	33.01	112.1	113.6	98.7
1875..........	34		104.1	107.8	96.6
1876..........	29		89.7	103.6	86.6
1877..........	29		90.6	98.4	92.1
1878..........	28		88.4	96.5	91.6
1879..........	29	31.35	92.5	96.0	96.4
1880..........	32		103.0	95.2	108.2
1881..........	30		97.5	94.5	103.2
1882..........	31		101.7	93.7	108.5
1883..........	27		89.4	92.9	96.2
1884..........	28	29.92	93.6	92.1	101.6
1885..........	26		87.6	91.2	96.1
1886..........	24		81.5	90.3	90.3
1887..........	26		89.0	89.3	99.7
1888..........	26		89.8	88.2	101.8
1889..........	28	28.72	97.5	86.8	112.3
1890..........	28		98.2	84.9	115.7
1891..........	22		77.7	82.0	94.8
1892..........	19		67.5	77.0	87.7
1893..........	21		75.1	70.2	107.0
1894..........	18	27.76	64.8	67.7	95.7
1895..........	18		65.2	66.0	98.8
1896..........	20		72.8	65.3	111.5
1897..........	18		65.9	65.0	101.4
1898..........	16		58.9	70.2	83.9
1899..........	17	27.03	62.9	76.5	82.2

TABLE 27a (*continued*)

	I	II	III	IV	V
1900............	26		96.5	83.4	115.7
1901............	22		82.0	89.8	91.3
1902............	23		86.0	94.7	90.8
1903............	28		105.1	98.7	106.5
1904............	31	26.53	116.8	102.5	114.0
1905............	24		90.7	106.1	85.5
1906............	28		106.0	109.5	96.8
1907............	31		117.6	112.8	104.3
1908............	27		102.6	116.0	88.4
1909............	29	26.26	110.4	118.3	93.3
1910............	37		141.0	119.7	117.8
1911............	33		125.8	120.1	104.7
1912............	30		114.4	120.1	95.3
1913............	33		125.8	119.9	104.9
1914............	30	26.23	114.4	119.6	95.7

Source of data: Up to 1866, W. S. Jevons, *loc. cit.*, pp. 148–49 (cotton — several varieties); from 1866, A. Sauerbeck.

Equation of the primary trend line:

$$y = 108.79 - 6.198\,x + 0.1163\,x^2$$

x in units of 5 years, origin at 1779.

Column IV: smoothed moving average of 7 years up to 1847, 5 years from 1847.

TABLE 28. CONSUMPTION OF TEA, UNITED KINGDOM,
1780–1920

Columns I and II in thousands of pounds

	I	II	III	IV	V
1770–1780..	4,770	6,814	70.0		
1781–1790..	10,329	9,283	111.3		
1791–1800..	17,263	12,632	136.7		
1801–1804..	24,016	16,142	148.8		
1805–1809..	23,325	18,240	127.9		
1810–1814..	24,265	21,239	114.2		
1815–1819..	24,997	24,713	101.2		
1820–1824..	26,957	28,736	93.8		
1825–1829..	29,402	33,824	86.9		
1830–1834..	31,678	38,742	81.8		
1835–1839..	36,764	44,910	81.9		
1840–1844..	37,588	51,991	72.3		
1845–1849..	47,200	60,093	78.5		
1850.......	51,172	65,500	78.1	78.6	99.4
1851.......	53,949		79.9	79.2	100.9
1852.......	54,713		78.7	80.0	98.4
1853.......	58,834		82.3	81.0	101.6
1854.......	61,953		84.3	82.0	102.8
1855.......	63,429	75,488	84.1	83.0	101.3
1856.......	63,278		81.3	84.0	96.8
1857.......	69,132		86.4	85.0	101.6
1858.......	73,196		88.9	86.1	103.3
1859.......	76,304		90.3	87.3	103.4
1860.......	76,816	86,816	88.5	88.8	99.7
1861.......	77,949		87.3	90.5	96.5
1862.......	78,794		85.7	92.2	93.0
1863.......	85,183		90.2	94.0	96.0
1864.......	88,599		91.3	96.3	94.8
1865.......	97,835	99,599	98.2	98.5	99.7
1866.......	103,165		100.6	100.6	100.0
1867.......	110,988		105.4	102.3	103.0
1868.......	107,085		99.0	103.5	95.6
1869.......	111,796		100.6	104.6	96.2

TABLE 28 (*continued*)

	I	II	III	IV	V
1870.......	117,551	113,948	103.2	105.4	97.9
1871.......	123,401		105.3	106.1	99.2
1872.......	127,661		106.1	106.7	99.4
1873.......	131,881		106.7	107.2	99.5
1874.......	137,279		108.3	107.6	100.7
1875.......	145,327	129,952	111.8	107.9	103.6
1876.......	149,164		111.7	108.0	103.4
1877.......	151,114		110.2	107.8	102.2
1878.......	157,396		112.0	107.6	104.1
1879.......	160,432		111.3	107.4	103.6
1880.......	158,326	147,758	107.1	107.1	100.0
1881.......	160,056		105.6	106.8	98.9
1882.......	164,958		106.1	106.4	99.7
1883.......	170,780		107.1	106.0	101.0
1884.......	175,060		107.1	105.5	101.5
1885.......	182,409	167,285	109.1	105.0	103.9
1886.......	178,891		104.3	104.6	99.7
1887.......	183,661		104.4	104.3	100.1
1888.......	185,600		103.1	104.1	99.0
1889.......	185,600		100.6	103.9	96.8
1890.......	194,008	188,653	102.9	103.7	99.2
1891.......	202,457		104.8	103.6	101.2
1892.......	207,114		104.6	103.5	101.1
1893.......	208,097		102.8	103.5	99.3
1894.......	214,341		103.5	103.5	100.0
1895.......	221,800	211,784	104.7	103.6	101.1
1896.......	223,067		102.9	103.7	99.2
1897.......	227,270		102.5	103.8	98.7
1898.......	235,354		103.8	103.8	100.0
1899.......	242,506		104.7	103.8	100.9
1900.......	249,751	236,604	105.6	103.7	101.8
1901.......	255,825		105.8	103.4	102.3
1902.......	254,399		103.0	103.0	100.0
1903.......	255,328		101.1	102.2	98.9
1904.......	256,467		99.6	101.4	98.2
1905.......	258,777	262,959	98.4	100.8	97.6
1906.......	269,503		100.6	100.4	100.2
1907.......	273,769		100.5	100.1	100.4
1908.......	275,240		99.4	99.9	99.5
1909.......	283,330		100.5	99.7	100.8

TABLE 28 (*continued*)

	I	II	III	IV	V
1910.......	286,892	286,512	100.2	99.6	100.6
1911.......	293,302		100.1	99.6	100.5
1912.......	295,223		98.5	99.6	98.9
1913.......	305,490		99.8	99.6	100.2
1914.......	317,478		101.5	99.7	101.8
1915.......	316,814	319,444	99.2	100.0	99.2
1916.......	302,033		92.8	100.5	92.3
1917.......	277,436		83.8	101.2	82.8
1918.......	310,687		92.2	102.0	90.4
1919.......	388,005		113.1	102.9	109.9
1920.......	392,339	349,022	112.5	104.0	108.2

Sources of data: G. Bienkowski, *Tee Produktion und Teehandel,* Braunschweig, 1913, p. 38; except for: 1801–49, *Journal of the Royal Statistical Society,* 1860, p. 51; 1912–20, *Statistical Abstract for the United Kingdom,* 1906–20, pp. 134–35.

Equation of the primary trend line:

$$y = \frac{771,256}{1 + 10^{1.91427 - 0.13567\,x}}$$

x in units of 10 years, origin at 1785.

Column IV: smoothed moving average of 7 years.

TABLE 29. COAL OUTPUT, BELGIUM, 1831–1913

Columns I and II in thousands of metric tons

	I	II	III	IV	V
1831........	2,305	2,356	97.8	95.5	102.4
1832........	2,281		91.5	95.5	95.8
1833........	2,531		96.2	95.6	100.6
1834........	2,437		88.1	95.8	92.0
1835........	2,639	2,904	90.9	96.0	94.7
1836........	3,074		99.9	96.2	103.8
1837........	3,229		99.4	96.4	103.0
1838........	3,260		95.3	96.6	98.7
1839........	3,479		96.8	96.8	100.0
1840........	3,930	3,767	104.3	97.0	107.4
1841........	4,028		101.2	97.2	104.1
1842........	4,141		98.8	97.4	101.4
1843........	3,982		90.4	97.6	92.6
1844........	4,445		96.2	97.8	98.4
1845........	4,919	4,832	101.8	98.0	103.9
1846........	5,037		99.0	98.3	100.7
1847........	5,664		106.0	98.6	107.5
1848........	4,863		86.8	98.9	87.8
1849........	5,252		89.7	99.2	90.4
1850........	5,821	6,114	95.2	99.5	95.7
1851........	6,233		97.2	99.9	97.3
1852........	6,795		101.2	100.3	100.9
1853........	7,173		102.3	100.7	101.3
1854........	7,948		108.7	101.2	107.4
1855........	8,409	7,612	110.5	101.7	108.7
1856........	8,212		103.3	102.1	101.2
1857........	8,384		101.2	102.5	98.7
1858........	8,926		103.5	102.8	100.7
1859........	9,161		102.2	103.1	99.1
1860........	9,611	9,303	103.3	103.4	99.9
1861........	10,057		104.0	103.7	100.3
1862........	9,936		99.0	104.0	95.2
1863........	10,345		99.4	104.2	95.4
1864........	11,158		103.6	104.3	99.3

TABLE 29 (*continued*)

	I	II	III	IV	V
1865........	11,841	11,138	106.3	104.4	101.8
1866........	12,775		110.9	104.4	106.2
1867........	12,756		107.2	104.4	102.7
1868........	12,299		100.1	104.3	95.9
1869........	12,943		102.2	104.2	97.5
1870........	13,697	13,047	105.0	103.9	101.1
1871........	13,733		102.3	103.5	98.8
1872........	15,659		113.4	102.8	110.3
1873........	15,778		111.2	102.1	108.9
1874........	14,669		100.7	101.4	99.3
1875........	15,011	14,948	100.4	100.7	99.7
1876........	14,330		93.6	100.0	93.6
1877........	13,939		88.9	99.4	89.4
1878........	14,899		92.9	98.8	94.0
1879........	15,447		94.2	98.3	95.8
1880........	16,867	16,758	100.7	97.9	102.9
1881........	16,874		98.7	97.7	101.0
1882........	17,591		101.0	97.5	103.6
1883........	18,178		102.4	97.6	104.9
1884........	18,051		99.8	97.6	102.2
1885........	17,438	18,412	94.7	97.7	96.9
1886........	17,286		92.4	97.8	94.5
1887........	18,379		96.7	97.9	98.8
1888........	19,218		99.6	98.1	101.5
1889........	19,869		101.4	98.3	103.7
1890........	20,366	19,867	102.5	98.5	104.1
1891........	19,491		96.8	98.7	98.1
1892........	19,583		96.1	98.9	97.2
1893........	19,410		94.1	99.1	95.0
1894........	20,534		98.4	99.3	99.1
1895........	20,458	21,103	96.9	99.5	97.4
1896........	21,251		99.7	99.7	100.0
1897........	21,492		99.9	99.9	100.0
1898........	22,088		101.7	100.1	101.6
1899........	22,072		100.7	100.3	100.4
1900........	23,463	22,125	106.0	100.5	105.5
1901........	22,213		99.7	100.7	99.0
1902........	22,877		101.9	100.9	101.0
1903........	23,797		105.2	101.1	104.0
1904........	22,761		99.9	101.1	98.6

TABLE 29 (*continued*)

	I	II	III	IV	V
1905........	21,775	22,949	94.9	101.0	94.0
1906........	23,570		102.1	100.9	101.2
1907........	23,705		102.1	100.7	101.4
1908........	23,558		100.9	100.5	100.4
1909........	23,518		100.2	100.2	100.0
1910........	23,917	23,600	101.3	99.9	101.4
1911........	23,054		97.3	99.5	97.8
1912........	22,972		96.5	99.0	97.5
1913........	22,842		95.6	98.7	96.9
1914........					
1915........		24,108			

Source of data: Bulletin de la Société de l'Industries Minérales; collected by H. G. Villard, National Bureau of Economic Research, Inc.

Equation of the primary trend line:

$$y = \frac{25,697}{1 + 10^{0.76503 - 0.12974\,x}}$$

x in units of 5 years, origin at 1840.

Column IV: smoothed moving average of 13 years.

TABLE 29a. PRICES OF COAL, BELGIUM, 1831–1913

Columns I and II in francs per ton

	I	II	III	IV	V
1831	8.71		80.4	101.0	79.6
1832	8.53	10.78	79.1	101.0	78.3
1833	8.56		80.5	101.0	79.7
1834	8.60		81.3	101.0	80.5
1835	9.48		90.0	101.0	89.1
1836	12.47		119.0	101.0	117.8
1837	13.10	10.45	125.4	101.0	124.2
1838	13.13		126.0	101.0	124.8
1839	12.97		124.8	101.0	123.6
1840	11.79		113.8	101.0	112.7
1841	10.55		102.1	100.9	101.2
1842	9.19	10.30	89.2	100.1	89.1
1843	9.09		88.5	98.0	90.3
1844	8.96		87.4	94.0	93.0
1845	9.60		93.8	91.0	103.1
1846	9.33		91.3	88.0	103.7
1847	9.23	10.21	90.4	85.8	105.4
1848	8.47		83.0	84.2	98.6
1849	7.52		73.8	84.0	87.9
1850	7.98		78.4	85.0	92.2
1851	7.98		78.5	89.0	88.2
1852	7.81	10.16	76.9	92.5	83.1
1853	8.67		85.3	95.5	89.3
1854	10.80		106.3	97.5	109.0
1855	12.35		121.4	99.5	122.0
1856	12.84		126.1	101.8	123.9
1857	11.98	10.19	117.6	103.3	113.8
1858	11.58		113.5	104.5	108.6
1859	11.35		111.2	105.7	105.2
1860	11.15		109.1	106.9	102.1
1861	10.94		106.9	108.1	98.9
1862	10.52	10.25	102.6	109.3	93.9
1863	10.13		98.6	110.4	89.3
1864	9.91		96.2	111.5	86.3

TABLE 29a (*continued*)

	I	II	III	IV	V
1865	10.45		101.2	112.5	89.1
1866	11.82		114.1	113.5	100.5
1867	12.40	10.39	119.3	114.5	104.2
1868	10.88		104.4	115.3	90.6
1869	10.51		100.6	116.1	86.6
1870	10.86		103.5	116.8	88.6
1871	11.20		106.4	117.3	90.7
1872	13.32	10.57	126.0	117.5	107.2
1873	21.40		201.5	117.3	171.8
1874	16.41		153.8	116.9	131.6
1875	15.31		142.8	116.3	122.8
1876	13.55		125.8	115.0	109.4
1877	10.97	10.82	101.4	113.0	89.7
1878	9.92		91.3	109.0	83.8
1879	9.39		85.9	103.5	83.0
1880	10.06		91.5	97.0	94.3
1881	9.70		87.8	91.0	96.5
1882	10.00	11.12	89.9	86.0	104.5
1883	10.17		90.9	83.0	109.5
1884	9.53		84.6	82.0	103.2
1885	8.87		78.3	81.5	96.1
1886	8.25		72.4	81.5	88.8
1887	8.04	11.48	70.0	81.5	85.9
1888	8.43		72.9	82.1	88.8
1889	9.45		81.2	83.5	97.2
1890	13.18		112.5	85.1	132.2
1891	12.58		106.5	87.0	122.4
1892	10.28	11.90	86.4	89.5	96.5
1893	9.34		77.9	91.0	85.6
1894	9.32		77.2	93.0	83.0
1895	9.45		77.6	95.0	81.7
1896	9.51		77.5	97.2	79.7
1897	10.26	12.37	82.9	99.5	83.3
1898	11.00		88.2	101.9	86.6
1899	12.43		98.9	104.0	93.7
1900	17.41		137.3	105.6	130.0
1901	15.23		119.1	107.0	111.3
1902	13.20	12.90	102.3	108.1	94.6
1903	12.99		99.8	108.9	91.6
1904	12.59		96.0	109.6	87.6

TABLE 29a (*continued*)

	I	II	III	IV	V
1905...........	12.64		95.5	110.1	86.7
1906...........	15.00		112.3	110.4	101.7
1907...........	16.86	13.48	125.1	110.7	113.0
1908...........	16.14		118.7	111.0	106.9
1909...........	14.37		104.7	111.2	94.2
1910...........	14.59		105.3	111.4	94.5
1911...........	14.76		105.5	111.6	94.5
1912...........	16.56	14.12	117.3	111.8	104.9
1913...........	18.34		128.6	112.0	114.8

Source of data: *Statistique des Minérales Belges*; collected by H. G. Villard, National Bureau of Economic Research, Inc.

Equation of the primary trend line:
$$y = 10.92 - 0.53\,x + 0.092\,x^2$$

x in units of 5 years, origin at 1827.

Column IV: smoothed moving average of 13 years.

TABLE 30. PIG IRON PRODUCTION, BELGIUM, 1845–1913

Columns I and II in thousands of metric tons

	I	II	III	IV	V
1845..........	135	190.5	70.9	65.5	108.2
1850..........	144	226.9	63.5	79.9	79.5
1851..........	154		65.4	83.9	78.0
1852..........	168		68.9	87.8	78.5
1853..........	220		87.1	91.4	95.3
1854..........	273		104.5	94.0	111.2
1855..........	294	269.8	109.0	96.5	113.0
1856..........	306		109.3	98.8	110.6
1857..........	288		99.3	101.1	98.2
1858..........	313		104.3	103.2	101.1
1859..........	309		99.6	105.1	94.8
1860..........	320	320.3	99.9	106.8	93.5
1861..........	312		93.9	108.4	86.6
1862..........	357		103.7	109.7	94.5
1863..........	392		110.0	111.0	99.1
1864..........	450		122.2	112.0	109.1
1865..........	471	380.3	123.8	113.0	109.6
1866..........	482		122.3	113.7	107.6
1867..........	423		103.7	114.2	90.8
1868..........	436		103.4	114.7	90.1
1869..........	534		122.6	115.0	106.6
1870..........	563	449.6	125.3	115.0	109.0
1871..........	609		130.8	115.0	113.7
1872..........	656		136.2	115.0	118.4
1873..........	607		121.9	114.6	106.4
1874..........	533		103.7	114.1	90.9
1875..........	542	530.2	102.2	113.0	90.4
1876..........	490		89.3	110.0	81.2
1877..........	470		82.8	103.0	80.4
1878..........	519		88.6	101.7	87.1
1879..........	389		64.3	102.0	63.0
1880..........	608	623.3	97.5	102.7	94.9
1881..........	625		97.0	102.8	94.4
1882..........	727		109.2	102.8	106.2
1883..........	783		113.9	102.8	110.8
1884..........	751		106.0	102.3	103.6
1885..........	713	730.2	97.6	101.0	96.6
1886..........	702		93.0	99.2	93.7
1887..........	756		97.0	97.0	100.0
1888..........	827		102.9	94.8	108.5
1889..........	832		100.5	92.4	108.8

TABLE 30 (*continued*)

	I	II	III	IV	V
1890..........	788	852.2	92.5	89.6	103.2
1891..........	684		77.8	87.7	88.7
1892..........	753		83.0	86.5	96.0
1893..........	745		79.7	86.0	92.7
1894..........	819		85.1	86.2	98.7
1895..........	829	989.9	83.7	86.6	96.7
1896..........	959		94.0	87.2	107.8
1897..........	1,035		98.5	87.9	112.1
1898..........	978		90.5	88.6	102.1
1899..........	1,025		92.2	89.4	103.1
1900..........	1,019	1,144.1	89.1	90.2	98.8
1901..........	764		64.8	91.1	71.1
1902..........	1,069		88.2	92.1	95.8
1903..........	1,216		97.6	93.1	104.8
1904..........	1,288		100.6	94.1	106.9
1905..........	1,311	1,314.9	99.7	95.3	104.6
1906..........	1,376		101.8	96.5	105.5
1907..........	1,407		101.3	97.7	103.7
1908..........	1,270		89.0	99.0	89.9
1909..........	1,616		110.4	101.0	109.2
1910..........	1,852	1,501.8	123.3	103.5	119.1
1911..........	2,046		132.7	106.0	125.2
1912..........	2,301		145.4	108.5	134.0
1913..........	2,485		153.1	111.5	137.3
1915..........		1,703.6			

Sources of data: *Annuaire Statistique de la Belgique, Annales des Mines*; collected by H. G. Villard, National Bureau of Economic Research, Inc.

Equation of the primary trend line:

$$y = \frac{5223.4}{1 + 10^{\,1.26393 - 0.15798\,x}}$$

x in units of 10 years, origin at 1855.

Column IV: smoothed moving average of 9 years.

TABLE 30a. PRICES OF PIG IRON, BELGIUM, 1845–1914

Columns I and II in francs per ton

	I	II	III	IV	V
1845.........	108.28		93.6	90.5	103.4
1846.........	134.74		119.0	91.2	130.5
1847.........	119.56	110.90	107.8	92.2	116.9
1848.........	93.75		86.2	93.5	92.2
1849.........	86.83		81.4	95.2	85.5
1850.........	80.09		76.6	97.2	78.8
1851.........	80.75		78.8	99.8	79.0
1852.........	78.44	100.32	78.2	101.6	77.0
1853.........	98.29		99.8	102.8	97.1
1854.........	116.12		120.2	103.7	115.9
1855.........	116.18		122.7	104.2	117.8
1856.........	113.89		122.7	104.4	117.5
1857.........	104.62	90.94	115.0	104.2	110.4
1858.........	95.22		106.6	103.8	102.7
1859.........	86.27		98.4	103.3	95.3
1860.........	82.16		95.5	102.6	93.1
1861.........	80.54		95.4	101.5	94.0
1862.........	80.12	82.78	96.8	99.9	96.9
1863.........	75.50		92.8	99.0	93.7
1864.........	78.98		98.7	98.6	100.1
1865.........	78.64		100.0	98.5	101.5
1866.........	79.82		103.4	98.4	105.1
1867.........	74.89	75.84	98.7	98.8	99.9
1868.........	70.38		94.2	99.5	94.7
1869.........	70.26		95.5	101.0	94.6
1870.........	72.90		100.7	103.5	97.3
1871.........	73.63		103.3	109.0	94.8
1872.........	99.79	70.11	142.3	113.0	125.9
1873.........	115.66		167.1	113.5	147.2
1874.........	89.16		130.5	112.8	115.7
1875.........	75.44		111.9	110.5	101.3
1876.........	67.47		101.5	104.5	97.1
1877.........	62.59	65.59	95.4	98.8	96.6
1878.........	56.33		86.8	94.9	91.5
1879.........	64.22		99.9	91.7	108.9
1880.........	61.30		96.4	89.7	107.5
1881.........	58.36		92.7	88.0	105.3
1882.........	60.25	62.29	96.7	86.5	111.8
1883.........	55.60		89.9	85.2	105.5
1884.........	50.32		81.9	84.0	97.5

TABLE 30a (*continued*)

	I	II	III	IV	V
1885.........	45.95		75.3	83.0	90.7
1886.........	44.02		72.6	82.5	88.0
1887.........	45.09	60.20	74.9	83.7	89.5
1888.........	48.97		81.6	85.6	95.3
1889.........	53.46		89.3	87.6	101.9
1890.........	63.56		106.5	89.8	118.6
1891.........	56.01		94.1	92.0	102.3
1892.........	51.40	59.32	86.6	94.2	91.9
1893.........	48.37		81.4	96.4	84.4
1894.........	49.88		83.9	98.6	85.1
1895.........	48.49		81.5	101.0	80.7
1896.........	53.60		89.9	103.2	87.1
1897.........	58.66	59.66	98.3	105.3	93.4
1898.........	59.10		98.5	107.1	92.0
1899.........	72.62		120.5	108.4	111.2
1900.........	89.87		148.3	108.6	136.6
1901.........	61.84		101.5	108.4	93.6
1902.........	58.90	61.22	96.2	108.0	89.1
1903.........	60.48		97.9	107.5	91.1
1904.........	59.09		94.8	106.9	88.7
1905.........	60.36		96.0	106.2	90.4
1906.........	71.46		112.7	105.6	106.7
1907.........	75.54	63.98	118.1	105.0	112.5
1908.........	67.60		104.4	104.4	100.0
1909.........	62.23		94.9	103.8	91.4
1910.........	64.80		97.6	103.2	94.6
1911.........	65.30		97.2	102.5	94.8
1912.........	69.89	67.96	102.8	101.8	101.0
1913.........	73.79		106.9	101.1	105.7
1914.........	67.87		96.9	100.4	96.5

Sources of data: Up to 1893, H. Denis, *La Dépression Économique et Sociale et l'Histoire des Prix, Bruxelles*, 1895, pp. 319–20; from 1893, *Annuaire Statistique de la Belgique*, successive issues (total value divided by the number of tons).

Equation of the primary trend line:

$$y = 122.70 - 12.408\,x + 0.607\,x^2$$

x in units of 5 years, origin at 1842.

Column IV: smoothed moving average of 9 years.

TABLE 31. STEEL PRODUCTION, BELGIUM, 1875–1913

Columns I and II in metric tons

	I	II	III	IV	V
1875....	54,420	57,726	94.3	116.9	70.7
1880....	132,052	98,053	134.7	113.1	119.1
1881....	141,640		124.9	111.7	111.9
1882....	182,627		141.8	110.0	128.9
1883....	179,489		124.5	107.5	115.8
1884....	185,916		116.5	104.8	111.2
1885....	155,012	174,977	88.6	100.4	88.2
1886....	155,169		78.4	93.9	83.5
1887....	216,186		97.8	90.9	107.6
1888....	231,847		95.0	88.7	107.1
1889....	254,397		95.2	86.7	109.8
1890....	221,296	290,214	76.3	84.9	89.9
1891....	221,913		68.1	83.7	81.4
1892....	260,037		72.0	83.5	86.2
1893....	273,113		68.9	85.9	80.2
1894....	405,661		94.0	91.9	102.3
1895....	407,634	467,146	87.3	97.4	89.6
1896....	598,974		115.2	99.3	116.0
1897....	616,541		107.7	99.7	108.0
1898....	653,523		104.5	99.7	104.8
1899....	731,249		107.8	99.7	108.1
1900....	655,199	731,239	89.6	99.7	89.9
1901....	515,780		63.8	99.7	64.0
1902....	769,030		86.9	99.8	87.1
1903....	969,230		100.8	99.9	100.9
1904....	1,090,770		105.1	100.1	105.0
1905....	1,227,110	1,114,787	110.1	100.3	109.8
1906....	1,395,140		114.0	100.7	113.2
1907....	1,466,715		110.1	102.3	107.6
1908....	1,198,000		83.2	106.4	78.2
1909....	1,580,350		102.1	109.9	92.9

TABLE 31 (*continued*)

	I	II	III	IV	V
1910....	1,892,160	1,657,482	114.2	112.4	101.6
1911....	2,028,170		112.2	114.9	97.7
1912....	2,442,420		124.8	116.9	106.8
1913....	2,402,780		114.0	118.9	95.9
1915....		2,400,488			

Source of data: *Annuaire Statistique de la Belgique*, successive issues.

Equation of the primary trend line:

$$\log y = 4.22802 + 4.75192(1 - 0.83333^x)$$

x in units of 15 years, origin at 1865.

Column IV: smoothed moving average of 9 years.

TABLE 31a. PRICES OF STEEL, FINISHED PRODUCTS, BELGIUM, 1880–1914

Columns I and II in francs per ton

	I	II	III	IV	V
1880......	167.4		112.9	102.4	110.3
1881......	163.1		111.3	100.5	110.7
1882......	160.5	144.86	110.8	99.2	111.7
1883......	151.3		105.4	98.0	107.6
1884......	133.9		94.1	97.0	97.0
1885......	124.2		88.0	96.2	91.5
1886......	116.2		83.1	95.5	87.0
1887......	113.7	138.57	82.1	95.0	86.4
1888......	121.9		88.5	94.8	93.4
1889......	136.0		99.3	94.7	104.9
1890......	154.5		113.5	95.0	119.5
1891......	141.1		104.3	95.5	109.2
1892......	132.5	134.50	98.5	96.2	102.4
1893......	128.3		95.7	97.0	98.7
1894......	117.8		88.1	97.8	90.1
1895......	115.3		86.4	99.0	87.3
1896......	121.6		91.4	100.6	90.9
1897......	132.3	132.67	99.7	102.5	97.3
1898......	134.9		101.6	105.1	96.7
1899......	151.7		114.2	106.9	106.8
1900......	184.6		138.9	107.5	129.2
1901......	146.8		110.4	107.6	102.6
1902......	130.7	133.07	98.2	107.2	91.6
1903......	125.6		94.0	106.2	88.5
1904......	123.5		92.1	105.0	87.7
1905......	129.6		96.3	103.8	92.8
1906......	145.1		107.3	102.6	104.6
1907......	158.6	135.70	116.9	101.6	115.1
1908......	139.3		101.9	100.6	101.3
1909......	124.5		90.5	99.5	91.0

TABLE 31a (*continued*

	I	II	III	IV	V
1910......	131.2		94.7	98.4	96.3
1911......	134.3		96.2	97.3	98.9
1912......	142.4	140.56	101.3	96.2	105.3
1913......	141.2		99.4	95.2	104.5
1914......	124.5		86.8	94.2	92.1

Source of data: *Annuaire Statistique de la Belgique*, successive issues (total value divided by the number of tons).

Equation of the primary trend line:

$$y = 153.39 - 9.642\,x + 1.1155\,x^2$$

x in units of 5 years, origin at 1877.

Column IV: smoothed moving average of 9 years up to 1897, 7 years from 1897.

TABLE 32. CRUDE ZINC PRODUCTION, BELGIUM, 1845–1913

Columns I and II in metric tons (thousands of tons from 1901)

	I	II	III	IV	V
1845........	7,221	10,633	67.9	70.0	97.0
1846........	8,963		79.2	76.5	103.5
1847........	10,241		85.0	83.0	102.3
1848........	10,850		84.7	89.0	95.1
1849........	13,579		99.5	94.1	105.4
1850........	14,808	14,517	102.0	98.1	104.0
1851........	15,250		99.1	101.0	98.1
1852........	16,672		102.2	103.5	98.7
1853........	18,817		108.9	105.5	103.2
1854........	19,553		106.8	107.4	99.4
1855........	20,633	19,409	106.3	109.8	96.8
1856........	22,900		111.8	117.6	95.1
1857........	24,526		113.4	119.6	94.8
1858........	34,191		149.7	119.9	124.9
1859........	28,631		119.3	117.1	101.9
1860........	22,027	25,446	86.6	110.4	78.4
1861........	28,150		105.2	101.7	103.4
1862........	25,861		91.9	95.6	96.1
1863........	28,978		97.9	95.9	102.1
1864........	30,718		98.6	98.2	100.4
1865........	34,244	32,763	104.5	102.0	102.5
1866........	34,659		100.9	106.0	95.2
1867........	38,684		107.5	109.7	98.0
1868........	44,347		117.5	111.0	105.9
1869........	47,407		119.8	111.3	107.6
1870........	45,754	41,469	110.3	109.2	101.0
1871........	45,623		105.3	102.6	102.6
1872........	41,838		92.4	98.7	93.6
1873........	42,314		89.4	95.5	93.6
1874........	46,088		93.2	92.9	100.3
1875........	49,960	51,666	96.7	92.3	104.8
1876........	47,981		89.1	94.0	94.8
1877........	55,923		99.7	96.0	103.9
1878........	61,227		104.8	98.1	106.8
1879........	57,157		93.9	99.8	94.1
1880........	59,880	63,425	94.4	101.3	93.2
1881........	69,800		105.9	102.4	103.4
1882........	72,947		106.5	103.6	102.8
1883........	75,366		105.9	104.4	101.4
1884........	77,487		104.8	104.3	100.5

TABLE 32 (*continued*)

	I	II	III	IV	V
1885........	80,298	76,795	104.6	102.5	102.0
1886........	79,246		100.5	100.0	100.5
1887........	80,468		97.4	97.5	99.9
1888........	80,675		94.1	94.9	99.2
1889........	82,526		92.8	93.2	99.6
1890........	82,701	92,220	89.7	92.3	97.2
1891........	85,999		90.3	91.9	98.3
1892........	91,546		93.0	92.2	100.9
1893........	95,665		94.1	94.0	100.1
1894........	97,041		92.5	96.0	96.3
1895........	107,664	108,415	99.3	97.7	101.6
1896........	113,361		101.4	98.8	102.6
1897........	116,067		100.6	99.3	101.3
1898........	119,677		100.1	99.1	101.0
1899........	122,843		100.1	98.1	101.7
1900........	119,317	126,620	94.2	97.2	96.9
1901........	127.2		97.6	96.4	101.2
1902........	124.8		93.0	95.9	97.0
1903........	131.7		95.4	95.7	99.7
1904........	137.3		96.6	95.6	101.0
1905........	142.6	146.35	97.4	95.7	101.8
1906........	148.0		98.4	97.1	101.3
1907........	152.4		98.7	99.4	99.3
1908........	161.9		102.0	102.0	100.0
1909........	174.5		107.0	104.9	102.0
1910........	181.7	167.52	108.5	108.4	100.1
1911........	198.2		115.3	112.0	102.9
1912........	205.9		116.8	114.9	101.7
1913........	204.2		112.9	117.0	96.5

Sources of data: W. R. Ingalls, *Production and Properties of Zinc,* New York, 1902, p. 71; checked from 1881 by the *Annuaire Statistique de France.*

Equation of the primary trend line:

$$\log y = 4.07814 + 2.03944(1 - 0.726085^z)$$

x in units of 23 years, origin at 1844.

Column IV: smoothed moving average of 5 years.

TABLE 32a. PRICES OF ZINC, BELGIUM, 1845–1914

Columns I and II in francs per metric ton

	I	II	III	IV	V
1845.........	540.9		91.1	82.0	111.1
1846.........	539.1		91.9	83.9	109.5
1847.........	561.9	579.92	96.9	86.3	112.3
1848.........	401.6		70.0	89.1	78.6
1849.........	436.1		76.8	92.3	83.2
1850.........	441.2		78.5	95.8	81.9
1851.........	432.9		77.8	99.7	78.0
1852.........	630.9	550.36	114.6	103.5	110.7
1853.........	541.6		99.3	106.3	93.4
1854.........	606.3		112.2	108.1	103.8
1855.........	621.6		116.1	109.3	106.2
1856.........	698.2		131.6	109.8	119.9
1857.........	703.4	525.49	133.9	110.0	121.7
1858.........	616.6		118.2	109.9	107.6
1859.........	548.6		106.0	109.5	96.8
1860.........	539.7		105.1	108.5	96.9
1861.........	488.5		95.9	105.5	90.9
1862.........	472.0	505.30	93.4	101.0	92.5
1863.........	477.6		95.1	101.5	93.7
1864.........	536.2		107.4	102.5	104.8
1865.........	551.7		111.2	103.8	107.1
1866.........	555.2		112.6	105.1	107.1
1867.........	539.0	489.80	110.0	106.2	103.6
1868.........	519.1		106.4	107.2	99.3
1869.........	506.1		104.2	108.2	96.3
1870.........	474.6		98.2	109.1	90.0
1871.........	445.6		92.6	109.9	84.3
1872.........	544.3	478.99	113.6	110.2	103.1
1873.........	610.1		127.7	110.3	115.8
1874.........	575.1		120.7	110.1	109.6
1875.........	597.2		125.6	109.5	114.7
1876.........	584.5		123.3	107.6	114.6
1877.........	495.4	478.85	104.8	105.0	99.8
1878.........	445.7		94.3	101.9	92.5
1879.........	418.1		88.5	97.7	90.6
1880.........	465.6		98.6	93.0	106.0
1881.........	408.6		86.6	88.0	98.4
1882.........	425.8	471.41	90.3	85.2	106.0
1883.........	394.6		83.6	84.4	99.1
1884.........	343.7		72.7	84.1	85.3

TABLE 32a (*continued*)

	I	II	III	IV	V
1885.........	334.3		70.6	84.2	83.8
1886.........	339.6		71.6	85.0	84.2
1887.........	360.8	474.65	76.0	86.0	88.4
1888.........	429.3		90.1	87.0	103.6
1889.........	465.3		97.4	88.1	110.6
1890.........	558.8		116.6	89.2	130.7
1891.........	561.3		116.7	90.3	129.2
1892.........	508.7	482.57	105.4	91.4	115.3
1893.........	414.0		85.3	92.5	92.2
1894.........	372.7		76.4	93.6	81.6
1895.........	357.6		71.7	94.8	75.6
1896.........	405.0		82.0	96.0	85.4
1897.........	428.0	495.18	86.4	97.1	89.0
1898.........	496.4		99.6	98.2	101.4
1899.........	607.5		121.0	99.3	121.9
1900.........	499.8		98.9	100.4	98.5
1901.........	419.7		82.5	101.5	81.3
1902.........	454.2	512.47	88.6	102.6	86.4
1903.........	512.7		99.2	103.6	95.8
1904.........	553.4		106.2	104.6	101.5
1905.........	620.8		118.1	105.5	111.9
1906.........	666.1		125.7	106.2	118.4
1907.........	589.6	534.45	110.3	106.7	103.4
1908.........	496.4		92.0	106.7	86.2
1909.........	545.4		100.1	106.3	94.2
1910.........	569.7		103.5	105.4	98.2
1911.........	625.6		112.6	104.4	107.9
1912.........	650.5	561.11	115.9	103.1	112.4
1913.........	565.8		99.7	101.7	98.0
1914.........	533.0		92.9	100.3	92.6

Sources of data: Up to 1890, H. Denis, *loc. cit.*, pp. 319–20; from 1890, *Annuaire Statistique de la Belgique*.

Equation of the primary trend line:

$$y = 614.16 - 36.58\,x + 2.3425\,x^2$$

x in units of 5 years, origin at 1842.

Column IV: smoothed moving average of 11 years.

TABLE 33. WHEAT CROPS, GERMANY, 1878–1914

Columns I and II in millions of metric quintals

	I	II	III	IV	V
1878.......	26.2		129.6	110.3	117.5
1879.......	22.9		109.1	109.1	100.0
1880.......	23.5	21.74	108.1	107.7	100.4
1881.......	20.7		92.0	106.2	86.6
1882.......	25.6		110.1	104.7	105.2
1883.......	23.6		98.3	103.2	95.3
1884.......	24.9		100.5	101.7	98.8
1885.......	26.0	25.53	101.9	100.1	101.8
1886.......	26.7		101.6	98.5	103.1
1887.......	28.3		104.7	96.7	108.3
1888.......	25.3		91.2	94.6	96.4
1889.......	23.8		83.6	91.3	91.6
1890.......	28.3	29.23	96.8	91.1	106.3
1891.......	23.3		77.8	94.0	82.8
1892.......	31.6		103.3	98.5	104.9
1893.......	34.1		109.0	101.0	107.9
1894.......	33.4		104.5	102.6	101.9
1895.......	31.7	32.65	97.1	103.2	94.1
1896.......	34.2		102.9	103.6	99.3
1897.......	32.6		96.2	103.6	92.9
1898.......	36.1		104.7	103.3	101.4
1899.......	38.5		109.8	102.6	107.0
1900.......	38.4	35.66	107.7	101.9	105.9
1901.......	25.0		69.1	100.7	68.6
1902.......	39.0		106.3	99.7	106.6
1903.......	35.6		95.6	98.8	96.8
1904.......	38.0		100.8	97.9	103.0
1905.......	37.0	38.22	96.8	97.1	99.7
1906.......	39.4		102.0	96.5	105.7
1907.......	34.8		89.1	95.9	92.9
1908.......	37.7		95.5	95.6	99.9
1909.......	37.6		94.3	96.1	98.1

TABLE 33 (*continued*)

	I	II	III	IV	V
1910.......	38.6	40.30	95.7	98.5	97.2
1911.......	40.7		100.1	101.1	99.0
1912.......	43.6		106.3	102.8	103.4
1913.......	46.6		112.8	103.8	108.7
1914.......	39.7		95.3	104.4	91.3

Source of data: *Annuaire Statistique de France*, vol. 36, 1919–20, p. 223*.

Equation of the primary trend line:

$$y = \frac{47.02}{1 + 10^{-0.21559 - 0.28113\ x}}$$

x in units of 10 years, origin at 1890.

Column IV: smoothed moving average of 5 years.

TABLE 33a. PRICE OF WHEAT, LEIPZIG, 1881–1914

Columns I and II in marks per 1000 kilo

	I	II	III	IV	V
1881..........	232.9		114.2	102.0	112.0
1882..........	214.0		108.0	102.0	105.9
1883..........	174.7	193.24	90.4	102.0	88.6
1884..........	176.4		92.9	102.0	91.1
1885..........	167.2		89.7	102.0	87.9
1886..........	162.6		88.8	102.0	87.1
1887..........	170.1		94.7	102.0	92.8
1888..........	180.9	176.34	102.6	102.0	100.6
1889..........	186.5		106.9	101.9	104.9
1890..........	191.7		111.0	101.8	109.0
1891..........	224.1		131.1	101.6	129.0
1892..........	188.3		111.3	101.3	109.9
1893..........	155.1	167.34	92.7	100.9	91.9
1894..........	133.3		79.8	100.2	79.7
1895..........	139.8		83.8	99.0	84.6
1896..........	157.8		94.7	95.5	99.2
1897..........	162.1		97.4	94.5	103.1
1898..........	189.6	166.24	114.1	93.9	121.5
1899..........	154.6		92.2	93.7	98.4
1900..........	146.3		86.6	93.7	92.4
1901..........	165.4		97.1	93.8	103.5
1902..........	164.1		95.6	94.1	101.6
1903..........	153.1	173.03	88.5	94.6	93.6
1904..........	171.9		97.7	96.3	101.5
1905..........	172.7		96.5	99.2	97.3
1906..........	172.7		95.0	102.7	92.5
1907..........	205.2		111.1	104.8	106.0
1908..........	206.9	187.72	110.2	105.6	104.4
1909..........	230.4		119.9	105.8	113.4
1910..........	205.4		104.4	105.4	99.1
1911..........	198.9		98.8	103.4	95.6
1912..........	209.1		101.6	100.5	101.1
1913..........	193.5	210.30	92.0	97.6	94.3
1914..........	211.1		97.6	95.0	102.7

Sources of data: *Statistisches Handbuch fuer d. Deutsche Reich*, Berlin, 1907, p. 474. *Statistisches Jahrbuch f. d. D. Reich*, 1907 and successive issues.

Equation of the primary trend line:

$$y = 218.03 - 28.738\,x + 3.94762\,x^2$$

x in units of 5 years, origin at 1878.

Column IV: smoothed moving average of 9 and 7 years.

TABLE 34. OUTPUT OF COAL, BITUMINOUS AND LIGNITE,
GERMANY, 1860–1914

Columns I and II in thousands of metric tons

	I	II	III	IV	V
1860......	16,730	17,988	93.0	97.0	95.9
1861......	18,755		97.7	99.0	98.7
1862......	20,661		101.2	102.0	99.2
1863......	22,366		103.4	104.5	98.9
1864......	25,613		112.1	106.5	105.3
1865......	28,553	24,071	118.6	108.0	109.8
1866......	28,163		109.7	109.4	100.3
1867......	30,803		113.0	110.6	102.2
1868......	32,879		113.9	111.7	102.0
1869......	34,344		112.7	112.5	100.2
1870......	34,003	32,068	106.0	113.0	93.8
1871......	37,856		110.8	113.4	97.7
1872......	42,324		116.7	113.6	102.7
1873......	46,145		120.3	113.4	106.1
1874......	46,658		115.4	112.0	103.0
1875......	47,804	42,538	112.4	110.6	101.6
1876......	49,550		109.5	109.2	100.3
1877......	48,230		100.6	107.8	93.3
1878......	50,520		99.7	106.4	.93.7
1879......	53,471		100.2	105.2	95.3
1880......	59,118	56,074	105.4	104.0	101.3
1881......	61,540		103.4	103.0	100.4
1882......	65,378		103.8	102.0	101.8
1883......	70,443		106.0	100.9	105.1
1884......	72,114		103.2	99.7	103.5
1885......	73,676	73,333	100.5	98.4	102.1
1886......	73,683		94.9	97.0	97.8
1887......	76,233		93.0	95.7	97.0
1888......	81,960		95.0	94.3	100.7
1889......	84,973		93.8	93.0	100.9
1890......	89,291	94,949	94.0	91.9	102.3
1891......	94,253		94.0	90.9	103.4
1892......	92,544		87.7	90.0	97.4
1893......	95,426		86.1	89.3	96.4
1894......	98,806		85.1	88.8	95.8
1895......	103,957	121,412	85.6	88.8	96.4
1896......	112,471		88.1	89.0	99.0
1897......	120,475		89.9	89.7	100.2
1898......	127,959		91.2	90.5	100.8
1899......	135,845		92.6	91.4	101.3

TABLE 34 (*continued*)

	I	II	III	IV	V
1900......	149,788	152,933	97.9	92.2	106.2
1901......	153,019		95.5	92.9	102.8
1902......	150,600		89.9	93.6	96.0
1903......	162,457		93.0	94.3	98.6
1904......	169,451		93.1	95.0	98.0
1905......	173,811	189,257	91.8	95.7	95.9
1906......	193,538		98.1	96.4	101.8
1907......	205,733		100.2	97.1	103.2
1908......	213,286		99.8	97.8	102.1
1909......	217,446		98.1	98.5	99.6
1910......	222,375	229,630	96.8	99.2	97.6
1911......	234,521		98.4	100.0	98.4
1912......	257,215		104.2	101.0	103.2
1913......	277,225		108.5	102.3	106.3
1914......	245,332		92.9	103.0	90.2
1915......		272,662			

Sources of data: Up to 1898, J. M. Swank, *History of the Manufacture of Iron in All Ages*, Philadelphia, 1892, p. 522; 1899–1905, *Statistisches Handbuch, f.d. D.R.*, p. 252; from 1906, *Statistisches Jahrbuch*, successive issues.

Equation of the primary trend line:

$$y = \frac{581,970}{1 + 10^{1.49628 - 0.13104\,x}}$$

x in units of 5 years, origin at 1860.

Column IV: smoothed moving average of 13 years.

TABLE 34a. PRICE OF BITUMINOUS COAL, GERMANY,
1860–1913

Columns I and II in marks per ton

	I	II	III	IV	V
1860.........	6.41		99.2	81.2	122.2
1861.........	5.72		89.6	83.0	107.9
1862.........	5.33	6.310	84.5	84.8	99.6
1863.........	5.06		80.8	86.6	93.3
1864.........	5.18		83.4	88.4	94.2
1865.........	5.53		89.7	90.2	99.4
1866.........	5.88		95.2	92.0	103.5
1867.........	5.77	6.071	95.0	95.0	100.0
1868.........	5.67		93.7	101.0	92.8
1869.........	5.82		96.5	109.2	88.4
1870.........	6.20		103.1	124.7	82.7
1871.........	7.43		124.0	129.1	96.1
1872.........	8.91	5.975	149.1	131.4	113.5
1873.........	11.09		185.3	131.9	140.5
1874.........	10.78		179.9	130.3	138.1
1875.........	7.95		132.5	127.6	103.8
1876.........	6.86		114.1	123.1	92.7
1877.........	5.78	6.021	96.0	115.6	83.0
1878.........	5.25		86.7	104.7	82.8
1879.........	4.89		80.2	90.0	89.1
1880.........	5.23		85.3	84.0	101.5
1881.........	5.18		83.9	82.0	102.3
1882.........	5.14	6.210	82.8	81.0	102.2
1883.........	5.25		83.7	81.0	103.3
1884.........	5.22		82.3	82.0	100.4
1885.........	5.19		81.0	83.5	97.0
1886.........	5.18		80.0	85.7	93.3
1887.........	5.16	6.542	78.9	87.9	89.8
1888.........	5.22		78.7	90.0	87.4
1889.........	5.72		85.0	92.1	92.3
1890.........	7.66		112.2	93.5	120.0
1891.........	8.00		115.6	94.9	121.8
1892.........	7.38	7.016	105.2	96.2	109.4
1893.........	6.75		94.6	97.2	97.3
1894.........	6.63		91.3	98.0	93.2
1895.........	6.81		92.2	98.8	93.3
1896.........	6.92		92.2	99.6	92.6
1897.........	7.13	7.633	93.4	100.4	93.0
1898.........	7.37		94.7	100.8	93.9
1899.........	7.77		98.0	101.2	96.8

TABLE 34a (*continued*)

	I	II	III	IV	V
1900..........	8.84		109.3	101.6	107.6
1901..........	9.35		113.5	101.9	111.4
1902..........	8.84	8.393	105.3	102.1	103.1
1903..........	8.62		100.5	102.2	98.3
1904..........	8.56		97.8	102.3	95.6
1905..........	8.66		96.9	102.4	94.6
1906..........	8.93		98.0	102.4	95.7
1907..........	9.74	9.295	104.8	102.4	102.3
1908..........	10.31		108.5	102.3	106.1
1909..........	10.41		107.2	102.2	104.9
1910..........	10.16		102.4	102.1	100.3
1911..........	9.93		98.0	101.9	96.1
1912..........	10.52	10.340	101.7	101.7	100.0
1913..........	11.23		106.2	101.4	104.7

Sources of data: *Statistisches Handbuch f.d. D.R.*, p. 252; from 1906, *Statistisches Jahrbuch*, successive issues.

Equation of the primary trend line:

$$y = 6.692 - 0.4531\,x + 0.07314\,x^2$$

x in units of 5 years, origin at 1857.

Column IV: smoothed moving average of 9 years.

TABLE 35. CONSUMPTION OF PIG IRON, GERMANY, 1860–1913

Columns I and II in thousands of metric tons

	I	II	III	IV	V
1860....	636	860	74.0	80.0	92.5
1861....	719		78.5	82.3	95.4
1862....	836		86.0	84.8	101.4
1863....	955		92.9	87.3	106.4
1864....	1,002		92.4	89.8	102.9
1865....	1,109	1,141	97.2	92.6	105.0
1866....	1,167		96.0	95.6	100.4
1867 ...	1,201		93.1	99.0	94.0
1868....	1,299		95.2	104.8	90.8
1869....	1,501		104.3	110.8	94.1
1870....	1,510	1,515	99.7	114.0	87.5
1871....	1,892		117.3	116.0	101.1
1872....	2,501		146.0	116.6	125.2
1873....	2,830		156.2	116.4	134.2
1874....	2,234		116.9	115.0	101.7
1875....	2,316	2,009	115.3	112.9	102.1
1876....	2,123		99.2	110.1	90.1
1877....	2,094		92.2	107.4	85.8
1878....	2,202		91.6	105.4	86.9
1879....	2,171		85.7	104.0	82.4
1880....	2,663	2,665	99.9	103.0	97.0
1881....	2,835		99.9	102.2	97.7
1882....	3,409		113.2	101.6	111.4
1883....	3,418		107.3	100.9	106.3
1884....	3,584		106.7	100.2	106.5
1885....	3,646	3,533	103.2	99.6	103.6
1886....	3,382		89.9	99.0	90.8
1887....	3,900		97.7	98.4	99.3
1888....	4,373		103.6	97.8	105.9
1889....	4,674		105.0	97.2	108.0
1890....	4,897	4,681	104.6	96.6	108.3
1891....	4,711		94.5	96.1	98.3
1892....	4,966		93.9	95.6	98.2
1893....	5,032		90.0	95.3	94.4
1894....	5,350		90.8	95.3	95.3
1895....	5,434	6,196	87.7	95.9	91.5
1896....	6,538		99.1	97.0	102.2
1897....	7,171		102.5	98.4	104.2
1898....	7,403		100.1	99.2	100.9
1899....	8,535		109.5	99.6	109.9

Table 35 *(continued)*

	I	II	III	IV	V
1900........	9,106	8,193	111.1	99.6	111.4
1901........	7,823		89.7	99.4	90.2
1902........	8,144		88.1	99.1	88.9
1903........	9,657		98.9	98.7	100.2
1904........	9,917		96.4	98.3	98.1
1905........	10,513	10,816	97.2	97.9	99.3
1906........	12,149		105.6	97.6	108.2
1907........	13,016		106.8	97.3	109.8
1908........	11,712		90.9	97.1	93.6
1909........	12,252		90.3	97.0	93.1
1910........	14,163	14,253	99.4	97.2	102.3
1911........	14,886		98.3	97.6	100.7
1912........	16,775		104.6	98.1	106.6
1913........	18,594		109.8	99.0	110.9

Sources of data: *Statistisches Jahrbuch f.d. D.R.*, collected by H. G. Villard, National Bureau of Economic Research, Inc.

Equation of the primary trend line:

$$y = \frac{439,934}{1 + 10^{1.96840-0.24661\,x}}$$

x in units of 10 years, origin at 1890.

Column IV: smoothed moving average of 9 years.

TABLE 35a. PIG IRON PRICES, GERMANY, 1850–1910

Columns I and II in marks per ton

	I	II	III	IV	V
1850..........	92.4		70.7	85.2	83.0
1851..........	87.0		68.9	86.1	80.0
1852..........	87.0	121.78	71.4	87.1	82.0
1853..........	116.0		98.3	88.1	111.6
1854..........	135.0		118.3	89.1	132.8
1855..........	135.2		122.5	90.1	136.0
1856..........	93.0		87.3	91.1	95.8
1857..........	99.0	102.73	96.4	92.1	104.7
1858..........	89.6		90.0	93.1	96.7
1859..........	85.0		88.2	94.2	93.6
1860..........	75.0		80.5	95.3	84.5
1861..........	70.0		77.8	96.4	80.7
1862..........	79.0	86.74	91.1	97.5	93.4
1863..........	81.0		96.1	98.9	97.2
1864..........	84.0		103.0	100.5	102.5
1865..........	89.2		113.0	102.6	110.1
1866..........	87.0		113.9	105.6	107.9
1867..........	75.2	73.80	101.9	114.0	89.4
1868..........	72.2		100.5	119.5	84.1
1869..........	77.6		111.1	123.2	90.3
1870..........	75.6		111.4	125.6	88.7
1871..........	82.0		124.5	126.3	98.6
1872..........	117.4	63.91	183.7	126.7	145.0
1873..........	125.2		200.2	126.8	157.9
1874..........	79.8		130.5	126.6	103.1
1875..........	69.7		116.6	126.1	92.5
1876..........	57.8		98.9	125.2	79.0
1877..........	61.0	57.07	106.9	122.0	87.6
1878..........	55.4		98.4	116.4	84.5
1879..........	51.7		93.1	110.7	84.1
1880..........	66.8		121.9	108.4	112.5
1881..........	55.6		102.9	106.8	96.3
1882..........	66.1	53.28	124.1	105.3	117.9
1883..........	57.8		108.8	103.8	104.8
1884..........	54.5		102.9	102.4	100.5
1885..........	48.3		91.4	101.0	90.4
1886..........	43.5		82.6	99.8	82.8
1887..........	49.5	52.54	94.2	98.6	95.5
1888..........	52.2		98.5	97.3	101.2
1889..........	58.5		109.4	96.1	113.8

TABLE 35a (continued)

	I	II	III	IV	V
1890.........	66.6		123.5	95.2	129.7
1891.........	48.2		88.6	95.1	93.2
1892.........	48.0	54.86	87.5	95.4	91.6
1893.........	50.2		89.8	95.7	93.8
1894.........	49.3		86.5	96.0	80.7
1895.........	48.3		83.2	96.3	86.4
1896.........	57.9		97.9	96.6	101.4
1897.........	61.3	60.22	101.8	96.8	105.2
1898.........	59.7		96.4	97.0	99.4
1899.........	72.1		113.4	97.2	116.7
1900.........	88.0		134.8	97.2	138.7
1901.........	66.5		99.2	96.8	102.5
1902.........	61.3	68.64	89.3	96.3	92.7
1903.........	60.5		85.3	95.3	89.5
1904.........	59.5		81.3	93.9	86.6
1905.........	59.8		79.2	92.3	85.8
1906.........	69.6		89.4	90.5	98.8
1907.........	77.6	80.11	96.9	88.5	109.5
1908.........	71.1		85.7	86.5	99.1
1909.........	64.2		74.7	84.3	88.6
1910.........	66.3		74.7	82.1	91.0

Sources of data: Up to 1881, L. Hertel, *Die Preisentwicklung d. Unedlen Metalen u. Steinkohle seit 1850*, Halle a. Saale, 1911, p. 114 (Schlesien); 1881–1905, *Statistisches Handbuch fuer d. D.R.*, p. 479; (Breslau iron); 1906, *Statistisches Jahrbuch, f.d. D.R.*, successive issues.

Equation of the primary trend line:

$$y = 143.87 - 23.621\,x + 1.5256\,x^2$$

x in units of 5 years, origin at 1847.

Column IV: smoothed moving average of 11 years.

TABLE 36. CRUDE STEEL OUTPUT, GERMANY, 1879–1913

Columns I and II in thousands of metric tons

	I	II	III	IV	V
1879........	478		81.2	100.7	80.6
1880........	624	662	94.3	100.7	93.6
1881........	840		114.3	100.7	113.5
1882........	1,003		124.3	100.6	123.5
1883........	860		97.8	100.0	97.8
1884........	863		86.1	93.0	92.6
1885........	894	1,124	79.5	84.8	93.6
1886........	955		76.7	82.5	93.0
1887........	1,164		85.1	82.4	103.3
1888........	1,299		87.1	83.0	104.9
1889........	1,425		84.3	83.6	100.8
1890........	1,614	1,894	85.2	84.4	100.9
1891........	1,841		87.8	85.4	102.8
1892........	1,977		86.0	86.7	99.2
1893........	2,232		89.3	88.4	101.0
1894........	2,608		92.1	90.5	101.8
1895........	2,830	3,163	89.5	93.3	95.9
1896........	3,463		99.1	96.6	102.6
1897........	3,863		100.9	100.0	100.9
1898........	4,353		104.7	105.9	98.9
1899........	4,791		102.0	110.3	92.5
1900........	6,646	5,239	126.8	116.4	106.4
1901........	6,394		110.6	119.2	92.8
1902........	7,781		123.1	120.4	102.2
1903........	8,802		128.3	120.6	106.4
1904........	8,930		115.5	120.4	95.9
1905........	10,067	8,608	116.9	119.0	98.2
1906........	11,308		119.3	114.5	104.2
1907........	12,064		116.5	109.3	106.6
1908........	11,186		99.6	105.2	94.7
1909........	12,050		95.4	101.0	94.5
1910........	13,699	14,027	97.7	99.2	98.5
1911........	15,019		97.4	99.6	97.8
1912........	17,302		102.8	101.4	101.4
1913........	18,935	18,226	103.9	102.9	101.0

Source of data: Stahl u. Eisen (data of the Verein f. Deutsche Ingen-
iere), collected by H. G. Villard, National Bureau of Economic Research,
Inc.

Equation of the primary trend line:

$$\log y = 2.71263 + 14.2547(1 - 0.967686^x)$$

x in units of 10 years, origin at 1879.

Column IV: smoothed moving average of 5 years.

TABLE 36a. PRICES OF INGOTS AND STEEL BILLETS,
GERMANY, 1877–1910

Columns I and II in marks per ton

	I	II	III	IV	V
1877......	304.8		159.9	123.0	130.0
1878......	192.1		107.1	111.6	96.0
1879......	140.9	167.99	83.9	101.5	82.7
1880......	146.3		91.9	93.0	98.8
1881......	143.2		95.2	85.0	112.0
1882......	133.7		94.3	82.9	113.8
1883......	109.0		82.0	82.4	99.5
1884......	98.8	124.22	79.5	82.0	97.0
1885......	84.6		71.7	82.0	87.4
1886......	76.5		68.4	82.1	83.3
1887......	75.9		71.8	85.0	84.5
1888......	83.7		84.1	88.0	95.6
1889......	86.8	93.32	93.0	91.0	102.2
1890......	96.3		107.3	94.0	114.1
1891......	85.8		99.6	97.5	102.2
1892......	79.0		95.7	101.0	94.8
1893......	74.7		94.7	104.0	91.1
1894......	72.0	75.31	95.6	107.0	89.3
1895......	71.0		95.6	109.5	87.3
1896......	77.7		106.1	112.0	94.7
1897......	84.2		116.6	114.5	101.6
1898......	85.6		120.2	117.0	102.6
1899......	91.9	70.18	130.9	118.6	110.4
1900......	107.2		152.8	119.0	128.4
1901......	88.4		126.0	118.9	106.0
1902......	80.0		114.1	118.1	96.6
1903......	78.4		111.8	116.5	96.0
1904......	78.8	70.12	112.4	114.0	98.6
1905......	80.1		105.7	110.0	96.1
1906......	84.8		104.1	106.0	98.2
1907......	96.7		111.0	102.0	108.8
1908......	86.3		93.0	97.0	95.9
1909......	85.6	98.51	86.8	92.0	94.3
1910......	87.0		82.7	87.0	95.1

Sources of data: Up to 1906, *Statistisches Handbuch f.d. D.R.*, p. 266;
from 1906, *Statistisches Jahrbuch*, successive issues.

Equation of the primary trend line:

$$y = 224.63 - 63.0833\,x + 6.4381\,x^2$$

x in units of 5 years, origin at 1874.

Column IV: smoothed moving average of 11 years.

TABLE 37. COPPER PRODUCTION, MANSFIELD WORKS,
GERMANY, 1860–1913

Columns I and II in metric tons

	I	II	III	IV	V
1860........	1,501	1,224	122.6		
1865........	2,113	2,202	96.0		
1870........	3,803	3,806	99.9		
1875........	6,039	6,189	97.6		
1879........	8,500	8,442	98.4	105.1	93.6
1880........	9,900	9,248	107.1	105.8	101.2
1881........	11,200		113.1	106.4	106.3
1882........	11,700		110.8	106.9	103.6
1883........	12,800		114.1	106.9	106.7
1884........	12,800		107.9	106.1	101.7
1885........	12,600	12,515	100.7	104.7	96.2
1886........	12,800		97.7	103.3	94.6
1887........	13,200		96.5	101.9	94.7
1888........	13,600		95.5	100.3	95.2
1889........	15,800		106.6	98.6	108.1
1890........	16,100	15,386	104.6	96.6	108.3
1891........	14,400		91.0	94.7	96.1
1892........	15,600		96.1	92.8	103.6
1893........	14,400		86.4	91.6	94.3
1894........	15,200		88.9	92.0	96.6
1895........	15,100	17,508	86.2	94.0	91.7
1896........	18,500		104.0	97.4	106.8
1897........	18,300		101.3	100.8	100.5
1898........	18,300		99.8	102.1	97.7
1899........	21,100		113.4	102.6	110.5
1900........	18,700	18,833	99.0	102.6	96.5
1901........	19,100		100.2	102.0	98.2
1902........	19,100		99.4	100.9	98.5
1903........	19,300		99.6	98.9	100.7
1904........	19,000		97.2	96.8	100.4
1905........	19,900	19,701	101.0	94.7	106.7
1906........	18,100		91.4	93.3	97.9
1907........	17,300		87.0	92.8	93.8
1908........	18,000		90.1	93.2	96.7
1909........	19,000		94.6	94.9	99.6

TABLE 37 *(continued)*

	I	II	III	IV	V
1910........	20,300	20,162	100.7	97.1	103.7
1911........	20,900		103.4	99.4	104.0
1912........	20,500		101.1	101.8	99.3
1913........	20,300		99.9	103.9	96.2

Source of data: F. W. Franke, *Abriss d. neuesten Wirtschaftsgeschichte d. Kupfers*, p. 45.

Equation of the primary trend line:

$$y = \frac{20,705}{1 + 10^{0.92453 - 0.27717\, x}}$$

x in units of 5 years, origin at 1865.

Column IV: smoothed moving average of 5 years.

TABLE 37a. PRICE OF COPPER, HAMBURG AND FRANKFURT,
1851–1914

Columns I and II in marks per 100 kilo

	I	II	III	IV	V
1851......	169.9		74.4	89.6	83.0
1852......	175.4		78.4	92.0	85.2
1853......	200.1	219.01	91.4	94.2	97.0
1854......	224.0		104.3	96.4	108.2
1855......	223.2		106.0	98.2	107.0
1856......	228.3		110.6	99.6	111.0
1857......	224.5		111.0	100.8	110.1
1858......	205.7	198.06	103.9	101.8	102.1
1859......	187.8		96.6	102.4	94.3
1860......	203.1		106.5	103.0	103.4
1861......	190.7		101.9	103.2	98.7
1862......	188.4		102.7	103.3	99.4
1863......	177.9	179.74	99.0	103.2	95.9
1864......	195.8		110.9	102.8	107.9
1865......	174.3		100.5	102.2	98.3
1866......	187.0		109.7	101.4	108.2
1867......	169.4		101.3	100.8	100.5
1868......	154.9	164.06	93.9	100.6	93.3
1869......	156.8		97.1	100.7	96.4
1870......	150.8		94.9	104.9	90.5
1871......	156.0		99.9	110.2	90.7
1872......	190.8		124.2	112.8	110.1
1873......	191.5	151.01	126.8	114.6	110.6
1874......	178.1		119.6	115.4	103.6
1875......	183.1		124.7	115.6	107.9
1876......	181.4		125.3	115.4	108.6
1877......	167.7		117.5	114.2	102.9
1878......	151.5	140.60	107.8	111.5	96.7
1879......	136.2		98.0	107.9	90.8
1880......	129.8		94.4	104.0	90.8
1881......	131.9		97.0	98.3	98.7
1882......	140.5		104.6	94.6	110.6
1883......	135.2	132.82	101.8	91.1	111.7
1884......	119.1		90.4	88.6	102.0
1885......	95.3		72.9	86.9	83.9
1886......	86.4		66.6	85.4	78.0
1887......	94.1		73.1	84.4	86.6
1888......	154.2	127.67	120.8	83.9	144.0
1889......	110.9		87.2	83.9	103.9

TABLE 37a (*continued*)

	I	II	III	IV	V
1890..........	121.3		95.8	83.9	114.2
1891..........	111.5		88.4	83.9	105.4
1892..........	97.9		77.9	83.9	92.8
1893..........	95.0	125.16	75.9	84.1	90.2
1894..........	85.8		68.5	85.0	80.6
1895..........	93.2		74.4	86.3	86.2
1896..........	100.6		80.3	88.3	90.9
1897..........	103.1		82.3	91.9	89.6
1898..........	110.2	125.28	88.0	95.3	92.3
1899..........	155.2		123.3	98.6	125.1
1900..........	153.3		121.3	101.8	119.2
1901..........	146.7		115.6	104.8	110.3
1902..........	111.5		87.5	106.4	82.2
1903..........	123.2	128.04	96.2	107.3	89.7
1904..........	123.7		95.8	107.8	88.9
1905..........	147.0		112.9	108.1	104.4
1906..........	183.1		139.5	108.3	128.8
1907..........	189.3		143.0	108.1	132.3
1908..........	124.6	133.43	93.4	107.6	86.8
1909..........	122.3		90.6	106.8	84.8
1910..........	120.0		87.8	105.8	83.0
1911..........	117.8		85.2	104.7	81.4
1912..........	153.4		109.7	103.5	106.0
1913..........	145.1	141.45	102.6	102.3	100.3
1914..........	152.3		106.1	101.0	105.0

Sources of data: Up to 1881, L. Hertel, *loc. cit.*, p. 116; 1881–1905, *Statistisches Handbuch fuer d. D.R.*, p. 479 (Frankfurt price); from 1906, *Statistisches Jahrbuch d. D.R.*, successive issues.

Equation of the primary trend line:

$$y = 242.59 - 24.901\,x + 1.317\,x^2$$

x in units of 5 years, origin at 1848.

Column IV: smoothed moving average of 9 years.

TABLE 38. CRUDE ZINC PRODUCTION, GERMANY, 1845–1913

Columns I and II in thousands of metric tons

	I	II	III	IV	V
1845.........	17.1	23.84	71.7	79.0	90.8
1846.........	22.3		88.9	81.3	109.3
1847.........	22.4		85.2	84.0	101.4
1848.........	20.2		73.1	87.1	83.9
1849.........	26.3		90.5	89.8	100.8
1850.........	28.7	30.38	94.4	92.3	102.3
1851.........	30.6		96.2	94.8	101.5
1852.........	34.7		104.2	97.3	107.1
1853.........	34.7		99.4	99.6	99.8
1854.........	36.9		100.9	101.9	99.0
1855.........	38.3	38.15	100.3	104.2	96.3
1856.........	38.3		96.2	106.4	90.4
1857.........	43.6		104.8	108.6	96.5
1858.........	52.8		121.5	110.7	109.8
1859.........	49.3		108.7	112.2	96.8
1860.........	55.3	47.24	117.2	112.9	103.8
1861.........	58.6		119.0	113.1	105.2
1862.........	59.8		116.6	112.5	103.6
1863.........	60.3		113.0	110.6	102.2
1864.........	59.2		106.6	108.0	98.7
1865.........	56.5	57.75	97.8	105.4	92.8
1866.........	60.2		100.4	102.7	97.8
1867.........	63.9		102.4	100.0	102.4
1868.........	66.1		102.1	97.3	104.9
1869.........	69.9		103.8	94.6	109.7
1870.........	64.0	69.76	91.7	92.1	99.6
1871.........	58.3		80.6	90.3	89.3
1872.........	58.4		77.9	89.0	87.5
1873.........	62.8		80.8	88.6	91.2
1874.........	70.4		87.5	89.8	97.4
1875.........	74.3	83.29	89.2	92.5	96.4
1876.........	83.2		96.6	95.8	100.8
1877.........	95.0		106.6	98.8	107.9
1878.........	95.0		103.0	101.1	101.9
1879.........	96.8		101.5	102.9	98.6
1880.........	99.6	98.39	101.3	104.5	96.9
1881.........	105.5		103.9	105.9	98.1
1882.........	113.4		108.2	107.2	100.9
1883.........	116.9		107.7	108.2	99.5
1884.........	125.3		112.2	108.9	103.0

TABLE 38 (*continued*)

	I	II	III	IV	V
1885..........	129.1	115.05	112.2	109.2	102.7
1886..........	130.9		110.5	109.0	101.4
1887..........	130.4		106.9	108.2	98.8
1888..........	133.2		105.9	106.8	99.2
1889..........	136.0		108.1	105.1	102.9
1890..........	132.3	133.39	104.4	103.4	101.0
1891..........	139.4		101.6	102.0	99.6
1892..........	139.9		99.2	100.6	98.6
1893..........	142.9		98.6	99.2	99.4
1894..........	143.6		96.3	97.9	98.4
1895..........	150.3	153.05	98.2	96.7	101.6
1896..........	153.1		97.4	95.5	102.2
1897..........	150.7		93.4	94.4	98.9
1898..........	154.9		93.5	93.7	99.8
1899..........	153.2		90.1	93.3	96.6
1900..........	155.8	174.27	89.4	93.8	95.3
1901..........	166.3		93.1	94.4	98.6
1902..........	174.9		95.5	95.4	100.1
1903..........	182.5		97.2	96.6	100.6
1904..........	193.1		100.4	97.9	102.6
1905..........	198.2	196.91	100.7	99.2	101.5
1906..........	205.7		102.1	100.4	101.7
1907..........	208.2		100.9	101.8	99.1
1908..........	216.5		102.5	103.3	99.2
1909..........	219.8		101.7	104.8	97.0
1910..........	221.4	220.93	100.2	106.6	94.0
1911..........	243.8		108.0	108.4	99.6
1912..........	269.2		116.7	110.2	105.9
1913..........	278.9	235.79	118.3	112.0	105.6

Sources of data: Up to 1900, W. R. Ingalls, *Production and Properties of Zinc*, New York, 1902, p. 71; from 1900, *Annuaire Statistique de France*.

Equation of the primary trend line:

$$\log y = 1.35608 + 1.760944(1 - 0.750518^x)$$

x in units of 23 years, origin at 1844.

Column IV: smoothed moving average of 7 years.

TABLE 38a. PRICES OF ZINC, BRESLAU, 1850–1913

Columns I and II in marks per metric ton

	I	II	III	IV	V
1850............	255		68.1	81.0	84.1
1851............	246		66.2	84.0	78.8
1852............	264	368.4	71.7	87.0	82.4
1853............	335		91.6	90.0	101.8
1854............	379		104.3	93.2	111.9
1855............	394		109.1	97.5	111.9
1856............	437		122.0	99.7	122.4
1857............	448	355.8	125.8	101.5	124.0
1858............	389		109.8	102.7	106.9
1859............	363		103.2	103.6	99.6
1860............	344		98.1	104.4	94.0
1861............	313		89.6	105.0	85.3
1862............	315	347.1	90.8	105.4	86.1
1863............	314		90.7	105.8	85.7
1864............	396		114.7	106.3	107.9
1865............	382		111.0	106.9	103.8
1866............	392		114.2	107.6	106.1
1867............	389	342.2	113.7	108.8	104.5
1868............	378		110.5	111.9	98.7
1869............	382		111.8	115.2	97.0
1870............	349		102.2	116.7	87.6
1871............	357		104.6	117.6	88.9
1872............	408	341.2	119.6	118.0	101.4
1873............	478		139.9	117.2	119.4
1874............	423		123.6	115.5	107.0
1875............	454		132.4	113.3	116.9
1876............	431		125.5	111.0	113.1
1877............	368	344.0	107.0	108.0	99.1
1878............	322		93.2	103.6	90.0
1879............	300		86.4	96.8	89.3
1880............	340		97.5	89.6	108.8
1881............	304		86.8	85.9	101.0
1882............	316	351.7	89.9	84.3	106.6
1883............	286		80.9	83.3	97.1
1884............	227		63.9	83.3	76.7
1885............	261		73.0	84.5	86.4
1886............	267		74.3	85.9	86.5
1887............	284	361.2	78.6	87.2	90.1
1888............	354		97.2	88.4	110.0
1889............	383		104.4	89.6	115.5

TABLE 38a *(continued)*

	I	II	III	IV	V
1890............	451		122.0	90.7	134.6
1891............	450		120.8	91.7	131.7
1892............	405	375.5	107.8	92.7	116.2
1893............	336		88.6	93.7	94.6
1894............	299		78.1	94.6	82.6
1895............	283		73.2	95.5	76.6
1896............	316		81.0	96.4	84.0
1897............	339	393.8	86.1	97.2	88.6
1898............	395		99.2	98.0	101.2
1899............	481		119.5	98.8	121.0
1900............	395		97.1	99.6	97.5
1901............	330		80.2	100.3	80.0
1902............	355	415.8	85.4	101.0	84.6
1903............	404		96.0	101.6	94.5
1904............	438		102.8	102.2	100.6
1905............	498		115.5	102.8	112.4
1906............	533		122.1	103.4	118.1
1907............	478	441.7	108.2	103.9	104.1
1908............	398		88.9	104.4	85.2
1909............	451		99.4	104.8	94.8
1910............	471		102.5	105.2	97.4
1911............	508		109.1	105.5	103.4
1912............	534	471.5	113.3	105.7	107.2
1913............	473		98.9	105.9	93.4

Sources of data: Up to 1892, L. Hertel, *loc. cit.*, pp. 116–17; 1892–1905, *Statistisches Handbuch fuer das D.R.*, p. 479; 1906 and on, *Statistisches Jahrbuch d. D.R.*, successive issues.

Equation of the primary trend line:
$$y = 382.81 - 18.346x + 1.224x^2$$

x in units of 5 years, origin at 1847.

Column IV: smoothed moving average of 11 years.

TABLE 39. CONSUMPTION OF RAW COTTON, GERMANY, 1836–1913

Columns I and II in tons

	I	II	III
1836–1840................	8,917	8,912	100.1
1841–1845................	13,246	12,735	104.0
1846–1850................	15,782	18,145	87.0
1851–1855................	26,441	25,087	102.5
1856–1860................	46,529	36,341	128.0
1861–1865................	46,831	51,001	91.8
1866–1870................	68,281	70,526	96.8
1871–1875................	116,390	96,522	120.6
1876–1880................	124,549	129,327	96.3
1881–1885................	152,329	169,886	89.7
1886–1890................	201,046	216,630	92.8
1891–1895................	252,381	268,529	94.0
1896–1900................	302,316	321,536	94.0
1901–1905................	361,701	373,308	96.9
1906–1910................	419,840	419,807	100.0
1911....................	436,928		98.4
1912....................	501,660		111.4
1913....................	481,156	459,878	104.6

Sources of data: Up to 1906, *Statistisches Handbuch f.d. D.R.*, p. 491; from 1906, *Statistisches Jahrbuch*, successive issues.

Equation of the primary trend line:

$$y = \frac{587889.5}{1 + 10^{1.81267 - 0.15787\,x}}$$

x in units of 5 years, origin at 1836–40.

Table 39a. Index of Wholesale Prices, Germany,
O. Schmitz, 1851–1913

Relatives, 1851–1913 = 100

1851–1855	105.96	1891–1895	83.04
1856–1860	110.24	1896–1900	84.04
1861–1865	108.89	1901–1905	90.97
1866–1870	108.04	1906–1910	101.27
1871–1875	118.08		
1876–1880	101.62	1911	107.43
1881–1885	92.54	1912	117.78
1886–1890	87.32	1913	114.76

Source of data: U.S. Bureau of Labor Statistics, Bulletin no. 284, p. 254, table 52.

TABLE 40. WHEAT CROPS, FRANCE, 1815–1913

Columns I and II in millions of hectolitres

	I	II	III	IV	V
1815...........	39.5	45.0	87.8	100.4	87.5
1816...........	43.3		94.0	100.6	93.4
1817...........	48.0		101.9	100.8	101.1
1818...........	52.7		109.4	101.0	108.3
1819...........				101.2	
1820...........	44.3	50.3	,88.1	101.3	87.0
1821...........	58.2		113.2	101.4	111.6
1822...........	50.9		96.9	101.5	95.5
1823...........	58.7		109.4	101.6	107.7
1824...........	61.8		112.8	101.6	111.0
1825...........	61.0	55.9	109.1	101.6	107.4
1826...........	59.6		104.5	101.6	103.4
1827...........	56.8		97.7	101.5	96.3
1828...........	58.8		99.2	101.4	97.8
1829...........	64.3		106.5	101.2	105.2
1830...........	52.8	61.5	85.9	101.0	85.0
1831...........	56.4		90.0	100.8	89.3
1832...........	80.1		125.5	100.5	124.9
1833...........	66.1		101.7	100.2	101.5
1834...........	67.0		101.3	99.9	101.4
1835...........	71.7	67.3	106.5	99.6	106.9
1836...........	67.6		98.7	99.3	99.4
1837...........	67.9		97.5	98.9	98.6
1838...........	63.7		90.0	98.5	91.4
1839...........	64.9		90.2	98.2	91.9
1840...........	80.9	73.1	110.7	97.7	113.3
1841...........	71.5		96.3	97.1	99.2
1842...........	71.3		94.6	96.7	97.8
1843...........	73.7		96.4	96.5	99.9
1844...........	82.5		106.3	96.5	110.2
1845...........	72.0	78.7	91.5	96.6	94.7
1846...........	60.7		76.1	97.0	78.5
1847...........	97.6		120.6	97.4	123.8
1848...........	88.0		107.3	97.9	109.6
1849...........	90.8		109.3	98.4	111.1
1850...........	88.0	84.2	104.5	99.0	105.6
1851...........	86.0		100.9	99.6	101.3
1852...........	86.1		99.8	100.2	99.6
1853.........	63.7		73.0	100.7	72.5
1854...........	97.2		110.0	101.4	108.5

TABLE 40 (*continued*)

	I	II	III	IV	V
1855............	72.9	89.4	81.5	102.0	79.9
1856............	85.3		94.4	102.5	92.1
1857............	110.4		122.1	102.7	118.9
1858............	110.0		119.0	102.6	116.0
1859............	87.6		93.8	102.5	91.5
1860............	101.6	94.4	107.6	102.3	105.2
1861............	75.1		78.8	102.0	77.3
1862............	99.3		103.2	101.6	101.6
1863............	116.8		120.2	101.1	118.9
1864............	111.3		113.5	100.8	112.6
1865............	95.6	99.0	96.6	100.7	95.9
1866............	85.1		85.2	100.6	84.7
1867............	83.0		82.4	100.9	81.7
1868............	116.8		115.1	101.7	113.2
1869............	107.9	103.2	105.4	102.7	102.6
		96.9			
1870............				103.7	
1871............	69.3		71.0	104.7	67.8
1872............	120.8		122.9	105.5	116.5
1873............	81.9		82.8	105.9	78.2
1874............	133.1		133.6	105.9	126.2
1875............	106.1	100.3	105.8	105.7	100.1
1876............	95.4		94.5	105.2	89.8
1877............	100.1		98.5	104.7	94.1
1878............	95.3		93.2	104.2	89.4
1879............	79.4		77.2	103.6	74.5
1880............	99.5	103.5	96.1	102.9	93.4
1881............	96.8		93.0	102.2	91.0
1882............	122.2		116.8	101.5	115.1
1883............	103.8		98.6	100.7	97.9
1884............	114.2		107.9	99.7	108.2
1885............	109.9	106.4	103.3	98.7	104.7
1886............	107.3		100.3	97.2	103.2
1887............	112.5		104.7	95.8	109.3
1888............	98.7		91.3	94.7	96.4
1889............	108.3		99.8	93.9	106.3
1890............	116.9	109.1	107.1	93.3	114.8
1891............	77.3		70.5	93.2	75.6
1892............	109.5		99.5	93.8	106.1
1893............	97.8		88.4	94.7	93.3
1894............	122.5		109.8	95.7	114.7

TABLE 40 (*continued*)

	I	II	III	IV	V
1895............	120.0	111.6	107.5	96.7	111.2
1896............	119.7		106.8	97.7	109.3
1897............	86.9		77.2	98.7	78.2
1898............	128.3		113.6	99.7	113.9
1899............	128.4		113.2	100.6	112.5
1900............	114.7	113.9	100.7	101.3	99.4
1901............	109.6		95.9	101.6	94.4
1902............	115.5		100.7	101.7	99.0
1903............	128.4		111.5	101.7	109.6
1904............	106.3		92.0	101.5	90.6
1905............	118.2	116.0	101.9	101.1	100.8
1906............	114.5		98.4	100.7	97.7
1907............	132.9		113.8	100.2	113.6
1908............	112.0		95.7	99.5	96.2
1909............	125.5		106.8	98.3	108.6
1910............	90.8	117.9	77.0	97.2	79.2
1911............	111.0		93.9	95.7	98.1
1912............	118.5		99.9	94.4	105.8
1913............	113.1	118.9	95.1	93.3	101.9

Source of data: *Annuaire Statistique de France*, vol. 36, 1919–20, pp. 50*–51*.

Equation of the primary trend line:

For 1815–70, $y = \dfrac{133.53}{1 + 10^{-0.00694-0.22523\,x}}$

x in units of 15 years, origin 1835.

For 1871–1913, $y = \dfrac{133.82}{1 + 10^{-0.47605-0.16879\,x}}$

x in units of 15 years, origin at 1875.

Column IV: smoothed moving average of 11 years.

TABLE 40a. WHEAT PRICES, FRANCE, 1815–1913

Columns I and II in francs per hectolitre

	I	II	III	IV	V
1815...........	19.53		98.0	122.1	80.3
1816...........	28.31		141.7	117.1	121.0
1817...........	36.16	20.04	180.4	112.6	160.2
1818...........	24.65		122.6	108.1	113.4
1819...........	18.42		91.4	104.1	87.8
1820...........	19.13		94.7	100.1	94.6
1821...........	17.79		87.8	97.1	90.4
1822...........	15.49	20.31	76.3	94.6	80.7
1823...........	17.52		86.1	92.3	93.3
1824...........	16.22		79.5	90.8	87.6
1825...........	15.74		77.0	89.7	85.8
1826...........	15.85		77.4	89.0	87.0
1827...........	18.21	20.53	88.7	88.6	100.1
1828...........	22.03		107.1	88.4	121.2
1929...........	22.59		109.6	88.3	124.1
1830...........	22.39		108.5	88.3	122.9
1831...........	22.10		106.9	88.3	121.1
1832...........	21.85	20.70	105.6	88.4	119.5
1833...........	15.62		75.3	88.6	85.0
1834...........	15.25		73.5	88.9	82.7
1835...........	15.25		73.4	89.3	82.2
1836...........	17.32		83.2	90.0	92.4
1837...........	18.53	20.84	88.9	90.9	97.8
1838...........	19.51		93.5	92.1	101.5
1839...........	22.14		106.0	93.4	113.5
1840...........	21.84		104.5	95.1	109.9
1841...........	18.54		88.7	96.8	91.6
1842...........	19.55	20.92	93.5	98.3	95.1
1843...........	20.46		97.8	100.3	97.5
1844...........	19.75		94.3	102.2	92.3
1845...........	19.75		94.3	104.1	90.6
1846...........	24.05		114.8	105.9	107.6
1847...........	29.01	20.95	138.5	107.3	129.1
1848...........	16.65		79.5	108.3	73.4
1849...........	15.37		73.4	109.2	67.2
1850...........	14.32		68.4	109.9	62.2
1851...........	14.48		69.1	110.5	62.5
1852...........	17.23	20.96	82.2	110.9	74.1
1853...........	22.39		106.9	111.1	96.2
1854...........	28.82		137.6	111.1	123.9

TABLE 40a (*continued*)

	I	II	III	IV	V
1855...........	29.32		140.2	111.1	126.2
1856...........	30.75		147.1	110.9	132.6
1857...........	24.37	20.88	116.7	109.9	106.2
1858...........	16.75		80.3	106.6	75.3
1859...........	16.74		80.3	102.1	78.6
1860...........	20.24		97.2	100.1	97.1
1861...........	24.55		118.0	99.3	118.8
1862...........	23.24	20.79	111.8	99.3	112.6
1863...........	19.78		95.3	99.9	95.4
1864...........	17.80		85.9	102.1	84.1
1865...........	16.94		81.8	106.6	76.7
1866...........	19.59		94.8	111.0	85.4
1867...........	26.02	20.64	126.1	113.1	111.5
1868...........	26.08		126.5	114.9	110.1
1869...........	20.21		98.2	115.9	84.7
1870...........				116.0	
1871...........	26.65		130.1	116.1	112.1
1872...........	22.90	20.45	112.0	116.0	96.6
1873...........	25.70		125.9	115.3	109.2
1874...........	24.31		119.3	114.1	104.6
1875...........	19.38		95.3	112.6	84.6
1876...........	20.64		101.8	110.9	91.8
1877...........	23.42	20.23	115.8	108.9	106.3
1878...........	23.08		114.4	106.9	107.0
1879...........	21.92		109.0	104.9	103.9
1880...........	22.90		114.2	102.9	111.0
1881...........	22.28		111.5	100.9	110.5
1882...........	21.51	19.93	107.9	99.0	109.0
1883...........	19.16		96.4	97.1	99.3
1884...........	17.76		89.7	95.4	94.0
1885...........	16.41		83.1	93.9	88.5
1886...........	16.54		84.1	92.5	90.9
1887...........	17.71	19.60	90.3	91.3	98.9
1888...........	18.79		96.2	90.3	106.5
1889...........	18.09		93.0	89.5	103.9
1890...........	18.96		97.8	88.9	110.0
1891...........	20.54		106.4	88.4	120.4
1892...........	17.84	19.23	92.8	88.0	105.5
1893...........	16.21		84.6	87.6	96.6
1894...........	14.84		77.8	87.2	89.2

TABLE 40a (*continued*)

	I	II	III	IV	V
1895...........	14.06		74.0	87.1	85.0
1896...........	14.33		75.8	87.1	87.0
1897...........	18.80	18.81	99.9	87.1	114.7
1898...........	19.62		104.9	87.3	120.2
1899...........	15.02		80.7	87.6	92.1
1900...........	14.45		77.9	88.0	88.5
1901...........	15.16		82.2	88.5	92.9
1902...........	16.21	18.34	88.4	89.1	99.2
1903...........	17.03		93.4	89.9	103.9
1904...........	16.31		89.9	91.1	98.7
1905...........	17.56		97.3	92.7	105.0
1906...........	17.61		98.2	94.6	103.8
1907...........	18.03	17.83	101.1	97.3	103.9
1908...........	17.25		97.3	100.0	97.3
1909...........	18.15		103.1	102.8	100.3
1910...........	19.10		109.1	105.9	103.0
1911...........	20.28		116.6	108.9	107.1
1912...........	21.29	**17.27**	123.3	112.9	109.2
1913...........	20.73		120.9	115.9	104.3

Source of data: *Annuaire Statistique de France*, vol. 36, pp. 50*–51*.

Equation of the primary trend line:

$$y = 19.73 + 0.335x - 0.0229x^2$$

x in units of 5 years, origin at 1812.

Column IV: smoothed moving average of 11 years.

TABLE 41. OUTPUT OF COAL (COMBUSTIBLES MINERAUX), FRANCE, 1810–1913

	I	II	III	IV	V
1810.......		590			
1811.......	774		123.3	117.5	104.9
1812.......	836		125.4	115.7	108.4
1813.......	772		109.4	113.9	96.1
1814.......	788		105.8	112.1	94.4
1815.......	882	784	112.5	110.3	102.0
1816.......	942		112.7	108.7	103.7
1817.......	1,003		112.9	107.2	105.3
1818.......	898		95.5	105.7	90.3
1819.......	964		97.2	104.9	92.7
1820.......	1,094	1,044	104.8	104.2	100.6
1821.......	1,135		102.0	103.5	98.6
1822.......	1,194		101.1	102.9	98.3
1823.......	1,195		95.6	102.4	93.4
1824.......	1,326		100.6	102.1	98.5
1825.......	1,491	1,387	107.5	101.9	105.5
1826.......	1,541		104.3	101.7	102.6
1827.......	1,691		107.9	101.6	106.1
1828.......	1,774		107.1	101.6	105.4
1829.......	1,742		99.7	101.6	98.1
1830.......	1,863	1,838	101.4	101.6	99.7
1831.......	1,760		90.0	101.6	88.6
1832.......	1,963		94.7	101.6	93.2
1833.......	2,058		93.9	101.6	92.4
1834.......	2,490		107.8	101.6	106.1
1835.......	2,506	2,427	103.3	101.6	101.6
1836.......	2,842		110.2	101.6	108.4
1837.......	2,981		109.1	101.6	107.4
1838.......	3,113		107.9	101.5	106.3
1839.......	2,995		98.6	101.4	97.2
1840.......	3,003	3,192	94.1	101.1	93.1
1841.......	3,410		100.6	100.7	99.9
1842.......	3,592		100.2	99.3	100.9
1843.......	3,693		97.7	98.3	99.4
1844.......	3,783		95.1	96.3	98.8
1845.......	4,202	4,175	100.7	94.3	106.8
1846.......	4,469		101.0	93.5	108.0
1847.......	5,153		110.3	93.2	118.3
1848.......	4,000		81.2	93.1	87.2
1849.......	4,049		78.3	93.0	84.2

TABLE 41 *(continued)*

	I	II	III	IV	V
1850.........	4,434	5,423	81.8	93.0	88.0
1851.........	4,484		78.2	93.0	84.1
1852.........	4,904		81.1	93.0	86.6
1853.........	5,938		93.4	93.2	100.2
1854.........	6,827		102.4	93.6	109.4
1855.........	7,453	6,982	106.8	94.1	113.5
1856.........	7,926		107.6	95.0	113.3
1857.........	7,902		102.0	96.4	105.8
1858.........	7,353		90.5	97.6	92.7
1859.........	7,483		87.9	98.6	89.1
1860.........	8,304	8,892	93.4	99.6	93.8
1861.........	9,423		100.8	100.4	100.4
1862.........	10,290		104.9	101.0	103.9
1863.........	10,710		104.4	101.5	102.9
1864.........	11,243		104.9	101.9	102.9
1865.........	11,600	11,176	103.8	102.2	101.6
1866.........	12,260		104.7	102.3	102.3
1867.........	12,739		104.1	102.4	101.7
1868.........	13,254		103.8	102.5	101.3
1869.........	13,464		101.2	102.3	98.9
1870.........	13,330	13,831	96.2	101.9	94.4
1871.........	13,259		91.9	101.3	90.7
1872.........	15,803		105.2	100.6	104.6
1873.........	17,479		111.8	99.9	111.9
1874.........	16,908		104.2	99.2	105.0
1875.........	16,957	16,816	100.8	98.4	102.4
1876.........	17,101		97.9	97.6	100.3
1877.........	16,805		92.8	96.7	96.0
1878.........	16,961		90.4	95.7	94.5
1879.........	17,111		88.2	94.7	93.1
1880.........	19,362	20,048	96.6	93.7	103.1
1881.........	19,766		95.4	92.6	103.0
1882.........	20,604		96.3	92.0	104.7
1883.........	21,334		96.7	91.5	105.7
1884.........	20,024		88.1	91.2	96.6
1885.........	19,511	23,413	83.3	91.1	91.4
1886.........	19,910		82.7	91.1	90.8
1887.........	21,288		86.0	91.1	94.4
1888.........	22,603		88.9	91.2	97.5
1889.........	24,304		93.1	91.4	101.9

TABLE 41 (*continued*)

	I	II	III	IV	V
1890.......	26,083	26,764	97.5	91.9	106.1
1891.......	26,025		95.0	92.5	102.7
1892.......	26,179		93.3	93.2	100.1
1893.......	25,651		89.4	93.9	95.2
1894.......	27,417		93.5	94.7	98.7
1895.......	28,020	29,972	93.5	95.4	98.0
1896.......	29,190		95.5	96.0	99.5
1897.......	30,798		98.9	96.4	102.6
1898.......	32,356		101.9	96.8	105.3
1899.......	32,863		101.6	97.2	104.5
1900.......	33,404	32,920	101.5	97.6	104.0
1901.......	32,325		96.7	98.0	98.7
1902.......	29,997		88.9	98.4	90.4
1903.......	34,906		101.2	98.8	102.4
1904.......	34,168		97.6	99.2	98.4
1905.......	35,928	35,530	101.1	99.6	101.6
1906.......	34,196		95.0	100.0	95.0
1907.......	36,754		100.9	100.5	100.4
1908.......	37,384		101.4	101.0	100.4
1909.......	37,840		101.4	101.4	100.0
1910.......	38,350	37,769	101.5	101.8	99.7
1911.......	39,230		102.9	102.2	100.7
1912.......	41,145		106.8	102.6	104.1
1913.......	40,844		105.0	103.0	101.9

Source of data: *Annuaire Statistique de France*, vol. 36, 1919-20, pp. 55*-56*.

Equation of the primary trend line:

$$y = \frac{46,406}{1 + 10^{0.87840 - 0.12657 x}}$$

x in units of 5 years, origin at 1850.

Column IV: smoothed moving average of 13 years.

TABLE 41a. AVERAGE PRICE OF COAL, FRANCE,
1814–1913
Columns I and II in francs per ton

	I	II	III	IV	V
1814............	10.02		101.4	107.0	94.8
1815............	10.82		109.3	106.8	102.3
1816............	10.40	9.92	104.8	106.5	98.4
1817............	10.57		106.3	106.2	100.1
1818............	10.73		107.7	105.9	101.8
1819............	10.82		108.4	105.5	102.7
1820............	10.54		105.3	105.1	100.2
1821............	10.73	10.03	107.0	104.6	102.3
1822............	10.46		104.1	103.9	100.2
1823............	10.53		104.6	103.1	101.4
1824............	10.16		100.6	102.3	98.3
1825............	10.12		100.0	101.3	98.7
1826............	10.52	10.14	103.7	100.4	103.3
1827............	10.35		101.8	99.5	102.3
1828............	9.98		97.9	98.7	99.2
1829............	9.70		94.9	98.0	96.8
1830............	9.75		95.1	97.3	97.7
1831............	9.66	10.28	94.0	96.6	97.3
1832............	9.56		92.8	96.0	96.7
1833............	10.26		99.3	95.4	104.1
1834............	9.49		91.6	94.8	96.6
1835............	9.60		92.4	94.3	98.0
1836............	10.29	10.42	98.7	93.8	105.2
1837............	10.09		96.5	93.3	103.4
1838............	9.93		94.7	92.9	101.9
1839............	9.68		92.1	92.5	99.6
1840............	9.75		92.4	92.1	100.3
1841............	9.70	10.58	91.7	91.7	100.0
1842............	9.30		87.6	91.3	96.0
1843............	9.12		85.7	91.0	94.2
1844............	9.66		90.5	90.7	99.8
1845............	9.45		88.3	90.4	97.7
1846............	9.84	10.74	91.6	90.1	101.6
1847............	9.70		90.0	90.2	99.8
1848............	10.06		93.0	90.9	102.3
1849............	10.06		92.7	92.5	100.2
1850............	9.74		89.4	94.1	95.1
1851............	9.60	10.93	87.8	96.3	91.2
1852............	9.50		86.6	98.0	88.4
1853............	10.05		91.3	99.2	92.0
1854............	10.96		99.3	100.4	98.9

TABLE 41a (*continued*)

	I	II	III	IV	V
1855...........	12.17		109.8	101.5	108.2
1856...........	12.87	11.12	115.7	102.6	112.8
1857...........	12.60		112.9	103.5	109.1
1858...........	12.46		111.2	104.4	106.5
1859...........	12.69		112.9	105.0	107.5
1860...........	11.61		103.2	105.2	98.1
1861...........	11.55	11.33	102.0	105.2	97.0
1862...........	11.51		101.2	105.0	96.4
1863...........	11.31		99.1	104.1	95.2
1864...........	11.28		98.5	102.8	95.8
1865...........	11.47		99.7	102.4	97.4
1866...........	11.79	11.55	102.1	102.3	99.8
1867...........	12.23		105.5	102.3	103.1
1868...........	11.63		100.0	102.5	97.6
1869...........	11.62		100.0	103.9	96.2
1870...........	11.69		99.6	106.0	94.0
1871...........	12.39	11.78	105.1	109.0	96.4
1872...........	13.46		113.8	110.5	103.0
1873...........	16.61		139.9	111.1	125.9
1874...........	16.53		138.7	111.4	124.5
1875...........	15.93		133.1	111.5	119.4
1876...........	15.33	12.02	127.5	111.5	114.3
1877...........	14.06		116.5	111.5	104.5
1878...........	13.46		111.1	111.2	99.9
1879...........	12.93		106.2	110.7	95.9
1880...........	12.74		104.3	109.4	95.3
1881...........	12.43	12.27	101.3	107.6	94.1
1882...........	12.36		100.3	104.9	95.6
1883...........	12.50		101.0	100.9	100.1
1884...........	12.33		99.2	97.5	101.7
1885...........	11.73		93.9	95.4	98.4
1886...........	11.19	12.54	89.2	94.0	94.9
1887...........	10.63		84.4	92.7	91.5
1888...........	10.31		81.5	91.5	89.1
1889...........	10.42		82.0	90.4	90.7
1890...........	11.94		93.6	89.3	104.8
1891...........	13.25	12.82	103.4	88.5	116.8
1892...........	12.40		96.3	88.0	109.4
1893...........	11.49		88.8	88.0	100.9
1894...........	11.22		86.3	88.9	97.1

TABLE 41a (*continued*)

	I	II	III	IV	V
1895...........	11.01		84.3	90.5	93.1
1896...........	10.84	13.11	82.7	92.1	89.8
1897...........	10.85		82.4	93.7	87.9
1898...........	11.22		85.4	95.1	89.8
1899...........	12.41		93.4	96.4	96.9
1900...........	14.05		105.2	97.7	107.7
1901...........	15.79	13.42	116.9	99.0	118.1
1902...........	14.65		107.9	100.3	107.6
1903...........	14.10		103.5	101.6	101.9
1904...........	13.37		97.8	102.9	95.0
1905...........	12.99		94.5	104.2	90.7
1906...........	13.70	13.73	99.8	105.4	94.7
1907...........	14.97		108.5	106.5	101.9
1908...........	15.84		114.3	107.4	106.4
1909...........	15.29		109.8	108.2	101.5
1910...........	14.50		103.6	109.0	95.0
1911...........	15.24	14.06	108.4	109.7	98.8
1912...........	15.51		109.8	110.3	99.5
1913...........	16.55		116.5	110.8	105.1

Source of data: *Annuaire Statistique de France*, vol. 36, 1919–20, pp. 55*–56*.

Equation of the primary trend line:

$$y = 9.75 + 0.15 x + 0.02 x^2$$

x in units of 5 years, origin at 1811.

Column IV: smoothed moving average of 13 years.

TABLE 42. CONSUMPTION OF PETROLEUM, FRANCE, 1866–1913

Columns I and II in thousands of quintals

	I	II	III	IV	V
1866...........	252	212	118.9	99.0	120.0
1867...........	151		63.6	99.0	64.2
1868...........	262		99.9	98.9	101.0
1869...........	311		108.1	98.6	109.6
1870...........	328	313	104.8	98.1	106.8
1871...........	316		89.4	97.4	92.8
1872...........	395		100.1	96.3	103.9
1873...........	483		111.0	95.1	116.7
1874...........	402		84.4	93.9	89.9
1875...........	394	577	76.2	93.2	81.8
1876...........	560		96.5	93.5	103.2
1877...........	729		113.3	94.4	120.0
1878...........	563		79.6	95.7	83.2
1879...........	746		96.8	97.2	99.6
1880...........	758	835	90.8	98.9	91.8
1881...........	1,081		116.5	100.1	116.4
1882...........	929		90.9	100.7	90.3
1883...........	1,128		101.1	100.9	100.2
1884...........	1,233		102.0	100.8	101.2
1885...........	1,374	1,303	105.5	100.6	104.9
1886...........	1,395		97.5	100.3	97.2
1887...........	1,518		97.5	99.7	97.8
1888...........	1,705		101.2	98.9	102.3
1889...........	1,821		100.5	97.9	102.7
1890...........	1,964	1,938	101.3	96.5	105.0
1891...........	1,921		91.8	93.4	98.3
1892...........	2,130		94.7	100.8	94.0
1893...........	2,588		107.7	104.4	103.2
1894...........	2,926		114.4	106.2	107.7
1895...........	2,908	2,711	107.3	107.2	100.1
1896...........	2,997		104.2	107.0	97.4
1897...........	3,155		103.8	105.8	98.1
1898...........	3,391		105.8	104.6	101.1
1899...........	3,364		99.8	103.6	96.3
1900...........	3,506	3,535	99.2	102.7	96.6
1901...........	3,834		104.0	101.6	102.4
1902...........	3,792		98.8	100.8	98.0
1903...........	4,255		106.6	100.0	106.6
1904...........	3,939		95.1	99.2	95.9

TABLE 42 (*continued*)

	I	II	III	IV	V
1905..........	4,878	4,298	113.5	98.6	115.1
1906..........	3,538		80.0	98.9	80.9
1907..........	4,307		94.7	99.6	95.1
1908..........	4,895		104.8	100.4	104.4
1909..........	6,011		125.4	101.2	123.9
1910..........	4,128	4,918	83.9	102.0	82.3
1911..........	5,206		103.9	102.8	101.1
1912..........	5,446		106.8	103.6	103.1
1913..........	5,461	5,190	105.2	104.5	100.7

Source of data: *Annuaire Statistique de France*, vol. 36, pp. 123*–24*.

Equation of the primary trend line:

$$y = \frac{6168.2}{1 + 10^{1.27249 - 0.23341\,x}}$$

x in units of 5 years, origin at 1870.

Column IV: smoothed moving average of 5 years.

TABLE 42a. PRICES OF CRUDE PETROLEUM, FRANCE,
1865–1914

Centimes per kilo

	I	II	III	IV	V
1865...............	45		105.4	99.6	105.8
1866...............	40		96.9	98.2	98.7
1867...............	36	39.82	90.4	97.4	92.8
1868...............	35		91.6	95.4	96.0
1869...............	35		95.5	94.6	101.0
1870...............	35		99.9	94.0	106.3
1871...............	28		83.7	94.6	88.5
1872...............	35	31.89	109.8	103.0	106.6
1873...............	32		104.7	110.0	95.2
1874...............	30		102.6	114.8	89.4
1875...............	30		107.5	118.0	91.1
1876...............	40		150.5	119.9	125.5
1877...............	35	25.24	138.7	119.9	115.7
1878...............	35		144.9	117.6	123.2
1879...............	19		82.3	110.0	74.8
1880...............	19		86.3	97.2	88.8
1881...............	18		85.9	92.0	93.4
1882...............	18	19.88	90.5	90.0	100.6
1883...............	18		94.4	89.4	105.6
1884...............	17		93.2	89.2	104.5
1885...............	17		97.5	89.7	108.7
1886...............	15		90.3	91.3	98.9
1887...............	13	15.81	82.2	95.0	86.5
1888...............	14		91.8	98.6	93.1
1889...............	17		115.7	100.4	115.2
1890...............	17		120.3	100.8	119.3
1891...............	15		110.5	100.0	110.5
1892...............	14	13.03	107.4	92.0	116.7
1893...............	7		54.9	82.7	66.4
1894...............	8		64.3	82.3	78.1
1895...............	11		90.5	83.6	108.3
1896...............	10		84.2	85.7	98.3
1897...............	9	11.59	77.7	88.4	87.9
1898...............	10		86.7	91.6	94.7
1899...............	12		104.4	94.2	110.8
1900...............	12		104.9	95.6	109.7
1901...............	11		96.6	96.0	100.6
1902...............	11	11.34	97.0	95.9	101.1
1903...............	12		103.9	94.7	109.7
1904...............	12		102.0	92.0	110.9

TABLE 42a (*continued*)

	I	II	III	IV	V
1905...............	10		83.4	89.0	93.7
1906...............	11		90.1	86.6	104.0
1907...............	11	12.43	88.5	84.7	104.5
1908...............	11		85.3	83.1	102.6
1909...............	11		82.3	82.1	100.2
1910...............	10		72.2	82.2	87.8
1911...............	11		76.8	91.0	84.4
1912...............	16	14.81	108.0	101.0	106.9
1913...............	20		128.7	106.8	120.5
1914...............	21		129.1	110.0	117.4

Source of data: *Annuaire Statistique de France*, vol. 36, 1919–20, pp. 102*–03*.

Equation of the primary trend line:

$$y = 49.05 - 9.871\,x + 0.6447\,x^2$$

x in units of 5 years, origin at 1862.

Column IV: smoothed moving average of 7 years.

TABLE 43. PRODUCTION OF PIG IRON, FRANCE,
1824–1913

Columns I and II in thousands of metric tons

	I	II	III	IV	V
1824..........	198		94.1	89.3	105.4
1825..........	199	220	90.5	88.5	102.3
1826..........	206		89.9	87.9	102.3
1827..........	220		92.3	87.3	105.7
1828..........	227		91.6	87.0	105.3
1829..........	219		85.2	86.7	98.3
1830..........	225	266	84.4	86.6	97.5
1831..........	229		82.5	86.8	95.0
1832..........	225		77.9	87.1	89.4
1833..........	236		78.7	87.5	89.9
1834..........	269		86.4	88.2	98.0
1835..........	295	323	91.4	89.2	102.5
1836..........	308		91.7	91.0	100.8
1837..........	332		95.0	94.0	101.1
1838..........	348		95.9	97.4	98.5
1839..........	350		93.0	100.3	92.7
1840..........	403	390	103.4	102.1	101.3
1841..........	436		107.4	103.3	104.0
1842..........	455		108.1	103.9	104.0
1843..........	478		109.1	104.0	104.9
1844..........	483		106.4	103.5	102.8
1845..........	498	470	105.9	101.3	104.5
1846..........	586		119.8	98.5	121.6
1847..........	592		116.4	97.4	119.5
1848..........	472		89.5	97.3	92.0
1849..........	414		75.7	97.3	77.8
1850..........	406	566	71.8	97.5	73.6
1851..........	446		75.8	99.0	76.6
1852..........	523		85.6	101.0	84.8
1853..........	661		104.3	105.0	99.3
1854..........	771		117.5	108.8	108.0
1855..........	849	679	125.1	112.5	111.2
1856..........	923		130.8	116.0	112.8
1857..........	992		135.5	119.0	113.9
1858..........	872		114.9	120.5	95.4
1859..........	864		110.0	121.3	90.7

TABLE 43 (*continued*)

	I	II	III	IV	V
1860..........	898	812	110.6	121.7	90.9
1861..........	967		114.7	121.8	94.2
1862..........	1,091		124.8	121.7	102.5
1863..........	1,157		127.8	120.8	105.8
1864..........	1,213		129.5	119.7	108.2
1865..........	1,204	968	124.4	118.5	105.0
1866..........	1,260		125.6	117.3	107.1
1867..........	1,229		118.2	115.4	102.4
1868..........	1,235		114.8	113.5	101.1
1869..........	1,381		124.2	111.5	111.4
1870..........	1,178	1,148	102.7	109.5	93.8
1871..........	860		72.3	107.5	67.3
1872..........	1,288		104.7	105.5	99.2
1873..........	1,382		108.7	103.7	104.8
1874..........	1,416		107.9	102.5	105.3
1875..........	1,448	1,354	106.9	101.7	105.1
1876..........	1,435		102.4	102.0	100.4
1877..........	1,507		104.1	104.5	99.6
1878..........	1,521		101.8	105.8	96.2
1879..........	1,400		90.8	106.8	85.0
1880..........	1,725	1,588	108.6	107.0	101.5
1881..........	1,886		114.9	107.1	107.3
1882..........	2,039		120.4	106.0	113.6
1883..........	2,069		118.5	103.0	115.0
1884..........	1,872		104.1	100.0	104.1
1885..........	1,631	1,851	88.1	97.0	90.8
1886..........	1,517		79.5	94.0	84.6
1887..........	1,568		79.7	91.8	86.8
1888..........	1,683		83.1	89.7	92.6
1889..........	1,734		83.2	87.7	94.9
1890..........	1,962	2,141	91.6	86.4	106.0
1891..........	1,897		86.1	86.4	99.7
1892..........	2,057		90.7	86.8	104.5
1893..........	2,003		85.9	87.5	98.2
1894..........	2,069		86.4	88.1	98.1
1895..........	2,003	2,457	81.5	88.8	91.8
1896..........	2,339		92.6	89.5	103.5
1897..........	2,484		95.8	90.3	106.1
1898..........	2,525		94.9	91.1	104.2
1899..........	2,578		94.5	92.0	102.7

TABLE 43 (continued)

	I	II	III	IV	V
1900..........	2,714	2,796	97.1	92.9	104.5
1901..........	2,389		83.3	93.8	88.8
1902..........	2,405		81.9	94.7	86.5
1903..........	2,841		94.4	95.6	98.7
1904..........	2,974		96.6	96.6	100.0
1905..........	3,077	3,150	97.7	98.3	99.4
1906..........	3,314		102.8	101.0	101.8
1907..........	3,590		108.9	104.0	104.7
1908..........	3,401		100.9	107.5	93.9
1909..........	3,574		103.8	112.5	92.3
1910..........	4,038	3,516	114.8	116.5	98.5
1911..........	4,470		124.5	119.5	104.2
1912..........	4,939		134.8	121.4	111.0
1913..........	5,207	3,734	139.4	122.8	109.1

Source of data: *Annuaire Statistique de France*, vol. 36, 1919–20, pp. 57*–58*.

Equation of the primary trend line:

$$y = \frac{7452.7}{1 + 10^{1.17173 - 0.08368\,x}}$$

x in units of 5 years, origin at 1845.

Column IV: smoothed moving average of 7 years.

TABLE 43a. AVERAGE PRICE OF PIG IRON, FRANCE,
1830–1913

Columns I and II in francs per ton

	I	II	III	IV	V
1830............	190		96.4	94.6	101.9
1831............	180		92.7	95.4	97.2
1832............	180	191.3	94.1	96.6	97.4
1833............	172		91.2	97.3	93.7
1834............	184		99.1	97.7	101.4
1835............	186		101.7	98.0	103.8
1836............	198		109.9	97.7	112.5
1837............	183	177.5	103.1	97.0	106.3
1838............	182		104.1	96.2	108.2
1839............	181		105.1	95.4	110.2
1840............	141		83.1	94.7	87.8
1841............	142		85.0	94.0	90.4
1842............	140	164.4	85.2	93.3	91.3
1843............	134		82.8	92.7	89.3
1844............	128		80.3	92.1	87.2
1845............	136		86.7	91.9	94.3
1846............	153		99.0	92.6	106.9
1847............	180	152.1	118.3	94.0	125.9
1848............	145		96.9	96.6	100.3
1849............	138		93.7	100.0	93.7
1850............	132		91.0	105.0	86.7
1851............	135		94.6	108.1	87.5
1852............	143	140.4	101.9	109.9	92.7
1853............	158		114.3	111.4	102.6
1854............	167		122.8	112.5	109.2
1855............	176		131.5	113.2	116.2
1856............	173		131.3	113.7	115.5
1857............	160	129.4	123.6	114.0	108.4
1858............	143		112.3	113.8	98.7
1859............	135		107.8	113.0	95.4
1860............	129		104.7	110.4	94.8
1861............	126		104.0	106.0	98.1
1862............	122	119.2	102.4	102.1	100.3
1863............	118		100.6	98.6	102.0
1864............	112		97.1	96.0	101.1

TABLE 43a (*continued*)

	I	II	III	IV	V
1865.............	106		93.4	94.5	98.8
1866.............	104		93.2	93.0	100.2
1867.............	96	109.7	87.5	92.5	94.6
1868.............	92		85.3	93.5	91.2
1869.............	91		85.8	96.5	88.9
1870.............	92		88.2	100.5	87.8
1871.............	98		95.5	105.0	91.0
1872.............	121	100.9	119.9	107.5	111.5
1873.............	137		138.1	108.5	127.3
1874.............	119		122.1	108.8	112.2
1875.............	108		112.6	108.5	103.8
1876.............	98	92.7	103.9	108.1	96.1
1877.............	95		102.5	107.5	95.3
1878.............	88		96.5	106.0	91.0
1879.............	85		94.8	104.3	90.9
1880.............	93		105.4	99.2	106.2
1881.............	91		105.0	95.6	109.8
1882.............	91	85.3	106.7	92.9	114.9
1883.............	81		96.5	90.6	106.5
1884.............	75		90.8	88.4	102.7
1885.............	62		76.3	86.7	88.0
1886.............	55		68.8	85.0	80.9
1887.............	57	78.7	72.4	83.4	86.8
1888.............	57		73.5	82.1	89.5
1889.............	61		79.9	80.9	98.8
1890.............	70		93.2	80.4	115.9
1891.............	65		88.0	80.9	108.8
1892.............	61	72.7	83.9	82.5	101.7
1893.............	58		81.0	84.5	95.6
1894.............	57		80.9	86.5	93.3
1895.............	55		79.3	89.1	89.0
1896.............	56		81.9	91.7	89.3
1897.............	58	67.4	86.1	94.5	91.1
1898.............	63		94.9	97.3	97.5
1899.............	72		109.9	100.1	109.8
1900.............	82		126.9	103.0	123.2
1901.............	70		109.9	108.0	101.8
1902.............	68	62.8	108.3	113.5	95.4
1903.............	64		103.2	117.5	87.8
1904.............	65		106.2	121.5	87.4

TABLE 43a (*continued*)

	I	II	III	IV	V
1905.............	68		112.6	125.5	89.7
1906.............	80		134.0	129.5	103.5
1907.............	87	59.0	147.5	133.5	110.5
1908.............	82		140.7	137.5	102.3
1909.............	82		142.4	141.5	100.6
1910.............	78		136.8	145.0	94.3
1911.............	76	56.4	134.8	148.0	91.1

Source of data: *Annuaire Statistique de France*, vol. 36, pp. 57*–58*.

Equation of the primary trend line:
$$y = 205.84 - 14.86\,x + 0.355\,x^2$$

x in units of 5 years, origin at 1827.

Column IV: smoothed moving average of 11 years.

TABLE 44. STEEL PRODUCTION (BARS, RAILS, PLATES, ETC.), FRANCE, 1870–1913

Columns I and II in thousands of metric tons

	I	II	III	IV	V
1870............	61	131.3	46.4	42.0	110.5
1871............	62		43.2	51.8	83.4
1872............	112		71.7	66.0	108.6
1873............	120		71.1	85.0	83.6
1874............	182		100.4	95.5	105.1
1875............	223	193.7	115.1	103.0	111.7
1876............	211		99.8	109.0	91.6
1877............	240		104.7	114.3	91.6
1878............	283		114.7	119.0	96.4
1879............	307		116.1	122.0	95.2
1880............	360	282.3	127.5	124.4	102.5
1881............	394		127.9	125.8	101.7
1882............	458		137.2	126.2	108.7
1883............	522		145.1	126.0	115.2
1884............	503		130.5	124.2	105.1
1885............	554	411.4	134.7	121.0	111.3
1886............	454		101.5	116.8	86.9
1887............	493		102.0	111.8	91.2
1888............	517		99.5	106.0	93.9
1889............	529		95.2	101.0	94.3
1890............	582	591.9	98.3	97.5	100.8
1891............	639		99.4	94.5	105.2
1892............	683		98.5	92.0	107.1
1893............	664		89.1	90.5	98.5
1894............	674		84.7	90.0	94.1
1895............	715	846.9	84.4	91.5	96.2
1896............	917		99.9	94.2	106.1
1897............	995		100.6	97.5	101.6
1898............	1174		110.8	99.0	111.9
1899............	1240		107.4	98.9	108.6
1900............	1227	1201.2	102.1	98.0	104.2
1901............	1175		90.5	96.8	93.5
1902....	1246		89.2	95.4	93.5
1903............	1306		87.3	93.9	93.0
1904............	1407		88.3	92.4	95.6

TABLE 44 (*continued*)

	I	II	III	IV	V
1905	1442	1690.8	85.3	91.0	93.7
1906	1684		92.2	91.0	101.3
1907	1860		95.0	91.0	104.4
1908	1852		88.4	91.5	96.6
1909	2040		91.5	94.9	96.4
1910	2324	2363.2	98.4	100.0	98.4
1911	2702		106.1	105.5	100.6
1912	3250		119.1	109.5	108.8
1913	3186		109.3	112.9	96.8

Sources of data: *Annales des Mines*, 1896, vol. 9, p. 406; from 1882, *Statistique de l'Industries Minerales*, collected by H. G. Villard, National Bureau of Economic Research, Inc.

Equation of the primary trend line:

$$\log y = 2.08416 + 7.98110(1 - 0.93784^z)$$

x in units of 15 years, origin at 1869.

Column IV: smoothed moving average of 7 years.

TABLE 45. CRUDE ZINC PRODUCTION, FRANCE, 1870–1913

Columns I and II in thousands of tons

	I	II	III	IV	V
1870............	3.4	7.08	48.0	80.0	60.0
1871............	3.5		46.2	86.0	53.7
1872............	8.2		101.4	93.2	108.8
1873............	12.6		144.9	106.8	135.7
1874............	12.9		138.7	117.5	118.0
1875............	13.7	9.91	138.2	125.1	110.5
1876............	13.7		130.3	125.5	103.8
1877............	11.9		105.6	124.1	85.1
1878............	13.8		114.9	122.1	94.1
1879............	14.8		116.0	119.5	97.1
1880............	16.2	13.51	119.9	116.7	102.7
1881............	18.5		129.8	113.5	114.4
1882............	18.5		122.2	109.8	111.3
1883............	15.9		98.9	105.0	94.2
1884............	16.9		99.5	98.0	101.5
1885............	15.1	17.89	84.4	90.6	93.2
1886............	16.1		85.7	84.4	101.5
1887............	16.7		84.3	83.0	101.6
1888............	17.0		81.2	82.4	98.5
1889............	18.0		81.7	82.1	99.5
1890............	19.0	23.15	82.1	82.0	100.1
1891............	20.6		84 9	82.5	102.9
1892............	20.6		80.8	83.4	96.9
1893............	22.4		83 6	88.0	95.0
1894............	23.4		83 3	93 0	89.6
1895............	24.2	29.42	82.3	97.5	84.4
1896............	35.6		115.8	101.2	114.4
1897............	38.1		118.5	103.7	114.3
1898............	37.2		110 5	104.7	105.5
1899............	39.3		111.7	104.9	106.5
1900............	36.3	36.70	98.9	102.5	96.5
1901............	37.6		98.4	99.8	98.6
1902............	36.3		91.1	97.6	93.3
1903............	37.4		90.0	96.0	93.8
1904............	41.6		96.1	95.2	100.9

TABLE 45 (*continued*)

	I	II	III	IV	V
1905............	43.2	44.99	96.0	95.1	100.9
1906............	46.5		99.5	95.7	104.0
1907............	47.9		98.7	96.7	102.1
1908............	47.9		95.2	98.0	97.1
1909............	49.7		95.1	99.4	95.7
1910............	51.5	54.19	95.1	101.1	94.0
1911............	57.1		101.8	103.2	98.6
1912............	62.7		107.8	105.7	102.0
1913............	67.9	60.26	112.7	109.0	103.4

Source of data: *Annuaire Statistique de France*, vol. 36, 1919–20, p. 271*.

Equation of the primary trend line:

$$\log y = 0.17858 + 2.51097 \, (1 - 0.72074^x)$$

x in units of 20 years, origin at 1850.

Column IV: smoothed moving average of 7 years.

TABLE 45a. PRICES OF ZINC (PREMIER FUSION),
FRANCE, 1860–1914

Columns I and II in centimes per kilo

	I	II	III	IV	V
1860	55		99.0	93.5	105.9
1861	46		84.1	94.2	89.3
1862	49	53.90	90.9	95.0	95.7
1863	48		90.1	96.0	93.9
1864	48		91.3	97.1	94.0
1865	53		102.0	98.3	103.8
1866	60		116.9	99.8	117.1
1867	52	50.67	102.6	101.7	100.9
1868	50		99.6	104.1	95.7
1869	48		96.5	107.3	89.9
1870	48		97.4	110.7	88.0
1871	45		92.2	112.5	82.0
1872	58	48.32	120.0	113.3	105.9
1873	66		137.4	113.3	121.3
1874	60		125.7	112.5	111.7
1875	62		130.7	111.3	117.4
1876	58		123.0	109.0	112.8
1877	53	46.86	113.1	105.1	107.6
1878	43		92.0	99.3	92.6
1879	40		85.8	94.5	90.8
1880	44		94.6	90.4	104.6
1881	38		81.9	88.0	93.1
1882	39	46.29	84.3	87.0	96.9
1883	35		75.5	86.8	87.0
1884	33		71.1	87.7	81.1
1885	39		83.9	89.4	93.8
1886	38		81.7	91.3	89.5
1887	40	46.60	85.8	93.1	92.2
1888	50		106.7	94.4	113.0
1889	50		106.2	95.4	111.3
1890	55		116.2	96.2	120.8
1891	55		115.6	96.9	119.3
1892	54	47.80	113.0	97.6	115.8
1893	46		95.4	98.3	97.0
1894	40		82.3	98.9	83.2
1895	37		75.4	99.5	75.8
1896	44		88.9	100.1	88.8
1897	46	49.89	92.2	100.7	91.6
1898	55		108.9	101.3	107.6
1899	64		125.3	101.9	123.0

TABLE 45a (*continued*)

	I	II	III	IV	V
1900..............	56		108.4	102.4	105.9
1901..............	46		88.0	102.9	85.5
1902..............	50	52.87	94.6	103.4	91.3
1903..............	53		98.8	103.9	95.1
1904..............	58		106.6	104.4	102.1
1905..............	65		117.8	104.6	112.6
1906..............	68		121.5	104.6	116.2
1907..............	60	56.73	105.8	104.5	101.2
1908..............	51		88.4	104.1	84.9
1909..............	56		95.5	103.3	92.4
1910..............	57		95.7	102.0	93.8
1911..............	63		104.1	100.4	103.7
1912..............	66	61.48	107.4	98.8	108.7
1913..............	57		91.1	97.0	93.9
1914..............	57		89.4	95.0	94.1

Source of data: *Annuaire Statistique de France*, vol. 36, 1919–20, pp. 101*, 103*.

Equation of the primary trend line:

$$y = 58.02 - 4.564\,x + 0.4435\,x^2$$

x in units of 5 years, origin at 1857.

Column IV: smoothed moving average of 11 years up to 1895, 7 years average since 1895.

TABLE 46. SALT OUTPUT, FRANCE, 1872–1913

Columns I and II in thousands of metric tons

	I	II	III	IV	V
1872..........	449	533	84.2	101.9	82.6
1873..........	599		109.2	101.9	107.2
1874..........	739		131.2	101.9	128.8
1875..........	604	579	104.4	101.9	102.5
1876..........	577		97.0	101.8	95.3
1877..........	590		96.5	101.6	95.0
1878..........	571		90.9	101.4	89.6
1879..........	539		83.7	101.2	82.7
1880..........	693	661	104.9	100.9	104.0
1881..........	751		110.7	100.6	110.0
1882..........	704		101.2	100.2	101.0
1883..........	737		103.4	99.8	103.6
1884..........	806		110.4	99.4	111.1
1885..........	701	748	93.7	98.1	95.6
1886..........	721		94.1	95.2	98.8
1887..........	718		91.6	94.2	97.2
1888..........	631		78.6	94.1	83.5
1889..........	747		91.0	95.7	95.1
1890..........	843	839	100.5	100.5	100.0
1891..........	811		94.6	101.7	93.1
1892..........	974		111.2	102.5	108.6
1893..........	1114		124.5	103.1	120.8
1894..........	990		108.4	103.5	104.7
1895..........	871	932	93.5	103.7	90.2
1896..........	1043		109.7	103.9	105.6
1897..........	948		97.8	104.0	94.0
1898..........	999		101.1	104.1	97.1
1899..........	1193		118.5	104.1	113.8
1900..........	1089	1025	106.2	104.1	102.0
1901..........	910		87.2	104.0	83.8
1902..........	864		81.4	103.8	78.4
1903..........	968		89.6	103.6	86.5
1904..........	1154		105.0	103.3	101.6

TABLE 46 (*continued*)

	I	II	III	IV	V
1905............	1162	1117	104.0	102.9	101.1
1906............	1388		122.3	102.5	119.3
1907............	1324		114.8	102.0	112.5
1908............	1173		100.2	101.4	98.8
1909............	1113		93.7	100.8	93.0
1910............	1051	1206	87.1	100.2	86.9
1911............	1339		109.5	99.3	110.3
1912............	1099		88.6	98.4	90.0
1913............	1282	1257	102.0	97.1	105.0

Source of data: *Annuaire Statistique de France*, vol. 36, p. 56*.

Equation of the primary trend line:

$$y = \frac{1904.8}{1 + 10^{0.36012 - 0.25602\,x}}$$

x in units of 15 years, origin at 1875.

Column IV: smoothed moving average of 7 years.

TABLE 47. WHEAT CROPS, AUSTRALIA, 1860–1920

Columns I and II in millions of quintals

	I	II	III	IV	V
1860.............	2.8	2.37	118.2		
1865.............	2.3	2.94	78.2		
1870.............	3.6	3.64	98.9		
1875.............	5.0	4.50	111.1	95.8	116.0
1876.............	5.1		108.3	98.6	109.8
1877.............	4.0		81.4	101.4	80.3
1878.............	5.3		103.3	104.4	98.9
1879.............	5.4		101.0	107.2	94.2
1880.............	7.8	5.56	140.3	109.9	127.7
1881.............	6.3		108.4	112.5	96.4
1882.............	5.8		95.5	114.6	83.3
1883.............	5.8		91.7	116.1	79.0
1884.............	9.7		147.2	117.0	125.8
1885.............	8.3	6.85	121.2	117.0	103.6
1886.............	7.4		103.4	115.3	89.9
1887.............	9.1		121.9	111.9	108.9
1888.............	9.2		118.2	107.0	110.5
1889.............	7.0		86.4	102.1	84.6
1890.............	9.2	8.41	109.4	95.3	114.8
1891.............	7.4		84.3	88.1	95.7
1892.............	7.0		76.5	80.9	94.6
1893.............	8.9		93.5	73.2	127.7
1894.............	1.9		19.2	56.1	34.2
1895.............	7.6	10.28	73.9	56.2	131.5
1896.............	5.0		46.7	58.1	80.4
1897.............	5.7		51.1	63.7	80.2
1898.............	7.7		66.4	69.3	95.8
1899.............	11.2		93.0	74.3	125.2
1900.............	10.9	12.50	87.2	79.2	110.1
1901.............	13.1		100.6	84.0	119.8
1902.............	10.5		77.5	88.6	87.5
1903.............	3.4		24.2	92.9	26.1
1904.............	20.2		138.5	96.9	144.3
1905.............	14.8	15.12	97.9	100.4	97.5
1906.............	18.6		118.3	103.4	114.4
1907.............	18.1		110.8	106.2	104.3
1908.............	12.2		72.0	108.9	66.1
1909.............	17.0		96.9	110.6	87.6

TABLE 47 (*continued*)

	I	II	III	IV	V
1910............	24.6	18.15	135.5	113.3	119.6
1911............	25.9		137.4	116.0	118.4
1912............	19.5		99.8	115.6	86.3
1913............	25.9		128.0	107 7	118.8
1914............	28.1		134.2	108.0	124.3
1915............	6.8	21.63	31.4	122.0	25.7
1916............	48.7		217.3	123.1	176.5
1917............	41.5		178.9	123.6	144.7
1918............	31.3		130.5	123.8	105.4
1919............	20.5		82.7	123.8	66.8
1920............	12.7	25.55	49.7	123.8	40.1

Source of data: *Annuaire Statistique de France*, vol. 36, 1919–20, p. 221*.

Equation of the primary trend line:

$$y = \frac{93.17}{1 + 10^{1.48749-0.38724\,x}}$$

x in units of 20 years, origin at 1865.

Column IV: smoothed moving average of 5 years.

TABLE 48. WHEAT CROPS, ARGENTINE, 1881–1920

Columns I and II in millions of quintals

	I	II	III	IV	V
1881.............	8.5		147.1	128.0	114.9
1882.............	8.5		134.7	118.8	113.4
1883.............	8.5		124.3	109.5	113.5
1884.............	5.8		78.7	102.5	76.8
1885.............	8.5	7.90	107.6	96.0	112.1
1886.............	8.5		98.4	90.8	108.4
1887.............	8.5		90.5	85.8	105.5
1888.............	8.5		83.8	81.0	103.5
1889.............	6.6		60.6	76.2	79.5
1890.............	8.7	11.64	74.7	74.7	100.0
1891.............	8.5		67.2	77.5	86.7
1892.............	9.8		71.8	80.5	89.2
1893.............	15.9		108.4	83.4	130.0
1894.............	22.4		142.9	86.3	165.6
1895.............	16.7	16.69	100.1	89.2	112.2
1896.............	12.6		70.1	92.1	76.1
1897.............	8.6		44.7	94.8	47.2
1898.............	14.5		70.6	97.4	72.5
1899.............	28.6		131.1	100.0	131.1
1900.............	27.7	23.11	119.9	102.6	116.9
1901.............	20.3		82.5	105.3	78.3
1902.............	15.3		58.6	108.1	54.2
1903.............	28.2		102.1	111.2	91.8
1904.............	35.3		121.1	115.3	105.0
1905.............	41.0	30.65	133.8	120.6	110.9
1906.............	36.7		113.7	122.4	92.9
1907.............	42.5		125.4	122.6	102.3
1908.............	52.4		147.6	120.1	122.9
1909.............	42.5		114.5	116.0	98.7
1910.............	35.7	38.75	92.1	111.5	82.6
1911.............	39.7		98.4	106.7	92.2
1912.............	45.2		107.9	101.4	106.4
1913.............	51.0		117.3	97.1	120.8
1914.............	31.0		68.8	92.8	74.1

Table 48 (*continued*)

	I	II	III	IV	V
1915............	45.8	46.63	98.2	89.3	110.0
1916............	46.0		95.8	86.0	111.4
1917............	19.1		38.6	84.2	45.8
1918............	60.9		119.8	85.2	134.0
1919............	46.7		89.4	97.0	92.2
1920............	58.3	53.61	108.7	105.0	103.5

Source of data: *Annuaire Statistique de France*, vol. 36, p. 221*.

Equation of the primary trend line:

$$y = \frac{73.04}{1 + 10^{0.72224 - 0.38765\,x}}$$

x in units of 10 years, origin at 1890.

Column IV: smoothed moving average of 5 years.

TABLE 49. WHEAT CROPS, JAPAN, 1877–1920

Columns I and II in millions of quintals

	I	II	III	IV	V
1877	2.4	2.49	96.4	93.2	103.4
1878	2.4		91.1	94.6	96.3
1879	2.6		93.5	96.0	97.4
1880	3.1	2.92	106.2	97.4	109.0
1881	2.8		91.4	98.9	92.4
1882	3.4		105.7	100.4	105.3
1883	3.3		97.9	102.0	96.0
1884	3.8		107.9	103.3	104.5
1885	3.4	3.67	92.6	104.2	88.9
1886	4.5		117.6	104.6	112.4
1887	4.2		105.5	103.9	101.5
1888	4.3		104.0	102.1	101.9
1889	4.5		105.2	99.7	105.5
1890	3.4	4.42	76.9	97.3	79.0
1891	5.0		109.6	96.3	113.8
1892	4.3		91.7	97.4	94.1
1893	4.6		95.3	99.9	95.4
1894	5.5		110.9	101.6	109.2
1895	5.5	5.09	108.1	102.6	105.4
1896	5.0		94.5	102.7	92.0
1897	5.3		99.5	102.8	96.8
1898	5.8		106.7	102.6	104.0
1899	5.8		104.5	102.3	102.2
1900	5.7	5.66	100.7	100.3	100.4
1901	5.9		102.6	92.8	110.6
1902	5.3		90.7	81.5	111.3
1903	2.5		42.1	77.5	54.3
1904	5.2		86.2	77.5	111.2
1905	4.9	6.11	80.2	81.7	98.1
1906	5.3		85.8	87.2	98.2
1907	6.0		96.0	90.8	105.7
1908	6.0		94.9	94.2	100.7
1909	6.1		95.6	97.4	98.2

TABLE 49 (continued)

	I	II	III	IV	V
1910	6.2	6.44	96.3	99.6	96.7
1911	6.8		104.7	101.1	103.6
1912	7.0		107.0	102.0	104.9
1913	6.9		104.6	102.6	101.9
1914	5.9		88.8	103.1	86.1
1915	6.9	6.69	103.1	107.9	95.6
1916	7.7		114.4	111.9	102.2
1917	8.9		131.6	116.3	113.2
1918	8.4		123.7	120.0	103.1
1919	8.3		121.7	123.5	98.5
1920	8.0	6.85	116.8	126.1	92.6

Source of data: *Annuaire Statistique de France*, vol. 36, p. 221*.

Equation of the primary trend line:

$$y = \frac{7.2}{1 + 10^{0.16568 - 0.18268\,x}}$$

x in units of 5 years, origin at 1880.

Column IV: smoothed moving average of 5 years.

TABLE 50. COPPER OUTPUT, JAPAN, 1879–1922

Columns I and II in thousands of metric tons

	I	II	III	IV	V
1879...........	3.9				
1880...........	3.9	6.68			
1881...........	3.9				
1882...........	4.9				
1883...........	7.7		88.0	95.0	92.6
1884...........	10.1		107.6	98.0	109.8
1885...........	10.1	10.12	100.3	100.5	99.8
1886...........	12.2		112.3	102.9	109.1
1887...........	11.2		96.5	105.0	91.9
1888...........	11.8		95.6	106.8	89.5
1889...........	15.2		116.0	108.3	107.1
1890...........	15.2	13.85	109.8	109.7	100.1
1891...........	17.3		115.2	110.0	104.7
1892...........	18.3		112.9	109.8	101.2
1893...........	18.3		105.2	108.8	96.7
1894...........	20.4		109.9	107.2	102.5
1895...........	18.7	19.76	94.6	105.6	89.6
1896...........	21.3		99.5	103.8	95.9
1897...........	23.4		101.6	101.8	99.8
1898...........	25.6		103.7	100.2	103.5
1899...........	28.8		109.5	99.0	110.6
1900...........	28.3	27.96	101.2	98.0	103.3
1901...........	27.9		92.4	97.4	94.9
1902...........	30.3		93.6	96.8	96.7
1903...........	31.9		92.1	96.6	95.3
1904...........	35.4		96.1	96.5	99.6
1905...........	36.5	39.06	93.4	96.4	96.9
1906...........	43.4		103.3	96.4	107.2
1907...........	49.7		110.7	96.5	114.7
1908...........	43.7		91.3	96.7	94.4
1909...........	47.8		94.2	97.2	96.9
1910...........	46.7	53.70	87.0	97.9	89.3
1911...........	55.9		97.4	99.1	98.3
1912...........	66.6		108.9	101.3	107.5
1913...........	66.4		102.3	104.6	97.8
1914...........	70.3		102.6	109.1	94.0

TABLE 50 (*continued*)

	I	II	III	IV	V
1915	75.3	72.30	104.1	114.0	91.3
1916	100.4		132.4	117.2	113.0
1917	107.8		135.6	117.6	115.3
1918	90.2		108.3	108.0	100.3
1919	78.3		90.1	93.1	96.8
1920	67.7	90.49	74.8	74.0	101.1
1921	54.0		56.0	67.0	83.6
1922	54.0	102.50	52.7	61.0	86.4

Sources of data: Up to 1913, F. W. Franke, *loc. cit.*, p. 45 (ore-metal content; 1879–87 — estimated); from 1913 — smelter production — Statistical Bulletins of the Imperial Mineral Resources Bureau of the British Empire, Copper, War Period, 1919–21, 1920–22.

Equation of the primary trend line:

$$y = \frac{296,183}{1 + 10^{1.47314 - 0.49105\,x}}$$

x in units of 15 years, origin at 1885.

Column IV: smoothed moving average of 5 years.

TABLE 51. COPPER ORE OUTPUT, CANADA, 1881–1922

Columns I and II in thousands of metric tons of metal content

	I	II	III	IV	V
1881..........	.5	0.62	80.7	74.0	109.1
1882..........	.5		66.8	87.0	76.8
1883..........	1.0		119.4	95.0	125.7
1884..........	1.0		99.1	100.5	98.6
1885..........	1.2	1.14	105.4	103.3	102.0
1886..........	1.6		111.9	105.6	106.0
1887..........	1.4		84.3	107.2	78.6
1888..........	2.3		114.3	108.8	105.1
1889..........	2.5		108.7	109.9	98.9
1890..........	3.1	2.59	119.5	109.8	108.8
1891..........	3.6		112.2	109.0	102.9
1892..........	3.6		94.1	106.1	88.7
1893..........	5.1		114.9	98.9	116.2
1894..........	5.1		101.0	88.5	114.1
1895..........	4.1	5.67	72.3	78.8	91.8
1896..........	4.1		60.2	73.9	81.5
1897..........	6.0		75.5	73.2	103.1
1898..........	8.2		90.1	74.7	120.6
1899..........	6.9		67.3	90.9	74.0
1900..........	8.6	11.38	75.5	103.0	73.3
1901..........	19.1		146.0	110.0	132.7
1902..........	17.8		120.4	113.4	106.2
1903..........	19.6		118.9	114.3	104.0
1904..........	19.5		107.2	113.8	94.2
1905..........	20.9	19.89	105.1	112.5	93.4
1906..........	25.9		118.1	110.5	106.9
1907..........	26.0		108.4	108.0	100.4
1908..........	29.0		111.4	104.5	106.6
1909..........	24.5		87.2	99.7	87.5
1910..........	26.1	29.11	89.7	97.4	92.1
1911..........	25.3		82.9	97.3	85.2
1912..........	35.3		110.4	99.2	111.3
1913..........	34.9		104.5	105.0	99.5
1914..........	34.4		98.7	118.6	83.2

TABLE 51 (*continued*)

	I	II	III	IV	V
1915............	45.7	36.22	126.2	123.2	102.4
1916............	53.2		143.4	124.0	115.6
1917............	49.6		130.7	123.8	105.6
1918............	53.9		139.1	118.0	117.9
1919............	34.1		86.0	100.0	86.0
1920............	37.0	40.41	91.6	83.0	110.4
1921............	21.6		52.9	70.0	75.6
1922............	19.5	41.25	47.2	58.0	81.4

Sources of data: Up to 1913, F. W. Franke, *Abriss d. Neuesten Wirtschaftsgeschichte d. Kupfers*, p. 45; from 1913, Statistical Bulletins of the Imperial Mineral Resources Bureau of the British Empire, Copper, War Period, 1919–21, 1920–22.

Equation of the primary trend line:

$$y = \frac{44,174}{1 + 10^{1.57749 - 1.11809\,x}}$$

x in units of 15 years, origin at 1885.

Column IV: smoothed moving average of 5 years.

TABLE 52. TONNAGE OF FREIGHT MOVED ON THE ERIE CANAL, 1837–1922

Columns I and II in thousands of short tons

	I	II	III		I	II	III
1837–40....	772	764	101.0	1893......	3,236		106.4
1841–45....	884	1,061	83.4	1894......	3,144		105.2
1846–50....	1,557	1,421	109.5	1895......	2,356	2,934	80.3
1851–55....	2,142	1,828	117.1	1896......	2,742		95.4
1856–60....	1,890	2,250	84.0	1897......	2,585		91.9
1861–65....	2,744	2,651	103.5	1898......	2,338		85.0
1866–70....	3,018	3,000	100.6	1899......	2,419		89.9
1870.......	3,083		99.0	1900......	2,146	2,630	81.6
1871.......	3,581		113.0	1901......	2,257		88.2
1872.......	3,563		110.4	1902......	2,106		84.7
1873.......	3,603	3,284	109.7	1903......	2,414		100.0
1874.......	3,097		93.0	1904......	1,946		83.1
1875.......	2,787		82.5	1905......	2,000	2,270	88.1
1876.......	2,418		70.8	1906......	2,385		108.6
1877.......	3,254		94.2	1907......	2,416		113.9
1878.......	3,609	3,493	103.3	1908......	2,177		106.3
1879.......	3,820		108.2	1909......	2,031		102.9
1880.......	4,609	3,570	129.1	1910......	2,023	1,900	106.5
1881.......	3,599	3,542.2	101.6	1911......	2,032		111.2
1882.......	3,694		105.3	1912......	1,795		102.3
1883.......	3,587		103.2	1913......	1,788		106.3
1884.......	3,390		98.4	1914......	1,362		84.6
1885.......	3,208	3,411	94.1	1915......	1,155	1,537	75.2
1886.......	3,809		113.1	1916......	918		62.4
1887.......	3,841		115.5	1917......	675		48.1
1888.......	3,322		101.1	1918......	667		49.9
1889.......	3,674		113.3	1919......	842		66.3
1890.......	3,304	3,200	103.2	1920......	891	1,203	74.0
1891.......	3,098		98.4	1921......	994		86.8
1892.......	2,979		96.3	1922......	1,485		136.5

Source of data: *Statistical Abstract for the United States*, 1922, pp. 330, 696.

Equation of the primary trend line:

$$1837\text{–}1880\text{:}\quad y = \frac{4000}{1 + 10^{1.10506 - 0.73596\,x}}$$

x in units of 20 years, origin at 1825.

$$1881\text{–}1922\text{:}\quad y = 4{,}000 - \frac{4000}{1 + 10^{1.24758 - 0.64553\,x}}$$

x in units of 20 years, origin at 1870.

TABLE 53. NUMBER OF RAILROAD MILES ADDED,
UNITED STATES, 1831–1922

	I	II		I	II
1830........		108	1865........	1177	2911
1831........	72		1866........	1716	
1832........	134		1867........	2249	
1833........	151		1868........	2979	
1834........	253		1869........	4615	
1835........	465	190	1870........	6078	3666
1836........	175		1871........	7379	
1837........	224		1872........	5870	
1838........	416		1873........	4097	
1839........	389		1874........	2117	
1840........	516	328	1875........	1711	4292
1841........	717		1876........	2712	
1842........	491		1877........	2274	
1843........	159		1878........	2665	
1844........	192		1879........	4809	
1845........	256	557	1880........	6711	4748
1846........	297		1881........	9846	
1847........	668		1882........	11569	
1848........	398		1883........	6745	
1849........	1369		1884........	3923	
1850........	1656	918	1885........	2975	5048
1851........	1961		1886........	8018	
1852........	1926		1887........	12876	
1853........	2452		1888........	6900	
1854........	1360		1889........	5162	
1855........	1654	1444	1890........		5237 / 5132
1856........	3642		1891........	4844	
1857........	2487		1892........	3656	
1858........	2465		1893........	4143	
1859........	1821		1894........	2899	
1860........	1837	2132	1895........	1895	4889
1861........	660		1896........	2053	
1862........	834		1897........	2163	
1863........	1050		1898........	2026	
1864........	738		1899........	3466	

TABLE 53 (*continued*)

	I	II		I	II
1900......	4628	4500	1910......	5908	3000
1901......	3324		1911......	4740	
1902......	4965		1912......	3301	
1903......	6169		1913......	3003	
1904......	6690		1914......	2511	
1905......	5084	3894	1915......	831	1688
1906......	5565		1916......	1653	
1907......	6188		1917......	350	
1908......			1918......	− 322	697
1909......	3238		1919......	−1826	
			1920......	− 526	250
			1921......	114	
			1922......	− 1277	

Sources of data: *Statistical Abstract for the United States*, 1881, p. 157; 1922, p. 310.

Equation of the primary trend line:

1831–90:
$$y = \frac{5500}{1 + 10^{0.69807 - 0.99877\,x}}$$

x in units of 20 years, origin at 1850.

1891–1920:
$$y = 5500 - y_1$$

$$\frac{1}{y_1} = \frac{1}{5500}(1 + 10^{0.24812 - 0.45692\,x}) - 0.00010376$$

x in units of 10 years, origin at 1910.

TABLE 54. COPPER OUTPUT, UNITED KINGDOM, 1854–1915

Columns I and II in thousands of tons

	I	II	III		I	II	III
1854.......	20		120.6	1885......	3	2.0	149.3
1855.......	21	16.2	129.5	1886......	1		54.0
1856.......	24		151.4	1887......	0.88		51.8
1857.......	17		109.8	1888......	1		64.8
1858.......	14		93.9	1889......	0.90		64.8
1859.......	16		111.4	1890......	.93	1.2	75.6
1860.......	16	13.8	115.9	1891......	.72		62.5
1861.......	15		113.2	1892......	.49		45.8
1862.......	15		118.3	1893......	.42		42.5
1863.......	14		115.5	1894......	.44		48.5
1864.......	13		113.1	1895......	.57	.825	69.1
1865.......	12	10.9	110.4	1896......	.55		70.6
1866.......	11		107.5	1897......	.51		69.4
1867.......	10		104.0	1898......	.64		92.8
1868.......	10		111.3	1899......	.63		97.8
1869.......	8		95.7	1900......	.76	.600	126.7
1870.......	7	7.7	90.7	1901......	.53		92.1
1871.......	6		83.2	1902......	.48		87.2
1872.......	6		89.4	1903......	.53		100.8
1873.......	5		80.6	1904......	.49		97.9
1874.......	5		87.8	1905......	.71	.477	148.8
1875.......	5	5.2	96.2	1906......	.74		159.5
1876.......	5		106.5	1907......	.66		146.5
1877.......	4		95.2	1908......	.57		130.3
1878.......	4		103.1	1909......	.43		101.5
1879.......	3		84.1	1910......	.44	.412	106.8
1880.......	4	3.3	122.7	1911......	.39		96.4
1881.......	4		135.5	1912......	.29		73.0
1882.......	3		113.4	1913......	.42		107.7
1883.......	3		128.5	1914......	.34		88.8
1884.......	3		138.2	1915		.377	

Source of data: W. Page (editor), *loc. cit.*, p. 181.

Equation of the primary trend line: $y = 20.6 - y_1$

$$\frac{1}{y_1} = \frac{1}{20.6}\left(1 + 10^{0.85759 - 1.09162\,x}\right) + 0.00089$$

x in units of 20 years, origin at 1850.

TABLE 55. LEAD OUTPUT, DOMESTIC ORE, UNITED KINGDOM, 1854–1915

Columns I and II in thousands of tons

	I	II	III		I	II	III
1854.......	64		95.4	1885......	38	42.65	89.1
1855.......	66	67.35	98.0	1886......	39		94.6
1856.......	73		108.9	1887......	38		95.3
1857.......	67		100.3	1888......	38		98.7
1858.......	68		102.2	1889......	36		98.0
1859.......	63		95.1	1890......	34	35.74	95.1
1860.......	63	65.97	95.5	1891......	32		92.6
1861.......	66		100.7	1892......	30		90.0
1862.......	69		106.0	1893......	30		93.3
1863.......	68		105.1	1894......	30		97.0
1864.......	67		104.3	1895......	20	29.76	67.2
1865.......	67	63.77	105.1	1896......	31		107.5
1866.......	67		106.2	1897......	27		96.7
1867.......	68		108.9	1898......	25		92.6
1868.......	71		114.9	1899......	24		92.0
1869.......	73		119.5	1900......	24	25.17	95.4
1870.......	73	60.43	120.8	1901......	20		81.6
1871.......	69		116.0	1902......	18		75.4
1872.......	60		102.5	1903......	20		86.1
1873.......	54		93.7	1904......	20		88.5
1874.......	59		104.1	1905......	21	21.94	95.7
1875.......	57	55.70	102.3	1906......	22		102.2
1876.......	59		108.3	1907......	24		113.8
1877.......	61		114.5	1908......	21		101.6
1878.......	58		111.5	1909......	22		108.6
1879.......	52		102.3	1910......	22	19.84	110.9
1880.......	57	49.60	114.9	1911......	18		91.9
1881.......	49		101.6	1912......	19		98.4
1882.......	50		106.8	1913......	18		94.7
1883.......	43		94.6	1914......	19		101.2
1884.......	40		90.8	1915......		18.52	

Source of data: W. Page (editor), *loc. cit.*, p. 181.

Equation of the primary trend line: $y = 69.4 - y_1$

$$\frac{1}{y_1} = \frac{1}{69.4}\left(1 + 10^{1.03892-0.69897\,x}\right) + 0.004463$$

x in units of 15 years, origin at 1865.

TABLE 56. TONNAGE OF SAILING SHIPS, ENTERED AND CLEARED, PORTS OF FRANCE, 1842–1915

Columns I and II in thousands of tons

	I	II	III		I	II	III
1842–50 [a]..	2,717	2,551	106.5	1883.....	4,228		107.9
1851......	2,930	3,284	89.2	1884.....	3,729		98.4
1852......	3,176		93.1	1885.....	3,383	3,662	92.4
1853......	3,315		93.6	1886.....	3,081		88.2
1854......	3,242		88.3	1887.....	3,023		91.0
1855......	3,515	3,800	92.5	1888.....	3,118		98.9
1856......	4,370		112.2	1889.....	2,723		91.3
1857......	4,499		112.8	1890.....	2,613	2,811	92.9
1858......	4,580		112.2	1891.....	2,778		104.9
1859......	4,862		116.4	1892.....	2,163		87.0
1860......	4,403	4,272	103.1	1893.....	2,077		89.4
1861......	5,028		116.0	1894.....	2,016		93.2
1862......	4,486		102.1	1895.....	1,623	2,000	81.2
1863......	4,431		99.4	1896.....	1,567		83.0
1864......	4,269		94.5	1897.....	1,538		86.6
1865......	4,535	4,578	99.0	1898.....	1,818		109.4
1866......	4,723		102.3	1899.....	1,531		98.8
1867......	4,879		104.9	1900.....	1,415	1,438	98.4
1868......	5,151		109.8	1901.....	1,385		100.7
1869......	4,920		104.1	1902.....	1,287		98.0
1870......	4,484	4,763 / 4,816	94.1	1903.....	1,247		99.6
1871......	4,446		93.2	1904.....	1,304		109.6
1872......	4,986		105.5	1905.....	1,291	1,128	114.4
1873......	4,968		106.1	1906.....	1,129		102.8
1874......	4,689		101.1	1907.....	1,060		99.1
1875......	4,527	4,593	98.6	1908.....	1,090		104.4
1876......	4,663		102.8	1909.....	953		94.4
1877......	4,517		100.9	1910.....	1,008	980	102.9
1878......	4,710		106.6	1911.....	981		101.5
1879......	5,300		121.6	1912.....	962		100.9
1880......	5,802	4,300	134.9	1913.....	955		101.6
1881......	5,164		123.8	1914.....	776		83.8
1882......	4,692		116.0	1915.....		913	

[a] Average for 9 years.

Source of data: *Annuaire Statistique de France*, 1914–15, p. 61*.

Equation of the primary trend line:

$$1845\text{–}70: \quad y = \frac{5,000}{1 + 10^{0.57013-0.53536\,x}}$$

x in units of 10 years, origin at 1840.

$$1870\text{–}1915: \quad \frac{1}{y_1} = \frac{1}{5,000}\left(1 + 10^{1.88564-1.11226\,x}\right) + 0.0000417$$

$$y = 5000 - y_1$$

x in units of 15 years, origin at 1865.

TABLE 57. OUTPUT OF ZINC ORE (CALAMITE AND BLENDE), BELGIUM, 1840–1913

Columns I and II in thousands of tons

	I	II	III		I	II	III
1840....	20.48	.12.00	170.7	1877...	44.99		108.4
1841....	18.38		119.2	1878...	45.29		115.5
1842....	18.47		98.0	1879...	42.69		115.7
1843....	25.67		109.4	1880...	38.81	34.62	112.1
1844....	22.69		80.8	1881...	23.55		71.8
1845....	30.03	33.62	89.3	1882...	20.44		67.1
1846....	42.37		108.2	1883...	20.74		73.0
1847....	47.66		105.9	1884...	27.61		104.9
1848....	48.58		95.7	1885...	18.19	24.25	75.0
1849....	49.71		88.9	1886...	19.04		84.3
1850....	69.50	61.16	113.6	1887...	20.88		99.7
1851....	80.28		123.0	1888...	24 54		127.2
1852....	78.35		112.9	1889...	21.18		120.0
1853....	80.09		110.7	1890...	15.41	16.00	96 3
1854....	79.47		105.6	1891...	14.28		96.4
1855....	81.27	77.55	104.7	1892...	12.26		89.9
1856....	83.27		108.7	1893...	11.31		90.8
1857....	76.24		100.7	1894...	11.59		102.7
1858....	75.39		100.8	1895...	12.23	10.11	121.0
1859....	70.39		95.3	1896...	11.63		124.8
1860....	66.14	72.92	90.7	1897...	10.95		128.4
1861....	73.16		102.2	1898...	11.48		148.3
1862....	74.01		105.4	1899...	9.5		136.7
1863....	61.77		89.7	1900...	8.7	6.17	141.0
1864....	58.07		86.0	1901...	6.6		115.8
1865....	56.19	66.13	85.0	1902...	3.9		74.4
1866....	54.52		84.8	1903...	3.6		75.3
1867....	58.05		92.9	1904...	3.7		85.6
1868....	68.70		113.3	1905...	3.9	3.86	101.0
1869....	66.92		113.7	1906...	3.9		110.8
1870....	57.10	57.00	100.2	1907...	3.5		110.1
1871....	61.13		111.5	1908...	2.1		73.7
1872....	55.54		105.5	1909...	1.2		47.6
1873....	42.58		84.4	1910...	1.4	2.19	63.9
1874....	43.30		89.7	1911...	0.8		40.0
1875....	42.50	46.06	92.3	1912...	1.2		65.9
1876....	37.71		86.1	1913...	0.9		54.9

Sources of data: W. R. Ingalls, *Production and Properties of Zinc*, New York, 1902, p. 64. Checked from 1890 and supplemented by the *Annuaire Statistique de France*, vol. 36, 1919–20, p. 270*.

Equation of the primary trend line:

1840–1855: $$y = \frac{85.0}{1 + 10^{1.61944 - 0.83530\,x}}$$

x in units of 7 years, origin at 1833.

1855–1913: $$y = 85.0 - \frac{85.0}{1 + 10^{1.25216 - 0.94345\,x}}$$

x in units of 20 years, origin at 1850.

INDEX

(See also lists of Charts and Tables)